Creative Report Writing

America's leadership must be guided
by the lights of learning and reason—
or else those who confuse rhetoric with reality
and the plausible with the possible
will gain the popular ascendancy.

JOHN F. KENNEDY

CREATIVE REPORT WRITING

Arnold B. Sklare

McGraw-Hill Book Company

New York
San Francisco
Toronto
London

Creative Report Writing

For I. S. S.

Preface

This is a book for people in business, professions, government, or colleges who want to improve their ability to communicate professionally.

Persons writing reports today have already received training in English. They have probably also achieved some standing in their own fields of professional endeavor. The present volume attempts to integrate the reader's broad knowledge of English with his special knowledge of his own work.

There is a cumulative approach in this text. Understanding of the principles of effective writing is needed before creative reports can be written. Though this book may be thumbed through for an occasional answer to a passing question, it should be read whole. The ability to write well—with form and substance—cannot be acquired casually. There is only good and bad writing, not good and bad report writing. Neither is there "technical writing" nor "business writing": there is writing.

Perhaps the word "creative" in the title needs explaining. Skill, mechanical proficiency, and ingenious execution are not the only aims of a report writer. Unless skill is accompanied by inventiveness, it becomes artifice; unless mechanical proficiency is tempered by vision, it degenerates into slickness; unless ingenious execution is animated by insight, it results in contrivance. A creative approach to report writing recognizes the claims of imagination upon reason.

It will be seen that both Mammon and Orpheus speak throughout this volume. The author has for some years earned part of his living as a professional writer and consultant in industry (Director, The Written Word: An Institute of Creative Communication) and part as a college professor (C. W. Post College). In industry, he presents programs to improve communication processes; on the campus, he teaches literature and writing. Wall Street and Olympus, alas, are still asunder!

Arnold B. Sklare

Acknowledgments

Many persons in industry, government, libraries, professions, and universities helped me with this book, as did many friends. I wish to thank them formally and acknowledge their aid.

I should like, first, to express appreciation to Mr. Meyer Feldman, Deputy Special Counsel to the late President of the United States, for making available to me as exhibits some of the reports included in Chapter 5.

My friend Dr. William E. Buckler, Dean of the Washington Square College of Arts and Science, New York University, offered useful suggestions throughout the genesis of this book. Likewise, my friend Gerald Gold, Bronx Borough Coordinator, New York Public Library, gave of his ideas. Jerry Cusamano, my attorney and friend, advised me on certain matters, as did my good friend Richard J. Halpern of the Ziff-Davis Publishing Company. On the basis of his outstanding business experience, my brother, Frank D. Sklare of Chicago, was also able to provide wise counsel and judgment.

I am grateful to Thomas J. Watson, Jr., of the International Business Machines Corporation for personally acknowledging my request for information. Robert M. Wendlinger of the New York Life Insurance Company was good enough to provide materials from his company's Effective Letters Program.

The men and women in my advanced composition graduate seminar, Fall, 1962–1963, at C. W. Post College, gathered the selected bibliography at the end of the book.

I have, I think, acknowledged all reproduced materials in the text. Nonetheless, I wish to thank the following journals, companies, and institutions for permission to use materials belonging to them:

Fortune, IBM Journal of Research and Development, Harvard Business Review, Yale Law Journal, Anesthesia and Analgesia, Journal of Accountancy, Chemical Abstracts, Dissertation Abstracts, and Psychological Abstracts.

National Industrial Conference Board; Chas. Pfizer & Co., Inc.; First National City Bank of New York; Chase Manhattan Bank; Pace College; Polychart Graphic Workshop of Brooklyn Heights, N.Y.; Allwin Resume Service, New York; Dun and Bradstreet, Inc.; American Pharmaceutical Association; E. I. du Pont de Nemours and Company; General Motors Corporation; Volkswagen of America, Inc.; Health News Institute; New York Life Insurance Company; Ziff-Davis Publishing Company; Oxford University Press; and Trend Finders, Inc., New York.

Lastly, I wish to express appreciation to my East Hampton summer neighbor, Mrs. Margaret A. Lamb, who faithfully typed the manuscript.

Arnold B. Sklare

Contents

PART II:
GENERAL PROBLEMS AND CONSIDERATIONS

PART III:
CREATING THE REPORT: PHASE I

PART IV:
CREATING THE REPORT: PHASE II

PART VII:
BIBLIOGRAPHY

I

Backgrounds

1

The Meaning of "Report"—Aims and Criteria

A Definition of a Report
Reports and the Crisis in Communication
Flexibility or Rigidity in Reports?

A DEFINITION OF A REPORT

A report is a creative communication between two people. It is an interaction that sets up a dynamic equilibrium between writer and reader. To make a report is to produce an original written creation characterized by the constructive actions of giving ideas and defining relationships. A flow of intellectual energy is released to form a two-way, reciprocal understanding between the creator of the report and his co-creator, the reader.

To define a report in these terms is to emphasize that writers of modern reports are not perfunctory recorders of statistics. Men who write reports today are often creators of vast industrial enterprises or originators of profound social, legal, or medical changes which may affect the lives of countless persons. In business, the professions, and universities, writers of reports are the movers and shakers of our lives.

Yet to have good reports we must have more than good ideas; we must have good writers, and we must have good readers. The writer must communicate his idea unblemished and undisturbed, and the reader must have the capacity to attain that fullest of satisfactions, understanding of the idea. Deterioration of communication between writers and readers of reports can lead to business, professional, or governmental decline. Creative thinkers do not write reports for fun or profit. They write with the serious purpose of informing and explaining to readers who want and need ideas.

REPORTS AND THE CRISIS IN COMMUNICATION

Reports have as their aim the communication of the steadily increasing flood of information developed and acquired by our creative thinkers; however, our business, professional, and scientific workers are failing to communicate clearly and adequately with each other and the public. There is, as a result, a serious deceleration in important research and development work in many areas.

Poorly organized and written reports, without doubt, cause millions of dollars worth of information to be lost or withheld from other creative workers and thinkers who need it. Obscure, wordy, pompous, fragmentary, disorganized, incorrect, and misleading reports cause thousands of valuable man-hours to be lost. With inadequate reports, unrealistic and even dangerous attitudes are developed within business, professional, scientific, governmental, and academic circles—and among the public at large. In short, failure of communication in reports is not only symptomatic of the decline of our social, political, professional, and business institutions—it is also the cause.

The aim of reports, then, is a higher intelligence for both writer and reader, a mutual intelligence acquired through the giving and taking of new ideas and freshly observed relationships. Not until the modern report writer can assimilate and control the explosion of information around him can he hope to creatively communicate it; and not until this information can be communicated and understood can we all hope to begin to learn how to live with it.

FLEXIBILITY OR RIGIDITY IN REPORTS?

Most people like to think that an easy answer can be found for a difficult problem. Particularly in our culture does this immature attitude seem most prevalent. Books on ten easy lessons to a million dollars in the stock market and five short steps to a successful marriage are popular and sell widely. Such pat treatments of challenging subjects appear to appeal to the human desire to gain the most but to do the least. Even more, seeing a complex subject apparently reduced to a simple formula seems to reassure readers that they are not so dumb after all and that they really can understand difficult subjects. We await publication of *Einstein's Theory for the Teen-ager*.

Whether what readers come to understand by these books has anything to do with the subject treated need not be our concern here. But we should be concerned about the state of mind engendered by the belief that if a person has a formula, follows it, lives right, and has good luck, he will succeed.

In talking about report writing, one can (and does) set forth rules, guidelines, and principles. If there is a pedagogical technique that permits otherwise, we should like to know about it. But there is no more a rigid formula for creative report writing than there is for any other kind of writing.

The report writer must be pliant, must be able to bend without breaking, he must be flexible. He must not be firmly fixed and set in an undeviating posture, he must not be rigid. One is not by this suggesting that each reporter see himself as Shakespeare but that the report writer be unafraid to depart from conventional treatment if it occurs to him that another presentation may better communicate what he wants to say.

Business and professional writing, as we all know, has become unyieldingly static, almost ironbound in its immobile fixity. This appalling dehumanization of language can be arrested in report writing if we approach it as we approach all good writing. Good writing communicates by its naturalness, by its quality of one man talking directly to another. The report writer, therefore, should unhesitatingly use his own language, his own pattern of arrangement, his own mode of presentation. He can never come to understand good writing if he blindly knocks out his reports in a rigid pattern just because they have always been done that way.

One cannot, naturally, break away from standard patterns without fully knowing and understanding what the classic forms are and how and why they came to be. The creative report writer can become more flexible only as he gains wider experience and comes to recognize the limitations of the established pattern. Then he will truly know the meaning of a report, its aims, its definition, and its standards of excellence.

2

The Relationship of Reports
to Other Forms
of Written Communication

REPORTS AS A LITERARY GENRE

The purpose of this chapter is to show the relationship of reports to other written forms of communication. Better reports probably cannot be written until we all understand more clearly what reports are and are not. Many a college freshman has been directed to write a theme the first day he enters his English class without being told what a theme is. In this same manner reports come to be written in emulation of a newspaper story, a publicity release, a familiar essay, an advertisement, a short story, or a piece of propaganda—other kinds of writing the report writer may know best.

Because a report is not and should not be any of these, the result is frazzled nerves, migraine headaches, and ulcers. The writer who wants to do a creative report owes it to himself to discover that the modern report is a new genre—a new form. It has borrowed extensively from older, more recognizable literary forms, it has undergone a formation of its own, and it has emerged as a unique literary archetype.

MASS MEDIA

Mass media of communication are newspapers, popular magazines, radio, movies, and television. Though we will talk only about the mass media that reach the receiver in written form, and only about the aspects of these which may usefully be discussed in an attempt to differentiate them from reports, the general characteristics of mass media apply to the unprinted forms as well.

The newspapers we all hungrily read have one striking similarity to reports—they, too, are written primarily to inform. But the nature of a newspaper organization, the relation of the newspaper reader to the source of information, and the scope of the information together with the style in which it is presented, make newspapers essentially very different from reports. Moreover, in that the contemporary newspaper has the added mission of entertaining as well as informing its audiences, the differences between it and a report are more marked.

The nature of mass communication is such that the creator speaks through an organization—a whole newspaper staff, a large magazine or book publishing house, a broadcasting network, etc. The person writing for the paper or magazine speaks in an institutional role through the facilities of his institution. Receivers of this information are unknown readers—you and I, everybody—and we have very little opportunity to talk back, disagree, or otherwise communicate with the writer. By the same token, the newspaper writer can only guess about the interests and intelligence of his readers. To heighten this rather broad, directionless relationship, as mass communication audiences we have sharply limited contact with other mass receivers of this information. Our opportunity to discuss, to test, to verify newspaper information is deplorably circumscribed.

Presumably, the newspaper undertakes to convey all the information available to it on all subjects so that there may be something in it of interest to anybody who reads it. Since the average person may not have a powerful intellect, and since the poor fellow is surrounded by a bewildering array of printed matter of all kinds, it is not likely that his level of attention will be very sustained. Accordingly, newspaper style emphasizes short, clipped sentences, monosyllabic words, and the maximal simplification attainable.

Now, many reports, like all newspapers, are also written in an organizational setting—a corporation, a governmental agency, a department, a special committee. However, there are fundamental differences between the relationship of the writer of a report in a business or institutional setting to his audience and that of a news writer to his audience. These differences establish the distinctive character of each kind of writing.

From the outset, the report writer knows his audience and its particular needs for a special kind of information. The report writer also has direct feedback from his audience—a striking factor in any communication situation. The report writer pretty well knows the intelligence level of his readers and their interest-motivation in the report. Hence, he can be directly selective in presenting his information, and he can adopt a style of presentation appropriate to adults. Lastly, the report writer is not burdened with the awful responsibility of entertaining an amorphous, unknown mass readership.

It follows that the report writer will treat a single subject in considerable depth and from a variety of angles rather than a great many subjects superficially. He will not essay to inform everyone about everything but rather will speak to a known, relatively small audience in a controlled situation. He will be directly responsible and answerable for what he writes, even though he is writing within an institutional framework. And he will not purposely adopt a breezy, journalistic style for fear of otherwise losing his audience.

In the final analysis, as the creative report writer will easily see, mass media tend to appeal to the least common denominator by way of audience. Rather than write up to a higher level of intellectual attainment, writers for the mass media will write down, in the certainty that information so presented will be widely understood. The report writer, too, must be deeply preoccupied with simplicity, directness,

9

and clarity in his writing, but it is simplicity of a totally different kind and in a completely different context. His simplicity needs to be that which is present in communication between a doctor talking to a doctor, top management talking to its personnel director; these people do not dilute the facts and speak in elliptical sentences. The report writer's simplicity is achieved through full disclosure, complete amplification, and logical relationships.

POPULAR READING

The term "popular reading" is here meant to designate fiction and nonfiction of all kinds other than that in newspapers and magazines. It is read by mass audiences seeking not immediately useful information so much as diversion from their everyday problems and pursuits. Detective books, Western novels, science fiction works, books on fishing and cooking, historical novels above love and sex, paperback books (other than the classics and serious works) available in drug stores and railroad waiting rooms—all are, by the present definition, popular reading. This category of literature includes the various how-to-do-it books; simplified treatments of history, electronics, psychoanalysis, and God; novels sent out by the big book clubs; comics; serials; and every book ever presented in the *Reader's Digest*. It does not include learned textbooks, particularly those on report writing.

Like the products of the mass media, popular reading is directed toward a big, unknowable readership. Popular nonfiction writing very often is of a high caliber and provides exceedingly useful information in compact form: how to refinish antique furniture, what restaurants to avoid in Istanbul. Information so presented is, generally, information to be used away from the office, in pursuit of a special interest, hobby, or penchant. Unlike that in reports, it is information not practically useful in carrying out daily business, professional, and academic functions. Popular treatments of the Civil War, the Presidency, and Zen Buddhism, likewise, often present valuable explanation and information in easily followed style.

Popular fiction is, as is well known, intended to satisfy frustrated emotional and imaginative needs. It deals with unreality, dream worlds, never-never lands into which persons temporarily withdraw as sanctuary against unpaid bills, crying babies, and unreasonable bosses. Popular fiction is, in short, the absolute reverse of reports, which depend on facts, reason, logic, and an approach which is preoccupied with knowing and improving our real world. The only lesson that the creative report writer can learn from popular fiction is how effectively the mind can be led away from pragmatic concerns into a preoccupation with fantasies. This is not to condemn fantasies, a part of life, but to emphasize that they need to be kept out of reports, another part of life.

From well-executed popular nonfiction, however, the report writer may learn a wealth of techniques worthy of imitation. Problems faced by writers of popular exposition are very much like those faced by creative report writers. True, a book on how to build your own sailboat cannot be used to forecast next month's supply of brass ball bearings. But popular expositions are often characterized by carefully worked-out patterns of organization, brilliant sequential unfoldings, strong transitions, firm handling of complex parallel processes, and a total sense of order and clearness seldom seen in business reports. The proficient slickness of the professional popular nonfictionist is truly enviable. Though his relation to the reader is looser, less structured than that of the report writer, a fact which imposes on him a wide middle road in language and depth of treatment, he usually succeeds most capably in informing and explaining. The creative report writer wants to achieve a similar success by imitating as many of the same expository techniques as possible.

PROPAGANDA

Propaganda is an expression of opinion by individuals or groups which is deliberately designed to influence opinions of other individuals with reference to predetermined ends. Since there are in these times few opportunities to view "pure" propaganda, the report writer should think of propaganda as a literary device and general approach rather than as a literary form. Rather than expecting to find propaganda isolated, as in an enemy's wartime pamphlet, the reader can anticipate finding it in more dilute, subtle forms in all kinds of printed matter—newspapers, magazines (and all the other mass media), popular reading, and serious books, as well as in publications of labor unions, business groups, churches, schools, and political parties.

Unlike reports, propaganda undertakes to convince, persuade, inform, and explain without asking us to examine the evidence. Whereas reports attempt to discover truth and fact, propaganda aims chiefly to convey its message, good or bad, and bring about a specific action. It therefore appeals to emotions rather than to reason. With our emotions aroused, we are less likely to seek facts and examine logic, and this emotional condition is what the propagandist strives to create.

Propaganda strives to arouse emotions through commonly employed devices which sophisticated readers soon come to recognize. Recognizing them is sufficient unto itself for the report writer; it is a warning and an alert that propaganda approaches have no place whatever in respectable reports.

"Name-calling" is a device to make us form a judgment without examining the evidence on which it should be based. Bad names are given to people, policies, practices, beliefs, and ideals the propagandist wants us to condemn and reject. Names such as Communist, Socialist, integrationist, labor agitator, rabble-rouser, egghead, Red, dictator, and degenerate are bandied about. The propagandist does not present the essential meanings of these names, with all their pertinent implications. Rather, by emotionally arousing readers through use of these names, he undertakes mainly to create a negative impression about those things or people to whom he applies the term.

"Glittering generalities" is a device which works like name-calling in reverse. Good rather than bad words are used—honor, liberty, love, freedom, brotherhood, loyalty, progress, democracy. On these bases we are asked to approve without thinking.

"Transfer" involves carrying over the authority, sanction, and prestige of something we respect to that which the propagandist would have us accept. For example, symbols such as the cross and flag, standing for church and nation, are used on his letterhead. It is the propagandist's wish to have us believe that all peace-loving Christians and all true-blue Americans approve his program and are on his side.

"Testimonial" devices employ names of respected public figures in support of the propagandist's program. The "plain folks" technique undertakes to show the propagandist as just one of the boys, playing poker or attending country picnics, a fellow just like us and therefore wise and good, worthy of our belief and support.

"Card stacking" is more dramatic; it stacks the cards against truth with lies, half-truths, deception, distortion, and sham. It deliberately tries to make real appear unreal and the unreal real. "The bandwagon" technique does this also in the attempt to move people as groups—Caucasians, Negroes, white collar workers, farmers. Prejudices and biases, fears and hatreds common to the group are emotionally exploited.

The report writer ought to realize, of course, that not all propaganda has evil, sinister ends. Particularly in our society, with its openly opposed groups of all kinds, with its lobbyists, its pressure groups, and its public relations men, are we exposed to propaganda which is truly not socially harmful, though one would not wish to pass over that point too lightly either. Nonetheless, nobody who can read in America today is unexposed to propaganda and the propaganda approach.

There are, fortunately, few reports fully pretending to be reports that employ propaganda devices openly and consciously. There are, however, many reports in business and the professions which are guilty of falling into the propaganda approach, i.e., there are many reports which attempt to convince rather than to inform and explain according to the facts. These are the reports long on one-sided opinions and short on objective facts, the reports that slip into name-calling, that rely upon glittering generalities, and that utilize the bandwagon psychology. Again, these techniques can be most effective, and they do have a place in writing that has a propaganda aim. Propaganda and its devices do not, however, have a legitimate place in reports; propaganda aims to end discussion and thought, not to stimulate them. Creative report writers, cognizant of the scientific method, ought to strive very strongly to avoid one single word or sentence tending toward the propaganda approach; and as readers of reports, all writers should be alert to spot propaganda, whenever and wherever it appears.

PUBLIC RELATIONS WRITING

"Public relations" aims to form and control public opinion in the interest of a particular enterprise in order to create goodwill. PR, as it has come to be known, is popularly thought to be chiefly a characteristic activity of big business in relations with its employees, customers, stockholders, government, national business organizations, and the general public. By no means is PR today confined to business. Public relations activities are energetically carried out on behalf of labor unions, churches, universities, professional societies, political parties, national foundations, governmental agencies, branches of the Armed Forces, civic organizations, fraternal groups, and social clubs.

The scope and proliferation of PR forms are gigantic and ingeniously varied; our discussion can only briefly touch on some public relations efforts planned to reach the receivers in printed form. Consideration of a few general aspects of these may serve to pinpoint certain problems of interest to the creative report writer.

Especially (but by no means only) in the business setting do PR publications assume characteristic expression in annual reports, company newspapers, magazines, tabloids, newsmagazines, picture magazines, bulletins, and handbooks. The avowed general purpose of all these printed communications is to establish goodwill for the company; to create a benevolent, friendly, human image of the company; to tell the company story to stockholders and employees; to encourage general industrial harmony within and favorable financial and legislative climates without. Examination of these broad objectives shows that they are essentially antithetical to the spirit of objective inquiry and scientific presentation required in report writing.

PR writing fails in its objective if it does not accentuate the positive, place disagreeable facts in the rosiest glow possible, assume a cheerful mien in the presence of negative circumstances, and generally create the impression that ours is the best of all possible worlds. Perhaps only the man who has successfully done this kind of writing for a living knows best that this is unimpeachably true.

The report writer has none of these preoccupations, just as the scientist and university professor do not and must not have them. The report writer's concern must be to disinterestedly search out and establish facts without regard for how they will influence labor negotiations and the stock market. The only credible way for a report writer to effectively maintain good public relations with himself is through presentation of an honest report that holds no predetermined brief for or against a problem or idea. To the degree that a writer can, throughout his inquiry and writing, remain aloof from the PR implications of his report, he is likely to make a useful contribution. In the business or professional situation where the public relations approach permeates the atmosphere, the report writer who does not consciously disengage himself from it is doing himself and his company a great disservice. Through an objective, rational report a vicious cycle may be broken. Recommendations and conclusions which are sustained by facts and not by their public relations implications are the strongest antidote for schemes conceived in the heat of mutual admiration between top management and the PR director. What is good for the PR department is not always good for the company—and for society.

ADVERTISING

Inevitably, discussion of mass media, popular reading, propaganda, and public relations leads on to advertising. So saturated is our culture with it that one may unhesitatingly plunge into consideration of advertising in relation to report writing without pausing to provide a working definition.

Mass advertising, like the printed mass media in which it appears and which it substantially supports, is addressed to the anonymous individual. Though the advertiser probably suspects that his prospective purchasers are heterogeneous in their tastes and walks of life, he nonetheless regards them as part of the mass, an anonymous, homogeneous group. All that was said, therefore, regarding the assumptions inherent in the content and style of mass media applies likewise to mass advertising. Yet the true parallels are between advertising and propaganda.

As we said, to be effective propaganda must ultimately aim at bringing about collective action rather than individual action. Herein lies perhaps the only fundamental distinction between it and advertising, for, in the final analysis, advertising must seek to influence individual purchasers—in large numbers, yes—but individual purchasers nonetheless. Aside from the modifications which this difference imposes upon each form, the practical rules of advertising and propaganda are much alike. And, again, just as a portion of the propaganda and public relations activity swirling about us may finally serve a socially beneficial purpose, so may advertising be said to have some constructive uses.

The acknowledged ground rules for advertising are pretty well known. Brief recapitulation of them may be helpful in further showing the report writer what his own problems are and are not.

Before advertising can implant a desire for a product, it must first attract the attention of readers. In print, attention is gained in many ways—the size of the advertisement, its position on a page and in the newspaper or magazine, color, illustration, typography, layout, or copy. The ad attempts to attract the reader to it through contrast, novelty, and distinction.

As a next step, the advertisement must quickly undertake to stimulate desire for the product. Mass advertising, in attempting to persuade mass customers to buy, appeals to the bedrock of human nature: consumer self-interest. It assumes that people are primarily interested in themselves and the things that pertain only to them—home, children, health, comfort, financial security, status, etc. Mass advertising does not assume for itself the mission of cultivating lofty attitudes of intellectual detachment in its readership; it purposefully tries to excite desire by appealing to that which is selfish and acquisitive in the individuals who make up the masses. But, of course, one may not condemn advertising for failing to do what it never set out to do.

Beyond these classic first two steps, advertising depends on favorable, appealing, simple, clear-cut images. With the images there must be continuous repetition of slogans and catchwords, persistent assertion and reassertion, assertion and reassertion.

For the report writer, review of advertising principles offers additional pointers on what to studiously avoid in reports. First, reports do not require catchy gimmicks to draw attention to them. This is not to suggest that reports are sufficient unto themselves like the Bible or Constitution. But reports have nothing to sell. The inherently pragmatic character of subjects treated in reports is usually such that persons have sufficient motivation to read them from the outset. It will become increasingly clear to readers of this book that the author is not advocating insufferably dull reports lacking luster and originality. One must only recognize that a report should not exist unless it offers useful information to one or many readers. The attention of those who choose or are obligated to read the report has already been drawn to it by the subject and the situation. The nature of the treatment given the subject, if dispassionate and logical in the desire to lucidly inform and explain, is the best assurance of sustaining reader interest.

Further, a report need not openly appeal to a reader's primitive self-interest. This is not to deny the existence and value of self-interest. Self-interest is the prime motivation to action in most humans, with the exception of saints. But it is well known that there are higher and lower levels of self-interest and higher and lower means of satisfying it. The fellow who robs a bank is self-interested, but so is the laborer who works hard all week for his money. Though most reports will, directly or indirectly, be connected with a profit motive of some sort, they seek to satisfy this need through the acquisition and dissemination of knowledge. Improvement of the human condition is gained by the sustained self-discipline required for the researching, organization, and writing of a report. The report itself should, essentially, be directed to the satisfaction of human reason.

Lastly, with regard to the use of repetition in advertising, the report writer will learn farther on that repetition is a conventional rhetorical device for gaining emphasis. He will see also, however, that repetition is not the only means of achieving emphasis and that it can be utilized effectively only as part of a comprehensive writing approach for making the main message in a report stand out clearly.

SUMMARY

Before considering reports in relation to belles lettres as a last exercise in elaborating their aims and criteria and in exposing their essential nature, a review of matters already covered in this chapter might be helpful.

1. A report is a literary form evolved in response to the needs of contemporary business and professional men for clear factual information and explanation of diverse simple and complex subjects. A report contains certain characteristics of other expositional literary forms; there are certain others which it does not contain.

2. A report is not an instrument of mass communication. It is undertaken with a specific purpose, for a definite, circumscribed objective, with a known, select audience in view. Reports are prepared with the knowledge that the writer bears direct responsibility, irrespective of his organizational-institutional role.

3. Popular expository nonfiction can teach the report writer about good techniques for clear explanation. Popular fiction is at the opposite pole from report writing.

4. Propaganda uses emotional, anti-intellectual devices which are openly malappropriate to the essentially scientific nature of reports.

5. Public relations writing, also, is carried out with a predetermined premise, i.e., all is well or will be well. Such an engaged hypothesis cannot allow for the judicious, impartial examination of facts needed in report writing.

6. Advertising, to satisfy its selling purpose, utilizes a psychology, technique, and language which essentially undermine reason and urge acceptance on the basis of self-interest. Report writing, on the contrary, is directed logically to the mind in a disinterested, impartial approach to objective truth; it is not chiefly concerned with material gains.

7. A report must essay to ward off the various corrupting influences of these other familiar communication forms and to be itself a document of truth.

BELLES LETTRES

Belles lettres refers to literature as one of the fine arts—fiction, poetry, drama—as distinct from technical and scientific writing and from the immediately utilitarian kinds of writing we have just talked about.

A report writer is not a belletrist any more than a textbook author is or an advertising copywriter is. Those who create fine, great literature are in a class apart from these. It may be said that all persons engaged in any kind of writing, no matter for what immediate purpose, are but scarecrows dangling in the empty field, or as lonely coyotes baying at the moon, unless they cultivate an appreciation of serious literature in all its forms.

What they gain from this appreciation, truly, has but little utilitarianism. As writers we gain from belles lettres a respect for ideas, a feeling for language, a sense of form, and so on. But to read good books in the primary quest for rewards such as these is to read for the wrong reason. One ought not to search out practical benefits from great books. One should not seek culture to satisfy social and economic demand. Nor should one read belles lettres in search of some moral motto to live by. One reads the world's great literature in the desire to increase the quantity and quality of his personal experience—to achieve the depth, breadth, and gentleness of mind and heart which are the real rewards of good reading.

The aim of life, philosophers agree, is happiness—a self-sufficient state of being which is not a means to obtaining some other state but an end in itself. One reads good books for personal happiness—the satisfaction that results from broadened emotional and intellectual experience gained through contact with rich minds. A man does not seek this broadening experience primarily to increase his market value, even though it does increase that value. To place practical above personal benefits in reading is to defeat the idea of happiness.

Good literature is distinguished by its enduringness and universality. A great book appeals to all times. Where is last year's best seller? Chaucer and Dante still endure after six centuries. What qualities of universality are there in today's novel? Sophocles and Goethe still provide that quality which appeals to the universal traits of humanity.

There are no absolute laws for good literature, a fact which prejudices many modern business and scientific minds against it. Nonetheless, literary works that have proved their universality by enduring are clearly works of the imagination that appeal to the emotions.

Literature, like all art, is a form of communication. The writer through his art communicates his experiences and feelings to others. He consciously does this. A sea gull swooping over the waves in search of food is a natural phenomenon, but this occurrence recreated in a novel, with feeling and interpretation, is art. The writer must first have the experience and then consciously find the words to re-create it. If he is successful, he finds recognition in the reader's mind, where the experience is vicariously duplicated. (This aspect of good reading ties in with the methodology of criticism, to be discussed in Chapter 18.) Belles lettres are intensely concerned with the individual experience and with the communication of knowledge, not logically, but intuitively through images. The man of business, the man of the professions, the man of science, cannot hope to be a whole man unless he cultivates through good reading this intuitive knowledge. Without it, his success with logical knowledge, the general relations between things and the laws governing those relations, is vacuously meaningless.

TECHNICAL AND SCIENTIFIC WRITING

There has come into being a particular kind of report called "technical" or "scientific." Having written a large number of them in his capacity of a professional industrial report writer, your author knows what these reports are. To this technical report as such Chapter 21 in this book is devoted. In addition, readers will find in Chapter 18 remarks on the nature of science and steps in the scientific method. Here, in line with the aims of the present chapter, the overall kinship of technical and scientific writing will be commented upon in broad relation to expository writing in reports.

Examples of scientific writing must include the works of Aristotle in the fourth century B.C., Galen in the second century A.D., Bacon in the sixteenth century, Faraday in the seventeenth, and Darwin in the nineteenth, as well as those of Whitehead, Russell, and Einstein in our own century. Technologists with a scientific education could, in writing their reports, gain much from familiarity with the general principles which animate classics of scientific prose. The style has altered in response to the time and place, and the corpus of knowledge has grown, but the principles of scientific writing are the same.

Scientific writing, of course, differs from belles lettres in that it pursues logical knowledge empirically and makes use of defined and agreed-upon sets of classifications and measurements. Though books have been written on "technical writing" and "technical report writing," and though many more will doubtlessly appear, technical writing is no more than scientifically oriented writing that consists of special terms used strictly with reference to an agreed-upon scheme. These special terms and agreed-upon schemes are efficiently cataloged in a growing storehouse of manuals, handbooks, dictionaries, guidebooks, encyclopedias, lists of specifications, and lists of standard technical abbreviations and terms for physicists, chemists, chemical engineers, geologists, mechanical engineers, electrical engineers, civil engineers, industrial managers, costs accountants, economists, foresters, industrial architects, and insurance actuaries. Use of these agreed-upon schemes and special terms is mandatory, and any technologist sufficiently competent to undertake a report will know what source books to consult for those in his own field.

But to be something more than a creature conceived for the purpose of feeding data into a digital computor, the technical writer should attempt to gain perspective on his position by study of both belles lettres and classical scientific writings. From scientific writing he may gain a view of the manner in which the scientific attitude expresses itself in words by rejection of conventional systems of ideas, by critical discrimination, by generality and system, and by empirical verification. These characteristics of scientific writing are those which all writers of reports, technical and otherwise, want to know about.

3

Needs for Reports in Modern Society

Professional Institutions
Communication in the Machinery of Constitutional Government
Communication in the Complex of Business Structures
External and Internal Communication
Vertical and Horizontal Communication

Need for reports has intensified proportionally with the complexity of organization of our society. Adam and Eve had only themselves and God to communicate with. When they failed to understand and to carry out a directive from their superior, the entire organization fell apart and went to hell. Ultimately, Adam and Eve came to understand that important message. But it took them a lifetime to try to regain what they had lost.

The purpose of the present chapter is to examine aspects of the structure of democratic society. This survey of phases of professional, governmental, and business organization strives to indicate parts of the societal pattern served by reports. Though the entire process of communication—both written and verbal—is concerned here, it is the role of written reports that interests us.

PROFESSIONAL INSTITUTIONS

Sociologists tell us our society consists of organizations or institutions which are distinctive and which, when taken together, provide for sustaining its life and reproducing its members. An institution may be said to consist of a common goal which a small or a large number of men have, together with an organization designed to seek this goal. Each institution has its *raison d'être*, norms, personnel, activities, material apparatus, and function. In these facets of an institution, reports figure most prominently.

The reason-for-being of a professional institution or organization—its goal, the end for which it exists—is perhaps its most important aspect. Persons in the professions, in scientific disciplines, and in the academic and scholarly pursuits have formed societies which have specific *raisons d'être*. Usually this goal is advancement of the profession for the benefit of the large body of society as a whole. A man will usually participate in a multiplicity of institutionalized activities in his community, social, familial, religious, and business or professional life, in each instance through an organization with an objective somewhat different from that of the others. Though reports are part of all institutionalized life, they come into the spotlight most often in professional organizations.

In the process of recognizing the need for organizing a group of professional people with some common interest into a society (for example, a legal society), in establishing the society, in sustaining it, and in perpetuating it, reports are essential. The major *raison d'être* of some professional societies is to foster preparation of reports which will increase the professional knowledge of those who belong.

When one speaks of the norms of an institution, one talks of the rules and regulations which members must follow if they are to remain members. Without norms the aims of the institution will not be served and its *raison d'être* will remain unfulfilled. It is in explicitly formulating and setting forth these norms through reports that charters are formed and constitutions are drafted which make the organization possible to begin with. And chief among the norms explicitly formulated through reports is often the rule that professional reports will be written by the society personnel for publication in the society journal.

The personnel of the institution consists of its leaders and its membership. The leaders are those with authority within the institution. Members occupy status and play roles in conformance with the norms of the institution. Men who wish to be more than members at large in the personnel of the society will recognize that the norms require writing creative reports. It is today a widely accepted fact of institutionalized professional life that any person aspiring to leadership in his profession must write and publish work. Writing reports and books is second to none as the most effective means of advancement to leadership within a professional organization.

If the norms of a professional society consist of what members should do, the activities are what they actually do. Infrequently are the two identical in every respect. Yet if the discrepancies between the norms and the activities are wide and serious, the institution will fail. Here again, reports are an integral part of the life of the institution, for these documents offer tangible and objective evidence of how closely the norms are being followed or deviated from. Through reports and their quality, the vitality of the institution can be constantly measured.

One refers to the material apparatus of an institution such as a professional organization as the particular equipment necessary to its operation. There is, of course, the utilitarian equipment, such as a building for administrative offices and meeting rooms, but there is also the symbolic apparatus, such as professional insignia and robes. In professional life, symbolic paraphernalia is fully as important as utilitarian apparatus. Clearly, some objects have both utilitarian and symbolic value, but some may be designated as having primarily one or the other. So it is with reports in a professional society; they possess strong utilitarian value, but they are symbolic of the institution's *raison d'être*, norms, personnel, and activities.

Finally, in considering reports in relation to institutionalized professional life, there is the matter of the function of the professional society. If *raison d'être* signifies what the members aim to accomplish, the function is what they actually do accomplish, the total results of the activities of the institution. These results are characterized by how closely the organization comes to achieving its purpose and by the side effects of these results for society as a whole. Reports, the results of the professional research of the society and its members, are often the most excellent measure of realized function. And the quality of the benefits which accrue to the body of society from these reports rounds out the assessment of the total results of the professional society's activities.

Within the structural organization of contemporary professional institutions, then, reports are vital. Not less important is the role played by creative reports in the machinery of constitutional government and in the complex of present-day business and industrial activities.

COMMUNICATION IN THE MACHINERY OF CONSTITUTIONAL GOVERNMENT

A system of constitutional government such as exists in America cannot live if it cannot function effectively. The core of effectively functioning constitutional government is bureaucracy, a term used here in no opprobrious sense whatever. Bureaucracy is intended to mean simply the administration of government through departments which have vital functions specified by law. Bureaucracy—administrative government—is a fundamental requisite of constitutional government. People in the service of government perform definite functions which the community at large considers necessary and worthwhile.

In order that bureaucracy may function well, there must be clearly defined relationships which are aimed at achieving integration and coordination of efforts of different groups. Three elements needed to establish and maintain these functional relationships are centralization of control and supervision, differentiation of function, and qualification for office. Creative reports figure prominently in each element.

As governmental organization grows larger and more complex, the number of officials who may exercise duplicated interests is endangered by irrational growth. To avoid this, detailed and specific functions of workers need continuous reinterpretation in terms of the larger objectives which the functions presumably serve. Also, the obstacles and difficulties encountered in the exercise of these specific functions demand continuing analysis with a view to possible improvement and alteration. Centralization of control permits coordination of spatially diffused functions of a bureaucratic unit.

Differentiation of function is another element requisite to the administration of present-day constitutional government. Constant experimentation and study are needed to keep the differentiation of functions of a governmental agency in line with changing public needs. The central authority acts as a control seeking to integrate technically and regionally differentiated functions of a governmental unit. Functional differentiation usually starts at the top of a governmental organization and proceeds downward.

Well-trained officials, qualified for appointment or election to civil service, are a third requirement of an efficiently working bureaucracy at the core of constitutional government. Technical qualifications today exist for many positions in government, an indication of the relation between a competent bureaucracy and good constitutional government. Of course, constitutional government could not long continue in the absence of a public educational system which serves to give persons the technical training needed for governmental service.

In the foregoing aspects of government administration, reports play a role of incalculable importance. It is doubtful that a competent bureaucracy could develop and continue without that phase of communication satisfied by reports. Hence, it may be said that constitutional government could not continue to function without reports clearly providing explanation and information. Each of the elements of democratic civil administration—centralized control and supervision, functional differentiation, and qualified officials—would atrophy and die were it not for continuous communication among the army of individuals comprising the interrelated groups. Reports undertake to effect the integration and coordination which are the objectives of the bureaucratic workings of constitutional government.

Federalism is the form of political organization in the United States. As we all know, federalism is suited to communities in which a territorially diversified pattern of objectives, interests, and traditions can be effectively implemented by joint efforts in pursuit of common objectives, interests, and traditions. The ingenious federal scheme combines a measure of unity with a measure of diversity; federalism expresses itself in an organizational pattern within which there is an urgent need for reports. Organizationally, the three elements of a federal pattern are a representative assembly, a common executive, and a judicial setup.

Congress deals with an immense bulk of business—thousands upon thousands of bills, joint resolutions, concurrent resolutions, and simple resolutions involving all phases of national and international life. To function well, both branches of Congress depend upon committees to which are referred, in accordance with their subject matter, all bills and resolutions. Frequently, a particular committee will form its own subcommittee to handle a designated piece of business. When action is taken on any proposition in hand, a committee report is prepared, recommending adoption with or without amendments, or reporting adversely. Reports, in the daily work of congressional committees, are at the vital center of the legislative process.

The President, in acting out most of the incredibly vast number of roles he plays, is frequently dependent upon reports which are often written especially for him. Some of these reports ultimately become items of public record, while others, owing to the nature of their subject, are sharply restricted to presidential scrutiny. President John F. Kennedy was said to have been an unusually talented, exhaustive reader of the vital reports presented to him. According to accounts, President Kennedy not only scrutinized the full body of an important report but, wherever appropriate to the situation, thoroughly studied appendixes of notes of conversations, statistical data, and like information. One may assume that the prodigious grasp of information President Kennedy possessed, which had so astounded Washington journalists, was acquired through this habit of reading reports searchingly.

The dual function of the American Supreme Court as guardian of the Constitution and as an executive organ engaged in interpretation, application, and enforcement of law is, in the end, carried out in written reports, documents called "opinions of the court." These reports, many of which have enduring historical value, contain the line of reasoning, citations of authority, and the final order in the disposition of the affair. Clearly self-evident, then, is the place of report writing in the judiciary element of a constitutional government in a federal form.

Lastly, in any consideration of the part reports play in the machinery of federal government, there are again the administrative agencies which were taken as the focus for our earlier general discussion of reports in a democracy. The task of carrying into force the Constitution, acts of Congress, Executive orders, decrees, and treaties is entrusted to this large number of administrative departments, commissions, and other agencies. It was seen previously in this chapter that reports constitute a great deal of the bread-and-butter daily routine that keeps these essential agencies in operation. So it is in the legislative, executive, and judicial branches of government: Reports keep the machinery of constitutional government rolling.

In state government certainly, and to a somewhat lesser degree in local government, creative reports are the staple of everyday administrative life. State and local governmental institutions in democratic countries provide an opportunity for closer citizen participation in governmental affairs than is possible in the bigger areas. As a consequence, these institutions provide political education that is valuable to the general politics of the country. Along with local meetings, direct confrontation, and verbal communication, reports serve not only to expedite the intragovernmental business but to prevent a chasm from developing between government and the people.

Primarily, state and local governments are providers of services.

Throughout the states and counties, these governments are concerned with the maintenance of roads and streets, parks and recreational areas, certain types of hospitals, social welfare institutions, and educational facilities. Likewise, state and local governments undertake to provide police forces, correctional institutions, fire-fighting services and, not less important, machinery for raising public funds to pay for these services.

However, before any of these essential services can be provided, government must make studies and prepare reports as a basis for communication with the people. Essentially, the people must determine how much of these services they want, the quality they want, and the degree to which they are willing to pay for them. It is unlikely that individuals can know this fully or be prepared to make sound judgments without reports that it is partly the function of state and local government to prepare and distribute. On many local governmental levels members of the citizenry will energetically initiate, or themselves actively participate in, the preparation of studies and reports for use in governmental service.

Though report writing is manifestly an inseparable, integral component of federal, state, and local intragovernmental activity, it operates also, though less apparently, as a basis for communication between the various levels of government and the people. The mass media are the chief vehicles for reporting governmental news and information. In general, information of government disseminated via mass media is concerned with day-to-day matters or things that are happening at the moment in Washington or the state capital or in county, municipal, or rural government. People who receive this information, though, are perhaps little aware that the affiliated news services and broadcasting-television networks which distribute it depend heavily upon documented reports prepared by and obtained from government. Without these reports, which are analyzed and filed by the research departments of the news agencies, there would be insubstantial bases for reporting daily events in government. Thus these documents likewise serve the daily workings of government by providing written evidence used as a foundation for communication with the people.

COMMUNICATION IN THE COMPLEX OF BUSINESS STRUCTURES

Business comprises all the activities associated with the production and sale of goods or services. The extent and nature of business activities are as varied as the social and economic interests of man. Three broad classifications of business are sometimes provided: commerce, industry, and service. To commerce is assigned all that activity concerned with the transfer of goods and the collecting, grading, warehousing, transporting, insuring, and financing of the transfer of goods. Industry is taken to be primarily concerned with the production of consumers' goods and producers' goods. Service industries are occupied with rendering the multiplicity of personal services.

A business undertaking is, depending on one's angle of vision, different things to different people. Local, state, and federal government, as well as the community, the worker, the owner, and the management of a business enterprise, all probably regard the primary function of the enterprise in a somewhat different light. Formal and informal verbal and written communication between the groups and the individuals comprising them helps assure mutual understanding of the goals of each interested segment. Reports aid in achieving coordination and successful operation of the business for everybody's benefit.

Regardless of the particular overall organizational form it assumes, a business has within itself various operating functions it must carry out. There are the functions of finance, manufacturing, production planning and control, purchasing, engineering, office management, personnel management, marketing, selling, etc. Ownership and structural forms of a business enterprise range from a single proprietorship through a general or limited partnership to a joint-stock company, business trust, or corporation. Each form has requirements for its effective operation. Internal structural organization is needed for the business enterprise to achieve its objective. Coordination is necessary between two or two thousand people if the enterprise is to gain maximal efficiency at minimal expense of human effort. It is the formal or informal structural relationship within which coordination takes place that is known as the organization.

Coordination must be the common objective in all organizations. The degree to which coordination is realized in any enterprise is directly related to the success or failure of communication within the organization and with the outside world. As this maxim has been more widely recognized, more and more feverish attention has been given by management to problems of communication. It may be said that improved communication has become the hue and cry of the present generation of business experts.

To produce a functioning organization, there must be a common objective, a control mechanism, fixed responsibilities, consideration of capacities and interests of involved personnel, and opportunities for individuals to express themselves and improve their position. Communication is needed in fulfilling each of these requirements.

Management needs to keep the personnel of an organization constantly aware of the major objective and mission of the enterprise. As an organization becomes increasingly larger this problem becomes more acute. Not only are business organizations in serious trouble when they lose sight of their basic institutional goals; so too are social, religious, educational, and governmental institutions set hazardously adrift by this same loss of sight of the chief institutional objective. Sound and clear written communication helps as nothing else does to prevent and overcome this wasteful groping of institutionalized man.

Control mechanisms in an organization are manifest through lines of supervision. Definite lines of supervision are needed to synchronize group effort. Organic unity of purpose and performance usually cannot be achieved without these lines. And in order to keep these lines open and functioning in both directions at all times, to keep them adjusted and adapted to meet the requirements and objectives for which the business enterprise is constructed, communication in written form is essential.

In establishing and maintaining definite lines of supervision within the organization, fixed responsibilities are placed. Sound organizational practice generally dictates that responsibility be fixed as low in the organization as competence exists to assume that responsibility. In building the organization for the future, careful selection and training of personnel are undertaken for the next-highest level of fixed responsibility. This operation of a functioning organization is exercised greatly through written reports. In large, complex organizations dispersed throughout a single large office building or throughout widely scattered plants and offices in this country and the world, a report may be the only face by which a man becomes known to those high in the organizational hierarchy.

Consideration of the capacities and interests among the personnel, together with provision of opportunity for a man to fully realize his personal objectives within the framework of the enterprise's objective, are equally fundamental to a successfully functioning organization. In the complex of business structures, report writing here, too, satisfies a basic need. Individual talents and interests are creatively articulated through written business and professional communication, a procedure which allows the writer opportunity to grow toward higher levels of attainment and recognition. Report writing in a complexly structured business organization may be the chief if not the only mode of communication and articulated participation an individual is regularly assured.

Multitudinous factors give rise to the need for improved organization and reorganization in all the foregoing business structures. Communication must occur at each of the interstices of the functioning organizational network. The overall institutional-organizational patterns which big business enterprises assume are commonly described as scalar organization, functional organization, and line-staff organization. A word will also have to be said about committees within these organizations.

Scalar, line, or military organization theoretically provides simple, direct authority and responsibility from top to bottom. Each unit is complete in itself as far as the functions it is required to perform. Coordination is achieved between heads of units or by a single executive controlling two cooperating units. Communication originates at the top of the hierarchy and travels vertically down the line as directives in the form of reports.

Functional organization undertakes to separate manual from mental requirements, especially in manufacturing industries. Between the manufacturing superintendent and the individual workmen are a number of specialists with specific functions bearing upon the labor of the entire manufacturing process. Supervisory and manual functions are sharply dichotomized. Where, in this organizational pattern, a worker must respond to a number of specialist-supervisors, communication downward and upward prevents shop management from breaking apart.

Line and staff organization, by far the most common form in business today, fuses some of the principles of both scalar and functional patterns. In contemporary practice the line-staff organization usually becomes a departmental-line organization with the staff functions added. The line portion of the line-staff organization operates essentially as a scalar structure from top to bottom, but line supervisors of functionally intact departments have at their command staff specialists to investigate, advise, and correlate interdepartmental relationships.

As may be abundantly clear, report writing is inextricably bound up with an effectively functioning line-staff organization. There is, first of all, the direct line of communication from the top to the bottom of the line. Next, there are the reports written to help fulfill a functional department's individual mission. Further, there is report writing as intercommunication between functional departments on the same line. Lastly, reports are at the heart of coordination and advisement efforts of the various staff specialists in their relationships with respective functional departments.

Within all forms of business structure and within every other kind of operating institution, work of the functioning organization is carried forward by committee—the policy committee, the administrative committee, and the safety, athletic, planning, grievance, and special committees. Appointment or formation of a committee is very often the initial step in getting any project started, in business and out. Professional societies and academic institutions—not to mention the various levels of government—would surely almost cease to function if committees ceased to be. While committees lack initiative, are time-consuming and slow, and are given to compromises which weaken their efficaciousness, they do offer a manageable approach to well-coordinated and balanced problem solution. Report writing, of course, is part and parcel of the committee's responsibility. Committees investigate, study, deliberate, discuss, advise, and recommend to those to whom they are responsible. And so here, again, reports cannot be eliminated in a business or any other institution which utilizes committees in its operation.

Business, viewed in perspective, may be seen as a social science. Business relationships in a good many of their aspects are group relationships. Understanding of fundamental group relationships is requisite to the solution of many business problems. In business, the basic unit of activity is the individual acting as a member of a group. The group can become effective only through the collective efforts of individual members. Each individual must become integrated into the cultural system (which includes the communication system) of the business organization.

Communication is a condition of all effective business activity. Information must be channeled upward so that the operation of the organization is not impaired by weak decision making. Delayed and distorted upward-directed reports jeopardize the judgments of those responsible for directing the enterprise. Modern business depends fully as much upon these group relationships as upon economic considerations. Each member of the group influences the other members and their activities. High on the list of ways in which any single business individual communicates with and acts upon the group— constructively or destructively—is the written report.

In this process there are yet to consider the additional aspects of reports in external and internal communication and in vertical and horizontal communication.

EXTERNAL AND INTERNAL COMMUNICATION

Our remarks so far have been directed toward intraorganizational reports. These comprise the vast preponderance of written communication prepared and circulated within an organization as part of the working function. In considering the movement of a report and its use by a company, however, one must also give attention to external reports, i.e., reports prepared within the organization proper but designed for distribution outside it. Yet among externally distributed, so-called company reports, only a very small number may be called true reports by the definitions we are using.

That reports which many contemporary organizations—professional, governmental, and business—prepare internally and distribute externally are not *primarily* reports is very evident: They are public relations, advertising, and propaganda releases prepared in the traditional format of reports. These publications, which we have already been at pains to identify, serve useful purposes of their own, but their main intention is not to scientifically offer objective information and explanation.

As an example of an external communication which is not a true report though it is called one, there immediately comes to mind a typical large corporation's annual report to its stockholders. Of course, since the stockholders actually own the company, the report is not external in a strict sense. But the annual report to shareholders, though it provides authentic financial and operational information, is in most instances today essentially a public relations document. It is prepared by the public relations department within the company or by an outside agency retained for the purpose. Pertinent information about company operations and finances is set off by rosy interpretation, lavish color illustrations, expensive paper and printing processes—all the standard PR devices to project a favorable company image. Again, it is not our intention to quarrel with these efforts; it is our main wish here to establish that the annual report is not the kind of true report in external communication we speak of.

In this connection it would be appropriate to remind readers that these same reservations apply to the entire bulk of internal reports referred to as "employee publications." These magazines, newspapers, tabloids, bulletins, and handbooks are legitimate reports only in that some do contain information of an educational sort. But the main intention of these publications is quite at variance with that of a true report.

Now, there are indeed external reports which *are* reports. Some of the kinds of reports discussed in the following chapter are used both internally and externally. It will be seen that some short, informal reports such as memoranda, some semiformal short reports, and a good many long, formal reports are written with a view to external communication with a limited sector of the general public, an outside governmental agency, the company's legal or financial advisors, etc. Further, it will be seen that concerns about the company image are, categorically, legitimate concerns of every creative writer of any report for external use. However, these considerations are best satisfied by attention to the form, style, and content of the external report, without diluting any of these with a view to making a "blue sky" impression,

That external report form which is chiefly used in the usual day-to-day external communication with company clients and customers is the letter report. It is a relatively brief, informal report form similar to, yet distinct from, the conventional business letter. (As a document separate from the letter report, the business letter is taken up in Chapter 19.)

VERTICAL AND HORIZONTAL COMMUNICATION

In the vocabulary of early classical studies of functioning bureaucratic and military organizations, "vertical" and "horizontal" appeared as descriptive terms. As these words apply to the nature and direction of information flow within present-day business and governmental organizations, they have received the attention of sociologists, industrial management experts, and personnel specialists. Assuming the hierarchy inherently necessary in the various organizational structures we have touched upon, vertical communication refers to information transmitted from the top to the bottom and information sent from the bottom to the top. This encompasses communication between any two different levels, no matter how closely or how widely separated on the organizational chain. Horizontal communication refers to that between units which are on the same plane of the organizational grid but are nonetheless separated by function and/or line of authority.

Traditional theory appears to hold that communication in organizations should and does move vertically throughout the hierarchy rather than that it cuts across lines of authority. Instructions move down a line of authority; information moves up. Assuredly, this pattern is essentially correct in broad practice, but there are certain critical variables.

In the scalar, functional, and line-staff business organizational configurations we spoke about, the downward communication is most often directive, instructive, or supervisory in nature. However, the quality of these communications is infrequently strictly official in tone. It is true that policies are pronounced, goals are projected, responsibilities are assigned, reassigned, or reaffirmed, schedules are established, etc., in downward communication. Nonetheless, it is not always emphasized in discussions of this process that these business reports, though directive in nature, consist chiefly of information or explanation in substance. These directives, more frequently than is supposed in business circles, actually state only facts and ideas, i.e., what is to be done, when, and by whom; less frequently will downward vertical communication actually instruct as to how to do it.

There is a view of the communication process within all kinds of large organizations which holds that there should be little if any formal written communication between personnel on the same level. Of course, this has nothing to do with informal small talk unrelated directly to work, or informal discussion about work problems. But if management executive X must formally communicate with management executive Y, the communication should go up one chain from X and then down another to Y, with their common vice-president linking the two chains at the top. Why?—so that higher officials may always be informed of things occurring beneath them.

In governmental bureaucracy, there can be no question of the validity of this theory and practice; there can be no strong centralization of control, accountability, and authority if those on top do not know exactly what is going on beneath them. Manifestly, though this need is as great in big business structures, the practice is not rigidly adhered to in a growing number of the modern big corporations. Chain of command is not as jealously guarded as it once was, chiefly because enlightened management, on the one hand, and well-educated men with specific business or technical specialties within the organization, on the other, recognize the awkwardness and slowness of acting out the circuitous up-down vertical routes.

Nonetheless, the problem still remains of informing those at the vertex of all that is occurring. This now tends to be accomplished informally, either verbally or in writing. But the formal up-down route, in a situation of the kind being described, could not be avoided initially if the personnel concerned were not confident of the rightness of their action. Streamlined, up-to-date personnel practice tends more to try to create structured organizational relationships which nevertheless allow staff personnel considerable freedom in executing business responsibilities, including the freedom to follow those routes for internal communication which seem most direct to them in a given situation. What has become apparent is that the necessity for a great rate of vertical communication decreases proportionally with a reduced need for close and continual supervision in any division of an organizational complex.

Horizontal communication among staff personnel of coordinate rank on the organizational chart thus appears to be increasing as relaxation of this rigid up-down-up practice occurs. In business and industrial job situations that require regular and close daily supervision, horizontal communication will be rare. But particularly in the contemporary business world, as distinct from the industrial-manufacturing world, horizontal communication that cuts across lines of authority seems more allowable, especially among coordinate but functionally separate staff persons in the lower and middle levels of organization.

For the creative writer of reports, problems inherent in vertical and horizontal communication reduce themselves to reasonably simple practical concerns. The present text does not undertake the task of instructing the individual as to whether a vertical or horizontal communication may be required in a given organizational situation. Though the reader may seek in specialized publications useful theoretical discussions of this problem, he would ultimately have to make an individual choice determined by the particular circumstances and practices within his own working organization.

Once the decision is taken as to whether a vertical or horizontal communication is wanted, the report writer may then be guided by thoughts developed in the following chapters. He will particularly need to have information about the function and composition of reports as they apply to up-down or across communication, a matter taken up in the following chapter.

4

Explanatory, Informative, Long Formal Reports

Anyone who has had the pleasurable but challenging experience of teaching report writing, either in a college classroom or in the field as a consultant, will have been struck by the stubborn way in which people cling to names of kinds of reports. A man will protest, "But we call that something else in my company—you can't be right in giving it that name!" Or, "We have always used a completely different system here for naming and identifying that kind of report!" Doubtless, these protests are sincerely motivated. But they reflect a rigidity of mind and even a sense of insecurity, however understandable, regarding new ideas. These qualities are not compatible with an open mind and the learning process.

All readers, regardless of their special interests and long experience in certain ways of doing and naming reports, will recognize their own particular kind of report in the descriptions which follow. First principles only have been followed in grouping them into large, broad categories—principles based on function and form. In all but the simple matter of providing a tag for discussion, the names given to these kinds of reports are quite inconsequential.

       ✿   ✿   ✿   ✿   ✿

Reports are categorized and described by their intended function or proposed arrangement and length, or by both. Function may be to inform or to explain, while arrangement and length may be informal and short or formal and long. Whether it is an external or internal communication, a horizontal or vertical message, and whether the intended setting for it is in industry, government, the professions, or school, the kind of report is satisfactorily denoted by these general modes of classification.

The function of an individual report not only will serve to classify it generally but also will influence if not determine its composition (arrangement and length), although certainly the arrangement and length by themselves may not be counted upon to make clear the function. Many a businessman, professional man, and student has most effectively obscured the intended function of his report by mismanagement of arrangement and miscalculation of length. Function and composition in a report—as in effective writing of all kinds—are inseparable.

CATEGORIES BY FUNCTION

Reports properly have one of two possible functions: to inform or to explain. Though the distinctions involved have already been touched upon in Chapter 2 and will be discussed more fully in Chapter 8, let it be clear now that reports also describe, narrate, persuade, and even argue. But to the extent that they do these things primarily and directly, they cease to be true reports and become misguided writing exercises and polemical tracts. Description or narration as an end in itself is malappropriate, but description and narration designed to integrally support information or amplify explanation in a report are both wanted and needed. Persuasion and argument, where they are the forces prompting and guiding the writing, may be expected only to befuddle the explanation and distort the information. The most irresistible argument in a report is that which is implicit in objective exposition of information. To the degree that a report contains special pleading on the part of the business executive, professional man, or student, the perceptive reader—be he the chairman of the board, president of the professional society, or college professor—will mistrust it.

That any of the forms of discourse—explanation (exposition), narration, description, and argument—be written in isolation from the others is neither possible nor desirable. Writers of reports are nonetheless well advised to confront at the outset the immutable fact that informing or explaining should always legitimately be their energetic preoccupation.

CATEGORIES BY COMPOSITION

Formal Long Reports

All the elements which may, at one time or another, have a place in a long, formal report are listed at the beginning of this chapter. It remains now to consider these elements individually—to provide a definition of each with an explanation of its function in relationship to other parts and to the whole of the report.

Front Matter

Cover. Since the long report may have some permanent reference value and may be handled and perused by a good many persons, the cover is needed to identify and protect it. Various materials—heavy paper, leather, cardboard, or plastic substances—are used. Author, title, completion date, and number (if part of a series) appear on the cover. In some organizations, printed forms for information which readily identifies and catalogs the report are attached to the cover.

Flyleaf. A blank sheet of thin, high-quality paper preceding the title page is the flyleaf. It is used when the report is prepared for a high officer or official, or when an impression of great correctness, formality, and quality is desired.

Frontispiece. The frontispiece faces the title page and may consist of a drawing, photograph, map, chart, or some other visual element (graph or table) closely relating to the subject matter of the report. This element serves to heighten the interest of the reader and to draw his attention to the subject at hand. It rarely if ever appears in an internal report.

Title Page. As a vehicle for fully identifying the report, the title page contains the title, subtitle, author (with his professional title and address), name and address of the individual or organization for whom the report is prepared, date of completion, and serial designation, contract, or project numbers, where appropriate.

Copyright Statement. If the material in the report is copyrighted, the statement indicating this will appear on the back of the title page. It will include the copyright date, the name of the publisher (if a professional press is used) or the name of the firm holding the copyright, and a statement to the effect that "all rights are reserved." Thus, parts of the report may not be legally reproduced. Since many firms are constantly fearful lest material from their reports be appropriated by their competitors, and since copyright is a complex legal problem, legally trained persons should be consulted as to the correct phrasing of the statement.

Letter of Authorization. The letter of authorization is written by the person requesting or authorizing the report to the person who is himself to do the report or is responsible to see that it is done. The authorization letter is included in the report only when it may be desired as a matter of record. The letter formally establishes authority for the report writer to proceed. To the extent that it may or may not outline concrete details and suggestions for executing the investigation and preparing the report, it is termed either a specific or a general letter of authorization. Though in practice most such letters are broadly general and merely request the report, the more specific letter of authorization is likely to initiate prompt, clearly motivated action by the report writer and to result in a report fully satisfying the needs of the person requesting it.

Letter of Acceptance. Though rarely included in contemporary reports, the letter of acceptance is a reply to the letter of authorization. Its function is to indicate that the person undertaking the project accepts the program of investigation and the writing of the report. If the letter of authorization was very general, the letter of acceptance will recapitulate the general request but will probably go on to outline specific plans for the project and seek approval for them. Questions in regard to time, expense, and procedure may be raised and resolved.

Alterations in the plans which were suggested by a specific letter of authorization may be offered. Clearly, the letter of acceptance is designed to establish close rapport and firm understanding between the report writer and report authorizer. Sharp, clear, unequivocal communication by both parties at the outset obviates misguided effort and establishes what is wanted and needed in the forthcoming report; the letter of acceptance should help achieve this solid foundation. In business practice, since early communication between those doing and those requesting reports is frequently carried out by a series of meetings, phone conversations, or short, informal letters, the letter of acceptance in its classic form seldom is drafted to appear in the final report. But there are without question many professional report-writing situations in which it is ill advised for the report writer to proceed before a formal letter of acceptance, summarizing all the areas of agreement, has been drafted and sent for approval to the report authorizer.

Letter of Approval. One kind of letter of approval is written in formal reply to the letter of acceptance and has the function of approving final plans, costs, techniques, time schedules, etc., for the report, giving the investigator the signal to proceed at once with the project. Again, this element does not frequently appear in the modern report.

Another kind of letter of acceptance may be written after the report is completed, accepting and approving it as satisfactory to the person who authorized it and commending it to the attention of other personnel in the organization or even to the public. This kind of acceptance letter will accompany the report. Particularly within large business enterprises, where the report may be prepared by a subordinate for a departmental chief, who may wish to approve and accept the document before it is sent on to the board of directors or some other higher-up group, will this kind of letter of acceptance come to be included in the final report.

Letter of Transmittal. The letter of transmittal serves as a formal forwarding vehicle of the completed report to the individual or persons who initially authorized it and then gave approval to the plans offered by the writer; thus, it is addressed to the report authorizer. The transmittal letter is usually bound into the report, but may also be sent separately. If it appears in the report, it should follow the title page and precede the table of contents; if other formal letters appear in the report, the letter of transmittal will be last, following the authorization, acceptance, and approval letters.

What the letter of transmittal—the one formal letter which is today invariably a part of the report—may be composed of depends largely, on one hand, on whether formal authorization, acceptance, and approval letters will also be included. On the other hand, contents of the transmittal letter will depend on the nature of the report and the business or professional setting for it.

If the other formal letters are excluded (as is often the case), the letter of transmittal will probably refer at least briefly to the mechanics of authorization, approval, and acceptance. Where a formal dedication, foreword, and preface may also be excluded from the report, the letter of transmittal can succinctly cover the functions of each of those elements.

Depending on various factors—the audience for the report, the purpose and scope of the report, the relationship of report writer to reader—the letter of transmittal may go on to present a short summary of the report, to review its scope and limitations, to sketch its history and background, to emphasize needs and uses for it, to survey its conclusions and recommendations, and even to articulate personal views, opinions, and attitudes of the writer which find no logical place in the report proper. A well-written and thoughtfully composed letter of transmittal can do much to awaken the reader's interest and to establish the writer's competence and authority for the report. There will be, nonetheless, occasions when the letter of transmittal will correctly be expected to do none of these things or to contain none of these elements. Then it will consist only of several sentences of submittal and forwarding of the report. The trend at present, however, in long, formal reports distributed both externally and internally, is to sharply reduce other front matter but to build the letter of transmittal along the lines and for the purposes mentioned above.

In front matter thus far discussed, additional information may be found in Chapter 10, Preliminaries and Essentials, and in Chapter 16, Presenting the Written Report. It should be emphasized here, in any event, that though formal presentation of some of the front matter is frequently abbreviated or omitted in line with a swing toward an uncomplicated, streamlined report format, the report writer is wise to review the functions of all these elements. He may in this way be assured, at least informally, that he is not failing to carry out basic communication processes which are essential prerequisites for an effective investigation and report.

Dedication.   Occasions may sometimes arise when a dedication of a professional or business report is appropriate. Obviously, this is a most formal element, suitable only for a report of considerable scope and depth reflecting an investigation covering an extended period. The dedication may be to an individual whose earlier work in the same field of investigation laid foundations for the report. It might be to a person who contributed much to the work of the report, but who died, fell ill, or moved to some other area before the report was completed.

It might, though infrequently (if ever) in a business setting, be to a personal friend or family member who provided support and encouragement. The dedication appears on a separate page, after the title page and copyright statement but preceding the other front matter.

Foreword. In reports, forewords are today often written by persons other than the report author. The foreword functions in much the same way as the letter of transmittal. Indeed, where a foreword is used, particularly in reports destined for wide external distribution, the letter of transmittal will usually be dropped to make place for the foreword. As a person who knows the report author and the quality of his work, the foreword author is able to commend the man and his work to the reader, commenting on the value and usefulness of the report. It would not be appropriate for the traditionally modest and self-effacing report writer to say these things about himself or his own work. But the foreword author needs to be someone who, by virtue of his own position, name, or reputation, commands the proper respect and attention for the report. Where the foreword is thus used, it is generally composed along the lines of a transmittal letter and complements the introductory matter of the text of the report. A good foreword, like a good letter of transmittal, can do much to urge the reader on and to orient him vis-à-vis the report author and the subject at hand. In requesting a foreword from an individual for these purposes, the report writer, having at first, of course, allowed the foreword writer to study the completed report, might courteously give him a free hand in its preparation. If, however, the report writer believes specific suggestions may be welcomed, he might indicate that he would be pleased to see the foreword touch upon some matters relating to the report such as these: purpose and magnitude, background to the development, qualifications and experience of the report author with an indication of his special interests, and relationships of the report to others in the field. The writer of the foreword can only be pleased if he is particularly invited to end his comments with a personal, objective, critical evaluation of the worth of the report.

Preface. The preface functions for the report author to provide a personal statement of his own philosophy and views. These, naturally, are simply presented in their relationships to the particular plan of attack or mode of execution of the report. The reporter has this opportunity to state clearly what he has tried to do and how he has tried to do it, so that he may be fairly judged and not censured, perhaps, for failing to do what he never wanted or wished to do. Prefaces are finding places in more modern long reports, especially those which are distributed externally. When the preface does appear, it will often replace either the foreword or the letter of transmittal, or both, but not always. If a preface lucidly sets forth the report author's personal statement, reasonable readers outside or inside the organization may certainly disagree as to whether the report was worth doing in the first place. But that consideration has more to do with the person requesting and authorizing the report than with the person preparing and writing it.

Acknowledgments.   Whether or not a separate acknowledgment page is included depends completely on the nature of the report and the purpose for which it is intended. Acknowledgments formally call attention to individuals, groups, and organizations which have cooperated and contributed in a significant way to any phase in the preparation and completion of the report. That acknowledgments should appear in many reports is clear. But whether they may be included in the letter of transmittal, preface, foreword, introduction, or in a separate page-listing is a matter for individual choice. If the acknowledgments are extensive they can clutter up and detract from whichever element they are combined with. However, presenting acknowledgments separately may overemphasize the help received, even to the point of embarrassing the people concerned.

Table of Contents.   Additional exploration of considerations relating to the table of contents will be found in Chapters 10, 12, and 16. Briefly, in its sequential relationship to other front matter of the long, formal report, the table of contents should be seen by the report author as the first view of the total architecture of his report that the expectant reader will gain.

As such, the table of contents may very well be in outline form. In this way, the major divisions can quickly be observed in their coordinated relationships to the whole of the plan. Subject headings under major divisions serve, in conventional outline pattern, to quickly indicate depth and detail of treatment among divisions and topics. Indentation common to the outline pattern of presentation should, accordingly, be used. Page numbers should be given for every topic listed; all considerations should be directed toward facilitating ready reference to any section or topic.

All front matter beyond the title page, as well as all back matter, is usually listed in the table of contents. Lowercase letters are customary for pagination of these sections and should be so shown in the table. In this fashion these components may be distinguished from the main body of the report.

It is also permissible, as any review of exemplary contemporary reports will testify, to abandon the outline technique in the table of contents and even not to list front and back matter. This is especially to be encouraged in a report covering small units of information related only in a very broad sense to one another although they are closely related to the central subject and purpose of the report. Forcing an outline upon sections dealing with, let us say, commodity price fluctuations, which are followed by a section covering, for example, available skilled labor would doubtlessly be artificial. It would be far better merely to list the necessary order of presentation in the table of contents by giving the major sections bold headings, with subtopics indented in a block and listed beneath. Page indications will nonetheless be required for all items listed even though the outline form is abandoned.

Table of Illustrations. The list of tables appears after the table of contents and all that it may contain. Since this list is a separate element, it may be presented on a separate page, or it may be appropriately labeled and spaced down from the table of contents on the same page. Depending, of course, on what the illustrative material consists of, the table may be called table of graphs, table of photographs, table of charts, etc., or table of illustrations. All items are given in order of appearance. Each is identified by the caption heading that appears with it on the page, and page numbers are given.

In addition to showing the caption, some report writers like to label each illustration as, say, Figure I, or Graph D, or Table 14; this is encouraged notably in technical reports or other reports which include many illustrations, or in reports which have a complex, intricate nature. Such numerical or alphabetical referencing, working with the caption (which is often lengthy), greatly simplifies and enhances identification. Further, some report authors wisely repeat in their table of illustrations the numerals corresponding to the main sections in the table of contents and then list the illustrations used under each section.

In a report containing very few illustrative materials, however, the writer may simply list them at appropriate points in the table of contents, relating them to the text they support and thereby eliminating need for a sketchy separate table of illustrations.

Text

Synopsis. Some of the distinctions among synopses, abstracts, précis, résumés, digests, and summaries will be mentioned in Chapter 25. In some ways, the differences are superficial and minor, perhaps only of academic interest. In other ways, because of the recognized importance of an objective, abbreviated statement containing the gist of a report, shorn of any embellishment or developmental material, one would do well to know these distinctions. Faced with the impossible task of knowing firsthand the profusion of literature presently being published, persons in all fields of endeavor, in order to keep abreast of developments in their respective fields, are obliged to depend more and more upon the reading of lucid, abbreviated statements of lengthier works.

For the moment, the synopsis should be regarded as a statement embodying a brief general view of the major ideas and facts contained in the report. It is obviously intended to provide the report reader with a helpful overall view which reveals, from a summit, the whole plan and main substance of the report. The synopsis, since it precedes the body of the report, is regarded by some writers to be an element of the front matter. This point serves to emphasize the fact that the synopsis must be able to stand alone—that one who reads it but not the report should nonetheless be provided with the heart of the matter. As a rule, however, any condensation appearing with the total report is chiefly useful through its ability to focus upon the main core of the report and to lead the reader confidently into a full illuminated reading of the whole. The synopsis, in other words, is properly part of the text and is a jumping off point for study of the entire body. By the synopsis, the mind of the reader is prepared to receive the information developed in each section of the report and to regard this information, even before a whole reading is accomplished, in relation to the whole view projected.

Body of the Report

> Introduction
> Materials and methods
> Discussion and commentary
> Conclusion
> Recommendation
> Summary

These elements are simply listed here. Since, in many ways, they are everything that this book is about, separate chapters elsewhere are devoted to each. The introduction to the report is discussed in Chapters 9, 10, and 12. Materials and methods are analyzed in Chapters 9 and 11 to 15. Discussion and commentary are developed in Chapters 8, 9, 13, and 15. Conclusions and recommendations appear in Chapters 9, 13, and 15. The summary is explained in Chapters 15 and 25.

Back Matter

Appendix. To some report readers, the appendix is fully as important as the text and the body of the report. For an intelligently selective and well-organized appendix can permit the reader to form his own judgments regarding the soundness of conclusions and recommendations in the report and to thereby assure himself about the competence of the report writer and the authority of what has been written. In reports on critical governmental matters this is unquestionably the case, but it holds equally in reports covering, for example, programs of financial investments, plans for extending product lines, investigations of new sites for location of plants, etc. It may be seen, then, that the classical view of the appendix as additional or supplementary material at the end of a report, relating to it but not essential to the main body of the work, no longer holds true in many instances. In some reports, the appendix *is* essential to the central work.

What, then, goes into the appendix? Any carefully selected material which will serve to illuminate the text and to verify its accuracy goes into the appendix. This may include copies and records of all communications central to the development of ideas and information put forward by the report. Included may be not only letters but telegrams, records of phone and personal conversations, and even recorded progress notes. If interviews or questionnaires were utilized to gather information for the report, notes on these with specimen samples may be placed in an appendix. Illustrative material and statistical information in logical support of the premises of the report may also be placed in the appendix. Newspaper clippings or other printed matter which may be of special value may also be included. Persons preparing technical or scientific reports will want to decide whether formulas and mathematical computations belong as notes within the text or as an appendix. Those doing legal or accountancy reports will be faced with similar decisions regarding full case citations and specimen balance sheets.

Each appendix is labeled. For example: Appendix A—Correspondence with Federal Bureau; Appendix B—Daily Progress Notes on Construction. If a great deal of matter is deemed necessary for the appendixes and it tends to make the report physically bulky and cumbersome to handle, appendixes can be separately bound and properly labeled. Many writers will prefer to handle large appendixes in this fashion.

This is not for a moment to suggest that all formal, long reports require appendixes of such detail, or require appendixes at all. Only the individual report author, in full grasp of the circumstances and materials of his report, can decide this matter. The chief rule is that the body of the report be as logically and compactly presented as is consistent with full understanding and credence on the part of the reader. Any material which seems essential but does not meet this criterion for the text of the report may be carefully weighed for the possibility of placement in an appendix.

Bibliography. The bibliography is a compilation of all the printed works used in the preparation of the report. It is offered so that the reader may verify original sources if he chooses and so that future report authors may find in one listing all the available material on the subject. Cumulative knowledge of a subject is thus gained, and repetition of searches is avoided. Bibliographies are presented alphabetically according to the last names of authors. They are, if comprised of many entries, broken down into sections. These may be units listing books, articles, and reference works.

As an acceptable alternative to the traditional bibliography, the report author may choose to offer a list composed only of references cited. In this situation, the listing at the end of the report will not be alphabetical or broken down into sections. Rather, each item will be numbered to conform to the number assigned it as a footnote in the individual pages of the report. This method is rapidly becoming more popular in reports not anticipated to have a very permanent value.

Variations on this method, however, are generally unsatisfactory. Some report writers judge that, since all the sources may be found consecutively numbered in the footnotes, a separate listing gathering them onto one page of the back matter is not required. Or they reason that although the sources are assigned footnote numbers throughout the body of the report, documentation need not be presented at the bottom of each appropriate page of the text but can be withheld for the final list of numbered references cited. The disadvantage of the first method of departure from the accepted streamlined form, of course, is that it does not conveniently provide references cited on one page; the reader must thumb through individual pages. The disadvantage of the second mode of departure is that the reader must turn pages backward or forward to make the necessary integration between a footnote number on an individual page and the reference list at the end of the report, and this can be an irritating chore. In general, some of these practices may be justified by the needs of publishers of journals to save on costs. But the practices have been perpetuated even in reports not destined for publication, a category which includes most reports.

The preferred method remains the traditional one of presenting the bibliography separately, alphabetizing and arranging it as first described, and making it independent of numbered citations in the footnotes. As will be seen in Chapter 16, the most widely accepted form for information in the footnotes is different from that of the bibliographic entry. Maintenance of this distinction has value. Further considerations of both footnoting and bibliography will be found in Chapters 11 and 26.

Index. Reports of unusual length and complexity, dealing with a multiplicity of data and destined for wide reading, require an index. As with all other components, the index is provided to enhance the value and to increase the usefulness of the report. The index is a detailed alphabetical key to the topics, names, and places in the report, with reference to their page location. It is the terminal component of reports in which it may appear.

Any report author preparing an index would do well to examine indexes of several reports or books containing them (including the one in this book), to gain a fuller idea of the general mechanics and of the variations exercised by authors in the degree of specific details offered. He should especially observe the system of indentation practiced in presenting the index in its final form. As with the principle followed in outlining, subtopics are indented below major topics.

Preparation of the index is perhaps best carried out with 3- x 5-inch filing cards. By scanning each page from the beginning of the report, the author can make entries of major and minor topics on individual cards and alphabetize them in the process. Final alphabetization of all the cards then becomes a fairly simple mechanical operation.

IBM

Personnel Research Studies
Effective Utilization of Older Workers:
A Review of the Literature

Office of Director of Personnel

TABLE OF CONTENTS

Summary

Although there are many varied results from studies on the
productivity of older workers and the majority of these report that
many older workers compare favorably with the younger worker in
all aspects of job performance, the question of aging and ability
can best be summarized by the following statement of the National
Committee on the Aging:

"Within the same individual as well as among individuals,
different abilities begin to decline at different ages and vary
in the rate in which they decrease. . . . Just as development
and growth are not uniform for all abilities nor for all people,
neither are decline and deterioration."

In addition, McFarland and O'Doherty point out that although
many studies show a steady decline in capacities with age, "it is
well to remember that this constantly changing balance between
physiological and psychological impairment, on the one hand, and
increased experience, wisdom, and judgment, on the other,
occasionally results in actual improvement of capacities. . . ."

The several means of utilizing the service of the older worker,
such as retraining, reassignment and job re-engineering are
examined in Section II. Although several sources contend that
not enough is really known about the psychological changes with
aging, a number of suggestions are made concerning the methodology
to be used which would be helpful in retraining programs.

Job reassignment and job re-engineering are two means used when
the ability to perform a customary job is impaired. Among several
types of jobs to which older persons might be transferred are:
jobs which require custom or quality work (an increase in quality
is often a compensation for decreased speed), less complex or
lighter jobs such as inspection work, etc.

When jobs are re-designed they may involve changing the pace of
the operation, breaking the job into simpler parts, using special
equipment to compensate for decreasing visual acuity, etc.

The introduction of materials handling and control equipment is
noted as a means of reducing physical demands on older workers.

The Department of Labor lists several reasons for the adoption
of flexible retirement programs: the allowance for individual
differences in productivity for all ages, the investment of time
and money in the development of a worker and the reduction of
pension costs.

These areas of the Federal Government are particularly concerned
with the problems of the older worker — the Department of Labor
which is involved in a broad research program concerning the

economic problems of the older worker; the Department of Health, Education and Welfare's Office of Vocational Rehabilitation and Office of Education, and the Federal-State employment service system.

On the question of displacement, the AFL-CIO contends that the older worker should be aided in two ways: 1) the Federal Government should assist in special research in the techniques of teaching and retraining older workers, 2) special attention should be given to job re-engineering, a matter for joint union-management agreement.

Among those companies which have given special consideration to developing programs for the utilization of older workers, the programs of Eastman Kodak, Con Edison, Convair and Macy's are cited.

In conclusion, it is suggested that additional research be conducted on several areas of the relationship between aging and the ability to be retrained, including specific methodologies of retraining and the investigation of retraining of non-industrial workers, such as salesmen, insurance agents, etc.

Introduction

The problem of effectively utilizing older workers has been magnified in recent years because of the rapid growth of this segment of the population. Since 1900 the number of persons under 45 has nearly doubled; those who are 45-65 tripled and the number who are 65 and over has quadrupled. In the decade 1960-1970, the labor force will grow by 13.5 million workers. Those workers under 25, with the least experience, will account for almost half of the manpower increase. There will be only a slight increase in the age group 25-44. And within that group, there will actually be a decrease in the group 35-44 which normally supplies the great bulk of highly skilled workers, foremen, managers and executives. Workers over 45 will increase by 5.5 million and account for 40% of the net gain in the labor force. It is estimated that by 1975 over half of the adult population will be over 45.

In an expanding economy it is important to utilize manpower fully and efficiently and to maintain consumer buying; it is therefore essential to consider this large and growing segment of the population who are or will be older workers as both producers and consumers.

It is the purpose of this paper to explore the literature available which deals with the effective utilization of the older worker. Most of the work done in this field in the 50's establishes bases in fact for the need to prepare the way for utilization of older workers through flexible hiring and retirement programs, job reassignment and retraining. However, the data on established programs by companies in all of these areas are unfortunately somewhat limited.

The method used in presenting this report is first to explore certain research data and reports by companies which deal with the characteristics attributed to the older worker which affect his ability to be reassigned or retrained to meet the changing demands of a technological age. Among the data studied are the psychological and physiological changes associated with the aging process which affect the ability to learn new methods of work, the relationship between age and productivity among different levels of occupations, and the records of older workers on absenteeism, accidents and turnover. Next, the several means of utilizing the services of the older worker are examined – retraining, reassignment, job re-engineering and flexible retirement – with greatest emphasis on retraining. Finally, the efforts of different groups to promote the concept of utilizing the older worker effectively are reported.

Although "older worker" is an ambiguous term which is used very freely in literature, throughout this report, "older worker" will generally refer to the skilled and semi-skilled worker who is 45 years old or older, unless otherwise noted. There will be specific references to studies of professional and technical people and to clerical workers and in one study of "older workers," the reference is to workers who are 65 and over.

The first part of this paper is concerned with the research material available on the relationship between job performance and the older worker in terms of productivity.

I. JOB PERFORMANCE OF OLDER WORKERS
    A. Productivity

Although there are variations in the results of research studies and reports by companies, the performance of older workers compares favorably with that of younger workers, as will be shown by the following reports.

Con Edison, in a merit rating study, found the peak performance of workers to be at the age of 45. Both the increase from 20 to 45 and the decrease from 45 to 65 were symmetrical. (8)

In a longitudinal study by a New England machine-shop firm, the work performance of workers ages 65 to 71 was compared with that of the same group at ages 60 to 65. Forty-six of 71 employees showed no decline that substantially affected their work. (8)

Alexander Smith and Sons, in a study of work output and age, found that differences between older and younger workers were not significant.

In the Ithaca Gun Company study, older workers showed up somewhat better than the younger workers. (8)

The H. J. Heinz Company found that where the job required accuracy or skill, the older workers could keep pace with the younger groups, but where raw materials were processed, the older worker shows a higher rate of output. Where transportation and warehousing operations are studied, particularly those involving incentive pay systems, the older worker is not as efficient. (8)

The Bureau of Labor Statistics conducted two studies on the relationship between age and job performance for factory workers and for office workers.

The first, a study of factory workers, (25) was conducted in two industries, covering 26 establishments and 5,000 production workers. The industries selected were the footwear and furniture industries which show a distribution of men and women throughout all ages which is similar to manufacturing as a whole. These industries make extensive use of incentive pay plans.

The methods used were based on those which had been developed previously for a pilot study by the Department of Labor. (23) Job performance was measured by three indicators: 1) output per man-hour 2) attendance 3) continuity of service.

The findings showed a different pattern for each aspect of job performance that was measured. For output per man-hour, there were greater variations within age groups than between age groups and substantial proportions of older workers outperformed the average of the younger groups. No relationship was found in the case of attendance. In continuity of service, length of time employed increased as age increased, with the exception of the oldest group.

Conclusions based on the wide variability of performance within age groups where many individuals perform far above and far below the average for the group, indicated the importance of individually evaluating a worker's performance.

The second Bureau of Labor Statistics' study (25) on the relationship between job performance and age, was conducted among 6,000 clerical workers employed by five Federal Government Agencies and 21 companies.

The production records were collected from the following clerical operations – typing, secretarial work, filing and key punch, business and duplicating machine operations. "An index of output was obtained for each worker by dividing his output per man-hour by the average output per man-hour of workers aged 35-44 years in

his same classification." Accuracy and consistency of
performance were also obtained. Incentive pay systems covered
about half of the employees.

Findings:

1) There was considerable variation in performance within age
groups; large proportions of older workers (those over 45)
exceeded the average performance of younger groups.

2) Differences between age groups were small.

3) Older workers had a steadier rate of output than younger
workers.

"For both groups of workers, there was relatively little
variation in average performance among age groups, but
considerable variation among individuals within age groups; a
large proportion of workers in the higher age groups exceed the
performance of the base group average." Once again, this study
points to the need for individual appraisal of the employee.

Although the results of the two BLS studies showed great
similarities, there were also several differences. Both studies
showed that nearly half of the workers in the ages 45-54 had output
per man-hour indexes greater than the average worker in the 35-44
age group. However, there was only a small number of office
workers over 45 having very low output indexes. Also there was a
difference in the individual performance of workers aged 55 and
over. Among clerical workers, the proportion of workers who had
output indexes that were greater than 100 was practically the
same as the proportion for the 45-54 age group. Among factory
workers, the proportion was lower. It was suggested that this
may be a reflection of the effect of the greater physical demands
of factory jobs.

Other findings of this study were: of the 10 occupational groups
studied, no differences were found in age-performance with the
exception that the key-punchers who were under 35 had much lower
average indexes than the other age groups. On routine jobs, such
as typing, sorting and filing, older workers, especially those over
55, had higher than average indexes of output.

Studies by Lehman (6) and Schaie (16) showed that men in
technical professions – engineers and chemists, did their best
work before the age of 40; their creative activity declined both
quantitatively and qualitatively after this age. This viewpoint
has supposedly received considerable support from a number of
people, including Dr. Raymond Stevens of Arthur D. Little,
Inc. (32)

To test the validity of Lehman's findings, Winston Oberg (13) studied the age-achievement relationship of engineers and scientists within an established organization. Oberg believed that it was more important to study the day-by-day work performance of a man than to draw conclusions from paper and pencil test scores which show a decline with age.

The subjects in Oberg's study were 909 people, 80% of whom were men and 97% of whom held one degree; 40% held advanced degrees. They consisted of almost the entire technical force of the company.

The method of evaluating performance was based on the annual order-of-merit rankings of technical men which were used for salary administration purposes. Although such rankings had disadvantages, it was felt that they deserved merit because they were the results of a series of independent analyses and they were prepared carefully as the basis for a man's salary increments. The engineers and scientists were rated separately according to the type of work engaged in – R & D or engineering. In the first stage of the analysis, both supervisory and non-supervisory technical people were studied. In the second stage, only 645 non-supervisory technical personnel were used.

In R & D work, the earlier findings of Lehman were supported – the performance peak was reached at ages 31-35. Ages 36-40 were almost as high. Then the rankings began to fall and declined more or less steadily.

However, the situation was quite different in the engineering departments. Here it was found that age and experience won out over youth and flexibility. Each group was rated higher than the next younger group.

Conclusions – in industrial R & D activities, peak performance is reached before the age of 40 and steadily declines thereafter. This conclusion supported Lehman and Schaie's findings.

In engineering work, performance appears to improve with age. This conclusion conflicts with the findings of Schaie. It is suggested that the reason for this is that an "engineer's work depends less on creativeness and innate ability than it does on the breadth and quality of his technical experience." The new problems he must solve are variations of those with which he has successfully coped in the past.

It may be noted that Lehman had studied the relationship of age to achievement in many fields – chemistry, poetry, art, literature and business management. For most of the occupations studied, he found that the best work of an individual's career had been accomplished by the time he reached 40. The two exceptions were novelists, whose peak was 41, and business executives who reached their peak in their late 50's.

The National Council on the Aging recently conducted a study (32) on the problem of utilizing trained professional and scientific workers who are over 65. On the subject of age and ability, the Council makes the following statement, "As a matter of scientific fact, there is no objective evidence to support any generalized relationship between age and ability as measured by productivity. "

The Council, which has noted the findings of Lehman, suggests that factors other than ability which are involved in a decline in productivity in older persons are "preoccupation with domestic, economic, vocational and emotional problems." Lehman himself recognized that the differences he observed in age groups may reflect changes in other circumstances and in motivation rather than in ability alone. And Dr. Stevens of Arthur D. Little, Inc. has acknowledged that the older person is superior in many traits, such as stability, dependability, and maturity of judgment.

Opinion surveys were conducted in 1939 and 1951 by the National Association of Manufacturing on the subject of age and performance. (10) In the first study, 85% of member companies rated the older worker's performance as equal or superior to that of the younger worker. In the second study, 93% of the companies indicated that the older worker equaled or surpassed the performance of the younger worker.

A Temple University survey (1) of 100 large Pennsylvania companies in 1953 showed that in assessing quality of production of older workers, 93% of the older workers were considered average or above (49% being considered above average). In quantity of production, 61% of older workers were average or above.

NOMA conducted surveys (11) in New York, San Francisco and Houston in 1957 and 1958 on the relationship between productivity and age. The range of replies was from 85% to 93% in stating that older workers are not less productive than younger workers.

In 1958, Factory Management and Maintenance magazine (14) asked employers of over 150 manufacturing plants whether or not workers over 50 "do the 'same' or 'better'" in the following aspects of work – overall performance, quality of workmanship and output. In overall performance, older men were rated higher by 97% of those responding; in quality of workmanship, higher by 99% and in output, higher by 78%.

B. Physical Capacity of Older Workers
In a study (20) that was conducted on retirement by the Institute of Adult Education and the Institute of Psychological Research of Teachers College, Columbia University, an investigation was

made into the area of the pressure effect of aging on work performance. For this study, union members in the garment industry aged 55 and over, were interviewed. They consisted of three groups — before, at and after retirement. Of those interviewed, about 40% of the first group and 70% of the last two groups indicated that they felt they were unable to turn out as good a day's work as they had 5 years previously. In addition to a decline in productivity, they also reported that they had to work harder to maintain the former level of performance. For the last two groups, there was also an indication that the reserve capacity for extended work is reduced with age. On all questions concerning job performance, the differences between the 3 groups are significant with progressive increases in the proportion who have to work harder, who tire more easily in getting to and from work and who worry about not being able to keep up with younger workers.

"The union workers' reports suggest that physiological declines are reflected in aspects of job performance." However, it was noted that it is dangerous to make generalizations from this data which appear to indicate a decline in productivity with age. The data are subjective and may be influenced by the stereotype that loss of productivity is always an accompaniment of the aging process. No production figures are available with which the subjective reports may be compared. There were great differences among those interviewed within age groups; there were some workers in their 70's who reported no decline in productivity while other respondents in their 50's did.

The National Committee on the Aging (8) suggests that tests be devised that apply to the work situation and which emphasize the factors involved in the ability to work.

The U. S. Department of Labor, in an evaluation of 4,000 typical jobs, found that about 86% required a minimum of strength or exertion. (22)

In terms of physical exertion, many employers are beginning to realize that most jobs can be handled by almost anyone and even when the physical requirements of a job are important, it should be recognized that individual capacities of older workers often equal or exceed that of younger workers.

C. Sensory, Motor and Mental Abilities

The most important consideration in hiring, retaining or retraining is whether or not the worker is physically and mentally capable of performing a job satisfactorily. Although the data are limited from both scientific and industrial sources, according to the National Committee on the Aging, the following research findings are available on sensory, motor and mental functions of aging. (8)

At 24, keenness of vision begins to drop off; after 50, it declines markedly. Hearing also drops with age, particularly after 65. General muscular strength begins to decline after 27; however, 82% of the maximum muscular strength remains at 50. Manual dexterity reaches its peak between 20-30 and then declines until age 50, after which the decline is steep. Test of co-ordination show the same curves; however, there are individual differences.

Although earlier studies indicated that intelligence declined after the early 20's, more recent investigation indicates that the peak is reached much later, the decline is more gradual, and the changes are small until the middle 50's. In one longitudinal study, a man at 50 showed higher scores on general intelligence than he had when tested at 19. A study by Bayley (2) indicates that verbal intelligence continues to grow until at least 50. Then when the peak is passed, the verbal intelligence declines more slowly than sensory and motor functions. After 29, the ability to remember declines gradually but steadily. Complex material and material that requires formations of new associations provide the most difficulty. Other mental abilities that decline with age are reasoning by comparison and analogy, the ability to understand and to adopt new ideas and working methods. Speed declines with age more rapidly than accuracy. Bowers (4) found that the ability to learn reaches a peak in the early 20's, falls off until age 45 and then drops off sharply. However, the change in the rate of learning was compensated for by an increase in dependability and steadiness. Most studies emphasized the need for individual appraisal since the tests indicate that the variations within age groups are more significant than age differences. The Committee stated, "Within the same individual as well as among individuals, different abilities begin to decline at different ages and vary in the rate in which they decrease. . . . Just as development and growth are not uniform for all abilities nor for all people, neither are decline and deterioriation."

A summary by experts of the effects of aging on work performance follows:

"The effects of aging vary so much from individual to individual that functional rather than chronological age is a more effective criterion in judging abilities. No method of measuring functional age has yet, however, been standardized. Most sensory changes do not interfere with performance, but changes in visual and auditory functions, though of less significance than is frequently supposed, are most likely to cause deterioration in performance. Changes in psychomotor skill suggest that older people should not be placed on work requiring continuous rapid action. This loss of speed, however, tends to be compensated for by greater accuracy and attention to detail." (9)

D. Attendance, Health and Safety

In a 1948 study, the Bureau of Labor Statistics reported that older workers had an attendance record that was 20% better than other workers. (21) The Bureau conducted additional studies in 1956 and 1957 and concluded that "age as a factor relating to a worker's attendance can be ignored." (24)

The National Association of Manufacturing's survey of attendance and safety records in 1939 and 1951 showed that employers felt that the record of older workers equaled or surpassed that of the younger worker. (10)

Ninety percent of respondents to the 1953 Temple University survey of private firms felt that the record of older workers was better than the average for younger workers on absenteeism. (23)

A Prentice-Hall Survey on employee attitudes indicated that deliberate absenteeism and turnover were considerably less for older workers than for younger workers. (28)

The National Committee on the Aging concluded from a number of research studies that "older employees may be less likely to be absent from work, but their absences, when due to illness, may be of longer duration. (8)

Although the results in the study of frequency of accidents are sometimes inconsistent, in most cases the older worker has a better record than the less experienced worker. (8) However, the consensus of reports seems to be that when older workers do have accidents, they are more likely to be severe.

E. Other traits Attributed to Older Workers

Belbin (3) studied employees in thirty companies to discover the negative characteristics attributed to older workers. According to this study, workers over 40 were considered unsuitable for acquiring new skills in industrial operations. The tasks they performed were subject to time stress, either by pacing or time pressure. The most difficulty was found in "unskilled operations and in those involving small parts and fine controls, or operations involving bodily movement or activity."

Bowers (4) analyzed the personnel records of employees aged 18-76 and found that employers thought older persons did not learn rapidly and were slow but they were better in attendance and conscientiousness.

According to Welford, (31) one of the sources of task difficulty for older workers involves the learning of new tasks. There was no evidence to discover whether specialized training, without stress, would lead to improved learning performance.

The Department of Labor conducted a study on "Adjustments to the Introduction of Office Automation" and found the following opinions among personnel officials regarding the selection and retraining of older workers. On the debit side was the opinion that older workers are less adaptable to change. Also to their disadvantage is their generally lower level of education. To their advantage, however, older persons appear to have a better attitude toward their jobs than younger people, with a greater sense of responsibility. Other traits mentioned were "mature judgment" and "care for details." (27)

In the National Committee on the Aging's study of 30 companies in the Cleveland area, it was indicated that "almost without exception, older employees were regarded very highly, especially because of their willingness to work, loyalty, backlog of experience, and lower rate of absenteeism and accidents." (8)

The Personnel Policies Forum of the Bureau of National Affairs made a survey of 200 companies which indicated that older workers match the performance of younger workers in almost all aspects of work behavior with the exception that there is a tendency on the part of the older worker to resist new ideas and a failure to make suggestions. However, an Eastman Kodak study revealed that although older workers suggest fewer ideas, the ones they do offer bring greater profit to the company. (8)

Although, as McFarland and O'Doherty point out, many studies show a steady decline in capacities with age, "it is well to remember that this constantly changing balance between physiological and psychological impairment, on the one hand, and increased experience, wisdom, and judgment, on the other, occasionally results in actual improvement of capacities. . . ." (9) It is unfortunate that those qualities in which the older worker is considered superior, such as stability, responsibility, loyalty and steadiness are not measureable.

The second section of this paper deals with the various means of effectively utilizing the services of the older worker.

II. MEANS OF UTILIZING OLDER WORKERS

A. Retraining

The preponderance of research data points to the wisdom of retaining older workers. However, in order for them to continue to be an economic asset to a company, the acquisition of new skills through retraining may be necessary. Older workers are often particularly vulnerable to displacement and the retraining problems and policies associated with the older worker deserve particular attention.

Comprehensive research on aging was conducted at Cambridge University by the Nuffield Foundation. (30) The purpose of these studies was to "point to ways of assisting the employment and training of people in their later years." According to A. T. Welford, Director of the Nuffield unit, the field studies of retraining do not in themselves clearly indicate the best methods to use in training older people. However, from results of experiments on learning and performance generally, Welford recommends the following:

1. "The subject should be given control of the pace of instruction and the amount required to be learnt at any one time should be limited.

2. "The relationship between instruction and task should, other things being equal, be as direct as possible. Thus, manipulatory skills should be neither taught nor tested by using words. . . . A verbal medium implies translation from words to action or vice versa which may be disproportionately difficult for older people.

3. "Care should be taken to ensure that the material presented is at all stages of training understandable to the subject so that he never has to perform a task he does not comprehend.

4. "Errors should be prevented during the early stages of training so that they do not become fixated and have to be 'unlearnt' later."

Welford notes that older people have more difficulty in learning through theoretical than through practical training, partly because the presentation is by lecture which imposes a pace for taking in information. Theoretical training is also more difficult because descriptions are verbal and abstract.

On the practical implications of training, the Nuffield studies conclude: wide variability among older people implies that some older people can be trained to a high standard of performance. Although training may take a little longer, the low turnover rate compensates for the cost of training.

From an empirical viewpoint, the main results of these studies, which appear repeatedly, are:

1. There is an "obvious slowing of performance that goes with age, a slowing manifested not only in sensori-motor tasks but in perception, problem-solving and other situations in which it is mental rather than the motor component which is stressed."

2. "There is the increasing variability between one individual and another as we go up the age scale, which means that more often than not we find a substantial number of old people performing at a level at least equal to that of the average of a group of younger subjects."

In the Handbook of Aging and the Individual, McFarland and O'Doherty point out that discouragement is the one most important factor to avoid in training older workers. (9) Therefore, "attention to the manner of presenting material and to the circumstances and pace of training" would seem to help not only in shortening the training time but also in avoiding discouragement among older workers.

This framework is suggested for formulating methods for learning: (9)

1. On perception, older people are helped considerably "by presenting the material in a way which will allow them to understand the essentials of the task. . . . Clarity of written instructions would also appear in many cases to be superior to verbal instructions, as the older person can go back to check his information."

2. "The pace of the instruction should be slowed down to enable full comprehension as learning progresses, or the pace should be under the trainee's control."

3. Learning by doing appears to be more effective than first memorizing instructions and then translating them into action.

4. Material should be broken into components which are clearly related to the whole task.

5. Since older people tend to show anxiety when learning in a competitive situation with younger people and are more reluctant to make mistakes than younger, perhaps older workers could be segregated in training programs.

Welford has suggested means of compensating for the shortcomings older people have in learning new skills. (30) The use of note-taking in solving problems helps to improve the performance of older persons when they are confronted with masses of data which call for insight. Older persons "should not be placed on jobs requiring continuous rapid action. They are particularly well suited for operations which demand a high degree of accuracy, since their deficiency in organizing new material is often more than offset by gains in quality and accuracy of performance once the material is assimilated." (30)

Dr. Nathan Shock made an investigation at the Harvard Business School on the effectiveness of advanced retraining courses. He concluded that "given the incentive, older people can retain and master information efficiently and contribute ideas and procedures." (32)

In a study of responses to inquiries regarding training and adjustment problems of older workers, 70% of employers questioned indicated that although many older workers present problems, once they are trained, they perform as well or better than workers who are younger. (14)

The National Committee on the Aging's study of 30 companies revealed that little or no training was given to older workers. However, it was determined that regular in-service training throughout the length of an employee's career enables him to shift more readily from jobs that require agility, speed and endurance to those which are less strenuous. The Committee also reported that "most firms think of training as an individual matter rather than as an age or group problem and, in some cases, express the opinion that formalized training programs for the older worker would be inappropriate and antagonistic to the purpose for which these programs are designed." (8)

"Training also motivates employees to work harder," according to Strauss and Sayles. "And the very fact that management is confident enough of their abilities to invest in training provides a sense of assurance that they are valued members of the organization. This is particularly important in dynamic companies undergoing changes in technology and methods. Such changes as automation are resisted when workers fear that they will not be competent to assume the new jobs that are being created." (19)

There is a great deal of work to be done on studies of aging and retraining. The field is new and therefore one of the least documented areas in the study of aging. What is known at present about psychological changes with age is not enough to develop a good method of training older workers. Research needs to be conducted on the relationship between attitudes on learning of older people and the way in which it affects their training. (9) The emotional demands of a job (which are often significant) cannot be measured at the present time and this is another area in which research might be conducted.

B. Reassignment and Job Re-engineering

When the ability to perform a customary job is impaired, two methods of retaining older workers so that they may continue to make contributions to a company are through job reassignment and job re-engineering.

1. Reassignment

When reassignments take place, they may be to jobs of the following type: those that are supervisory in nature where

judgment, knowledge and experience are important; jobs that
require custom or quality work; jobs in which older workers train
the new employees; jobs which are similar in nature but which are
not on the production line; part-time jobs or shift jobs which are
more convenient for the worker; less complex or lighter jobs such as
inspection work. (28)

2. Job Re-engineering

Changing the content of the job or job modification is perhaps
more desirable for the worker but it is not used as often as job
transfer because of the expense involved and because physical
deficiencies are not uniform. Re-designing the job to suit the
worker may involve changing the pace of the operation, breaking
the job into simpler parts, changing the height or location of
the equipment, using special equipment to compensate for
decreasing visual acuity, etc. The New York Legislative
Committee on the Aging reported that 15% of companies polled had
reported the use of job modification for their older workers.
These companies also reported higher production and lower costs
as a by-product of job re-engineering (28).

Of greater impact than job re-engineering on the reduction of
physical demands has been the introduction of materials handling
and control equipment. Although not directly related to the
utilization of older workers, automation increases the emphasis
on repair and maintenance, functions which use skills possessed
in abundance by older workers. A Department of Labor study notes
that automation ". . . also promotes the retention of older
workers by placing increasing reliance on maturity and
dependability" (26).

One manufacturer made the following statement regarding
mechanization of the job:

"The search for efficiency has resulted in the introduction of
machinery which has greatly reduced the number of back-breaking
jobs in the plant. Speed has become much more essential to
production efficiency, but this comes with experience. Thus,
the older worker has benefited tremendously by modern
technology which not only has reduced the physical labor
involved but has also placed a premium on experience. In
addition, technological advances have reduced the necessity of
transferring older workers to lighter work, for almost all jobs
can now be performed equally well by either young or old.
Intraplant transfers have only arisen because of inqury or
incapacity, not age." (26)

C. Flexible Retirement

The subject of flexible retirement has received considerable
study in recent years and industry has shown significant trends

in this direction. The Department of Labor (28) cites some of the reasons for promoting flexible retirement as a means of effectively utilizing older workers.

1. There are great individual differences in productivity for all ages.

2. The investment of years and money in the development of a worker are lost under compulsory retirement policies.

3. Pension costs are lower under a flexible retirement system. (One study estimates that there is a 40% savings in pension costs when a man is retired at 70 rather than at 65.)

4. Since people are living longer, many workers can effectively work to a later age than earlier generations could.

Section III is concerned with the efforts of various groups to promote the effective utilization of older workers.

III. EFFORTS IN BEHALF OF THE OLDER WORKER

A. Government

The Federal Government has conducted pilot studies on productivity, absenteeism, accident rates, and labor turnover by age groups. Seven metropolitan areas were studied to determine employer practices and policies in utilizing older workers; the collective bargaining agreements covering 7,500,000 workers were analyzed to determine the effects on older workers.

The Department of Labor is engaged in a broad research program into every economic aspect of the problems of the older worker. The Department's Bureau of Apprenticeship and Training encourages and aids in the development of training and retraining programs for journeymen, many of whom are middle-aged and older workers.

The Department of Health, Education and Welfare's Office of Vocational Rehabilitation grants funds to conduct research and demonstration projects and the Office of Education promotes job training and retraining for older persons.

The Federal-State employment service system is a nationwide program to combat discrimination on the basis of age and includes employment counselling, job solicitation and placement. When aptitude testing indicates the acquisition of new or additional skills, training facilities are recommended.

The following statement from the Governor's Conference on Automation (New York State) is on the subject of vocational retraining:

"Vocational retraining is required for the newer industries. The urgency of the latter program is highlighted by the trend in industry away from the type of semi-skilled employments for which the displaced had been prepared. There are openings

available even in major areas of unemployment which could be
filled by the appropriate training. The unemployed need to be
retrained for these newer jobs. In some instances complete
retraining is not necessary as upgrading and updating of
information is all that may be required. But there must be
facilities and finances to sustain these training programs. . . .
Prospective employers aware of the possibilities of such
retraining programs are likely to be attracted by localities
which conduct such programs. The retraining programs of Utica,
New York, stand out as an undertaking which did much to accelerate
the adjustments of people for the newer type of employments
which came into that community." (18)

B. Unions

The AFL-CIO's Director of Research, S. H. Ruttenberg, presented
a statement before the Subcommittee on Unemployment and the
Impact of Automation in March 1961 in which the questions of
displacement and the responsibilities for retraining older
workers were discussed. (15)

Although the responsibility for actually carrying out retraining
programs rests with the unions and employers, communities and the
states, the AFL-CIO contends, the Federal Government must take
the initiative in providing financial and technical assistance,
guidance and coordination. The unions claim that the Federal
Government should provide, as a guide for retraining programs,
technological outlook studies which would give such information
as which job classifications will be displaced and which new
skills will be required in the future. The AFL-CIO representative
stated that efforts to assist the older worker who has been
displaced should be in two directions, both with federal
assistance. The first is in special research in the techniques
of teaching and training older workers.

"Sufficient information on this subject is now lacking. If
most older workers are to be given a fair chance to be retrained
successfully, adequate education and training methods for
older workers should be developed. The funds for such a
comprehensive effort — to subsidize university research
programs in this area, for example — should come from the
federal government. If this research effort is to be meaningful,
it should be co-ordinated by a federal government agency.
Improved methods of teaching and training older workers are
essential for the successful retraining of older workers for
gainful employment in this period of radical technological
change."

The second approach, which has been mentioned earlier, job
re-engineering, is a matter for joint union-management agreement.
However, the union points out, the Federal Government can be of

service in this area by publishing the experiences of unions and companies and by educating the public to the need and possibilities of such efforts.

Older workers who are union members usually seem to fare better than non-union members with regard to opportunity for retraining. Under the UAW-Ford contract, apprenticeship training programs were amended to provide for older seniority employees. Older applicants who pass certain mental and aptitude tests satisfactorily are eligible for retraining, regardless of age. They are protected by being placed on a separate waiting list for training so that they will not be competing with younger applicants. (29)

C. Industrial Programs

The following companies are among those which have acknowledged the need for retaining and effectively utilizing older workers and have implemented programs to this end.

Eastman Kodak, which is unorganized, has a record of pioneering advances in employee welfare and utilization of older workers, including on-the-job training programs and flexible retirement. "The older employees are not segregated as a group, nor is a magnifying glass focused upon them." In none of its policies or programs does Eastman Kodak try to place its older workers in a special category, "but rather thinks of each person in terms of a total individual in relation to a particular occupation and to an employee-employer and community-home situation." (8) The National Committee on the Aging's report on "Flexible Retirement" outlines rather fully the work done by this firm on job requirements, appraisal of employees' capacities, work-evaluation criteria, job modification and re-design and flexible retirement.

Consolidated Edison in 1952 adopted a policy for effectively utilizing its older workers through flexible retirement which has proved to be economic for the company, the older worker and the Government. In a recent study of 337 older employees retained under its program, the company found that if these employees had retired at 65, $400,000 in Social Security benefits and $710,000 in pension funds would have been paid to them. In addition, these workers were able to earn $2,500,000. (28)

Lockheed Aircraft employs a large proportion of older workers and has found from experience that "chronological age is not a valid criterion for retirement, and the staff has found it equally unreliable as a placement criterion." The most successful approach has been to consider each employee as a total individual in relation to a particular job. (8)

Consolidated Vultee Aircraft Corporation of San Diego since 1942 has made use of its physical-placement program to ensure the effective utilization of its older workers and thus to solve its problems of an increasingly short labor market. With refinement of its placement program, a greater number of jobs has been found suitable for older workers. Convair's policies have resulted in great savings to the company, have contributed to the control of injuries and illnesses among older workers and have made it possible for the company to hire older workers and employ them longer. (8)

The American Sterilizer Company has instituted a program of diminishing work-load to employ its older workers in their late 60's or early 70's six months of the year. (8)

Macy's in April, 1961, signed the first union contract requiring that department store employees whose jobs have been eliminated by automation be retrained at company expense. Macy's employees average 12 years' service; with this length of service and the union ruling on severance pay, it is more economical to retrain employees than to dismiss them. The training period shall not exceed the number of weeks of severance pay the employee has earned. So far the longest period required has been a month – for training key punch operators. (7)

IV. CONCLUSION

The consensus of research studies and reports by industry suggest that the older worker compares favorably with the younger worker in all aspects of job performance. The single significant point made in each analysis of older worker performance is the importance of individually evaluating a worker on the basis of ability rather than age as substantial numbers of older workers out-perform the average of younger workers. Efforts should be directed toward eliminating prejudice against those workers who have superior abilities but who are held back by traditional attitudes that equate aging with a decline in performance.

Although important advances have been made in the area of effective utilization of older workers, additional research is needed on such controversial subjects as a specific methodology of retraining older workers and criteria for success in retraining. Most studies of retraining have been conducted in light and heavy industries; investigation of retraining of non-industrial workers, such as salesmen, insurance agents, etc. deserves attention.

As a matter of scientific fact, no standardized test has been formulated which accurately measures functional age. There should be devised a substitute for chronological age which will combine both physiological and psychological measurements.

"The one conclusion that seems confirmed by all the available data on the relation between age and ability is that any generalization that associates increase in age with a uniform decline in the ability to contribute to a professional or technical job is not valid. On the contrary, there is abundant and growing evidence that there are definite areas of ability in which the older group excels and definite patterns of conditions under which their increasing abilities can be translated into increasing productivity." (8)

V. BIBLIOGRAPHY

1. Aichele, Sylvester, "Older Worker Productivity, Accident Proneness and Sickness Records," Proceedings of the Second Joint Conference on the Problems of Making a Living While Growing Old, Temple University, September 1953, pp. 292-305.
2. Bayley, Nancy, "On the Growth of Intelligence," The American Psychologist, December 1955.
3. Belbin, R. M., "Older People and Heavy Work," British Journal of Industrial Medicine, 1955, pp. 309-319.
4. Bowers, William R., "An Appraisal of Worker Characteristics as Related to Age," Journal of Applied Psychology, October 1952.
5. Clay, Hilary M., The Older Worker and His Job: Problems of Progress in Industry, No. 7, Department of Scientific and Industrial Research, London, January 1960.
6. Lehman, H. C., Age and Achievement, Princeton, N. J.: Princeton University Press, 1953.
7. "Macy's Contract Pledges Re-Training," Business Week, April 29, 1961, p. 81.
8. Mathiasen, Geneva (ed.), Flexible Retirement, New York: G. P. Putnam's Sons, 1957, 225 p.
9. McFarland, Ross A. and O'Doherty, Brian M., "Work and Occupational Skills," Handbook of Aging and the Individual, University of Chicago Press, 1959, p. 496.
10. "NAM Urges Broader Acceptance of Older Jobseekers," National Association of Manufacturing Employee Relations Department Newsleter, July 1957.
11. National Office Management Association, Houston Chapter, Hiring Older Workers in Houston, Texas, July 1958.
12. National Office Management Association, San Francisco Chapter, Hiring Older Workers in San Francisco, August 1958.
13. Oberg, Winston, "Age and Achievement – and the Technical Man," Personnel Psychology, v. 13, no. 3, Autumn 1960.
14. "The Plain Truth About the Older Worker," Factory Management and Maintenance, v. 116, no. 3, March 1958, pp. 85-96.
15. Ruttenberg, S. H., Statement by Stanley H. Ruttenberg, Director of Research, AFL-CIO, Before the Subcommittee on Unemployment and the Impact of Automation of the Education

and Labor Committee of the House of Representatives, March 29, 1961.

16. Schaie, K. W., "Rigidity-Flexibility and Intelligence: A Cross-Sectional Study of the Adult Life Span from 20 to 70 Years," Psychological Monographs, No. 9, 1958.

17. Shriver, Beatrice M. and Miles, Walter R., "Aging in Air Force Pilots," Journal of Gerontology, April 1953.

18. State of New York, Governor's Conference on Automation, held at Cooperstown, New York, June 1, 2, 3, 1960.

19. Strauss, George and Sayles, Leonard R., Personnel, the Human Problems of Management, New Jersey, Prentice-Hall, Inc., 1960.

20. Tuckman, Jacob and Lorge, Irving, Retirement and the Industrial Worker, Columbia University, 1955.

21. U. S. Dept. of Labor, "Absenteeism and Injury Experience of Older Workers," Monthly Labor Review, 67: 17-18, July 1948.

22. U. S. Dept. of Labor, "The Functional Occupational Classification Project: Matching Men and Jobs — A new Look," Labor Market and Employment Security, BES, May, 1956, pp. 7-12.

23. U. S. Dept. of Labor, Job Performance and Age: A Study in Measurement, BLS Bulletin 1203, Washington, D. C., September 1956.

24. U. S. Dept. of Labor, Comparative Job Performance by Age, Bulletin No. 1223, BLS, Washington, D. C., November 1957.

25. U. S. Dept. of Labor, "Comparative Job Performance by Age," Monthly Labor Review, December 1957, pp. 1467-1471.

26. U. S. Dept. of Labor, Employing Older Workers; A Record of Employers' Experience. BES No. R-179, May 1959.

27. U. S. Dept. of Labor, Adjustments to the Introduction of Office Automation; A Study of Some Implications of the Installation of EDP in 20 Offices in Private Industry, With Special Reference to Older Workers, Bulletin No. 1276, May 1960.

28. U. S. Dept. of Labor, Meeting the Manpower Challenge of the Sixties with 40-Plus Workers. BES No. E-189, November 1960.

29. U. S. Dept. of Labor, Impact of Automation: A Collection of 20 Articles about Technological Change, from the Monthly Labor Review, Bureau of Labor Statistics, Bulletin No. 1287, Washington, D. C., November 1960.

30. Welford, A. T., Ageing and Human Skill, London, Oxford University Press, 1958.

31. Welford, A. T., Skill and Age, London, Oxford University Press, 1951.

32. Wolff, Harold, Utilization of Older Professional and Scientific Workers, National Council on the Aging, New York, May 1961.

Prepared by:
Margaret M. Schauer
Basic Personnel Research
Corporate Staff
August 1961

5

Short, Informal Reports

Routine Form Reports
Brief Nonreports
Memoranda
Semiformal Short Reports
Letter Reports

ROUTINE FORM REPORTS

By virtue of its straightforward function to inform with brevity and simplicity, the short, informal or routine report is the one which every person in any responsible phase of modern institutionalized life will encounter. Confusion often results from the term "routine" in that some persons intend it to designate any report which mechanically appears on specified occasions or at established time intervals, while others take the word to describe a report written out on a prepared form. Depending on the degree of sophistication of the organization complex which establishes standing authorization for them to appear automatically at definite intervals, reports included in this category are communications invariably called record, periodic, or progress reports. Governmental, professional, and academic organizations will favor the former two terms; large international corporations with stockholders will tend toward the more euphemistic latter term.

Though it may on the surface appear contradictory that reports such as these—which often are filed on prepared forms in line with controlled organizational practices—should be considered "informal," they are nonetheless judged to be so, at least by upper echelons of management. In the sense that these reports are everyday stuff, the bread-and-butter practice of organizational routine, they are informal. Often they are directed upward toward the next higher level of the organization, but almost as often they are directed horizontally or downward. Occasionally, the established form of such a report requires that the report filer give recommendations for action, but generally it does not.

Little can be said to edify the writer of short, routine reports on prepared organizational forms; the bulk of our attention here will be more productively directed toward those short reports whose composition is not rigidly programmed by the organization—those reports, in other words, prepared by individuals ascending toward or arrived at the policy-making plateau.

However, failure of a person to reach this plateau may be virtually guaranteed by his not giving the fullest information in the clearest fashion on each occasion of filing a routine report. Failure so to do is ultimately to invite censure. Writers of these short, informal reports within many organizations have developed the abominable practice of using fragmentary and elliptical sentences in a kind of telegraphic style. This habit can serve merely to communicate half-expressed information, to display the writer's lack of concern for details which may be important, and to reflect negatively upon his knowledge of the relationships among the facts.

The foregoing remarks would not apply to that routine report which provides only small fill-in or check-off spaces. However, those persons charged with responsibility for preparing a form for routine short-reporting will wish to consult carefully the section on Making the Questionnaire which appears in the Appendix. Where short form reports invariably fail to yield the desired information, the preparer of the form is undoubtedly more at fault than its filer. As in the preparation of a questionnaire, close scrutiny must be given by the form preparer to the precise phrasing used to elicit specific and exact information from the form filer as well as to the logical order utilized for seeking out a necessary series of data. Covering instructions may be as central to obtaining the desired information in acceptable form as the report form itself.

BRIEF NONREPORTS

Inside the complex of an organization, a multiplicity of "nonreports," frequently written by hand, serve to communicate small pieces of information along horizontal and, less frequently, vertical lines of administration. Nonreports often contain pertinent information of a valuable kind, but because the information may consist of no more than a short series of current sales figures, or the names of three new competitors who have just entered the field, it is not felt necessary to commit the isolated and transitory facts to semipermanent form. The nonreport, many times written on a sheet of pad paper imprinted "From the Desk of Peter Quince," is usually sent around with an attached "buck slip" containing names of persons to whom the non-report is to be passed before it is either destroyed or returned to the sender.

Though the advantages of the nonreport are clearly manifest, many an originator of one has later experienced the not-so-clear disadvantages. These are: (1) lack of control over time and sequence of circulation, and (2) lack of a record or a copy, in the event these may unexpectedly be needed. If practices are instituted to guard against such contingencies, then in the mass and welter of papers passing across a desk the nonreport may indeed usefully serve its sender and recipients.

Only the individual person within the framework of a particular organization can properly judge when and if a nonreport is permissible and desirable. In some settings it may be used consistently, in others only on certain occasions, and in others perhaps not at all. Where nonreports can convey information rapidly, clearly, and safely, they should of course be allowable. When they are employed continuously, particularly when a memorandum might serve better, they

Figure 5-1 A routine form report. Fill-in and check-off form reports are common in a variety of forms. Space is usually provided for additional comments. (*Reproduced with permission.*)

RATING SCALE   *Oct. 3*
                                          Date

GRADUATE STUDENTS - GUIDANCE AND COUNSELING PROGRAM

C. W. POST COLLEGE   HAPPAUGE EXT. _____
BROOKVILLE, NEW YORK

Master's Degree ___✓___
Certification: Prov._____ Perm.__✓__
Other: _____
Confidential Rating for: ___*Henrietta Taylor*___

R = Recommended   NR = Not Recommended   IBR = Inadequate basis for Rating

1. Personality Characteristics:	R	NR	IBR	REMARKS
a. Personal Appearance	✓			
b. Friendliness	✓			
c. Sincerity	✓			
d. Sense of Humor	✓			
e. Enthusiasm	✓			
f. Poise	✓			
g. Emotional Stability	✓			
h. Vitality	✓			
i. Tactfulness	✓			
j. Objectivity	✓			
k. Alertness	✓			
l. Integrity	✓			
m. General Promptness		✓		*habitually late*
n. Initiative	✓			
o. Open-mindedness		✓		*narrow views*
2. Professional Competence:				
a. Organizational Ability	✓			
b. Judgment	✓			
c. Intelligence	✓			*unusually bright*
d. Ability to get things done		✓		*unreasonable delays*

	R	NR	IBR	REMARKS.
e. Contribution to Class	✓			
f. Creativity in Assignments				
g. Work in Comparison with other class members	✓			
h. Apparent regard in which held by instructor	✓			
i. Apparent regard in which held by class members			✓	*difficult to determine*
j. Clarity of Expression - Oral			✓	*small opportunity to observe*
k. Clarity of Expression - Written	✓			
l. Evidences background of knowledge in education, guidance and/or related fields	✓			*weak but adequate*
m. Evidences sensitiveness to needs of young people	✓			*exceptionally understanding*
n. Professional attitudes and values				

Conference Recommended: Yes _____ No __✓__. If yes, please state
how this student can best be helped:

Additional Information, if any:
Still somewhat intellectually immature, but striving to widen her horizons.

Rated by: *Jack P. Rockwell*
Title: *Professor of English*

may be construed as slothful habits, attempts to evade responsibility, or inability to exercise judgment about business procedure.

MEMORANDA

Memoranda are both the gas and oil as well as the lubricating grease of the intraorganizational machine. Memos provide the power for action and motion, and they keep things running smoothly without shocks of dead-end stops. The nonreport is a one-shot missile asking for or giving a simple yes or no answer; its value next week will be much that of today's weather report.

Information communicated in a memorandum, however, is of a character to be committed to semipermanent records, and its distribution concerns people other than merely the sender and receiver; the others will receive a carbon copy. In general, when a prepared form is not available for the information which is to be conveyed in the report, when the nonreport is clearly not appropriate for the communication, and when a short, formal report is not required by the circumstances and subject, the memorandum will be made to serve admirably.

Again, the distinct occasion for a memorandum, as with any form of professional communication, can be properly determined only by an individual fully conversant with the prevailing practices and customs within his own sphere of business or professional practice. Memos are written to cover every aspect and phase of business life. Little is to be gained by attempting to speak of "routine" or "special" memos, "periodic" or "progress" memos, or "administrative" or "directional" memos. Both by definition and function, the memorandum is a report designed either to help one remember facts just established and decisions just made or, more commonly, to remind someone for the record that facts, decisions, and actions are wanted in the future. In both instances, the memo may travel horizontally, or up and down the chain of command in the organization.

Length of the memorandum may vary from one sentence to three to five or more pages. The memorandum should, for filing and record keeping, cover only one subject. Frequently, its use is to report a single phase of a continuing project. If the scope of the single subject reported is such as to require more than five pages, however, the writer is well advised to consider presenting his information composed as a short report; the tighter structure of the short report can frequently provide a conciseness the long memorandum may have difficulty in achieving. For the memo must enunciate facts and ideas precisely, elaborate details logically and fully, and indicate areas of responsibility unmistakably; otherwise it has no legitimate excuse for existing.

Almost every organization, large and small, has a prepared imprinted form for the recording of a memorandum. Since the elements which comprise this memo letterhead are few and simple, they can be typed on a plain sheet of paper in those few instances that a form may be unavailable. Beneath the organizational or divisional name and usually to the left margin, the words "To," "From," and "Subject" will appear, each beneath the other. An imprinted space for "Date" and sometimes for "File" or "Reference Number" will appear at the top right margin. Only minor variations, in the form of additional spaces for information which is needed because of the special size or nature of the organization, will appear. The To and From spaces obviate the need for the salutation used in a business letter; the complimentary close is also omitted at the conclusion of the memo. Likewise, memoranda need not be signed, though in actual practice they frequently are signed or initialed by the sender in ink at the close, particularly if the subject dealt with is considered of especial importance. Convention also prescribes that the subject be phrased cogently and typed in capital letters in the space provided. If the memo is directed upward, it is considered good practice in some companies to provide the title after the receiver's name while omitting it after the sender's name; if the memo is directed to subordinates, this practice is frequently reversed; and if the memo is going out on a horizontal plane, all titles are customarily omitted. Though not always followed, a final rule says the memorandum need not use indentation at the beginning of each paragraph.

Beyond these fixed elements and general considerations is a blank sheet of paper, and the memo writer is on his own. However, present readers who give thought to the language and logic of reports as presented in Chapters 6 to 9 and the development of reports covered in Chapters 9, 12, and 13 will be well equipped to face that blank sheet of paper. It should perhaps, within this section on the various forms of routine internal communication, be recalled that the memo, like the form report and nonreport, is utilized on everyday occasions and is, to that extent, informal in conception. Memoranda are presented crisply, concisely, and without ceremony—in accordance only with those fixed rules and conventions governing all forms of clear, good writing.

SEMIFORMAL SHORT REPORTS

Readers of the foregoing review of kinds of reports for internal distribution will have observed the short report referred to interchangeably as formal and informal. This demonstrates more the uncertainties of today's creators of short reports than uncertainties of the present writer. For, though it is both recognized and accepted throughout the business and professional world that internal communications of special importance or scope require a form of composition more structured than that allowed by the conventional memorandum, question exists as to how formal or informal that special report beyond the memorandum should be. It will be seen, in this context, that "informal" or "formal" merely indicates the various kinds and numbers of component elements the report will contain. Short or long, the formal report conventionally and traditionally includes all or some of those special elements discussed in Chapter 4 which are completely omitted from

Figure 5-2 A brief nonreport (opposite). Often such a report is accompanied by a circulation slip (below).

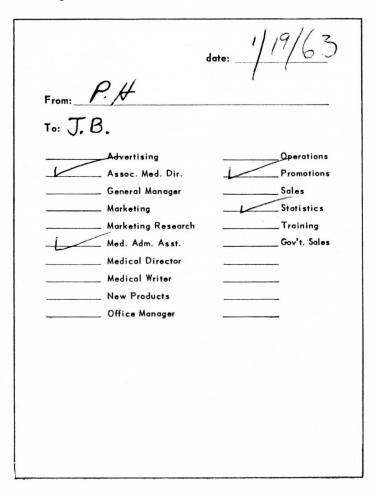

From the desk of: Pete Heister

To: Jim Black

Meeting with
New Products group
has been set for
Thursday at 2 p.m.
in Conference Room.

Please bring
latest data on
product LA-2914

P.H.

Figure 5-3 A memorandum signed by the late President of the United States, John F. Kennedy. (*Reproduced with permission.*)

THE WHITE HOUSE

WASHINGTON

June 22, 1961

MEMORANDUM FOR THE HEADS OF
DEPARTMENTS AND AGENCIES

SUBJECT: Minimum Wages for Government Employees

In response to my urgent request, Congress has recently enacted legislation to raise minimum wages which must be paid by private employers in interstate commerce. Although this legislation spe- cifically exempts the federal government as an employer, I believe that the social and economic reasons underlying this Congressional action are equally compelling and applicable to wage earners employed by federal departments and agencies.

In my view it is both desirable and in the public interest to establish the same minimum rates of $1.15 an hour, effective September 3, 1961, and $1.25 an hour, effective September 3, 1963, for all reg- ular federal employees paid from appropriated funds. I want to make clear these minimum rates should apply to federal laundry workers, even though such workers in private employment are specifically exempted by the law.

These new minimum rates should be applied to federal employees in the United States not later than the effective dates specified in the legislation. It is my wish that the head of each department and agency review this matter promptly and take appropriate action unless clearly prevented from doing so by law.

the fully informal report. To the degree that all or some of these components are included or omitted from a short special report, the report is formal or informal. For this reason, the term "semiformal" will be used arbitrarily for our discussion of this important intraorganizational report.

All or some of the elements which may appear as distinct units in the front matter of the long formal report will be omitted in the short semiformal report. Those elements which are utilized will be sharply abbreviated, and most probably, some of them will be amalgamated into a single unit which will appear as no more than a paragraph or two serving as a background headnote which quickly covers some of the formal functions of the omitted or abbreviated elements. Such a headnote, well prepared, can effectively satisfy the functions fulfilled in a long formal report by separate letters of authorization, acceptance, approval and transmittal, and a foreword and preface. Though the report is already earmarked as a special internal message by virtue of its abandonment of the memorandum form, the number and degree of formal components it utilizes will be determined by particular circumstances and the individual writer.

The text of the short, semiformal internal report of a special nature may require no more than a page or two, but very generally, it will require five to seven or ten pages. There are, of course, no rules for this, but the fact of varying length is intended to underscore the consideration that short reports are adopted in lieu of memoranda on the basis of the subject's importance and not of the breadth or scope of text alone. As in all writing, length is determined only by the number of words needed to treat any given subject with logic and organic wholeness.

Except for the synopsis and introduction, then, virtually all the elements of the text of the long formal report are retained in the short semiformal report; but there is frequently a departure from the classic formal order of this presentation. Because the synopsis is often dropped and, though less frequently, the introduction is also bypassed as unnecessary, it has become common good practice to present the conclusion, and sometimes the summary of results, as the opening elements of the text.

Next will come the material and methods section reviewing the procedures and plans or the course of logic or investigation followed to reach the conclusion. Discussion, usually brief, may follow to further amplify the conclusion. Recommendations will frequently (but not always) occupy the terminal position of the semiformal report. Good current practice permits the writer of the short formal report to place the summary after the recommendation section, where it can serve as both the recapitulation and the terminus of the communication. In general, the only supporting matter from the formal report which is retained in the semiformal report are selected, clearly labeled charts and illustrations: performance curves, photographs, drawings, sketches, etc.

Although flexibility and wide variations are and should be the rule, it is nonetheless possible on the basis of business practice to delineate the outline of components comprising a typical short semiformal intraorganizational report. Properly these should be considered only against the backdrop of the long formal report, since they represent accepted modifications of that form:

Front Matter
> To and From Indications
>> The To and From pattern of the memorandum is retained but is typed and not imprinted as in a memorandum.

> Title
>> This may or may not be presented on a separate cover or front page. In the interest of brevity and economy of space and time, it often appears merely as Subject, as in a memorandum.

> Headnote, Background Information
>> The To and From indications help obviate the need for a formal letter of transmittal and other front matter of the formal report. If the report has been prepared even for twenty or more persons, all their names (with or without individual titles) are neatly listed in several columns under To. Equally good practice permits the writer to direct the report to the chairman or head of the committee or board and to indicate at the bottom of the first page of the report rather than at the end those others who must receive copies. The opening paragraphs will follow immediately after the To and From indications and will succinctly provide all introductory information necessary to the what and why of the report.

Text
> Conclusions, Materials and Methods, Discussion, Recommendations, Summary

Supporting Matter
> Charts and Illustrations

Information necessary to the planning, execution, style, and presentation of each of these aspects of the text and supporting matter may be found in the separate chapters that follow. Most often, the nature of the information developed in the short semiformal report allows that footnotes can be safely omitted. If the information developed clearly demands supporting references by virtue of its controversial or iconoclastic content, footnotes and bibliography must be handled in the same fashion as in the long formal report. Full information regarding this may be found in Chapters 16 and 26.

Though we have chosen to speak of the short semiformal report as an instrument of internal communication, it is of course understood that this form of report can be and is used for external correspondence. When it is so used, certain formal elements omitted above must be included—for example, the conventional letter of transmittal. The report tends to become, on the whole, more formal if it is destined for external distribution. A separate cover and title page will probably be included under these circumstances, and a table of contents may also appear. Though the text as such will remain unchanged, supporting matter may be enlarged to include a bibliography.

To the extent that the semiformal report is expanded in these directions to fulfill the peculiar image-creating functions of the external communication, it shades into the long formal report, which was the subject of Chapter 4. Short semiformal reports for external use, however, are more often than not abandoned in favor of the letter report, which has a particular utility of its own, as we shall now see.

LETTER REPORTS

Because of their broad familiarity with the mechanics, form, and style of the standard business letter (readers may review these in Chapter 19), many writers of letter reports make fundamental errors in approach. Letter reports, indeed, retain many parts of the business letter—even some of the same general form and layout. But there are notable differences between a business letter and a business letter report as to style of writing and organization of contents.

Like the vast preponderance of all reports prepared in industry, the professions, and universities, letter reports are written for concrete and pragmatic ends. That is to say, reports are written not to please or titillate either the writer or the reader, but out of response to a request from the reader—be he boss or professor—for specific, useful information or explanation regarding a given subject. And since the reader will have requested or, by virtue of his position, will routinely expect or require the information, the report must necessarily be dependent upon and shaped to the reader's or readers' demands.

This dependence on the reader, though it is basic to the nature of report writing in contradistinction to other forms of writing (see Chapter 2), is nowhere more clearly manifest than in the letter report. Within the organization, the form report or memorandum is most routinely used to transmit required information. The letter report, on the other hand, serves as the vehicle for routine responses to demands

Figure 5-4 A governmental semiformal short report with a covering memorandum (below). (*Reproduced with permission.*)

THE WHITE HOUSE
WASHINGTON

July 20, 1961

MEMORANDUM FOR HEADS OF DEPARTMENTS AND AGENCIES
SUBJECT: STANDARDS OF CONDUCT FOR CIVILIAN EMPLOYEES

In section 6 of Executive Order 10939, dated May 5, 1961, the President directed that "Each department and agency head shall review or issue internal directives appropriate to his department or agency to assure the maintenance of high ethical and moral standards therein."

Attached for your guidance in the establishment of such internal instructions is a statement of minimum standards of conduct for civilian employees which was prepared by the Civil Service Commission with the assistance of departmental representatives. As indicated in Part VI of the statement, these standards will have to be supplemented to meet special problems peculiar to the responsibilities of individual agencies. These provisions apply to all civilian employees of the federal government and may be applied by each department to the extent applicable to part-time and intermittent employees, such as consultants. Presidential appointees are also subject to the foregoing Executive Order.

As soon as your internal directives are reviewed and reissued this office should be supplied with two copies.

Each department and agency head will be responsible to bring the proper minimum standards of conduct to the attention of all of its employees as soon as such standards are issued, and at least semi-annually thereafter. New employees shall be informed of these standards at the time of their employment.

Frederick G. Dutton
Special Assistant to the President

*   *   *   *   *

MINIMUM STANDARDS OF CONDUCT

I. INTRODUCTION

The maintenance of high moral and ethical standards in the public service is essential both to efficiency in the conduct of Government business and to assuring the confidence of the public in their Government. Unwavering integrity and standards of behavior that reflect credit on the Government are required of all members of the public service.

Agencies should include in the standards of conduct which they are to provide for their employees:

  a. A list of the important laws and rules on employee conduct pertinent to employees of the agency.

  b. Information to employees as to how and from whom they may get additional clarification of standards of conduct and related laws, rules, and regulations.

  c. Assurance that appropriate disciplinary action will be taken when employees violate laws, rules, or regulations on conduct.

II. CONFLICTS OF INTEREST

The elimination of conflicts of interest in the Federal service is one of the most important objectives in establishing general standards of conduct. A conflict of interest situation may be defined as one in which a Federal employee's private interest, usually of an economic nature, conflicts or raises a reasonable question of conflict with his public duties and responsibilities. The potential conflict is of concern whether it is real or only apparent.

It is essential that consideration be given to two key objectives: (1) ethical standards of the Federal government must be beyond reproach; (2) the Federal government must be in a position to obtain the high quality personnel needed for effective, representative government in the modern age.

There are a number of statutes which deal with conflict of interest in Federal employment. Generally, these statutes:

  a. Prohibit officials from assisting outsiders in the prosecution of claims against the United States.

  b. Forbid employees to assist others for pay in any matter which is before a forum of the executive branch and in which the United States is interested.

  c. Restrict certain post-employment activities involving prosecution of claims against the U. S.

d. Require officials to disqualify themselves from acting in government matters in which they have a conflicting interest.

e. Prohibit outside pay for government work.

In addition to these statutory restrictions, the following general standards on conflicts of interest seem desirable:

1. Outside employment

Employees may not engage in any outside employment, including teaching, lecturing, or writing, which might reasonably result in a conflict of interest, or an apparent conflict of interest, between the private interest of the employee and his official government duties and responsibilities.

2. Gifts

No employee may solicit or accept, directly or indirectly, any thing of economic value as a gift, gratuity, or favor, which might reasonably be interpreted by others as being of such nature that it could affect his impartiality, from any person, corporation, or group, if the employee has reason to believe that the person, corporation or group —

(a) has or is seeking to obtain contractual or other business or financial relationships with the employee's agency; or

(b) conducts operations or activities which are regulated by the employee's agency; or

(c) has interests which may be substantially affected by such employee's performance or non-performance of his official duty; or

(d) is in any way attempting to affect the employee's official actions.

3. Financial interests

Employees may not (a) have direct or indirect financial interests that conflict substantially, or appear to conflict substantially, with their responsibilities and duties as Federal employees, or (b) engage in, directly or indirectly, financial transactions as a result of, or primarily relying upon, information obtained through their employment. Aside from these restrictions, employees are free to engage in lawful financial transactions to the same extent as private citizens. Agencies may, however, further restrict such transactions in the light of the special circumstances of their individual missions.

III.   OUTSIDE EMPLOYMENT

In the absence of a condition distinguishing public service from private employment pertinent to the particular case, Federal employees are entitled to the same rights and privileges as all

other citizens. There is, therefore, no general prohibition
against Federal employees holding outside jobs if they wish to,
or if they feel the economic need for doing so.
However, it is important that:
  a. The employee's performance on his government job not be
     adversely affected by the outside work.
  b. The employee's outside employment not reflect discredit on
     the Government or on his agency.
(The question of conflict of interest in outside employment has
been dealt with in an earlier section of this issuance.)
The following general standards on outside employment should
apply.

1. General

Employees may engage in private outside employment, with or
without compensation, provided that such employment does not, in
the opinion of the agency head concerned: (a) interfere with the
efficient performance of the employee's Government duties, or
(b) bring discredit upon, or cause unfavorable and reasonable
criticism of, the Government or the agency concerned. Where
special circumstances exist, agency heads may place additional
restrictions on outside employment.

2. Teaching, writing and lecturing

Teaching, writing and lecturing by Federal employees are
generally to be encouraged so long as the laws, general standards,
and agency regulations pertaining to conflicts of interest and
the standards and regulations applying to outside employment are
observed. These activities frequently serve to enhance the
employee's value to the Government as well as to increase the
spread of knowledge and information in our society. However,
such activities must not be dependent on information obtained as
a result of the employee's official government position if such
information is not available to others at least on request.
This provision does not, of course, prevent the head of the agency
from authorizing an employee to base his writings or lectures on
non-public materials in the agency files (not involving national
security) when this will be done in the public interest.

IV. EMPLOYEE CONDUCT ON THE JOB

The manner in which an employee conducts himself on the job is
frequently relevant to the proper, economical, and efficient
accomplishment of his official duties and responsibilities. In
addition, those employees who are in direct contact with the
public play a most significant role in determining the public's

attitude toward the Federal service, both by the manner in which they serve the public and the way in which they conduct themselves generally in the view of the public.

The following standards seem generally appropriate:

1. General Standard of Conduct on the Job

   Federal employees must conduct themselves in such a manner that the work of the agency is effectively accomplished and must also observe the requirements of courtesy, consideration, and promptness in dealing with or serving the public or the clientele of their agency.

2. Use of Federal Property

   Employees may not use Federal property of any kind for other than officially approved activities. They also have a positive responsibility to protect and conserve all Federal property, including equipment and supplies, which is entrusted or issued to them.

V.   OTHER STANDARDS OF CONDUCT

In addition to the major topics covered above, the following standards should be observed in certain special areas:

1. Protection of Information

   Employees may not disclose official information without either appropriate general or specific authority under agency regulations.

2. Misuse of Information

   Employees may not, directly or indirectly, make use of, or permit others to make use of, offical information not made available to the general public, for the purpose of furthering a private interest.

3. Indebtedness

   Employees are expected to meet all just financial obligations.

VI.   ADDITIONAL DIRECTIVES

In addition to the foregoing standards, Presidential appointees are subject to E. O. 10939 dated May 5, 1961.

Further, individual Departments and Agencies will supplement the foregoing standards for all civilian employees and the special standards for Presidential appointees with specific standards of special applicability within that particular agency because of its functions and activities.

for information from outside the organization. However, just as the semiformal report is used in both external and internal communications but in the main serves for internal communications of a special nature, so, as the alert reader will quickly recognize, the letter report may also be utilized both externally and internally but has its chief utility in the realm of routine external correspondence.

In shaping the letter report to provide, explicitly and cogently, the precise information wanted by an outside agent, whether customer, client, or government inspector, the writer encounters the first major departure from the standard business letter: that of style. Where all enlightened writers of modern business letters (which include brief answers to simple inquiries, claim and adjustment letters, credit letters, collection letters, sales letters, and application letters) studiously practice an informal, personal technique, the writer of the letter report properly should not. The style of the letter report is factual, objective, and impersonal (a discussion of style occurs in Chapter 6). Only the requested facts are supplied, devoid of embellishments, irrelevancies, or trimmings. The singular you-I approach is discarded either for the impersonal, third-person point of view (see Chapter 6) or for the corporate, plural we-you. Indeed, the proper and most effective means of achieving personalization in the letter report is by adherence to and respect for the particular facts requested by an extra-organizational individual or group.

This same essentially courteous desire to faithfully provide the reader only with what he has asked for, without digression and empty, time-consuming personal exchanges, likewise establishes need for the other departure of the letter report from the business letter: that of content organization. In the considerate wish to effectively provide the reader with concrete facts, the writer of letter reports depends heavily upon his knowledge of the principles that control order, arrangement, internal design, and outline of the text (see Chapter 9). Material in the letter report will be presented in short, compact, sequential units, labeled clearly with headings (and subheadings, where needed) which are numbered or alphabetically labeled in accordance with the rules of logical development. The reply to each aspect or phase of the inquiry is given in step-by-step fashion. Moreover, as a further gesture of understanding the basic function of the letter report, the writer may wish to provide his recommendation at the very outset as the first unit of information.

Another attribute of content organization of the letter report is the integrated inclusion of tables and graphs in the text where a purpose useful to the explanation may be served. Inserted at junctions where they may most appropriately help to elucidate the textual facts they are offered in support of, such tabular arrangements and visualizations, though alien to a business letter, are quite correct in a letter report.

Aside from these distinct deviations in style and organization, which should at once help mark it for what it is intended to be, the letter report does in almost all other respects retain the traditional trappings of the standard business letter: company letterhead, date, inside address, salutation, complimentary close, and signature. The chief departure from this format which may be seen is in the salutation. It occurs particularly when a single letter report is distributed to a large number of addressees, such as to the stockholders of a corporation or the participants in any common endeavor (alumni association, community chest, etc.). In such a case the salutation will often appear as "To Holders of Our Common Stock," or "To Members of the University Alumni Association," and the inside address will not be used.

Subject lines (common to memoranda and semiformal reports) are used in the letter report as in a business letter, according to the choice of the writer and the prevailing practices of the organization. Justification for subject lines in letter reports is greater than in letters. As in the letter, the subject line will usually appear in the report dropped a line below the salutation and either flush with the left margin or centered on the page.

In sum, several common archetypal patterns for presentation of the units of the letter report are as follows. Analysis and discussion of each component occurs elsewhere in this book.

Pattern I
1. Authorization for writing the report
2. Statement of problem
3. Summary of findings
4. Materials used and methods followed
5. Conclusions and recommendations

Pattern II
1. Authorization for the report, including restatement of problem
2. Conclusions
3. Materials used and methods followed
4. Summary
5. Recommendations

Pattern III
1. Authorization for the report, including restatement of problem
2. Summary of findings
3. Materials used and methods followed
4. Conclusions and recommendations

✿　　✿　　✿　　✿　　✿

The chapters in this part of the book, which has been concerned with backgrounds, have tried to show the reader in unmistakable terms what a report is and should be, and how and why it relates to other forms of written communication in the society of which we are a part. The two chapters just concluded have outlined the chief patterns that contemporary reports assume.

Considerations of substance and form as they apply to creative report writing will be covered in the three chapters that now follow. For language *is* the substance of the report, and from statements about language, discussion of effective usage and style flows naturally. As to form, the report writer without a grasp of the essentials of logic may simply be putting a chaotic mind on full display for his boss and his professional associates to view. With the application of logic to his form, however, the report writer is displaying the facility expected from all enlightened minds dealing with problems of organization and development.

Figure 5-5 A letter report from a marketing research company to one of its clients, an advertising agency. Data and names are fictitious. (*Reproduced with permission.*)

TREND FINDERS, INC

9 5 7   P A R K   A V E N U E,   N E W   Y O R K   2 8,   N. Y. • Y U K O N   8 - 5 3 7 1

CAROL P. GELB

PHILLIP S. GELB

January 15, 19__

Mr. Zachary Burns-Jones,
President, Vortex Advertising Agency
3912 Maple Ave.,
Columbus, Ohio

Dear Mr. Burns-Jones:

The study you commissioned us to perform has now been completed. Tables of data will be sent to you, but, in brief, the pertinent finding of our survey is:

ONE-FOURTH ($\frac{1}{4}$) OF THE 150 INTERVIEWED MARTINI-DRINKERS DID COMPREHEND THE INTENDED MEANING OF THE TESTED ADVERTISING SLOGAN.

Review of Problem and Procedures

Problem

Your advertising agency prepared a campaign for the Valery Company, distillers of Kensington Gin. The slogan for the campaign was: "Martini's with Kensington Gin are not guaranteed to cure your ulcer, (but we aren't selling antacids)."

Question

Do martini drinkers comprehend the intended meaning of this advertising slogan?

Procedure

Approximately 1 out of 3 males contacted were qualified "martini drinkers" and were willing to be interviewed. These 150 male "martini drinkers" in Westchester, Suffolk, and Kings Counties (New York) were interviewed in a comprehension study of the Kensington Gin advertising headline.

2.

Summary of Data

Respondents' Martini-Drinking Habits

Of the 150 interviewed "martini drinkers"

14% drank martinis "often"
41% drank martinis "occasionally"
45% drank martinis "seldom"

Respondents' Rating of Kensington Gin

"one of, or, the very best gin" -- 49%
"a better than average gin" -- 20%
"an average gin" -- 27%
"a poor gin, or, don't know" -- 4%

DEMOGRAPHIC ANALYSIS OF RESPONDENTS

Age

13% were below 30 years of age
28% were between 31 and 35 years of age
25% were 36 to 40 years of age
23% were from 41 to 50 years of age
10% were over 50 years of age
   (One respondent declined to state his age)

Education

6% had only a grammar school education
33% were high school graduates
16% had 2 years of college
28% were college graduates
16% had professional or graduate degrees
   (One respondent declined comment)

Income

10% were earning from $5,000 to $7,000 annually
39% were earning from $7,000 to $10,000 annually
38% were earning from $10,000 to $15,000 annually
   (Three respondents declined to state their income)

Review of the data reveals that, in the interpretation of the Kensington Gin advertising headline, only 25% of the respondents understood the advertisement correctly.

This information will doubtlessly help you formulate decisions regarding present and future advertising plans for your client.

Yours sincerely,

Carol P. Gelb

Carol P. Gelb

CPG/sab

II

General Problems and Considerations

II

General Problems and Considerations

6

Meaning and Style

THE LOGIC OF MEANING

"Meaning" is what is meant—what is intended to be, or in fact is, signified, indicated, referred to, or understood. Under the descriptive term "logic of meaning" can be discussed some report-writing problems bearing on the machinery for expressing meanings fully and ensuring their adequacy and clarity.

Style

Style is the manner or mode of putting thoughts into words. Though it may be meaningfully discussed on diverse levels, style will be considered here as it must be shaped by the writer's main purpose: the choice and arrangement of words as a response to the needs of the audience addressed and the specific purpose at hand.

Already it has been said (in Chapter 4) that reports explain or inform. Chapter 8 will explore the purposes of exposition, while Chapter 13 will analyze the techniques thereof. Here we will consider the characteristics and attributes—the requirements—of a writing style which has an expository purpose, and we will discuss some of the ways to realize these.

In the main, desirable expository prose has the qualities of clarity and conciseness. To help achieve these, the writer may:

1. *Adjust the length of sentences.* This does not say that all expository sentences should be short, for an adult need simply review a child's third-grade reader containing short sentences exclusively to appreciate how boring and ludicrous this would seem to other adults. Variety in length and structure of sentences is required, although in report writing the emphasis should be upon brevity of sentences. This urges upon the writer the necessity to prune excess verbiage and to choose his words most carefully. Ponderous and pontifical sentences can easily be broken up in the interests of clearness and shortness. Relationships expressed between ideas may frequently thus be made sharper. The skilled report-writer learns to weigh the value of a period against that of a comma, an "and," a "but," or a "which," in his concern for projecting meanings unmistakably.

2. *Select the simple rather than the complex and the familiar rather than the unfamiliar word.* Obviously, this idea slavishly carried out would also lead writing back to the third grade. Complex and unfamiliar words are as indispensable to the logical meaning, clarity of expression, and variety in texture of writing as are the balanced and judicious use of both long and short sentences. Chiefly, the point is stated to suggest that good exposition does not thrive on polysyllabic ponderosities. Explanation is enhanced and facilitated by easily recognized, concrete words that

stand as old friends and signposts in otherwise unfamiliar terrain. Unjustifiably long sentences and deliberately selected unfamiliar words (alas! why do some textbook authors insist upon these?) only get in the way of explanation.

3. *Balance active verbs against passive verbs.* Exposition depends on facts, and verbs express the necessary relationships among the facts. More is said about this role of verbs in Chapter 9, The Logic of Reports.

As aids in achieving expository clarity and conciseness, verbs should be balanced as to voice, which is the modification of the verb that indicates whether the subject of the verb is acting or is acted upon. The active voice—for example, "he sees"—indicates that the subject is acting. The passive voice—"he is seen"—indicates that the subject of the verb is acted upon.

The passive voice quite naturally is used frequently and legitimately in report writing. It falls easily onto paper when the impersonal, third-person point of view is used, as it properly is in most reports. The passive voice helps emphasize the subject of the sentence in which it is used and helps maintain a consistent point of view.

For example: Reports provide the vital information required for business decisions. As a consequence, they *are* carefully *read* by management executives.

Here, use of the passive voice enables the writer to maintain a consistent point of view and to keep the same subject throughout his two sentences. Had he not used the passive *are read,* he would have been obliged to shift to *management executives* as the subject of the second sentence. Doing so would have shifted emphasis from *reports,* the topic under discussion.

Though the passive voice may do a great deal to support the main expository intention of report writing, it is easily overused and misused. Improperly employed, it weakens the force of the verb, or it throws more emphasis on the subject of the sentence than the subject warrants or can bear within the framework of the writer's chief purpose. Why say, "Authorization for the report was granted by the board of directors," when one might say, "The board of directors granted authorization for the report"? Placing active emphasis on the board, the doer of the action, makes the expression more vigorous, adding clarity to the explanation.

Tone

The report writer's attitude and posture toward his audience and toward his material are reflected by his tone of writing. As tone of voice can reveal the degree and quality of the speaker's state of mind and feeling, so tone of writing can be a dependable index to these. The proper tone for report writing is formal and objective. Tone in reports may be fully reflected by the sum total of diverse components—choice of words (diction), sentence structure, use of metaphor, and grammatical point of view. Since each of these elements except the last is discussed in separate chapters, only the grammatical point of view will be treated here. It will be followed by some additional general considerations pertinent to formal and objective tone.

Point of View

By point of view is meant the grammatical person of the report. Point of view takes note of the basic fact that a message is transmitted from a person with one point of view to a different person with another. Point of view for the report writer centers upon consistency in: (1) tense, voice, and mood of verbs, and (2) person and number of pronouns.

1. Verbs
   a. Tense
      Wrong: During April, three members of the department *were* either *attending* regional sales meetings in California or *went* to the shareholders' meeting in New York.
      Right: During April, three members of the department either *attended* regional sales meetings in California or *went* to the shareholders' meeting in New York.
   b. Voice
      Wrong: This *report has summarized* activities initiated and completed during the last year.
      New *activities will be discussed* in an interim report now in preparation.
      Right: This *report has summarized* activities initiated and completed during the last year. An interim *report* now in preparation *will discuss* new activities.
   c. Mood
      Wrong: These recommendations were made:
      (1) *Reorganize* the program for maintaining complete contact with the trade press.
      (2) The functions of the staff *should be realigned* in accordance with the proposed new program.
      Right: These recommendations were made:
      (1) *Reorganize* the program for maintaining complete contact with the trade press.
      (2) *Realign* staff functions in accordance with the proposed new program.
2. Pronouns
   a. Person
      Wrong: The *head of the department* formulated a manual of procedures for staff members. *You* may examine the copy attached. *I* will revise this manual as fresh needs arise.

Right: The head of the department formulated a manual of
procedures for staff members. *He* attaches a copy for
examination. As new needs arise, *he* will revise this
manual.

b. Number

Wrong: *Each* new staff member has *their* responsibilities clearly
outlined and *know* how to carry them out.

Right: *Each* new staff member has *his* responsibilities clearly
outlined and *knows* how to carry them out.

In the foregoing examples marked as being wrong, inconsistencies
in point of view occur. The shifts in point of view are: 1. *a. Tense*—
shift from past-progressive to past tense, *b. Voice*—shift from active
to passive voice, *c. Mood*—shift from imperative to subjunctive mood,
2. *a. Person*—shift from third- to second- to first-person pronouns,
b. Number—shift from singular- to plural-number pronouns.

While writers of novels and short stories may freely shift point of
view for dramatic effect, writers of reports may not. Sudden and illogical shifts in point of view tend to obscure the meaning and to slow
down the exposition. It is pointed out elsewhere in this text that shifts
in point of view, let us say from the active to the passive voice of
verbs, are a valuable stylistic device for occasionally gaining emphasis.
A shift in voice almost always involves a shift in subject. Shifts in
person and number of pronouns are also allowable under special circumstances, but not within the same paragraph; each paragraph must
consistently adhere to the same point of view, and shifts between
paragraphs should be kept at the minimum required by the nature of
the report.

Need for disinterested objectivity of tone in a report has already
been emphasized. Writing in the third person—he, she, it; his, her,
hers, its; him, her, it; they, their, theirs, them—is the general rule for
most reports and other business and professional communication. Indefinite pronouns—each, either, any, anyone, some, someone, one, few,
all, everyone—are frequently employed in pursuit of this same objectivity. The report writer traditionally refers to himself in the third
person—the writer, the author, one, etc.; singular first-person pronouns—I, my, mine, me—seldom appear, but, as will be seen, may on
occasion. However, plural first-person pronouns—we, our, ours, us—
are used more and more in reports, especially when the writer is
enunciating or setting forth a company or corporate policy. These
practices all are designed to place distance between writer and
reader, to preserve the objective anonymity of the report.

In the final analysis, there is but one sane policy to adopt toward
writing problems arising from point of view: a policy of flexibility, one

which freely allows the writer to rationally create a point of view consistent with the main purpose and the nature of the report. To hide blindly behind the third person or the corporate "we," without attempting to use other points of view where these are appropriate, is to write awkwardly and uncreatively. As a rule of thumb, the writer may routinely adopt the third-person singular or plural (the singular is the most practicable) in all formal reporting. This is virtually mandatory in certain sections of the formal report: the conclusion section, the recommendation section, the result section, and the summary. However, depending on the particular circumstances and the judgment of the individual writer, there may very well be paragraphs or whole sections in which interesting stylistic variation can be achieved by shifting to the second person—you, your, yours—or to the first person.

For instance, an introductory section or a commentary and discussion section might speak to "you as engineers," or "you as cost accountants," and so on. So long as this is done consciously and in a controlled, purposeful fashion, and so long as it is self-contained within paragraphs or sections, no impairment of formality need occur. By the same logic, personal observations or views in commentary and discussion sections of the report can occasionally in all propriety be presented from the "I" point of view.

Semiformal and informal reports permit even greater elasticity in the use of first- and second-person points of view, although in general the third person is here also the conventional view. Since it is one of the fundamental tenets of this text, the author does not hesitate to repeat again that in decisions about point of view, and in other decisions concerning clear, concise writing, the creative report writer adopts flexible rather than rigid approaches in judging the most effective mode of fulfilling his main purpose.

General Considerations

The names given to reports by way of classifying them in Chapters 4 and 5 are in many ways indicative of the appropriate tone which might be adopted for each. Short informal reports, whether written for distribution horizontally or vertically, externally or internally, could present a different tone from semiformal reports or formal long reports. As already indicated, informal reports are such, in one sense, because they constitute the regular routine of business. Accordingly, it may be guessed that writers of these might reflect a somewhat personal and familiar attitude toward both their material and their reader. Relaxation of full formality of tone certainly need not indicate lack of regard for the seriousness of the occasion.

Formality and objectivity of tone are signs of a formal, structured relationship between report writer and reader; a tone of formal objectivity serves to reassure the reader that the report writer is disinterested. For only a disinterested writer could be expected to conduct a complete and logical investigation and follow it up with an impartial and unbiased presentation of facts. Probably nothing works more insidiously to render a report suspect and to negate its usefulness than a belief, aroused by the writer's tone, that he may not be disinterested.

Regardless of whether the report writer is, in fact, admirably disinterested, doubt as to his objectivity may nonetheless spring from many sources: poor choice of words, undue emphasis by length of treatment or by structure of sentences, unintentional overstatement, unfortunate juxtapositions of information, and many, many more. If the report writer, however formal and objective, innocently slips into any of the devices of the propagandist (Chapter 2) or of the fallacious reasoner (Chapter 9), his tone is probably seriously enough impaired to negate his report. Proper tone should not suggest anxiety to stress one point or desire to underplay another.

Three further general considerations of tone may be mentioned. The first of these has two aspects, that of a tone of superiority and that of a tone of inferiority. A tone of superiority implies writing down to the reader of the report. This involves use of strained, oversimplified statements and unctuously careful explanation. If the report writer deliberately takes a tone of writing down, the reader may rightfully be insulted and revolted. If this tone is taken because of honest miscalculation of the reader's ability to understand, it may be equally mischievous in effect.

A tone of inferiority in a report addressed to business and professional superiors can only harm the writer by irritating the reader. This tone involves excessive self-effacement in one posture and undue elegance in another. The posture of exaggerated humility is implied by overuse of phrases such as "it is the humble opinion of," "inexperienced as the writer is," "can only in all humility suggest," "reluctant as the writer is to venture an opinion," and so on. Overelegance involves not only euphemisms—high-sounding words in place of the ordinary (commode for toilet)—but use of poetic devices—onomatopoeia, alliteration, etc.—and overlong sentences calculated to reach up to the cultivated, superior taste of the boss. Need more be said?

A second general hazard to actively avoid in tone is simulated enthusiasm. Sales, advertising, and marketing reports, not to mention corporate annual reports, are particularly prone to this depressing falseness. By seeking to place the best possible light on sales figures or marketing trends or company progress, these reports can lose control of themselves and get completely out of tone. Superlatives start to fly.

Good fellowship overflows. Sprightliness and snappiness crackle off the page. This becomes the best of all possible worlds for those readers who will just be good guys and accept the lopsided plan, the cross-eyed logic, and the ersatz enthusiasm of the report.

A confident tone of authority, even of affirmation and positiveness, may be much admired in a business or professional report. But it can probably best be gained by disinterestedly permitting the facts to lead the writer on, rather than vice versa. If one chooses by his plan or method of development in the report to judiciously weigh both the good and the bad import of the facts, that is often the most excellent way to proceed. One may, however, accept almost as a certainty that phony enthusiasm will creep in or even permeate the tone when the writer fails to consider the negative as well as the positive aspects of a problem.

Sentimentality of attitude toward reader or subject, though less often seen than false enthusiasm or writing up and down, seriously injures the tone of some reports. Businessmen and students more frequently than professional men exhibit this defect in their exposition. It consists in displaying a greater feeling for a thing, idea, or situation than it reasonably merits. In reporting on products or processes that have made money for them but are now obsolete, writers of business reports tend to become sentimental in tone. (Interestingly enough, personnel reports dealing with people usually exhibit the opposite extreme of tone: They are deadpan and cold-blooded.) Sloppy gushiness or mawkishness—that is, sentimentality—occurs when the writer of the report expects the reader to experience for something an emotional response which is, in actuality, unjustified.

LEVELS OF USAGE

To distinguish between the different types of English each of us uses on different occasions, the term "levels of usage" is employed. Formal English is the language used to satisfy serious and dignified occasions. The formality is seen in the words, the expressions, and the structures of the language. Colloquial English is that used in informal but polite conversation of cultivated people. Illiterate English, the language of the uneducated, need not concern us here. Formal English is required for report writing.

Since words, expressions, and sentence structures are the elements which indicate either formal or colloquial usage, the report writer can work through these to achieve the desired formality. For the propriety of words and expressions about which he may have doubt for formal occasions, a good dictionary is indispensable. The dictionary does not *determine* which words are formal or colloquial; it merely records the current practices. Therefore, the dictionary is the best guide to the words and expressions which other serious, enlightened members of the community are admitting or not admitting to formal usage.

The sentence structure of formal English in many ways presents no knotty problem for the writer. Since colloquial English may be thought of as that used in polite, civilized, everyday conversation, one would not expect it to be consistently and meticulously thought out, structured, and arranged, even when spoken by the best-organized mind. Grammatical niceties are not always refined; elliptical sentences may be used because the speaker may depend on the context, gesture, tone of voice, facial expression, etc., to complete his meaning. The language is, generally, less precise and more discursive and rambling, to suit the needs of shifting conversation and pursuit of a variety of interests.

Much of the inherent informality of civilized, conversational English naturally slips away when one puts pencil to paper. For when the report writer has a plan and an objective and consistently expresses himself in complete sentences, the structure of formal English is created. And this, of course, is the beauty of the written word—that it strives toward correctness and permanence. An error in usage committed to paper is ever there, in black and white, to damn the writer. The pressures upon him to be correct, therefore, serve admirably as discipline.

Consistency in use of formal English is the mark toward which the writer must strive. Lapses in words, expressions, and structure, when they occur, can jar the reader of the report. Injection of a word like "guy" or "swell" into an otherwise formal context can spoil the whole serious effect. A grammatically incomplete sentence can do much the same harm. In the maintenance of homogeneously formal consistency in diction—choice of formally acceptable words and expressions— there is the problem that no fixed dividing line exists between the levels of use. There are a goodly number of words admissible both colloquially and formally. But there are probably a larger number properly restricted in contemporary practice to colloquial levels, and these the report writer would strive to keep from appearing in large numbers in his report. The dictionary, in the absence of any other definitive arbiter accepted by all, must serve.

Neologisms—words or expressions newly coined for the occasion by the writer—necessarily have to be excluded from formal use, though there are occasionally exceptional circumstances. These arise chiefly in technical and scientific reports describing entities and phenomena not previously given nomenclature. Names for new entities are, generally, agreed upon by appropriate professional-society boards set up to deal with these matters. And it of course goes without saying that technical reports will use a vocabulary quite apart from consideration of formal or colloquial levels. Need for a technical vocabulary is properly determined and justified by the occasion. Where technical reports are destined for the nontechnical reader, the writer will need to define special terms for the layman. Here, comparisons through analogy and metaphor, together with visualizations, will prove most helpful. But no question can arise as to the appropriateness of technical usage in a report for technically initiated readers.

However, in the great body of reports in business which do not require a technical writer or reader, neologisms are inconsistent with formal usage. They may not only impair the tone of the report but may well form barriers to understanding. Where a normal phrase such as "coated with plastic" can be quickly understood by all, a neologism like "plasti-coated" may cause some readers to stumble. Neologisms do not support the main intention of exposition. A word such as "finalized" has not yet appeared in all dictionaries as correct for formal use, even though the form—a neologism—is widely used colloquially. Yet, since it now appears in many reports, there is small doubt it will rapidly gain formal acceptance. Dictionaries, necessarily not reissued each year, always lag somewhat behind in recording up-to-the-minute, formally acceptable words. Terms must also be in use formally for some time before the dictionary can so record them. To avoid possible misunderstanding and a breakdown in the expository process, the report writer might well adopt a conservative attitude toward use of neologisms.

SEMANTICS

Semantics may be defined as the science of the meanings of words. Brief discussion of it may serve to direct attention to the fact that words have a specific meaning (denotation) and also have implied meanings (connotations) through associations they may carry in a reader's mind.

A writer who wishes to convey information will select words which are relatively free of connotations; a writer who wishes to mold opinions will deliberately choose words with connotations. Reports are denotative writings concerned with communicating information. The word "shoe" means or refers to any member of the class of shoes (denotation); the word "shoe" means a man-created article of clothing fashioned to protect and adorn the foot (connotation). A word *denotes* a specific thing, person, place, or act, or a general set of things, persons, etc. "Babe Ruth" *denotes* that man. "Athlete" *denotes* any and all men and women with great proficiency in sports. It becomes evident that in talking about semantics and of the denotation and connotation of words, one is concerned with the *abstract* and the *concrete*, and with the *general* and the *specific*, aspects of language relating to the logic of meaning.

Abstract terms name ideas and qualities. "Protectability," "durability," "comfortableness," "stylishness" are abstract qualities without reference to any specific object such as "shoe." We can consider each of these qualities without a specific reference to a shoe. Concrete terms ("shoe") name what can be perceived by the senses: definite things, acts, persons, places.

A general term ("athlete") names a class or group; a specific term names a member of the class ("Babe Ruth," "baseball player"). A general word—"athlete"—stands for generalized qualities or characteristics: proficiency, poise, control, balance. A specific term—"baseball player"—singles out more definite and individual qualities: competitiveness, aggressiveness, professionalism. "Babe Ruth" renders still more specific qualities and characteristics: hitting power, judgment, shrewdness, patience. There are, as can be seen, relative degrees of specificity. The individual word is general or specific only in relation to some other word. "Athlete" is a general term in relation to "baseball player," but "baseball player" is general in relation to "Babe Ruth."

Concrete, specific words—"Babe Ruth," "baseball player," "moccasin"—usually refer to *particular persons* and *objects*, while *general* words—"athlete," "shoe"—usually name *classes of objects, actions*, etc. Words that refer to ideas, qualities, and characteristics, such as "durability" or "shrewdness," are usually abstract; these point less clearly to particular objects.

In a report, general terms such as "business," "government," "labor," "personnel," "management," etc., are nebulous and are capable of being interpreted in many different ways. These words denote particular things in a vague, general way, and they also connote many different things for different readers. Being abstract, these words communicate in a fuzzy, amorphous way. They weaken exposition, whereas substitute terms such as "sales figures," "federal taxes," "union representatives," "laboratory technicians," and "board of trustees," being relatively more specific, are more exact and vigorous; terms even more specific than these could also be used to move away from the abstractions and the diverse connotations inherent in the original terms. When an abstract term is relatively clear—"union representatives," "laboratory technicians"—it will still communicate less precisely and exactly than an even more specific word—"union president and vice-president," "chemical analysts," and so forth.

Where a choice exists, and for the report writer it often does, between abstract and specific words, he should choose the relatively most specific. He is wise to avoid language which may have hazy and shifting connotations, for indefinite language is open to misunderstanding. Some words are constantly in the process of shifting their meanings through the extension of meaning which individual writers and readers may attach to them by connotation. By hewing to specific and concrete words, the denotation of which is relatively stabilized, the writer may greatly improve his exposition.

It is much to be desired that report writing exclude slanted, value-judgment words loaded with unfavorable or favorable connotations. Terms such as "muckraker," "outside agitator," "rabble-rouser," "troublemaker," "Red," "alien," "Utopian," "economic royalist," and "left wing," which are loaded unfavorably, or "honor," "liberty," "American way," "social justice," "public service," "progress," "democracy," and "Constitution defender," which are loaded favorably, are grotesquely out of place in reports. Each carries a multiplicity of meanings by extension, and the meanings are all disturbingly vague and generalized. As seen in Chapter 2, emotionally charged words are the stock-in-trade of the propagandist.

THE SENTENCE

Most discussions of logic of meaning would probably begin with talk about the sentence, and all would necessarily lead to it. For when one considers what is *meant*—style, tone, levels of usage, and semantics—one is considering the sentence, the basic unit of communication. A sentence is an independent group of words which make a statement. It contains a subject and a predicate, either or both of which may be implied rather than expressed. The subject of a sentence is a word or group of words which denotes the thing about which something is affirmed or predicated. The predicate of a sentence is a word or group of words which asserts (predicates) something—makes a statement—about the subject.

The fixed word order (syntax) of the normal sentence is subject, verb, indirect object (if any), and direct object or other verb complements (if any). Adjectives precede the substantive they modify. Adjectival phrases and clauses follow the substantive they modify. Adverbs and adverbial modifiers (also participial phrases) are not fixed as to position, but movable. Movable modifiers placed at the beginning or end of a sentence modify the whole sentence; placed internally, they modify the relation between the words preceding and the words following them.

In exposition, the normal pattern of sentence structure with fixed word order is used most often. Deviations from it are reserved for purposes of emphasis and variety. Departures from the norm, as stated above, are achieved through manipulation of the movable modifiers and by variation in the basic pattern itself.

A common, simple way to emphasize the subject is to start the sentence with "It is" or "There is." "Reports are the foundation for every business decision" would become "There are reports at the foundation of every business decision." The rephrasing throws emphasis on "reports." A method for throwing emphasis on the indirect or direct objects of verbs was mentioned in the discussion of style—the use of passive verbs. Instead of saying "Reports communicated information to us," one says "We had information communicated to us by reports," or "Information was communicated to us by reports," depending upon where one would wish the emphasis to fall.

Incomplete, fragmentary sentences communicate incomplete, fragmentary information. Some rather fantastic advice to business writers has of recent date been offered by certain writing "experts." In essence, the advice says, "Forget about grammar and concentrate on what you have to say. Never mind if you violate the rules, so long as you get the message across. Don't worry about your sentence, worry about your ideas." This is such unmitigated know-nothingism that it should not be dignified by comment. Yet there are adult writers who not only accept but welcome this counsel of despair. It helps them rationalize their unwillingness to learn the fundamentals of grammar. But it is nonsense to even suggest that thoughts can be fully communicated when the communicator is ignorant of the integrity of the sentence. "Sentences" without verbs or subjects affirm or deny nothing about nothing. Reports containing even one fragmentary sentence may well raise doubts in a sophisticated reader about the writer's grasp of grade school grammar.

Now, if in abjuring grammar and proper sentences these modern advisers mean that *some* of the so-called rules of grammar can be safely ignored, then we are in agreement. If, for example, they are counseling writers to forget about the horrors of split infinitives or prepositions at the end of sentences or conjunctions at the start of sentences, then there is no quarrel. No violence whatever occurs to the sentence as a result of a split infinitive or of a preposition at the end. These are trivial considerations which most writers have long since made peace with. They have no connection, however, with fundamental grammar violations leading to fragmentary sentences, which are simply not allowable.

Apropos of other sentence matter: A sentence which contains the chief idea germane to a paragraph—the pertinent point around which the paragraph is constructed—is the topic sentence. It may be stated at the outset of the paragraph, be reserved for the last, occur in the middle, or be merely implied rather than explicitly stated anywhere. "The cost of the laminating process is attributable to two factors," for example, clearly indicates the topic to be discussed in the paragraph and probably in the paragraph that follows. The writer and the reader are alerted to the topic and guided to the explanation. The topic sentence is to the paragraph what the thesis sentence (Chapter 9) is to the whole report, and it is a natural outgrowth of a logical, overall design. The outline lays out the entire pattern for the report, a pattern indicated by the thesis sentence. The topic sentence, as the foundation for a paragraph which is a logical structural link in the whole design, deserves careful attention from the report writer. Further reference to the topic sentence will be made in Chapter 13 in discussion of the logical development of the report.

THE PARAGRAPH

The paragraph is a device to show the structural units of a piece of writing. Between outlining (Chapter 9) and paragraphing there is a close relationship. The paragraph will develop a particular heading or subheading of the outline. The heading itself, or a rephrasing of it for stylistic purposes, will thus become the topic sentence or, at least, the topic of the paragraph.

Only by regard for the paragraph as a unit of thought can the report writer construct it effectively. If the paragraph is approached mechanically as conventional practice for breaking up the page by arbitrarily marking off units of writing, it becomes rather absurd. As with other writing techniques, paragraphing is intended to serve the convenience of the reader. Simply marking off segments without regard to structural patterns will probably confound the reader.

In relation to the full report, individual paragraphs will have specialized functions. The opening paragraph, or paragraphs, to the report as a whole and to separate sections may be an introductory paragraph. This paragraph will survey in general terms the essential points to be subsequently developed. It will give the reader a comprehensive but concise overall view of that which will, piece by piece, follow in logical developmental order.

To delineate relationships between two sections of the report, a transitional paragraph may be needed. Such a paragraph undertakes to emphasize logical connections between that which has been completed and that which will follow. This kind of paragraph serves as a station for a brief rest on the way to the summit; the reader may glance back to see how far he has come, catch his intellectual breath, and then proceed to the next station or to the top.

The final paragraph of a section or of the report may sum up what has just been said. This terminal paragraph serves to bring the section to a suitable conclusion by briefly recapitulating main ideas and their connections. When the report writer provides a good introductory paragraph at the jumping-off point, a solid summarizing final paragraph at the rendezvous point, and skillful transitional paragraphs between sections, the reader is able to go confidently through the report.

UNITY, COHERENCE, AND EMPHASIS

Unity, coherence, and emphasis are concepts inseparably bound up with the logic of meaning. The three ideas are applicable equally to sentences, paragraphs, and the report as a whole.

Unity as a principle of correct writing demands that sentences, paragraphs, and the full report stick to the subject at hand. There should be nothing in a paragraph which does not clearly serve to support the topic sentence, and there should be no information in the report that does not logically fall within the circle drawn by the thesis sentence. Reports that digress or drift in any degree from the stated subject lack unity and are doubtless judged to be productions of a scatterbrain. Digression from the subject being explained is a manifest sign of uncontrolled thinking which can only annoy and bore even the most charitable reader who is seeking the specific information promised to him.

Paragraphs and reports that stick together have coherence. Sentences and paragraphs are in themselves orderly but are also woven together with others of like kind. Each element should flow into the other without jarring the reader and disturbing the flow of information.

Coherence is attained by various devices, none of which should obtrude upon the writing. One technique is enumeration, i.e., (1), (2), (3), and so forth. There can be no mistake here regarding how one thing leads to another. A second technique to help make the report stick together involves the reference of pronouns. Words like "these," "their," "they," "it," "those," etc., referring back to nouns in preceding sentences, serve to bind these sentences and paragraphs together. A third device, one commonly seen, is use of words whose function is to indicate specific relations between sentences and sentence parts. "But," "however," and "nevertheless" indicate a contrast. "So," "therefore," and "consequently" establish a result. "Moreover," "furthermore," and "accordingly" lead to additions and elaborations.

In addition to the foregoing connectives and coordinators, there are conventional stock phrases which establish cohesiveness and continuity in the report. Some of these are "for example," "for instance," "on the contrary," "of course," "on the other hand," "in addition," and "that is to say." A fourth device is the repetition of key words, phrases, and ideas as a means of achieving coherence. Where the writer succeeds in echoing key words—or suitable synonyms—in successive paragraphs, he is both unifying and binding together.

Lastly, parallel grammatical structure serves to give sentences, paragraphs, and total reports coherence. For example, coherence is promoted by parallel structure in verb tenses: "has guided," "has spanned," "has furnished," "has given," "has increased," etc. This idea carries over into parallel grammatical structure for terms following correlatives: "either-or," "neither-nor," "not only-but also," "both-and," "whether-or." Parallelism will be discussed further in Chapter 13, Logical Development.

Emphasis is as important to logical meaning as are unity and coherence. The principle involves techniques for firmly but undramatically revealing to the reader the relative scale of importance of elements in the report. Techniques for emphasis properly do *not* involve use of superlatives or of exclamatory words like "fantastic" and "fabulous."

Perhaps the most reasonable way to gain emphasis is through flat statement: "The most important step in the process is molding," or "Two factors of prime importance are. . . ." Emphasis can also be gained through the position of the elements of a sentence, paragraph, or report. Usually the terminal position is most emphatic, for it makes the final impression on the reader's mind. In a sentence, emphasis requires a word order which withholds the core idea until the final phrase. In a paragraph and in the total report, this means leading up to the main idea through logical build-up. The first position may also prove emphatic, but the middle position seldom does.

Repetition, of course, serves both coherence and emphasis. But probably emphasis can best be gained by proportion, that is, by giving the important elements the fullest treatment. The report reader can only assume that topics most fully detailed and elaborated are of greatest importance. Emphasis can also be achieved through style—through sharp, vivid phrasing of meticulously selected words or figures of speech arranged in clear but striking order.

❖   ❖   ❖   ❖   ❖

This chapter has consisted of elements *to be used* by the creative report writer to express meanings fully and to ensure their adequacy and clarity. The following chapter will continue to treat the logic of meaning, but from a different approach—that of the elements of writing *to be avoided* in reports.

7

Structure and Word Choice

THE ILLOGIC OF MEANING

Grammatical and stylistic writing practices which hinder the communication of full meanings will be considered under the descriptive term "illogic of meaning." Writers of clear, concise expository prose will assiduously avoid these deviations from good standard practice.

Lamentably enough, although bad writing can be found just about anywhere one may look, some of the very worst appears in reports and in other business and professional communications. One would not be starry-eyed enough to believe that any writer could in a single stroke eliminate all poor practices from his reporting. The process of improvement and growth must be continuous. Knowledge of what to avoid is the necessary first step.

Nongrammar. By nongrammar is meant deviation from the established rules for writing correct English. The reader deficient in knowledge of grammar should take the necessary steps to correct that deficiency; it is not the purpose of this text to provide grammatical instruction. Three serious grammatical lapses seen fairly commonly in reports may, however, be cited here. Other nongrammatical practices to which report writers seem particularly prone, such as making shifts in point of view, are taken up in other chapters.

1. *Lack of agreement between subject and verb*

    Wrong: *Repetition* of main ideas *help* provide emphasis.
    Right: *Repetition* of main ideas *helps* provide emphasis.
    Wrong: *Armatures* on the wheel *enables* continuous rotation.
    Right: *Armatures* on the wheel *enable* continuous rotation.

2. *Lack of agreement between pronoun and antecedent*

    Wrong: *The board of directors manages* the corporation. *They are* responsible only to the stockholders.
    Right: *The board of directors manages* the corporation. *It is* responsible only to the stockholders.
    Right: *The board of directors manage* the corporation. *They are* responsible only to the stockholders.

3. *Misplaced parts*

    Wrong: The tests were carried out successfully, *performing on time and completing the cycle.*
    Right: We carried out the tests successfully. The device *performed on time and completed the cycle.*
    Right: *By performing on time and completing the cycle,* the device successfully passed the tests.
    Wrong: To complete the report on time, *a good schedule is needed by the writer.*
    Right: To complete the report on time, *the writer needs a good schedule.*

Wrong: Differences of opinion have often prevented contract negotiations *over technicalities* during the peak production period.

Right: Differences of opinion *over technicalities* have often prevented contract negotiations during peak production periods.

Fragmentary Sentences, Fused Sentences, and Comma Splices

1. *Fragmentary sentences*

   Wrong: Work began on August 15. *First in the basement and then on the upper floors.*

   Right: Work began on August 15. The *carpenters started* in the basement and then *proceeded* to the upper floors.

   Wrong: Progress was slow. *Because of the shortage of heavy building equipment.*

   Right: *Because of the shortage of heavy building equipment,* progress was slow.

   Wrong: New problems were encountered. *Such as acquiring and orienting new personnel.*

   Right: New problems were encountered, *such as acquiring and orienting new personnel.*

   Right: New problems, *such as acquiring and orienting new personnel,* were encountered.

2. *Fused sentences*

   Wrong: The market expanded rapidly there was ample opportunity for profit taking.

   Right: The market expanded rapidly; there was ample opportunity for profit taking.

   Right: The market expanded rapidly. There was ample opportunity for profit taking.

3. *Comma splices*

   Wrong: The report proved *erroneous, however,* a wave of selling ensued.

   Right: The report proved *erroneous; however,* a wave of selling ensued.

   Wrong: The new process was *satisfactory, in fact* it was superior.

   Right: The new process was *satisfactory. In fact,* it was superior.

   Right: The new process was *satisfactory; in fact* it was superior.

The Use and Misuse of Commas. Many report writers use commas "intuitively" rather than rationally. There is nothing either mysterious or personal involved in comma usage; there are established rules for using them. The creative report writer should learn the rules and apply them intelligently.

1. Main clauses joined by one of the coordinating conjunctions—"and," "but," "or," "nor," "for"—are separated by a comma.

   Wrong: Other methods of analysis did not prove *necessary for* the client was satisfied with the original suggestion.

   Right: Other methods of analysis did not prove *necessary, for* the client was satisfied with the original suggestion.

2. A subordinate clause or a long phrase preceding the main clause is followed by a comma.

   Wrong: *Although the system did not prove to be effective* it helped point the way to one that would be.

   Right: *Although the system did not prove to be effective,* it helped point the way to one that would be.

3. Words, phrases, or clauses in a series are separated by commas.

   Wrong: The results of success are seen in *increased sales enlarged profits and reduced inventory.*

   Right: The results of success are seen in *increased sales, enlarged profits, and reduced inventory.*

4. Nonrestrictive (nonessential) clauses or phrases and other parenthetical elements are set off by commas; restrictive (essential) clauses or phrases are not.

   Wrong: The executive committee *which has six members* is empowered to vote on financial matters.

   Right: The executive committee, *which has six members,* is empowered to vote on financial matters.

   Wrong: The publisher *expecting there would be great demand for the pamphlet* printed 7,000 copies.

   Right: The publisher, *expecting there would be great demand for the pamphlet,* printed 7,000 copies.

   Wrong: The electric typewriter, *which is located in Mr. Black's office,* must be repaired.

   Right: The electric typewriter *which is located in Mr. Black's office* must be repaired.

Jargon (Businessese and Reportitis). By jargon is meant here the specialized vocabulary and idioms of those in business and the professions. Implied by jargon is writing which, although not ungrammatical, is incomprehensible, outlandish gibberish because of the vocabulary, idiom, and syntax used. Jargon is writing characterized by insipid, empty wordiness. Even authors of books on report writing must be on guard against it. The Glossary of Terms for Nonusage in the last section of this chapter contains some of the words and expressions peculiar to the jargon of report writing and of other business and professional communication. By avoiding these terms—and by striving to write sentences which directly, clearly, and concisely express his meanings—the report writer can reduce the hazards of jargon.

Circumlocution.   Circumlocution is a roundabout, indirect, lengthy way of expressing something. Instead of saying, "I accept your offer," one says, "Because of these socioeconomic factors presently at work and in view of the fact that other negotiations were not consummated and brought to fruition, other things being equal, the writer will be agreeable to accept the proposals advanced in your prior communication."

Euphemistic Writing.   A euphemism is a word or a phrase that is less expressive or direct, but is considered less distasteful or offensive, than some other word. The writer speaks of being "separated" from a job rather than fired or dismissed. Laborers are called "unskilled personnel" or "non-white-collar men," a job is a "position," and so forth. Euphemistic writing tends to be vague and inaccurate. Plain, familiar words are more suitable for exposition and are less likely to irritate or offend the reader than overuse of euphemisms.

Hyperbole.   Hyperbolic language exaggerates for rhetorical effect but is not to be taken literally. There are "mountains of unwashed tools behind the factory" and the equipment is "as old as time." Specific, concrete language is wanted in reports; hyperbole should be discarded.

Equivocation.   Here is another practice to avoid in report writing, for it involves using the same term in different meanings in the same report. "In the interest of hygiene for all employees, paper towels have been installed in the locker rooms. Interest in hygiene also prompts the reminder that employees are permitted to smoke only in areas where nonflammable materials are in use." In the first sentence, hygiene—measures to preserve health—is used in its conventional sense. In the second sentence, the meaning of hygiene is distorted so that it is made to stand for "safety" or "fire prevention." This is equivocation, and it results in ambiguousness in any explanation. Used deliberately by the propagandist, equivocation may purposely mislead the reader and obscure the writer's real meanings.

Hackneyed Language.   Hackneyed language is that made trite, stale, and commonplace by overuse. It is filled with clichés, platitudes, and aphorisms; as such, it is language devoid of vigor and remote of meaning—it is deadwood. Hackneyed language is jargon: It is the gobbledygook of businessese and the symptom of reportitis. It bogs down the exposition, befuddles the explanation, and befogs the meaning. Terms in the Glossary for Nonusage which follows are hackneyed.

GLOSSARY OF TERMS FOR NONUSAGE

Probably no writer of reports and other business and professional communications is completely liberated from the use of clichés. Though strict avoidance of clichés has been striven for in this book, sensitive readers will surely, nonetheless, be able to spot some. Can you, as a creative report writer, recognize your own clichés?

Clichés

all in the day's work
all sorts and conditions of men
all the relevant considerations
all things considered
all through the ages
all to the good
almighty dollar
almost incredible
ample opportunity
and something to spare
any port in a storm
appears to be without foundation
apple of discord
approximately correct
arrangements have been made
as a matter of fact
as a matter of form
as every schoolboy knows
as far as that goes
as good luck would have it
as the crow flies
as well as can be expected
at long last
at one fell swoop
at the crossroads
at the psychological moment
at this juncture
at your earliest convenience
auspicious occasion
average ability
awkward alternative
axe to grind
be that as it may
beaten track
bed of roses
beginning of the end
believe it or not
better and better
between two fires
beyond the shadow of doubt
bite off more than one can chew

bitter complaint
blessing in disguise
blind leading the blind
blunt instrument
bone of contention
break the ice
bring home to
build upon sand
burden of proof
bury the hatchet
business as usual
by fits and starts
by hook or by crook
by leaps and bounds
by no manner of means
by no means certain
by rule of thumb
by the same token
by word of mouth
call a halt to
call a spade a spade
call in question
can safely say
change of heart
change of scene
cherished belief
circumstances over which I have
    no control
clean sheet
clear the air
close on the heels of
cold light of reason
come to pass
common understanding
considered opinion that
consign to oblivion
constant communication with
controversial question
curious to relate
curiously enough
dark horse

dead and done
dead certainty
delicate negotiations
deliver the goods
desperate situation
devoted solely to
discerning reader
discuss ways and means to
do or die
doubtful advantage
doubtful cause
down and out
down to the last detail
draw the line at
draw to a close
due consideration
dyed in the wool
each and every
earnest consideration
economic factor
eminently successful
entertain hopes
every effort is being made
explore every avenue
express concern
fact of the matter is
fair and square
far and away
far from accurate
far-reaching effects
far-reaching policy
few and far between
finishing touch
firm footing
first and foremost
first and last
flash in the pan
for better or worse
force to be reckoned with
foregone conclusion
formulate a plan
from A to Z
from bad to worse
from start to finish
give and take
give pause to
go by the board

go to the other extreme
gone but not forgotten
graphic description
grateful acknowledgment
grave concern
grave issue
grievous error
gross exaggeration
guiding light
hang by a thread
hard and fast line
hard facts
have a wholesome respect for
have too many irons in the fire
head and shoulders above
heart of the matter
hearty congratulations
heavy responsibilities
high and dry
high hopes
highly confidential information
hold no brief for
honest penny
honest truth
horns of a dilemma
immeasurably superior
implicit confidence
important inside information
in a nutshell
in a word
in my opinion
in no uncertain manner
in round numbers
in the affirmative
in the event of emergency
in the extreme
in the light of recent events
in the negative
incontrovertible fact
inevitable consequences
ins and outs
irreducible minimum
irreparable loss
it goes without saying
it may interest you to know
it stands to reason that
justly famous

keep at arm's length
keep the ball rolling
knock the bottom out of
knotty point
know full well
last but not least
last extremity
latest intelligence
lay down the law
lay one's cards on the table
leave much to be desired
lifeblood of industry
link in the chain of progress
long and short of it
look facts in the face
major phenomenon
mark of recognition
matter is receiving the closest
   attention
missing link
naked truth
needle in a haystack
needs no introduction
not without reason
of the first magnitude
on unimpeachable authority
or words to that effect
other things being equal
outstanding features
over and above
par excellence
part and parcel
personal factor
prepared to state
purely and simply
rank and file
receive every consideration
reliable source

ruling precedent
second to none
select few
shape of things to come
shoulder the burden
signed, sealed, and delivered
simple truth
sooner or later
sound policy
square peg in a round hole
stand or fall
steady improvement
step in the right direction
stress and strain
strictly accurate
striking example
strong support
stupendous success
substantial agreement
sum and substance
take immediate steps
telling effect
things to come
to the bitter end
too numerous to mention
unavoidable delay
undetermined origin
unmistakable symptom
unsubstantiated report
unwritten law
ups and downs
weighed in the balance and found
   wanting
weighty reasons
wishful thinking
with flying colors
within limits
your earliest convenience

Archaic, Obsolete, and Obsolescent Terms

Archaic language is that belonging to an earlier period; it is ancient, antiquated, and old-fashioned. As distinguished from archaic language, obsolete language is that no longer properly in use or practice—language which is out of date and no longer in fashion at all. Obsolescent language is that in the process of becoming obsolete: in the process of passing out of good general use.

The New York Life Insurance Company prepared the following list of such phrases and expressions and urged its employees to abandon these in business correspondence. This list, therefore, should be particularly remembered in connection with Chapter 19, The Business Letter. The lists of words that people like and dislike are also from materials prepared by The New York Life Insurance Company and reproduced here with permission.

acknowledge receipt of
acknowledge with pleasure
advise (meaning to tell) and oblige
answering yours of
anticipating your favor
as captioned above
as per
as regards
as stated above
assuring you of
as to your favor
at an early date
at hand
at the present writing
attached hereto
attached herewith
attached please find
awaiting your reply
beg to acknowledge
beg to advise
carefully noted
check to cover
complying with your favor of
concerning yours of
contents noted
deem
desire to state
due to the fact
duly noted
enclosed find
esteemed favor
even date
for your files
for your information
hand you herewith
has come to hand
have your kind favor
hereby advise
herewith enclose

hoping for your favor
I have your letter of
in answer to same
in conclusion would state
in connection therewith
in due course
in re
in receipt of
in reference to
in the amount of
instant (inst.)
kind favor
kindly confirm same
of above date
past favor
per
please be advised
pleasure of a reply
pursuant to
re
recent date
referring to yours of
regarding the matter
regret to advise
said (the said regulation)
same (regarding same)
take pleasure in
take the liberty of
thanking you in anticipation
the writer
ultimo
under separate cover
up to this writing
we remain (ending last sentence)
we trust
with reference to
would advise
your favor has come to hand
yours with regard to above

Words People Like

ability	distinction	ingenuity	recommend
abundant	diversity	initiative	reliable
achieve	ease	integrity	reputable
active	economy	intelligence	responsible
admirable	effective	judgment	salient
advance	efficient	justice	satisfactory
advantage	energy	kind	service
ambition	enhance	lasting	simplicity
appreciate	enthusiasm	liberal	sincerity
approval	equality	life	stability
aspire	excellence	loyalty	substantial
attainment	exceptional	majority	success
authoritative	exclusive	merit	superior
benefit	expedite	notable	supremacy
capable	faith	opportunity	thorough
cheer	fidelity	perfection	thoughtful
comfort	fitting	permanent	thrift
commendable	genuine	perseverence	truth
comprehensive	good	please	unstinted
concentration	grateful	popularity	useful
confidence	guarantee	practical	utility
conscientious	handsome	praiseworthy	valuable
cooperation	harmonious	prestige	vigor
courage	helpful	proficient	vital
courtesy	honesty	progress	vivid
definite	honor	prominent	wisdom
dependable	humor	propriety	you
deserving	imagination	punctual	yours
desirable	improvement	reasonable	
determined	industry	recognition	

Words People Dislike

abandoned	collapse	evict	hardship
abuse	collusion	exaggerate	harp upon
affected	commonplace	extravagant	hazy
alibi	complaint	failure	ignorant
allege	crisis	fault	illiterate
apology	crooked	fear	imitation
bankrupt	deadlock	flagrant	immature
beware	decline	flat	implicate
biased	desert	flimsy	impossible
blame	disaster	fraud	improvident
calamity	discredit	gloss over	insolvent
cheap	dispute	gratuitous	in vain

liable	prejudiced	split hairs	unfair
long-winded	premature	squander	unfortunate
meager	pretentious	stagnant	unsuccessful
misfortune	retrench	standstill	untimely
muddle	rude	straggling	verbiage
negligence	ruin	stunted	waste
obstinate	shirk	superficial	weak
opinionated	shrink	tamper	worry
oversight	sketchy	tardy	wrong
plausible	slack	timid	
precipitate	smattering	tolerable	

8

The Effective Use of Language

KINDS OF PROSE WRITING

According to controlling purpose or main intention, prose is by tradition divided into four kinds: exposition, argumentation, narration, and description. All four are important to people interested in the technique of clear writing, whether for reports or anything else. Yet exposition, the purpose of which is to explain, is especially important in report writing. To understand the technique of exposition, the reader may refer to Chapter 13. To more clearly appreciate the fundamental purpose of exposition, one must consider it briefly side by side with the other forms of prose discourse.

All four kinds of prose complement one another and, of course, do not appear or function in reports as isolated phenomena. The skilled writer adapts the techniques of all forms and fashions them to his particular needs. The basic character of the writing will nonetheless be determined by its primary purpose. Although all four forms of prose will appear together in most pieces of writing, including reports, the role of the other three will be to support the chief form demanded by the main intention of the communication.

Exposition

Exposition is the kind of prose writing which explains or clarifies a subject. Expository writing undertakes to answer questions such as: What is it? What does it do? How does it work? Where and when does it occur? These questions are either explicit or implicit. The knife and fork of exposition are how? and why? The expositor (the report writer) is the man confronted by questions which challenge his understanding and that of others; he sets out to answer them with explanation and information that appeal to reason through evidence and logic.

Only when the report writer knows *who* he is (his unique position in the specific report-writing situation), *why* he exists (the precise function he and his report are supposed to fulfill), and *what* are the most direct means for his report (how he must carry out his assignment), can he fully appreciate that he is indissolubly wedded to exposition.

Argumentation

As its main purpose, argumentation seeks to persuade. It uses the tools of reason and logic to convince.

Both argumentation and exposition are grounded in facts, logical evidence, and valid rational processes. There is, indeed, sometimes only a hairline between the place where exposition ends and argument begins. Neither form, utilized properly and legitimately, is dependent upon subjective and emotional appeals indigenous to propaganda and advertising (see Chapter 2); both are, rather, sharpened on the grindstone of the objective and scientific wheel. The close interrelationship between the two forms is spelled out in the following chapter, The Logic of Reports. It will be seen that inductive and deductive processes of reasoning work to accomplish the purposes of both exposition and argumentation. Exposition in reports does frequently exist to persuade, while argument may sometimes serve to explain. Narration and description, the other kinds of discourse, likewise may serve the main expository intent of the report.

Narration

Narration is the kind of writing which has for its controlling purpose the telling of a story. It is concerned with spinning a yarn, recounting an episode; as such, it is made up of action and motion designed to answer the question, "What happened?" Within the scope of narration fall the elements of movement, time, and meaning.

For the report writer, acquisition of a sense of the main intention of narration is acquisition of a sense for organizing the parts of a thing into their natural order: beginning, middle, and end. This will be elucidated in Chapter 12, which covers the final organization of the report. By the same token, the technique of narration called "flashback" similarly has a place in report writing. Arrangement of the report by chronologic sequence in reverse, when this may satisfy the particular needs of the report writer, is a carryover from narrative technique. While exposition *explains* a process, narration *presents* the process. Exposition talks *about* a thing; narration *reveals* the thing as part of life in motion, for narration is the main form of discourse employed by writers of prose fiction: stories and novels.

Description

Description has for its purpose the re-creation of a thing perceived through the sensory faculties—sight, sound, etc.—or through the imagination. It involves translating perceptions into words.

In practice, there are two kinds of description: technical-objective and suggestive-subjective. The latter kind is impressionistic and involves selectivity of details as well as interpretation by the writer. It deals in particulars designed by the writer to convey the feeling and mood evoked in him by the object perceived. Suggestive-subjective description is used by poets and novelists, but not by report writers.

Technical-objective description, however, manifestly may serve the main intention of exposition—to explain or to inform—and most assuredly has a place in many reports. Such description gives valuable information about an object. It tends toward completeness in listing the qualities of the object, with emphasis on those attributes which are of special interest within the report context. The technical-objective description will be organized according to a scheme or plan stemming from the object described (left to right, outside to inside, etc.) and consistent with the special needs of the report.

In technical-objective description, concern is always for the *object* described and not for the report writer's personal interpretation, evaluation, or feeling about it; unvarnished facts, enumerated fully and arranged schematically, are at the core of technical-objective description.

✿   ✿   ✿   ✿   ✿

The fact that knowledge of the main intentions of the major forms of prose discourse is essential to the successful report is readily apparent. Lacking wisdom about the purposes and limitations of the different kinds of prose, one may simply not use language effectively. Equally fundamental is the necessity for understanding figures of speech and rhetorical devices. All too often the report writer, fearing the unknown, will avoid these tools, thinking them the province of poets and fools only. Poets, however, are not the only writers who need be concerned about the richness and flavor of language. Used appropriately, figures of speech may serve the author of reports as they do the poet—to extend the boundaries of language. For the report writer, they can serve to vivify the explanation and to heighten the interest of the communication.

FIGURES OF SPEECH

One may provide a definition of figures of speech which will seem at once to legitimately exclude them even from discussion in a book on report writing. It may be instructive to proceed that way, simply to show how the traditionally accepted thinking about figures of speech is crusty, lopsided, and restrictive. For the usual definition (accepted by many report writers and by some who offer instruction in report writing) of figures of speech—or figurative language, or language used figuratively—says that it includes all uses of language for stylistic effects, i.e., variations for effect from the plain, everyday, normal, straightforward manner of writing.

Those two figures of speech which have the widest potential application in reports are metaphor and simile.

Metaphor and Simile

In metaphor and simile, the characteristics and attributes of an object which is familiar are compared with those of another object which is less familiar, for purposes of making clear the explanation or description of the less familiar object, situation, or idea.

> Examples: Microscopically enlarged, the tissue *is* a checkerboard (metaphor).
> Microscopically enlarged, the pattern of the tissue appears *like* that of a checkerboard (simile).

These figures of speech serve to explain or describe the unfamiliar in terms of the familiar, and they are characteristic expressions of the way in which the human mind proceeds from the known to the unknown.

The standard view of metaphor and simile, which is only broadly correct, subscribes to the notion that these devices are not essential to the text in which they occur—that they provide decorative but only tangentially helpful touches which can safely be omitted without altering basic meanings. Indeed, some writers would insist that since comparisons are necessarily imperfect, they may even be misleading in writing that strives for simplicity and accuracy. Metaphor and simile, in this view, are judged to be so much window dressing. Particularly as it applies to report writing, this point of view ignores the fact that metaphor is frequently not merely an embellishment, even in scientific and technical writing, and that there is needed in report writing a kind of psychological accuracy, as distinct from mathematical precision.

Obviously, when a writer says, "H_2O is the chemical formula for water. Water is composed of two parts of hydrogen to one part of oxygen," there is no need for metaphor. The example, of course, represents what some refer to as "purely scientific" or "purely technical" writing, or even "pure exposition." In many ways, it is not that metaphor is unrequired in this type of writing so much as it is that words themselves tend to become unnecessary, and only a set of special symbols or formulas is needed. But as anyone who has ranged the broad world of report writing knows, the abstract scientific realm—and one does not speak deprecatingly of those who live, work, and write in it—is not a universal province.

In much report and other writing which is no less grounded in the scientific and technical but which is destined for a less restricted, selected audience, the case is quite different. For example, C. A. Coulson, Rouse Ball Professor of Mathematics at Oxford University, in speaking about *The Age of the Universe,* says:

> But this is not all; for our galaxy, large as it may seem to be, is only one among some hundred million others, most of them roughly the same size as our own. These galaxies—or nebulae, though the word is not a very happy choice, since their cloud-like appearance is merely the result of great distance—are immensely separated from us and from each other, the space between them being practically devoid of any concentrations of matter. We might be tempted to liken them to lonely wanderers in an arid and almost empty desert. And as far as we can see into this "desert" there are galaxies. The light from some of the more distant among them has taken no less than a thousand million years to reach us. Such is our universe, as we know it now.

"Liken them to lonely wanderers in an arid and almost empty desert" is, as a simile, not added for trimming, since it is manifestly an essential and integral piece of the explanation. The nature of the abstractions requires this comparison; otherwise the unknown could not be adequately brought into focus for the average, nonmathematically oriented reader for whom the writing is destined.

Another example of the manner in which metaphor, used properly, may be seen to be fundamentally necessary to the main intention of factual, scientifically oriented exposition is in the following passage from Rachel Carson's *The Sea around Us:*

> The central oceanic regions, bounded by the currents that sweep around the ocean basins, are in general the deserts of the sea. There are few birds and few surface-feeding fishes, and indeed there is little surface plankton to attract them. The life of these regions is largely confined to deep water. . . .

As one may judge even from this single passage, the main intention of the writing is expository. But this exposition about the sea is built on the metaphor which compares the central oceanic regions with a desert.

The creative report writer will perhaps begin to envisage the many situations within his own experience in which figures of speech, used judiciously, will enhance his explanation as nothing else can. He will recognize that metaphor involves the use of a concrete term set in relationship to wider meanings which he is seeking to communicate. The metaphor will not be used for rhetorical effect, nor will it be used in the belief that it precisely and accurately provides scientific and technical measurements or concepts. Yet, as seen by the examples, well-used metaphor has an organic and psychological accuracy of its own which the mind enjoys and is able to accept while recognizing the scientific and technical limitations. One may properly aspire in report writing to a language usage which is accurate and simple and which includes metaphorical language as one of the means to achieve accuracy and simplicity. As invaluable techniques for explaining through both comparison and contrast the prime nature of an object, situation, or idea which may be central to a report, metaphor and simile should be regarded not as the glossy veneer but as part of the natural grain of exposition.

Analogy

Fruitful discussion of analogy could occur either here, since an analogy is an extended figure of speech (simile), or in the following chapter on the logic of reports, since analogy is a type of induction. Because the view we take of analogy is closely allied to our view of metaphor—i.e., that it has a legitimate place in report writing, if the writer employs it expositorily (to explain) rather than argumentatively (to prove)—we will discuss it here.

Analogy is the explaining of something by comparing it point by point with something else. Analogical reasoning is based on the idea that if two instances are alike on a certain number of important points, they are probably alike on the point in question. Emphasis must be placed on the *probability*, for analogy cannot prove conclusively that the instances *will* prove alike on the point in question.

For example, a report from the new product development section might legitimately explain by analogy that since production difficulties have in the past made it economically unfeasible to proceed with development of product X, the same kind of difficulties would discourage future development of product Y. The analogy would be between production requirements for X and Y. The points of similarity might be the limited supplies of the basic substance, high cost of the extraction process, need for additional heavy equipment, and likely future availability of less expensive substitutes in the market. Then if X has already proved economically unfeasible, it may be judged from the points of similarity that Y would also prove so.

The ultimate value of the report, and its entire usefulness to management in providing the basis for a final decision, would depend, of course, upon the tests applied to the analogy:

1. Are the two instances which are compared sufficiently similar in important respects?

2. Are the differences between the two instances accounted for as being unimportant?

The report based on the analogy would *prove* nothing. But as a basis for *explaining* the hazards of proceeding to develop product Y, the analogy is quite indispensable. The analogy, indeed, might even be given more teeth by increasing the number of similarities used in the point-by-point comparison.

Thus two things in a report may be profitably compared analogically if the intention of the comparison is to explain or clarify but not to prove. For analogies can only establish some degree of probability that two things having some properties in common will have further common properties. That there is a strong basis for resemblance between the two things offers no certainty that the ultimate truth regarding one will also be true of the other. No matter how many attributes two things or situations may have in common, it cannot be assumed or inferred that all characteristics of one of them will also be characteristics of the other.

As in the case of figures of speech, analogy is a valuable aid to the report writer striving for the most effective use of language. But a prerequisite to making language a tool rather than a stone is knowledge of what the different forms of discourse and figures of speech can legitimately hope to achieve and what they cannot.

LOGICAL OR RHETORICAL LANGUAGE?

The preceding chapter on structure and word choice spoke of the pitfalls of jargon and of businessese and also of the dead weight of now meaningless expressions and locutions in report writing. It tried to show how language in reports can become merely language for language's sake rather than language for logical communication. Techniques for overcoming these problems were offered, and the present chapter has thus far given further consideration to some of the background knowledge necessary for using language effectively. Final thoughts on the uses and abuses of language—logical versus rhetorical language—may now be presented.

Figures of speech which are trite and hackneyed—whose meaning has been deadened by constant and unthinking use—have no place in reports or any other kind of serious professional writing. The more familiar a metaphor is, the less appropriate it is for setting down on paper. Shopworn figures of speech used in reports are not only dull but dangerous, since writer and reader are unlikely to be sharply aware of just what is being compared and contrasted and what the objective is.

In reports, comparisons expressed in vigorous metaphor may serve admirably to illustrate, to elucidate, to amplify, to add emphasis, and to suggest possibilities which may lead on to further profitable lines of investigation while helping to make clear a difficult point at hand. Clichés, which lack aptness and originality, can provide none of these advantages. Metaphor newly created to mark the essential quality of a thing is indispensable in extending the language of a report to meet the needs of a new situation. One does not anticipate a point-by-point series of literal likenesses between the things compared. The ultimate value and usefulness of the metaphor may be appreciated only within the full context in which it occurs and against the backdrop of the writer's main purpose.

Yet certain steps can be taken in using figures of speech to help prevent their becoming the handmaidens of rhetoric rather than of logic. First of all, the report author should not overexploit a metaphor by hanging onto it too long. If he fails to let the comparison go quickly after having made his desired expository point, the attributes of the familiar object may cease to bear comparison with the idea he is trying to elucidate. The figure may become contrived and extravagant—that is, rhetorical. If, for example, the writer cited in a foregoing section had not been satisfied to refer to the tissue under the microscope as a checkerboard but had insisted upon going on to speak of "the red and black organisms maneuvering to jump one another and to win the game" or of "upsetting the checkerboard by tilting the agar-dish table and adding chrome blue," his metaphor would have become rhetorical, degenerating into words led on by words for the sake of words themselves rather than for the sake of conveying meanings designed to illuminate the explanation.

Just as figures of speech should not be overdeveloped, neither should they be mixed to a point of incongruity. "Our managerial team blocked the tackle of competition and landed the big fish of increased sales. We made the touchdown and hauled in our big catch of green-backs." Those intoxicated by either cheap liquor or words are likely to have a difficult time getting home.

❖ ❖ ❖ ❖ ❖

From exploration of various aspects of substance in the report, we will now move on to principles which should control the form.

9

The Logic of Reports

LOGIC OF THE OVERALL DESIGN

The Thesis

While a well-prepared outline does not assure an effective report, lack of one virtually guarantees failure. The former is true because preparation of the outline is only a means to an end and not the end in itself. And the latter is a certainty because a report undertaken without even this guide to a formal, overall design can end only by being an amorphous hodgepodge.

It is inconceivable that an outline for a report can be prepared in the absence of a carefully formulated thesis. The first step in outlining must be to reduce to the simplest and most direct single sentence possible a lucid statement of the controlling purpose, the core idea, the central objective—the thesis—of the report. Any attempt to create a plan is logically impossible before this is done.

For the thesis sentence (or whatever else one might choose to label it) is the lighthouse beacon. It at once sets the direction and defines the limits for the report. All material not organically and integrally necessary to the fulfillment of the thesis will be eliminated. Meandering, directionless, wasteful foundering will be avoided, and decisions regarding what should and should not be included can be made objectively. In short, with thesis in hand the report writer has the way cleared for creation of a logical overall design.

Assume, for the example, that the new director of sales, following five months on the job, has been directed by the members of the board to prepare a report based upon a comprehensive investigation which he had been given a completely free hand to undertake. His appointment to the job in the first place was clearly the result of the failure of his predecessor to produce the sales demanded by management. Much of the new director of sales' future success in the company will be contingent upon his report. The board has specified that the report should embody his analysis of the reasons for failure of the former sales program and should present his forthright recommendations for a plan to meet the quotas assigned.

After having carefully carried out all the necessary investigative and other procedures, and after intensive thought and many unsuccessful attempts at precise phrasing, the new director of sales has finally formulated the following thesis, and from it he has derived his outline.

Thesis for the Report. Achievement of future yearly sales goals will require a well-trained and properly motivated field force, practical and imaginative selling aids, a generous but controlled sampling

138

program, and a thoroughly planned and coordinated advertising campaign.

The Outline

I. Sales personnel will be well schooled in current effective methods for selling the line of goods.
   A. New salesmen will be trained into an established program.
      1. The district manager will orient any new man by accompanying him on calls during the first two weeks in the field.
      2. Following this, the new man will spend two weeks in a training center to be established in the home office.
   B. Experienced sales personnel will be retrained and then will receive regular refresher training.
      1. Monthly informational training letters will be sent from the training-center office.
      2. Each salesman will undergo a sales-retraining refresher course following eighteen months in the field.
II. Sales personnel will be offered stimulating selling incentives.
   A. Well-defined bonus programs that provide attractive rewards will be inaugurated and enlarged according to needs.
   B. Field promotions will be postulated on a point system based on sales performance.
III. Selling aids will be adequately geared to effectively support the sales effort.
   A. Plastic scale models of each product unit will be designed and procured.
   B. Compact visual aids for each program will be devised.
   C. Lucid descriptive literature will be created.
   D. Conveniently carried and easily usable catalogs and file cards will be designed and utilized as leave-behinds after each sales visit.
IV. Product-sampling programs will be expanded but better controlled.
   A. Each salesman will be granted increased supplies of samples.
      1. Samples for shipment will be selected monthly by each man to suit his individual territorial needs.
      2. Follow-up reports will be instituted to indicate final use and disposition of samples in line with sales obtained.
   B. Future quotas of samples allowed will be geared to individual sales accomplishments.
V. Advertising campaigns will be better integrated to coincide with quarterly sales efforts for individual products.
   A. Journal advertisements will be planned and executed six months in advance of scheduled appearance.
      1. Closer liaison with the advertising agency will be required.
      2. Sharper scrutiny of advertising copy will be undertaken in line with selling needs.

  B. Direct-mail pieces will be sent with greater frequency during planned periods of individual product emphases, but more carefully screened mailing lists will be utilized.

  C. Sales personnel will be provided with full advertising schedules as well as copies of individual advertisements and mail pieces prior to their appearance or release.

The full circle of the report is drawn by the thesis, and each of the main supporting spokes is a major section of the outline.

From this properly constructed outline may be seen the most widely accepted system of notation:

I. Main headings
 A.
  Main subheadings
 B.
  1.
   Subsidiary headings (first degree)
  2.
   a.
    Subsidiary headings (second degree)
   b.
    (1)
     Subsidiary headings (third degree)
    (2)
     (*a*)
      Subsidiary headings (fourth degree)
     (*b*)

An inflexible and consistent method for indenting and labeling major headings and all subheadings of equal rank is required. Subsidiary headings beyond the second degree are infrequently used except when the report writer prefers to devise the outline with considerable developmental detail, perhaps saving himself this work later on.

Since a major justification for outlining is to enable the report writer to lay out the structural design of his project—to see the relationship of each major and minor element to all the other elements—balanced, dichotomized treatment is needed. Each heading, of whatever rank, requires a heading of the same rank as a balance. The whole, in other words, must be divided into equal halves at the least.

The relative values for each element may be quickly perceived in the outline. A main subheading under Roman numeral I, for example, is of coordinate value with any subheading of the same rank under Roman numeral II. If these values are carried through logically in the report, parallel and coordinate development is assured.

Any report created through valid inductive and deductive processes and structured to the sort of logical overall design demonstrated above will possess the ring of authority and good sense.

        ❋   ❋   ❋   ❋   ❋

Reports exist to provide explanation or to communicate information. Every report therefore presents certain facts so that substance may be provided as a basis for conclusions. Accordingly, the report author gathers the necessary data as evidence. From these data he proceeds to a conclusion.

Reasoning is the process by which the report author moves from the data (certain items of information) to the conclusion he offers in his report. Logic may be defined here as the particular quality or kind of reasoning process used by the report writer—the particular way in which his mind operates in establishing the facts and utilizing them for the drawing of conclusions.

Certain reports may be superficially convincing even though they ignore orderly reasoning processes and defy recognized conventions of logic. Doubtless, much of the work of our world is accomplished haphazardly, without resultant cataclysm and holocaust. But it is also possible that dire consequences can stem from a report built upon the quicksands of illogic. As the bases for formal logic, there are two kinds of reasoning: induction and deduction.

KINDS OF REASONING

Induction

Generalizations

Induction implies the collection and arrangement of data and the formulation of generalizations or rules (conclusions) to cover a number of data and possibly to account for them. The mind moves from particular facts or instances to general formulations or conclusions about them.

Except in certain fields, such as mathematics or physics, generalizations arrived at inductively are necessarily imperfect. That is to say, the substance of many reports dealing with the conduct of human affairs does not provide data sufficient for extraction of a universal rule or truth. At best, the conscientious report author can merely strive to avoid errors based on the faulty generalizations to which many persons are susceptible.

Sources of error contained in the generalizations which are often the conclusions of reports can usually be traced to three causes: (1) generalizations from single or isolated instances, (2) generalizations from selected instances, or (3) generalizations arising from ignorance or prejudice.

Though it may appear absurd that a report author might be misguided enough to base the conclusion of his report upon a single or isolated instance, this does occur. A report, for example, may offer an impressive body of facts supporting the superiority of site X over site Y for the location of a new plant for the production of citric acid. But because there has been an instance involving violence in a strike of union workers employed in citric acid production at another plant at site X, the report will conclude that site Y is superior.

Infrequently will the illogic be as clear as the example suggests. But the alert reader, having waded through the welter of pseudorationalizations and tortured evidence common to a report of this kind, will ultimately judge that the final conclusion is, in fact, forced from the single or isolated instance of violence in a labor dispute.

Generalizations from selected instances, moreover, are so common in business reports of some kinds that they have almost become the rule. Assume, for example, a situation in which advanced management has indicated to the marketing research department its determination to market a new detergent product specially created for washing plastic dishes and kitchenware rather than china and glassware. Management asks for a report on the potential sales in the plastic dish market, indicating the desirability of diversifying the product line into this area.

Deciding—erroneously, perhaps—that what is truly wanted is a report testifying to the wisdom of the management decision, market research prepares a report based on a selected sector of the potential market, a report which will be favorable to the intentions of management. A burgeoning suburban community, for example, may be chosen for study and sampling, in the belief that young couples with growing children will favor inexpensive plastic ware over breakable chinaware. From the selected survey impressive figures or statistics may be projected, figures designed ostensibly to give management a clear and comprehensive grasp of the facts. To support the generalizations and statistics, charts may be prepared in a convenient and intelligible form. The report readers, indeed, will neither have much opportunity nor feel the need to explore the assumptions or principles on which the figures are based. They will not check whether all the relevant figures have been taken into consideration or whether there is causal connection between different sets of figures.

The example is entirely mythical. But only the naïve person will fail to recognize that well-intentioned reports calculated to please the reader and to satisfy what is anticipated to be his point of view have produced some disastrous consequences in our times. Essentially, an error of inductive logic traceable to generalizations from selected instances may be the basic problem.

Generalizations arising from ignorance or prejudice, on the other hand, are often well concealed in reports and are sometimes difficult to isolate. Usually they are ascribed to other errors in generalization. The man preparing the report referred to earlier, the one covering sites for construction of a new citric acid plant, may really have been led to the illogical conclusion because of his prejudice against unionized labor.

Of course, it could happen that a report might honestly conclude, let us say, that process A is superior to process B and should be the design for retooling the plant, out of ignorance of the fact that process C exists and is superior to both process A and process B. But this fatally illogical conclusion would probably be attributed to selected instances rather than to ignorance.

To avert any of these egregious errors, the sagacious and honest report author will test his conclusions arrived at inductively by asking himself:

1. Has my investigation covered a wide enough field?
2. Are the conditions I have observed typical of general conditions, or are they special conditions prevailing only in the sphere of my investigation?
3. Is my conclusion one that could reasonably be supposed to exist?

Before the report author can profitably apply these simple tests to his generalizations, he will have to work back to the particular instances, facts, or information upon which they are based. Here he will have to test the validity of his generalizations by asking:

1. What are the relative number of the unobserved instances or facts?
2. Do the instances or facts observed or developed form a fair and sufficient sample? Are no exceptions discoverable?
3. What is the degree of probability of the validity of the generalization I am offering?

With these awarenesses and simple tests, the report author is likely to utilize effectively in his report that phase of inductive reasoning which involves formulation of generalizations as a logical procedure.

Cause and Effect

Once particular facts have been properly noted, sorted, classified, and tested, and once the general rules established from them have been subjected to the foregoing tests of validity, the next natural step is to try to explain these facts and conclusions. In other words, when the writer perceives that certain things are generally so, or that they generally happen in a certain way, he wants to know why. Once the "how" is known, search for the "why" follows in the nature of things. This leads the writer, inductively, to trace effects back to causes.

Problems arise here. Though an effect is the consequence of a cause—and the cause is an antecedent to an effect—report authors may be prone to assume the two events or conditions are causally connected. Suppose the writer discovers that, following the imposition of a new government tax, sales volume in industry Z fell to an unprecedented low. He may, therefore, erroneously conclude that all governmental taxes cause sales volume to decline. He will probably conclude this without searching to discover whether other economic factors were at work in industry Z, in other industries, and throughout the country. He may even overlook consideration of possible good effects of other kinds and amounts of governmental taxes, or he may neglect to find out whether the effect noted has, historically, occurred generally following imposition of taxes.

This example demonstrates the importance of applying two tests for the validity of cause-effect logic used in reports:

1. Does what the writer calls the cause adequately explain the effect?
2. Are there any other forces or factors that may have been involved?

Creative report writers are obliged constantly to recognize that the human desire to simplify things—to reduce them to a single cause—tempts authors into illogical reasoning. Conditions found side by side or in conjunction may indeed be causally related; as often, they are not.

❖ ❖ ❖ ❖ ❖

The distinctive characteristics of expository writing as differentiated from other forms of discourse were elaborated in Chapter 8. The patterns of development which may be used by the report writer in explanatory writing will be analyzed in Chapter 13 on logical development. Inductive reasoning as the basis for the logic of the report depends mainly upon exposition for (1) the presentation of facts, (2) the formulation of conclusions, and (3) the depiction of relationships between causes and effects. Effective exposition depends upon the judicious use of logical patterns for the development of the thoughts.

Deduction

As in induction the mind moves from a number of particulars to a generalization, so in deduction it moves from the generalization to the particulars. Though one is accustomed to consider induction and deduction separately, they are, of course, really complementary. Deduction is not possible without previous induction, and induction is of no particular value unless it is followed by deduction.

Traditionally, study of deduction is associated with study of valid argumentation and methods of providing rational proofs for the purpose of convincing or persuading. The report writer, primarily concerned with explanation, is naturally drawn to deductive logic because of its insistence on proper form and structure. Is the principle sound? Is the conclusion valid? Even more important, the writer finds deductive logic useful because it forces him to examine the content on which his conclusions are based.

A report contains certain items of information. These facts are presented in statements. For example, a report might assert, "Hand-operated punch presses are now obsolete." Analyzed logically, two basic questions arise from this statement (or any other): (1) What is its substance, or content, or subject (what is it about?) and (2) what is affirmed or denied about the subject or content (what does it say about its content? what is the relationship between the various terms?).

Information to answer the first question can be found in the terms (subject-content) of the statement's nouns and modifiers: Hand-operated punch presses . . . obsolete. These words comprise the content. The statement is about a class of things (hand-operated punch presses) and another class of things (things that are now obsolete).

The answer to the second question, regarding the relationship between the terms of the two classes of things, is contained in the verb (*are*). This affirms that the first class of things is included in the second class of things.

Formal deduction would involve applying the information contained in this proposition to a particular circumstance and then drawing a conclusion:

(All) Hand-operated punch presses are now obsolete. (Major premise–general concept)
Punch presses at factory X are of the hand-operated variety. (Minor premise–particular case)
Punch presses at factory X are therefore obsolete. (Conclusion)

This is presented as a syllogism: two premises and a conclusion. Before the major premise could be formulated, the inductive method of investigation had to be carried through. If the major premise is true to begin with (has valid content), the conclusion deduced from it is valid and must follow from the structure and form.

Now, the report writer of course knows that facts are infrequently served up in classic deductive forms. Syllogisms are implicitly, rather than explicitly, presented. In a report the example above would doubtless be much telescoped and quickly passed over so that the writer could undertake consideration of the important business: How much will it cost to retool? But the entire report would nonetheless stand or fall on the validity of the major assumption (as it happens, incidentally, all hand-operated punch presses are *not* obsolete).

Deductive processes oblige the writer to examine the structure of his explanation and to question the assumptions (content) upon which his conclusions are based. The report based on the erroneous premise above would appear sound even though built upon a fallacy—an error in reasoning. The fallacy stems from an error in the *content* of the deduction. Such *material* fallacies (as distinct from *formal* fallacies stemming from erroneous syllogistic structure) present strong challenges for report writers with a concern for rational expression of relationships among terms (facts, things, ideas) in the report. If the matter is illogically handled, proper structure or statement of relationships is only of academic interest. Common material fallacies, those concerned primarily with the matter rather than with the form of the report, merit consideration.

COMMON FALLACIES

Fallacies of Composition and Division

Errors which offend against the following logical rules are called fallacies of composition and division:

> *a.* What is true of one or more parts of a whole, taken separately or distributively, is not necessarily true of the whole; and conversely,
>
> *b.* What is true of the whole is not necessarily true of the parts taken separately.
>
> (*a*) For example, a report may present data showing that a particular measure instituted by the personnel department has greatly improved employee relations with management at the Eastern production center of the corporation. It might then be plausibly recommended that the same measure instituted at the Southern and Western production centers could be calculated to produce the same salutary effects at those points and throughout the whole company.
>
> (*b*) Or, conversely, it might be thought that a personnel measure instituted throughout the nationwide chain of production centers would improve employee relations as a whole, and that these improvements would be experienced and reflected equally at each of the production centers.

Though reports by and for top-level management executives may often contain such fallacious reasoning, any reader willing to examine the underlying logic can readily spot the error. Basically, this fallacy involves thinking in "lumps." Certain specific advantages gained from the plan under way in the Eastern plant might be gained equally in the South or West. But since particular circumstances are bound to vary from region to region, the advantages as a whole are mathematically unlikely to be equally distributed either throughout other regions or throughout the full company, even though the report writer determines otherwise by lumping all the advantages together.

Fallacies of Accident

Neglect of the following rules gives rise to fallacies of accident:

a. What is true of a thing generally is not necessarily true of it in some accidental or peculiar circumstance; and conversely,

b. What is true of a thing in some accidental or peculiar circumstance is not necessarily one of its general or essential properties or characteristics.

(*a*) For example, a memorandum is prepared to set forth corporate policy in regard to participation of all key personnel (from all departments) in business and professional-society meetings appropriate to individual areas of specialization. Corporate policy generally encourages full and open engagement of all personnel in such outside activities. It does not thereby follow that research personnel or production experts in possession of valuable confidential information are at liberty to participate, for they are in a peculiar position as possessors of precious private information. Were the memorandum to leave this matter to individual interpretation, serious consequences might follow.

(*b*) Or, to use another example for the converse, it would be logically unjustifiable for a report to recommend the permanent downgrading of materials used in product X on the grounds that present sales and price competition from a leading competitor justify it and that the public will be none the wiser. Deterioration of company quality standards and indifference to public trust are essentially serious matters, but the need to prevent company bankruptcy in these peculiar circumstances may temporarily overrule these essential and general considerations, making the action temporarily a logical necessity but not defensible as a general pattern of procedure.

Reduced to essentials, decisions of these kinds arrived at through logical processes and reasoning by the report author take cognizance of the fact that circumstances alter cases.

Begging the Question

When the report writer integrates into his premises the conclusion he is striving to deduce, he is begging the question. When he says, "Reasonable and conservative management officials are unanimously agreed that . . . " or "All expertly trained sales managers may safely assume that . . ." or "It is manifestly not open to disagreement that . . ." or "The recommendation is beyond dispute in that . . . ," he is unconsciously (or consciously) asking the report reader to agree without seeing the factual proof. The report writer, in other words, is stating a general rule and assuming, without offering adequate factual proof, that it covers the particular case at hand.

If the report begins its conclusion by saying, "Technicians grounded in ethical precepts prefer to use the quantitative analytical laboratory procedure," the issue is already prejudged and the conclusion is already assumed. The question is begged in that moral judgments—personal notions of good and bad—which have nothing to do with the subject of the report are allowed to obscure the picture and circumvent the issue at hand. Only the report writer who recognizes the necessity for precise definition of terms can be assured of avoiding this trap. If the writer defined "grounded in ethical precepts" in the context given, it would probably become clear that the terms are essentially equatable with those technicians who prefer to use the quantitative system of analysis. If vital terms are given careful definition at the beginning of the report and are adhered to throughout, the report is unlikely to be guilty of begging the question in this manner and of failing to satisfy its intended objective.

Complex Questions

"Have all major U.S. auto manufacturers ceased to utilize the air cooling system?" Here, no satisfactory reply to the rhetorical question in the report is possible. The fact assumed in the question is not a fact at all.

"Is it possible to retain our present position of leadership in the market without increasing advertising appropriations?" Unless the assumption built into the complex question is unequivocally established beforehand by proof, the reader of the report is asked to assent to the interrogative question-begging and to accept the affirmation buried in the question. Errors in reasoning of this kind, wherever they appear in reports, cast grave doubts upon the report author's presumed objective, be it to explain or to inform.

❖   ❖   ❖   ❖   ❖

This chapter has indicated that reports which are consciously created within the framework of logical principles will possess a structure that is inherently whole. In accordance with this same logic, there will necessarily be in the report an attention to the expression of the proper relationships of facts and ideas (substance) through the avoidance of common fallacies. In the abstract, these logical considerations might sum up the logic of the report. In the concrete realm, principles involved in logical overall design may be considered from the other angle of vision—that of the outline.

III

Creating the Report: Phase I

10

Preliminaries and Essentials

Thus far, we have talked about the report in rather general terms mostly descriptive of finished products. Now, we will move in more closely and examine the specific steps to be followed in getting started.

THE OBJECTIVE

Many an advertisement is written without the writer clearly knowing what he is trying to sell, and many a letter is dispatched without the sender knowing precisely what it is he is supposed to be trying to communicate. Similarly, many a report is completed without an objective clearly defined in the mind of the writer. Since reports are usually longer than either ads or letters, the waste is all the greater.

Because we already spoke fully in the preceding chapter about the thesis and outline, it remains here only to point out that the objective should be the end toward which all efforts are directed. Reports undertaken with vague, uncertain objectives are bound to be structurally flabby. There should be a goal perceived vividly enough so that one may make a direct line for it, refusing to be diverted. It is particularly desirable that the objective of the report be agreed upon from the outset by all persons concerned with it.

Is the objective to determine the effects of A upon B under C circumstances only, or under D circumstances as well? Since reports always involve at least two persons—reader and writer—it is well to have the objective adequately defined between them before the pen is even taken in hand. Very often several persons together will be responsible for creating a report. This is indeed a most common situation today when so much business activity and decision making are conducted by groups rather than individuals. It may be that a division of labor will be decided upon among the group, with each person working more or less independently to complete his or her section. Obviously, the various segments of the report will be woefully out of kilter unless all persons agree in advance upon the precise nature of the objective. This should be thoroughly discussed, and disagreements should be fully aired. In many ways, unless the objective for a report is seen clearly and then fully realized, the report has no legitimate *raison d'être*.

THE PROTOCOL

Formal studies leading to reports which may be published are frequently undertaken with a protocol. Reports to be based on studies done for fixed remuneration will also require a protocol. In fact, the protocol assimilates the functions of the letters of authorization, acceptance, and approval (Chapter 4).

The protocol is a preliminary communication, usually in the form of a memorandum or letter report, transmitted by the report writer to the person authorizing the report. Following preliminary discussion, the report writer prepares a protocol which sets forth a record of the points regarding the study on which agreement has been reached.

The protocol states the objective of the study and outlines the steps planned for achieving it. Frequently, when the report is to be of a scientific character, the writer will outline the specific steps he will take to introduce controls so that variables will be eliminated as much as possible from the final report. Also included in the protocol may be statements regarding the materials to be used, methods to be followed, and estimated time required to complete the study and prepare the report. A preliminary survey may be offered of the mathematical procedures which it is planned to follow by way of providing statistical analysis of data developed. An estimate of cost may also be included, if this is a factor. Though the precise format and content of a protocol are by no means rigidly fixed and are largely determined by the nature of the individual report, the function of the protocol is nonetheless clear. It stands as a compact of agreement between report writer and authorizer. It is designed to obviate false starts, wasted time, and misguided effort.

Certainly, protocols serve to crystallize thinking about a report during the preliminary stage. Even though their use is limited to formal reporting situations, the service they perform is one necessary to informal reports as well. One would certainly do well to have the protocol for an informal report clearly in mind if not on paper.

THE PRELIMINARY PLAN

For a report of any magnitude a preliminary plan is needed. Depending on the scope of the report and the working habits of the writer, the plan may be nothing more than an informal listing of ideas on a sheet of paper. Other writers will prefer to prepare a quite complete outline, feeling that the more structured guide will make the job easier.

Some writers may be sceptical as to how a plan can be made at all for a report yet to be written. There are, of course, problems, but none that is unresolvable. It must be kept in mind that the preliminary plan is really no more than a projected guide. Rarely if ever will the completed report conform in every way to the preliminary outline. It must be anticipated that structural changes will be made as the work progresses and the writer's knowledge grows.

As a foundation for the preliminary plan of a report on a subject quite unfamiliar to the writer, it is often wise to initially spend several hours reviewing general articles on the subject. Articles in the general or special encyclopedias may serve most admirably to provide this overall view. Use of appropriate handbooks, dictionaries, atlases, and other standard reference tools can also be immeasurably productive of basic subject information during preliminary planning. These reference works—and especially the encyclopedia articles, which conclude with bibliographic sources—also help launch the writer on the preliminary bibliography.

Though it may still to some writers seem difficult or even unnecessary to make a preliminary plan, the great help this device ultimately provides in writing the report more than justifies it. Without an early plan, writers may spend aimless hours in the library, dissipating their time and effort for lack of a research objective that can be systematically pursued. No matter how crude the plan may be at first, it nonetheless provides some anchor for the writer from the very beginning. The more complete the plan, the more direct may be the writer's attack upon the reading.

As the gathering and noting of data commences (Chapter 11), the preliminary plan becomes the working plan. It provides the guide for ordering and arranging the material as it is collected. Each note card finds its way into some sort of reasonable sequence, and as a result the report begins to gradually shape itself into a definite framework.

Probably the most useful form for the preliminary plan is the outline, starting with a thesis (Chapter 9). In this regard, it is just as important at the beginning as it will be in the later stages that a sharply enunciated thesis be established. The preliminary plan will serve the writer at the outset and through the entire research phase of the report, right up to the point before which the preparation of the first draft is begun. At this final stage, of course, the writer will review the knowledge acquired through research and set down his final plan as it has emerged from the preliminary and working plan. At that point the thesis must be enunciated with absolute clarity, since preparation of the final outline depends upon it. If the substance of the thesis has already been stated in the preliminary and working plan, setting it up with carefully selected language to stand at the head of the final outline will prove a relatively simple task. Moreover, the report for which the thesis has been clearly framed starting from the preliminary stages will have a solidity of structure it might not otherwise possess.

THE SCHEDULE

In many instances reports will be valueless unless completed by designated dates. Any one report may be part of a comprehensive program of testing and development which will be delayed if each part does not come through on time. Necessity for scheduling, planning, and programming is especially urgent when a group of persons is responsible for the report. Not only must individual responsibilities be delineated, but dates must be carefully determined so that separate parts of the program can be completed in proper sequence and on time. Dates should be established realistically, yet time should be allowed for unforeseen delays and setbacks.

With full knowledge of the purposes and objectives of the report, the writer first plans his investigation. He analyzes the problem and decides upon effective procedures for gathering data. Next, he amasses material through bibliographical research, questionnaires, interviews, observations, experiments, and correspondence. He records his data systematically and tabulates, analyzes, and further organizes them, after which he establishes conclusions and recommendations. Next, he organizes the material suitably for presentation in a report. Once the report is written, he revises, edits, and improves it. Finally, he sees that it is typed and presented in acceptable format. Clearly, if all these steps are to be completed on time, a schedule is required.

During planning, definite procedures for carrying out the investigation and writing the report are established. Policies relating to the objective, scope, cost, time limit, and outline of the report are established. The situation, the problem, and the reader for the report are analyzed. Definite limitations are determined. And then the work schedule is drawn up to show the target dates for completing each step in the process.

In practice, the work schedule may include a great many elements beyond the sequential dates projected for completion of individual phases. The schedule is an outgrowth of the preliminary plan, and by the same token it leads inevitably to the preliminary bibliography (see Chapter 26). If the work schedule is to be submitted for approval, it may be fairly elaborate and include such elements as statement of the problem, need and use for the report, purpose and objective, scope and limitations, and methods and procedures projected for gathering data. Along with this information the preliminary bibliography will often be submitted.

Scheduling by dates and by personnel for specific duties will help eliminate mixups and confusion. Charts can be drawn indicating job assignments scheduled for individuals in relation to dates. Or, of course, simple listing can be used. Some firms prefer to use a master-board, prominently displayed and accessible to all concerned, which graphically shows the full work progress schedule for the project report. Only through such scheduling controls can all the human and natural resources be coordinated with maximal efficiency.

11

How to Control and Shape Materials

159

Unless the report writer can resolve the challenges inherent in the controlling and shaping of his information, he is certain to produce an incomplete and chaotic product for his readers. Although there are today many mechanical devices and trained personnel available to assist the writer, the individual reporter is most often required to develop his own technique for controlling and shaping the information he amasses for a report. Or, if this is not the case, then he may have available to him the vast information stored by mechanical methods by the industrial information department operating within his own organization. The writer may be expected to retrieve such information himself from the storage system, in which case a thoroughgoing knowledge of the system is required. If the data are retrieved for him by specially trained personnel in the information service group, the report writer must be equipped to systematically resort, reclassify, reorder, and interpret such data within the framework of his particular report needs. In this eventuality, also, the writer needs knowledge of the various technics employed today for keeping up with the enormous literature which characterizes most specialized fields of interest.

THE INDUSTRIAL INFORMATION DEPARTMENT

So spectacular has been the growth in importance of reports that many medium- and large-sized organizations have installed highly specialized units dedicated to the report function. A firm may undertake to set up an industrial information department without any outside aid, but since few companies are prepared to tackle this complex installation, services of an outside creative communication consultant are usually purchased. Though information service groups require special equipment and employ professionally trained personnel, the cost of these departments is overwhelmingly justified by the services they render.

Whatever form an industrial information department takes, its broad function is generally to write, edit, duplicate, and distribute reports. As a functional corollary to this mission, information groups frequently also carry out literature research, make surveys, establish and operate punched card files, engage in machine coding, handle translations, furnish bibliographies, and organize information programs. Organization of research informational departments can be effectively carried out only after survey of the special needs and particular problems of a specific divisional operating unit or of the overall company.

As a basic source of raw material, the library (see Chapter 26) is available to the industrial information department. But, depending on the depth of the operation, the research information group may have many data sources beyond its book collection, reference shelves, and current and bound periodicals.

There are the technical files, the repository for soft-cover materials which cannot be fitted into the book and periodical categories. Such materials will consist of trade catalogs, government publications, photographic or processed copies of articles and papers, clippings, reprints, and other like material which may yield vastly helpful information to the report writer. To be of maximal usefulness to a searcher, technical files must be indexed from a suitable subject-heading listing. Materials which appear to possess reasonably permanent value are eventually indexed on file cards arranged alphabetically by author under subject; other materials must be weeded out periodically.

Microcopy machines of one kind or other are today part of the resources of most industrial information departments. Microfilm, microcards, and microprint make accessible to the report writer information which would be otherwise lost, out of print, or commercially unavailable. The cost of microcopy is usually far below that of the original document.

Also available to the report writer utilizing the facilities of the research information unit may be slides, films, and sound recordings. Lectures given at professional meetings by research staff members, talks devised for company training programs, and a host of different kinds of tapes, slides, and films may be part of the visual and auditory materials for which the industrial information department acts as depository and custodian.

A most vital source reference retained by many industrial information units are research and technical reports. These are the reports whose numbers have vastly multiplied since World War II, reports frequently sponsored by government funds or by grants from philanthropic foundations, reports representing the final results of costly planning, research, and effort. Because of their great value, research and technical reports are usually indexed accurately and in detail from every point of view of possible interest. No report writer with access to these important documents can afford to overlook them.

Not always included in the armamentarium of the research information unit, but often of enormous value to the report writer when they are, are laboratory notebooks and research records. These notebooks and correspondence files may provide valuable background information on the early phases of research projects and may furnish details not found in the more formal reports ultimately prepared and issued by an individual or group of writers.

The list of basic sources of information which might be available to

161

an individual report writer through the resources of an industrial information department is expandable. And the many services performed by this department, such as the preparation of translations, the obtaining of interlibrary loans, and the making of literature and patent searches, are equally varied. The creative report writer fortunate enough to work within such a unit, or to have the facilities and services of such a unit available to him, is many furlongs ahead both in the business of getting raw materials and in the task of controlling and shaping them to his particular needs.

In relation to the functions of the information service group within a large or medium-sized organization and its possible role in providing aid to the report writer in the control and shaping of data, a further note can be added here regarding the part the information service group plays in internal communications. Many information service groups are charged with the periodic review of organizational reporting practices. Such responsibilities usually extend beyond simple standardization of report formats and style to studies of the informational needs of management and staff and to problems of internal organizational security. Where there is in large organizations an editorial section within the information service group, this section may have the tasks of ghostwriting, editing, and even publishing the reports of management and staff. The scope of this activity varies, but it is often very comprehensive and goes well beyond mere quality control of reports and standardization of format.

Finally, a fundamental service of the information group in internal communication may be that of providing instruction to the management and staff in creative report writing. Regularly scheduled seminars and short courses may be given on a rotating basis to different sections. Instructional materials, including audiovisual aids, may be employed. As often as not, an outside report-writing consultant may be invited to prepare and give the course. The presence of an outside established authority on creative report writing usually does much to enhance the interest of company personnel in receiving instruction.

INFORMATION STORAGE AND RETRIEVAL

At bottom, a storage and retrieval system in report writing is an organized method for putting items away in a manner which permits or facilitates their expeditious recall or retrieval from storage in orderly sequence for the drafting of the report. A storage and retrieval system is a single system, not a storage system plus a retrieval system. The effect of the logical and physical design of the storage on the design and performance of the retrieval apparatus or method is quite direct.

The report information being controlled and shaped may be such that the classical technique of using 3 by 5 or 5 by 7 filing cards is feasible. As will be seen, this method has for ages been the traditional device of scholarly researchers, particularly in the humanities, working on long-term projects such as a doctoral dissertation. On the other hand, punched cards are often preferred, especially if the data being stored for retrieval are of a scientific or technical nature. Regardless of which method is used, the report writer must carry out the fundamental steps of analyzing his items in terms of their important features so that they may be properly classified and indexed.

Classification

As the individual cards containing pieces of information grow in number, the writer may arrange them according to a system of classification. Classification will be discussed fully in Chapter 13 as one of the logical ways in which the report may be developed. It will be seen that classification is a system of interrelated classes, arranged in a chain or lattice such that each class includes or is included in another class, or both. The classification may correspond to an apparent natural order, or it may be arbitrary. A so-called natural system is used in, for example, biological taxonomy. The inclusive chain would proceed from a division (phylum) to a variety, moving through class, order, family, genus, and species.

For the report writer, an arbitrary or specially designed classification system is probably the best. In such a system the grouping together of related classes reflects the habits and viewpoints of the writer rather than the sequence of any "natural" order. The subject classes of terms are tailored to the viewpoint and language of the report writer. The system mirrors only those areas of a subject to be encompassed by the report, even if, objectively, there are gaps in the classification.

Classification is the placing together of those items between which some form of identity has been detected. Whenever a class is formed, in other words, multiplicity is reduced to unity. Oftentimes, the report writer engaged in tailor-making his own classification system for controlling his information is led on to new paths. He may creatively discover himself developing an association of related ideas and seeing relationships between parts earlier thought of as separate. The ordering of concepts for purposes of classifying information for storage, and the listing of various parts of a concept in their relation to the whole report subject, can stimulate a creative report writer to broaden the scope of his investigation.

Indexing

For facilitating the rapid location of needed information, the other widely used method of storage for retrieval is indexing. In this method each recorded piece of information is inspected with regard to various points of interest which may figure in different parts of the report. A word or a phrase is adopted to designate each important feature of the piece of information being indexed. The words or phrases are then alphabetized so that each may have placed after it the series of arbitrarily assigned symbols, numbers, or letters which key it to the growing store of individual items of information. During the first drafting of the report, each indexed item may be retrieved and inspected with regard to its usefulness in any one or several different sections of the report.

Where there is report information relating to a large number of individual items, for example, as in chemistry, the indexing technique is usually the most effective means of controlling and shaping data. The report writer who installs his own classification or indexing system must, however, resolve the basic problem of identifying those characteristics of each item that are important or may be of importance before the report is completed. The writer must himself envisage which subgroup or subgroups in his classification scheme, or which heading or headings in his alphabetized index, will ultimately come nearest to providing him with the specific datum he may be required to retrieve when he drafts any individual aspect of the report.

THE FILING CARD METHOD

Probably every college student in his freshman course of English composition is exposed to the filing card method of recording information gathered for a research paper (the research paper is discussed in Chapter 26). Certainly every person who has written a dissertation as part of the requirements for a master's, doctoral, or other advanced academic degree knows the technique. The file card system of storing information may be made as simple or as complex, in terms of classification or indexing, as the ingenuity or needs of the individual report writer permit.

As the researcher examines each primary printed or other source of information, he abstracts or digests the pertinent ideas and data, recording their essence on 3 by 5 or 5 by 7 file cards. (Abstracts and précis are discussed in Chapter 25; for discussion of the role of filing cards in gathering bibliography and in taking notes, refer to Chapter 26.) It may be recognized at once that this method is the best if perhaps not the only one for a research report that deals chiefly with abstractions, concepts, and ideas which demand individual interpretation and analysis from various points of view. Factual scientific data, on the other hand, can perhaps best be stored by hand- or machine-sorted punched cards.

The report writer, as his number of research note cards grows, establishes a system for filing and arranging them in drawers or bins in accordance with his plan of classification or indexing. A particular advantage of filing the cards according to this method is that as the information grows and the researcher's thinking expands and modifies, the file cards can be reshaped and reordered in line with the altered vision. This flexibility is a great boon to the creative thinker in that it gives him freedom to achieve new dimensions of thought without losing control of information based on an earlier perspective which he may have gathered at the outset of his research.

Recorded information is indexed and encoded with individually developed notations which appear someplace on each file card. The information may also be cross-referenced during storing procedures to facilitate exploitation of data during the retrieval phase of the report writing. The creative writer, during the weeks, months, and years of researching which often precede the actual writing of the paper, thus has the satisfaction of being on top of his information at all times. He does not lose control of it should he be obliged to temporarily suspend his researches and then resume them at a later time.

In consideration of the general approach to storing and retrieving data, whether by the old file card method or the newer punched card system, it is helpful to distinguish between the preparation and the exploitation phases of the operation. During the preparatory period there are the indexing, editing, encoding, and recording steps to be carried out. It should be quite clear that even where machine-sorted punched cards are to be used, people and not machines must resolve the various intellectual problems. It is chiefly in the exploitation period that the tremendous value of the hardware may be appreciated. But here also, human ratiocination processes are basic in defining and interpreting the scope of the problem before the machines begin searching. The creative report writer is thus always at the helm even though he utilizes the magnificent tools available today for storing and retrieving data.

A Filing System

Though not every report will deal with data that require a file of material housed in ordinary office filing cabinets in addition to or in place of conventional 3 by 5 or 5 by 7 filing card or punched card systems, such a drawer-housed file can often be very helpful. There will be many materials which come into the report author's hands which offer possibility of future utility. There will be internal and external communications directly or indirectly related to the report project which need to be reviewed before the final draft is prepared. Additional materials which it may be more convenient to study and abstract at a future date will also come along. Reports similar in nature to that in preparation will perhaps be retained. And so it is frequently advisable to institute a filing-drawer system in conjunction with the report in progress or with a report that may be wanted in the future.

An obvious way to organize such a file is according to the exact system of classification or indexing used in the 3 by 5 or 5 by 7 card system the author develops. Usually, however, it is not convenient or necessary to make the file-drawer system as detailed or elaborate as this. Perhaps a file keyed only to the large outline divisions of the proposed report will serve sufficiently well, if the quantity of file-drawer material is unlikely to be very great.

Subject filing, that is, the indexing of papers by content instead of name, is usually quite difficult to administer, unless particular care is exercised in the selection of main subject headings. All headings have to be clear, concise, and mutually exclusive. As with the filing cards, the range of headings must be sufficiently broad to handle anticipated needs but not so broad as to confuse subdivisions with main headings. After the indexing is established, it is most wise to prepare a manual of operations to be followed throughout. It is undoubtedly best for one person to code the material for filing, and the report writer himself is probably the best person.

A variety of systems—numeric and alphabetic—are possible in drawer filing. Various colored tabs may be used to identify materials of a certain kind during the retrieval phase of the writing. Commercially available filing kits utilize terminal and middle-digit filing with specially prepared tabs for indexing according to sequence, folder, and cabinet numbers. These systems are adaptable to cross-referencing with both the report writer's bibliography cards and his note cards. The report author who takes the time to institute and maintain a drawer filing system of reasonable proportion in support of his writing project will find himself exercising fuller control over the shaping of his material throughout the storage and retrieval phases.

PUNCHED CARD SYSTEMS

A punched card system employs individual record-keeping facts which are punched in paper cards; equipment is utilized to mechanically, electrically, or electronically combine and organize the facts to prepare reports. The punched card method is fast, versatile, and economical. Two general types of punched cards, hand-sorted and machine-sorted, are in common use.

Our discussion will be limited strictly to general aspects of hand- and machine-sorted cards without reference to any specific commercially available card system or machine. Abundant detailed literature is always available from a manufacturer.

Hand-sorted Punched Cards

Hand-sorted punched cards may be obtained in a variety of sizes. Whatever the size, there are usually several rows of punched holes parallel to the edges of the cards. With all brands of hand-sorted edge-punched cards, the holes along the edges occupy only a small fraction of the total card area. Most of the surface on both sides of the card is available for writing, typing, or printing information, references, abstracts, numerical data, coded information, etc.—even for attaching pictures or clippings that are small or sufficiently reduced in size. One of the corners of each card is cut off so that it is possible to determine at a glance before beginning the sorting operation that all cards are right side up and facing the same way.

Probably a large number of seasoned report writers have become very facile in establishing hand-sorted punched card systems for their own and perhaps their departmental use during the execution of a particular research project. Information for all parts of the report can be programmed in one system which is the responsibility of a single person to maintain. Or just as often, different parts of a report project can be broken up into several sets of cards, with each set being kept up by a different member of the team.

Of course, in setting up his punched card file, the report writer must carefully analyze the ways in which the data on the cards are to be used. Various coding principles may be followed. Direct coding assigns a separate meaning to each hole, allowing sorting of the cards with a single pass of the sorting needle through the appropriate punched hole. But there may not be enough holes on the card to code all the desired data, so that several passes of the sorting needle through different sets of punched holes may become necessary. Numerical and alphabetical codes make use of combinations of punched holes known as fields. One or more holes may be punched to represent a single number or letter, permitting by this combination technique the encoding of greater amounts of information. Other encoding and sorting techniques are also possible, all of which permit the writer the satisfaction of knowing that information for his report is being directly controlled and shaped under his creative aegis at all times.

The mechanical sorting possible with punched card systems is much more rapid and less tiring that the card-by-card inspection and handling required to sort conventional card files. Also, the time-consuming job of refiling cards in exact order is eliminated, since punched cards need not be filed in any special order. Where abstracts or précis are recorded on the punched cards, rescanning of original sources is obviated at the time of writing the report. During the final stages of report drafting, punched cards also provide the considerable advantage of expediting the preparation of the bibliography. Cards used in the report are simply removed from the file and alphabetized, and the bibliography is typed directly from them.

Machine-sorted Punched Cards

The several commercially available machine-sorted punched card systems generally consist of pieces of card stock in which holes are punched throughout the body of the card to indicate codes. The information is stored so that sets of term codes for items are grouped together, while the items (units of information) are themselves arranged randomly. The system provides sequential access to each card during a sorting-searching operation. With special equipment, in many instances more than fifty such operations can proceed simultaneously. Codes are matched by passing the cards through a machine selecting device which has been programmed to select cards punched with the desired codes.

It is outside the aim of the present chapter to attempt a detailed discussion of the intricacies of machine-stored and -retrieved data. The operation of data processing equipment is usually relegated to personnel especially qualified to handle it. This is not to say that the report writer is free of responsibility in the matter. It is essential that the scope of the search to be performed by the machine be concisely and accurately defined. The person charged with conducting the machine search must be given by the reporter a precise definition of the desired scope.

If the search objective has been well defined, the data processer is able to efficiently interpret it in terms of machine operations. Data processing personnel will have good knowledge of the indexing and coding system of machine methods, so that maximal machine instructions can be set up for conducting the needed operations to satisfy the writer's request. Usually, a well-designed system will permit inquiries to flow rapidly through the machine. Once the identification of the items requested by the writer has been completed by the machine, the writer himself in most instances can withdraw the documents from the proper files. From then on, it is his responsibility to use the data to best advantage.

Data processing equipment clearly offers superb advantages of direct relevance to the report writer concerned with the storage and retrieval of large amounts of information. If massive amounts of data might otherwise produce unwieldy files, machine equipment allows dense packing of codes and thus reduces the size of the store. Then, of course, rapid machine matching of the store against the question greatly reduces time required for the search. As with hand-sorted punched cards, it is also possible to maintain constant updating of the store by simply eliminating cards with information that has become obsolete during the period of report preparation. A singular advantage of machine-sorted over hand-sorted cards, however, is the ability to match many-termed questions against a large store in one searching operation. There is with machine-sorted cards, in short, a great increase in the degree of parallel access as compared with hand-sorted punched card systems.

PERIODIC ASSESSMENT

Lastly, in connection with the storage and retrieval of data by machine- or hand-sorted punched cards, the writer may be profitably reminded of the need for adhering to a work schedule and timetable (see Chapter 10). Some report writers have mistakenly believed that retrieval of information is today merely an automated process, quickly and mechanically accomplished. They have therefore allowed less than ample time for this process, believing that its accomplishment is chiefly a foregone conclusion. But this frame of mind is unrealistic.

No system of information control is foolproof. Only the most fortunate of writers will find that, at the final report writing, every pertinent piece of necessary information is at his disposal. Further last-minute searches may be needed for a stray bibliographic reference, some tiny statistic, or a like piece of information. And even if all the data are at his command, the report writer must always allow time for a translation of an important paper from a foreign language or for statistical analysis of raw data developed earlier in a laboratory.

Periodic assessment of the information being gathered is therefore an important part of controlling and shaping information for the report. It is unwise for a writer to mechanically and uncritically store information with the belief that all of it will miraculously be present in exactly the desired amount and form at the time of writing. It is more prudent to at least partially evaluate the quality and completeness of data throughout the storage operation. If further searches or additional experimentation are wanted, they will therefore be completed before Phase II of creating the report is undertaken. Periodic assessment of information is a legitimate part of Phase I; it goes hand in hand with getting raw materials and with shaping them.

IV

Creating the Report: Phase II

12

Final Organization

In creating the report, the writer may be guided in the final stages preparatory to writing by traditional patterns for organizing and arranging information. A final outline will be invaluable, for the rough preliminary plan will probably have undergone various alterations during the information-gathering and note-taking phase of the work. Guided by conventional patterns for putting final facts and ideas into good working order, the writer may feel secure in knowing that his final organization will enhance the explanation and command critical admiration. Before discussion of the controlling patterns of arrangement, a short word is needed about organic wholeness of the report.

BEGINNING, MIDDLE, AND END

Ever since Aristotle told us, in the fourth century B.C., that a piece of creative writing is one "which has a beginning, middle, and end," the incontrovertible fact has been there as a challenge and a reminder. The problem has been, of course, to *understand* what beginning, middle, and end are, for the concepts are quite abstract and must be more sensed than understood. If the report writer, however, will at least take cognizance of these necessities as he lays out his final pattern of arrangement, the chances are great that the completed report will have a satisfying roundness, a sense of proportion, and qualities of symmetry and balance it might otherwise not possess.

For the beginning is the starting and commencing—the point of originating. We do not, as in the classical dictum, plunge immediately into the middle of things. To initiate the report, one must determine just that point and degree of foreground information required for full understanding of the main ideas to be exposed in the course of the work. In shaping the beginning of the report, the writer is setting into motion a process the full unfolding and unraveling of which he has clearly in mind.

And the middle of the report is the part halfway between the beginning and the end. It is the *center*, the point of greatest interest, the fulcrum upon which the full material is dynamically poised and balanced. But the middle matter, though it is the heart of the report, cannot intelligibly exist without the proper perspective provided by the beginning matter. Since the middle matter is the most original part of the report, it must be set off in a balanced relationship to other work in the field that has gone before it—it must be given a suitable frame for understanding. For, to fully comprehend the middle matter, one cannot be given a view of it unconnected with the rest of the world. The middle of the report is the *mean*—the middling—that which is in equipoise in the intermediate position.

174

The end position is the last part of the report, the conclusion which closes the circle traced two-thirds of the way by the beginning and middle. As the natural, inevitable follow-up to the earlier portions, the end marks a simple termination to the writing. The end is the outer boundary of the report, and it will not extend, overlap, or reach beyond any point not organically related to the beginning and middle.

Whatever traditional pattern of final organization the reporter uses as an ultimate guide, the end result can be organically whole only when the writer has acquired an Aristotelian sense of the beginning, the middle, and the end.

PATTERNS OF FINAL ARRANGEMENT

Chronological Sequence

Chronological arrangement is the simplest and most popular form of organization. It is merely a presentation of steps or events in the order in which they occurred. For many reports which explain business and technical processes, chronological sequence of presentation is best.

In making the chronological pattern, the report writer should retain in mind several considerations: (1) The entire chronology has a controlling purpose or direction—it leads toward a consequence and has a meaning which transcends the individual steps, (2) selected steps or events require greater or less amplification in terms of the needs of the intended audience, and (3) each step in the explanation must be suitably linked to the preceding and following one and to the process as a whole.

The consideration that a chronological arrangement of steps leads toward a consequence is helpful in determining the emphasis and proportion the writer may wish to establish in the exposition. For example, the report may be an explanation of how the new mixture of X and Y chemicals rather than X chemical alone performed throughout the manufacturing process and in the finished product. Since the purpose is to present data on X and Y, the new mixture, each step will present these data most fully. On the assumption that X data are well known to the reader, only enough of these to provide a meaningful base for comparison with X-Y are needed. If the audience for the report is likely to be more interested in relative costs than in performance, then cost factors will be stressed throughout the chronology. Imposition of control and purpose upon chronological patterning results in reporting with a clean expository thrust.

The linking of chronological steps is achieved through the several devices spelled out in Chapter 6 under Unity, Coherence, and Emphasis. Mastery of these devices is needed lest the chronological explanation falter or break down for lack of integration. No step is meaningful in itself, but it becomes so when linked to others in the chronological chain.

There will be occasions when two variations upon the straight chronological pattern may prove useful. These are the chronological sequence in reverse and the flashback arrangement. Certain kinds of reports, notably annual reports of large companies and personnel résumés, often provide current information first and then proceed methodically backward to the starting point. By spotlighting in the primary position the present degree of attainment or growth of a company or person, reports thus arranged provide a convenient format for the reader most interested in the here and now.

The flashback technique in expository report writing is borrowed from narrative writing. It allows the writer to begin recounting steps, let us say, halfway through the process in time, and then to bring the exposition up to the present. Then the writer may flashback to the very beginning and chronologically continue the exposition up to the halfway mark which was the starting point. Need for this pattern might arise in explaining a process in which the greatest complexity might occur halfway through the chronology. By starting at that point, proceeding forward, and then flashing-back to the earlier, simpler steps of the process, the difficult and important steps can be stressed rather than buried in the midst of the chronology.

Spatial Patterns

In a spatial arrangement the exposition moves from area to area rather than from time to time. This pattern permits organization of the report by geographical section, by idea, and by function or responsibility.

A report surveying the market potential for a new product for control of hay-fever symptoms, for example, might organize its material under the headings Southern, Eastern, and Midwestern. Since sectional climatic conditions are reflected in seasonal variations affecting the appearance of hay fever, the area-to-area pattern of organization could best reveal the effects of these upon the market potential. Though the report moves from section to section of the country, the reader must be kept constantly aware of the totality. But this cannot be reasonably accomplished unless the report takes up the details of each area in a parallel structure of presentation.

Spatial arrangement by idea is suitable for any investigative report concerned with two or more alternatives or possibilities for examination. Suppose that the writer were asked to report upon various means available to a nonprofit hospital to raise funds through voluntary contributions. The organizational headings might be: direct-mail solicitation, charity dances and card parties, endowments. Each idea would be systematically explored with a view to yielding a meaningful total picture.

Function or responsibility as the basis for a spatial pattern of arrangement possesses the same useful flexibility for the reporter as the organization by geographical area or idea. Reported plans for the yearly sales program might have the headings sales manager, marketing manager, advertising manager, convention manager, purchasing agent, office manager, and production chief. In turn, the functions or responsibilities in each area would be reported in terms of their relationship to the projected total objective.

In exploiting any pattern of the spatial organizational arrangement, the report writer should certainly not assume that a helter-skelter program is permissible. Any such arrangement should logically be justified by a controlling principle imposed upon it by the writer. For instance, geographical areas may be dealt with simply in the order of their spatial arrangement on the map. Or on the other hand, the writer may elect to consider each in terms of its relative importance to the purpose at hand. But it is the responsibility of the writer to let the reader know what is happening. If functions or responsibilities are to be the foundation pattern, these should be set up, for example, in order of importance, or in an order indicating those responsibilities which must be met on the earliest dates.

Causal Connections

The chronological pattern of arrangement depends upon the *when*, and the spatial pattern concerns itself with the *where;* the causal pattern unfolds the answer to *why*. The report organized in the causal pattern moves from cause to effect.

Organization from causes to effects is best used in a report dealing with concepts and ideas. In practice, this means the writer is called upon to explain the forces that produce a situation, or, contrariwise, to explain the results produced by a particular situation. Clearly, this pattern goes beyond mere sequences in time and space and calls for causal analysis.

Two questions are at the core of causal analysis: (1) Why did this happen? (What caused this?) and (2) In given circumstances, what effect is likely to follow? It would be wise for the report writer to think of "cause" as the connection between events—as those things or that thing which produces an effect or result. By connection we mean a link between ideas and events: In the absence of X, Y would not occur, or when X is present, Y will also be present. The reporter would most probably build his organization around the connections which were most immediate.

Let us assume that through a breakdown in communication within a large corporation, an important piece of sales literature has been released to the public without prior review by the legal department. The literature claims for a product certain benefits and advantages over other competitive products. But these advantages are not justified by the facts, and a costly lawsuit has followed as the result, with much unfavorable publicity. The corporate board of directors has authorized a report to determine the cause of the breakdown in communication.

The report, first of all, explores the established machinery for clearing sales literature through the legal department. It then goes on to examine the steps involved in the preparation of sales literature, tracing the participation of the various departments within the company and that of the outside advertising agency. The report, in toto, examines the degree of effective communication possible in a complex organized group effort involving many persons. From this—the cause—the consequences are traced until the immediate connection between the cause and the particular effect resulting in the lawsuit is determined. The report deals with concepts of departmental responsibilities, subordination and command, differentiation of function, and so forth. The "why" of the breakdown in communication is established through the cause-to-effect pattern of arrangement.

Inductive or Deductive Patterns

Induction and deduction as methods of reasoning are taken up in Chapter 9, The Logic of Reports. Here the inductive and deductive methods may be cited as useful patterns for imposing a final organization upon a report.

Induction is a method of reaching a conclusion based on a particular set of observable facts. At the point of final organization, the report writer has already gathered and ascertained his facts. To successfully lay them out inductively as a basis for analytical development, the various techniques are: (1) illustration by an example (or by several examples), (2) enumeration of particulars and details, (3) definition, (4) elaboration by comparison and contrast, and (5) combination methods. Since all these are essentially techniques for development, they will be taken up in detail in the following chapter on logical development. Here, since they are fundamental to any decision about whether the inductive or deductive final arrangement of a report is indeed practicable, we may consider the differences between fact and opinion.

The bases of induction are particular facts; facts must be (1) verifiable, and (2) attested by a reliable authority.

To verify is to prove to be true by demonstration. That which is offered as a fact, if it is indeed a fact, can be confirmed and substantiated by the report reader. Obviously, on the basis of common sense and experience, the reader will not feel impelled to verify certain assertions in reports. There will seem no need to affirm or deny the truth of most facts which are nonpolemical. For example, if a report on methods for training new sales personnel asserted that a positive, affirmative approach in selling is the best one, few readers would think it necessary to require substantiation through demonstration to verify this. However, if a report were to assert as fact that the salesman who wears a bow tie makes fewer sales than the man who wears a regular tie, the reader who favors bow ties could by demonstration show that the assertion is not verifiable as fact and is merely the writer's opinion.

The point here, of course, is that one would be most unwise to undertake an inductive approach in a report which advanced as observable facts what were really nothing more than a series of unverifiable personal impressions. If these were to be the basis for the report, the writer would be wise to adopt a spatial arrangement by ideas. In such a pattern, the report writer could effectively consider, evaluate, and entertain certain opinions and ideas without being obliged (as the inductive pattern would require him) to assert them as facts.

Even though the bulk of the writer's assertions may be either noncontroversial or verifiable, he had best give some thought to the other aspect of differentiation between fact and opinion before he undertakes an inductive pattern of arrangement. This second aspect involves the reliability of the sources he invokes to support his facts.

The report may say, "Mr. Rodney Wifenpou, executive director of the Sales Training Institute, supports the view that successful salesmen are those who do not wear bow ties. He states this fact in his most recent bulletin." Or it may say, "Professor J. H. P. Eggmorton-Hones of the Harvard Business School states in his book, the standard work in the field, that according to the Bible and the American Constitution, union negotiations must be carried out. . . ." Since it is not frequently feasible for readers to themselves verify facts, they may accept or reject evidence on the basis of attestation by authority.

Questions which arise are: (1) Is the authority rightly quoted? (2) Is the authority testifying in a field where he is competent? (3) Is the authority supported by other authorities in the same field? and (4) Does the authority have a record of success and recognized achievement?

None of these questions is particularly difficult to find answers to. Whether the authority is quoted out of context, is inaccurately quoted, or is rightly quoted but in a passage irrelevant to the fact being developed in the report, can readily be determined by a checkup. The writer will be obliged to provide references for the reader. Answers to the remaining three questions may be found through library research in standard reference works which provide biographical and other data about important people. Sources unknown to the reader and not sufficiently known to be listed in conventional reference works are not likely to be considered reliable.

These factors surrounding the nature of the evidence—on the one hand, facts which are verifiable or are attested by reliable authorities, or, on the other, opinions which are offered for evaluative consideration—should help the report writer decide which organizational pattern is most suitable, the inductive or the spatial. Elements regarding the choice of a deductive arrangement are essentially the same as for the inductive. The deductive pattern is structured to move from a general concept to a particular case. But if the general concept is not soundly built on fact, then the particular conclusion which follows will lack validity.

Climactic Importance

Where the report chooses to bypass arrangements based on time, space, causal, or logical sequences, it may adopt the pattern of climactic importance. This organization is based on presentation of data either from the least important to the most important, or vice versa. Importance is determined solely by the main purpose of the report, irrespective of chronologic or other considerations.

For example, a yearly report to the company manager might be called for from each department. The purpose of the report is to provide full information on activities and accomplishments throughout the year. The report will be used as a partial basis for salary review. By way of gathering the requisite information, a department head has asked each of the six persons in his department to prepare individual listings of his personal activities and accomplishments. All told, there are some one hundred individual items for use in the report to the company manager.

Now, the department head may choose the climactic pattern of organization. One good method would be to group all the items into, let us say, three areas of importance determined by the contribution to the sales effort of the firm. The headings as they appear in the report might be: routine activities, special accomplishments, and most important achievement. Each section might merely list the appropriate items and then provide a summarizing paragraph, or a summarizing remark might be provided after each item. By withholding for the climactic and terminal position the item of most importance in the report, the department chief has gained maximal impact and emphasis. If he had simply presented all one hundred items in a chronological sequence, the report could not possibly have fulfilled its purpose as effectively.

Combination Arrangements

All these arrangement patterns for final organization of the report are presented to call to the attention of the writer the variety of meaningful possibilities available. Analysis of any good report, however, shows that not one but several methods of arrangement have been used. No one pattern or combination of patterns is superior to another except as determined by the nature of the utilizable facts and the specific purpose of the report. The creative report writer must see these arrangement patterns as tools available for use. As with other methods shown to him in this book, he should be able at any moment to utilize, alone or together, whatever techniques will most effectively accomplish the purpose at hand.

The case is the same as that of the various forms of prose discourse presented in Chapter 8. Exposition does not subsist independently and in isolation from description, argumentation, and narration, despite the fact that the main intention of a report is expository. By the same token, even though the main pattern of arrangement may be spatial by idea, certain subsections may call for chronological sequencing or climactic ordering. The inseparability of form and substance has been emphasized at various points in this book. Perhaps the point can be made again, as an epilogue to analysis of patterns of arrangement and as a prologue to patterns of development.

13

Logical Development

Expository writing undertakes explanation and clarification of a subject. Questions about the "what" and the "how" and the "when" of things we seek to understand are systematically answered. A report that satisfies its expository purpose will tell us unmistakably what a thing *is* and what it means, or how a thing *works* and how it is put together. These questions rarely appear barefaced, yet if one will examine even cursorily the various reports at hand, regardless of their apparent complexity he will recognize these questions behind them.

Each facet of an explanation presents different problems for the report writer; there are a variety of solutions available. Every paragraph must be amplified suitably by the developmental method which best serves the particular segment of matter at hand and the overall intention. As each paragraph in the explanation is individually shaped by a selected principle, the total report is gradually developed into the overall design planned beforehand by the writer.

ELABORATION AND AMPLIFICATION

Development of the report is achieved through orderly elaboration and amplification in paragraph form of facts and ideas. To elaborate is to give details—to provide full and adequate treatment. To amplify is to enlarge, expand, and extend through use of particular instances and illustrations. Delicate judgment must be exercised by the report writer to determine the degree of development required in each paragraph. Explanations short on details—lacking information about why a certain step is called for or how it may be executed—can produce misunderstanding. Overcondensed explanation may be little better than none at all.

The topic sentence has been said (Chapter 6) to contain a statement of the point which a paragraph is created to explain. A topic sentence is usually a general statement, such as "There is a disadvantage to the system" or "Rotation of crops helps prevent soil erosion" or "Additional personnel are required by the headquarters staff." The writer is clearly obligated to establish the validity of such generalizations through elaboration and amplification with details.

The length of the paragraph is determined by the nature of the subject, the type of topic sentence, the main intention of the writer, and the character of the audience. To accommodate the modern reader, whose attention span is usually limited, good report writers will break up their material into small paragraph units. But adequate development is nonetheless incumbent upon the writer.

Regarding insufficiently developed paragraphs—and therefore, insufficiently developed reports—this much can be said with impunity: The writer is displaying directionless thinking, poverty of imagination, deficiency of observation, or lack of knowledge.

Illustration and Example

An illustration or an example is the commonest way to make a thesis clear. Some reports may be developed almost wholly by this method, and others will surely utilize the technique occasionally. Thus, if the writer wishes to elaborate the contention that lack of supervisory control is producing inefficiency in the payroll section, he will cite examples of duplication of work effort. As was pointed out in Chapter 9 on logic of the report, the illustrations and examples will need to be sufficiently typical to establish the point. Convincing development frequently requires several examples, but the number will vary with the contentiousness of the thesis and the complexity of the subject.

Illustration and example are basically a way of explaining the general by presenting the particular. The method is manifestly allied with inductive logic (Chapter 9) and patterns of organization (Chapter 12). A report covering, for example, the general value of a punch card system for assembling research data will probably be developed through a series of particular instances of usefulness. Instead of generalizing about qualities of the system, the report will aim to illustrate these through particular examples. Essentially, the explanation is dealing with a general type, class, or group of things (punch card systems); but communication of what that general thing is and how it works is accomplished through concrete illustrations and instances. Used to give the report substance and tangibility, illustration and example are invaluable developmental aids.

Enumeration of Particulars and Details

The writer of successful reports must inevitably make peace with innumerable particulars and details. Concrete specifications, facts, and reasons, selected and arranged to accomplish a specific purpose, are the substance of many well-developed paragraphs. Enumeration of steps in a process, parts of a structure, qualities of an object, divisions within a classification, reasons for a procedure, causes producing an effect, and results occurring from a cause, is a helpful way of providing the specifics which almost all reports require.

Just as certain kinds of topic sentences almost cry out for development by illustration and example, others demand enumeration. For example, if the topic sentence says, "The brick foundation is constructed with systematic care," enumeration of the particulars and details in the steps of the process must surely follow. Or if the topic sentence announces, "There are four kinds of membership presently possible in the organization," enumeration of these kinds is the natural follow-up in development. Or if the topic states, "Economic cooperation is particularly important in this nuclear age," enumeration of particular reasons will be required. Or if the topic asks, "How can we explain the fact that almost identical sealed bids were frequently submitted?" enumeration of examples would be expected. Or where the topic sentence declares, "Manufacture of the textile has three stages," the details of the stages will then be developed.

Should report writers be reminded that details in themselves are not lovely things? Judging from many reports, it would seem that a reminder is necessary. Some report writers appear to forget that the occasion of the writing demands information aimed to enlarge the reader's understanding. The function of details is to make exposition more meaningful by making it less abstract. Details selected to fit the writer's purpose help him to make himself clear to the reader. But details which have no relation to the writer's purpose—those that pad the exposition without improving it—will be worse than useless. Clearly, details must be purposefully selected. Only if the reporter remains constantly alert to the nature (rather than the number) of details and their relationships to one another (and to his main purpose) can he use them successfully.

Definition

Definition is of much importance in the development of reports. As a method of elaboration and amplification, it sets the limits of meaning of a thing. A formal definition is based upon a logical pattern consisting of three parts: (1) The term (word or phrase) to be defined, (2) the genus—the class, object, or concept to which the term belongs, and (3) the differentiae—those characteristics which differentiate or distinguish it from all others of its class. Informal definition often explains the meaning of a term by a synonym or other substitute expression, but both informal and formal definition must classify logically.

For example, a management executive (term to be defined) is a policy-making company officer (class to which he belongs) whose function is to formulate, administer, and direct overall activities of the enterprise (characteristics which distinguish him from others—comptroller, sales manager, etc.—of the same class). In making any concise definition—one that permits a maximum of information in a minimum of space—there are definite steps to follow.

First of all, one must name the smallest class that will include the term to be defined. To say that a management executive is "any person responsible for supervising the affairs of a company" is to create too broad a class. Included in this class would be the office manager and the purchasing agent. Narrowing the genus to policy-making company officer makes it large enough to include all the members of the term (management executive), but no larger.

Secondly, the differentiae must be essential, i.e., they must truly exclude other members of the class. Incomplete differentiation would exist between classes included in the definition if one said the function of the management executive is "to run the company." That is also the function of the sales manager and comptroller. By adding the differentiae "formulate, administer, and direct the overall activities," adequate differentiation is accomplished.

Thirdly, the report writer should not let his explanatory definition depend for its meaning upon a repetition of the term. It is not enlightening to say that "a management executive is a specialist in management." Other words—policy-making company officer—are needed if the definition is to really help the reader.

It is necessary, as yet another step in definition, to balance the term by another which is the same part of speech. The writer must avoid in his definition the error of "is when" or "is where." He may not say, "A metaphor is when the writer uses a figure of speech," or "A secretarial pool is where all the typists work for all the staff members." A noun (*metaphor, secretarial pool*) must be defined by a noun: "A metaphor is a figure of speech. A secretarial pool is an arrangement." A verb must be defined by a verb, an adjective by an adjective, and so forth.

A fourth requisite in making a definition is to exclude emotional or moral judgments. We have all seen "definitions" like these: "Capitalism is an economic system of free enterprise and private ownership which allows a God-fearing, freedom-loving people to have the highest standard of living. Socialism is a politico-economic theory which in practice destroys the individual's belief in God, respect for home and family, and love of democracy." Reports may lapse into biased definition when they strain to make a particular point. If the writer will merely attempt to define his terms as objectively as possible, recognizing that pertinent facts and judgments may, in their turn, be given separately in appropriate sections of the report, there will be no confusion to render the definition valueless.

So often, reports prepared by specialists in this or that field of study fail to provide effective definitions. Failure results from the unwillingness of the specialist writer to establish common ground and common language between himself and his nonspecialist reader. Only the report writer who offers a definition with an awareness of what his particular audience knows or is willing to learn can hope to succeed with this mode of development. It is the perceptive report author who, not forgetting that his objective is to enlarge his readers' understanding, will use words that his readers are acquainted with or can readily learn. He must also, in defining, employ information the reader is likely to have knowledge of. There can be no common ground when the definer defines a term in words as unfamiliar as the word defined.

As the author of reports comes more fully to understand the purpose and technique of definition in the development of his material, he will come to use not only simple but extended definition. There will be instances when establishment of common ground between the writer and reader may not be readily possible. In this case the reporter must attempt to reach understanding by developing and extending his own definition in detail. Extended definition is developed from simple definition into a full-scale discussion which may employ many methods. In its effort to add fullness and interest to basic data, the extended definition in a report may take advantage of numerous expository methods. It may extend itself through details, examples, comparison and contrast, and analysis, to cite but a few ways. So long as the extensions are judged to truly aid the readers' understanding of the basic material, they will be helpful. When the extended definition even suggests that the writer is trying to evade coming to grips with his original terms, then it has gone off the track.

There are today few reports of any consequence that in some way do not require use of simple or extended definition. In one sense, the mere step of formulating a thesis and establishing an objective for a report involves definition—setting limits of intended meaning for the report. But in the usual give-and-take of report writing, many individual terms will be defined. Experience teaches the writer that many terms essential to a report may be familiar to the reader but not thoroughly understood by him. Even terms from our everyday vocabulary—communism, fission, trajectory, collective bargaining, skilled labor, closed shop, technocracy, automation—may bear defining in exposition of which they are a part. Familiar as a term may be, it can have a particular personal meaning to the reader which will be at variance with that of the writer. It may indeed happen that a report reader will reject in his mind a particular definition offered by the reporter. As with many other things, there are definitions about which reasonable people may agree or disagree. But though there may be disagreement about the particulars of a writer's definition, there will be none regarding his knowledge of methods of effectively developing his report.

Comparison and Contrast

The technique of comparison and contrast involves holding up two similar but not identical objects, situations, or ideas for the sake of discovering their similarities and their points of variance. Since many reports weigh several alternatives in order to arrive at recommendations for a proper course of action, the salient points leading to a reasoned choice of one over the others may be made clear through comparing and contrasting.

Of course, none of the basic methods of paragraph development is simply a means for developing a report; each represents a method for thinking. Whenever you are faced with a choice, you carefully examine the possibilities, noting their likenesses and differences. Which car should you buy? Which route should you take? Which secretary should you hire? Explanation of similarities and dissimilarities between two or more things will, in a report, simply require that you present your comparison and contrast systematically.

In the imposition of a system by which you can compare and contrast, you will first have to decide the purpose. Is your purpose to inform the reader about one item? If so, you will have to relate it to another item with which he is already familiar. Is your purpose to inform the reader about two items? If so, you will compare and contrast both of them in relation to some general principle with which the reader is already familiar and which would apply to both items. Or is your purpose to compare and contrast items with which the reader is already familiar, in order to inform him about some general principle or idea? If you enumerate likenesses and differences without due understanding of the prime purpose, you are certain to be uninstructive.

As an example of a comparison which undertakes to inform your reader about one item by holding up another with which he is already familiar, assume that you are an executive in a shoe manufacturing business. You have just returned from an international shoe fair in Mexico. You wish to report to your colleagues on a European innovation in shoe styling that you think has great merit. As you initiate your written explanation, you may say, "In general, the model we now have which resembles the European style most closely is Model MM 348. But individual features of the European model more closely resemble those of various others of our models." Then you compare the new item systematically with models your readers are already familiar with.

Your systematic handling of the comparison should satisfy its purpose—to inform the reader about the new model he has never seen.

In the same situation, assume that there are two items involved: European and Latin American stylings that your colleagues are not familiar with. Here, you might systematically compare and contrast both unfamiliar styles with general, classic principles of shoe styling and manufacturing known to your readers. Or, contrariwise, if there are new principles of styling and manufacturing you wish to report, you might compare and contrast various shoe models known to your readers, for purposes of revealing the nature of the new process.

There are two general ways you may organize information for comparison and contrast. In what may be called the opposing pattern, you may fully present one item and then fully present the other. In an alternating pattern, on the other hand, you may present a part of one item and then a corresponding part of the other, until you have touched upon all the relevant points for comparison and contrast.

Usually, the opposing pattern is best when your material is not of great complexity. Emphasis is thus gained for the broad picture of contrast between two items. If your comparison is to be of some length and complexity, you might best choose the alternating pattern. Otherwise, the details about one item will not stay clearly in the reader's mind while you elucidate the other. The alternating pattern may best serve to stress the particular points of the comparison rather than the overall picture. When items are compared and contrasted in an alternating pattern, you may sometimes wish to present them visually in a table (Chapter 14). You will occasionally find this technique of laying out the two items side by side in a tabular arrangement to be very useful.

You will have already recognized that comparison and contrast are closely allied to metaphor, simile, and analogy (Chapter 8). Metaphor and simile you may think of simply as highly compressed comparisons, while analogy is an amplified comparison useful in explaining and informing. Though you may now begin to see comparison and contrast as an effective method for developing the substance of a report, this technique is really, after all, a formalized recognition of the way in which the mind seeks to understand the unknown in terms of the known.

ANALYSIS

Analysis is a logical method of breaking down a thing or a concept into its component parts for purposes of understanding its meaning.

We speak of two kinds of analysis, physical and conceptual. In physical analysis we break down an object until it is spatially separated into its components. For example, one might take apart an electric vacuum cleaner and explain the relationships among the parts. Clearly, doing so would provide an explanation of what a vacuum cleaner is and how it works. In conceptual analysis we perform in the mind, through use of reason, the breaking down of abstract ideas which cannot be physically apprehended. For example, a report cannot be fruitfully explained by physically grouping and counting the words, paragraphs, sections, and pages which may appear in various parts. These figures would not reveal the meaning of the report. We can analyze a report only by understanding the function of each of its parts. This is achieved through conceptual analysis.

A thing cannot be analyzed if we do not apprehend it as having a structure. Structures may be perceived by regarding the necessary relationships of the parts to one another and to the whole. Complete analysis not only divides things into their component parts; it indicates the relation among the parts and their place in the structure.

As a method of development in reports and other kinds of writing, analysis can be approached by two different techniques commonly employed: classification and partition.

Classification

Classification may be thought of as the dividing of a group into the kinds of units which comprise it. A class is a group whose members have significant characteristics in common. A system is a set of classes ranging from a most inclusive class down through less and less inclusive classes. He who undertakes the process of classification starts with individual units, arranges them in groups, and then relates those groups to more inclusive groups.

To the uninitiate, any body of information may appear formidably chaotic. For example, the number and kind of pathogenic organisms which may cause respiratory infections would make the layman despair of his physician's ever choosing the proper drug to control the infection. But once the laboratory technician has isolated, identified, and classified the causative organism, the physician will know which class of antibiotic drugs is most likely to be effective in treatment. To the microbiologist, the various classes of infection-causing bacteria have a high degree of order. To the physician, the spectrum of activity of different classes of antimicrobial agents is also seen as having order.

A classic example of admirable classification is the Dewey decimal system, by which libraries catalog the titanic masses of printed matter contained within their walls. First, all books are classified into ten broad groupings according to subject:

000–099	General works	500–599	Natural science
100–199	Philosophy	600–699	Useful arts
200–299	Religion	700–799	Fine arts
300–399	Sociology	800–899	Literature
400–499	Philology	900–999	History

Each of the ten categories is then subdivided into ten divisions. For example, literature is subdivided as follows:

800	General literature	850	Italian literature
810	American literature	860	Spanish literature
820	English literature	870	Latin literature
830	German literature	880	Greek literature
840	French literature	890	Minor literatures

Each of these classes is further subdivided into groups whose members have significant characteristics in common. For example, the breakdown on class 820—English literature—is comprised of the following less inclusive classes:

820	English literature	825	English oratory
821	English poetry	826	English letters
822	English drama	827	English satire
823	English fiction	828	English miscellany
824	English essays	829	Anglo-Saxon

Decimals are used to make any further subdivisions into still less inclusive classes. In addition, each book is given a number within its classification. This number is usually made up of an identifying letter plus a number showing the book's place in the library's collection.

Certain kinds of reports in every field of endeavor will present a massive amount of data for classification and interpretation. Much of this may be accomplished by mechanical means, i.e., punch cards, as seen in Chapter 11. To be maximally useful, any scheme of classes which the writer creates for use in classifying material for the development of his report should conform to the following simple rules: (1) There can be only one principle of division applied at each stage; (2) the subgroups under any group must exhaust that group; (3) the same principle of division that is applied in the first stage must be continued through successive stages, if such exist.

For an example of rule 1, assume that we might like to discover and exhibit in our annual personnel report to the board of directors the proportion of Negro college graduates among our corporation's 5,867 employees around the world. There are two principles here: Negro and college graduate. We would first divide all the employees on the basis of race, whether they work in the Brooklyn plant or the plant in Australia. Then we would divide the Negro class of employees into college graduates and non-college graduates to obtain our desired information. One could, obviously, first apply the principle of college graduates to all the data and from this extract the information regarding Negro college graduates. Whichever order is followed, the second principle should not be applied until the first has been fully worked out, if meaningful analytic classification is to be achieved. As in outlining, the report writer should strive to avoid overlapping of divisions of classes.

Rule 2 serves to remind us that we must account in our subclasses for all members of the class. Dividing employees on the basis of race into Caucasian and Negro does not account for all employees if there are also members of the Mongolian race to be accounted for. To the extent that this subclass is unaccounted for in our first subclass, our final classification will be inaccurate.

Rule 3 simply indicates that the classification must be consistent. For example, having in the first stage classified all employees on the basis of race, we would not decide to discover the proportion of Negro Protestant college graduates without starting all over again and applying the principle of religious affiliation to all the data.

Partition

In speaking of classification as an analytic method of developing the body of a report, we have, necessarily, already spoken of partition. While classification is concerned with the dividing of a group into the kinds of units which comprise it, partition works by focusing on a single unit and breaking it down into the parts of which it is composed. The example of physical analysis cited in the preceding sections— breaking down a vacuum cleaner into its component parts—is actually an example of partition.

The most valuable use of analysis by partition lies in determining the parts or phases of a subject to be explained and the logical order for treating them. Consider these topic sentences:

1. The executive, legislative, and judicial comprise the three branches of American government.
2. The reticuloendothelial system of the human body includes endo-

thelial and reticular cells of the liver, the reticuloendothelium of bone marrow, and the clasmatocytes.

3. A casting rod is made up of four main parts: a handle, a reel set, a length of rod, and several guidelines.

Partitioning or dividing the single unit into its component parts immediately provides a basis for logical development. The method lends itself admirably to reports of diverse kinds. The pattern of development consists of three stages, the first steps of which can be seen in any of the three topic sentences just cited: (1) Statement of the thesis, (2) Discussion (enumeration and amplification) of each factor in turn, and (3) Restatement of thesis or concluding summary (optional but usual).

It may be seen that partition provides a neat package as a method of development. Classification and partition, separately or together, serve well to bring out the full implications of a report's main thesis. But the writer must constantly remember that neither classification nor partition is analysis in itself. Breaking down things into parts is a purely mechanical process which yields no meaning unless the writer is creatively aware at all times of the main purpose which lies behind his particular piece of writing.

COMBINATION METHODS

Most paragraphs combine several methods of development. The writer will perhaps commence with definition, move off to enumeration, provide a contrast, offer examples, return to definition, amplify with additional illustrations, advance a comparison, and conclude with definition. Methods of amplifying information are closely allied with processes of thinking and the manner in which the mind flexibly ranges over matter it is seeking to understand.

But the same kinds of differences which exist between formal and informal usage (Chapter 6) and between the written and spoken word (Chapter 17) also exist between the way the mind thinks through a problem and the method by which information is articulated in a report. The mind may leap over connections, partially explore examples, elliptically frame definitions, incompletely develop contrasts— yet nonetheless reach full understanding. But the discipline of writing, though it freely encourages the writer to flexibly use all suitable methods of natural development, demands that the information be offered in systematic, fully structured order. Success of a report depends as much upon the way in which information is developed as upon the quality of the information.

INTERNAL DESIGN

Parallelism and Coordination

Necessity for a lucid thesis and a logical outline was stressed in Chapter 9. The overall design for a report provides the structural framework without which any experienced writer would not proceed. As we have seen thus far in the present chapter, development of the report from the plan involves putting meat on the bones.

An outline provides the report writer with what is essentially an undetailed general plan that lays bare the relationships and values of all of the parts. It provides, at a glance, a guide which alerts its creator to the relative degree of development logically required of each part so that the report will be neither top-heavy nor bottom-heavy but well balanced.

It will be recalled that the system of notation in outlining provides for main headings, subheadings, and subsidiary headings, determined by the relation of each part to the main thesis. Further, subheadings or subsidiary headings of one rank at any point in the outline are equal in value to all others of the same rank at any other point in the outline. Hence, parallel, equal developmental treatment is needed for parts with the same values.

Parallelism as a concept of internal design applies to words, sentences, and paragraphs as well as to whole sections of a report. The idea embodies patterns of consistency and correspondence. Reduced to the simplest formulas parallelism says: (1) Like meanings should be put in like constructions, and (2) like values should be exhibited by like (equal) development.

On the level of words and sentences, parallelism requires that sentence elements which are parallel in thought be expressed in parallel form. Examples are:

1. In business, ability *to listen* is as important as ability *to talk*.
2. The branch manager is responsible for *taking* inventory and *replenishing* stock.

Considered on the level of paragraphs and sections of the report, parallelism requires, as we have said, that structural elements of the same rank be given the same degree of amplification. This consideration springs as much from writing convention as from logic; it is by way of an implicit contract between writer and reader. Where the writer first discusses the disadvantages of system Z, the reader quietly anticipates parallel treatment for the advantages. If the subheading under one main division explains how to control the temperature of the iron during the initial stage of processing, parallel development for the same subject will be anticipated under the other main division in which it may occur. Parallelism, then, as a vector of internal design, helps the report reader to recognize units of equal importance. By providing the balanced treatment expected by the reader accustomed to this archetypal pattern of conventional exposition, parallelism helps make clearer the meaning of the explanation.

Coordination as a component of development in a report calls for placement or arrangement of parts in due order and proper relative position. As its objective, coordination strives for harmonious combination of the various parts of the report.

Coordination is another device for making the reader's task easier. In individual sentences and paragraphs, development of facts in such a way that the less important will be subordinated to the more important will provide a useful index to interpretation. If the writer critically sifts his ideas so that they may be arranged with precision, the reader is guided to the important relationships among them.

For example, in amplifying an explanation of a new process, one might say, "The vats are thoroughly cleaned and the molds are given an acid bath for 120 minutes." There is here no pattern of subordination to indicate the relative importance of the ideas; they are presented as being of equal importance. By rephrasing, the lesser idea can be subordinated: "After the vats are thoroughly cleaned, the molds are given an acid bath for 120 minutes." Through the arrangement of the parts in proper relative position, coordination is achieved.

Extended to the report as a whole, coordination requires that two or more units of the plan be of coordinate and equal rank wherever they happen to fall in the overall design. They must be developed accordingly. Conversely, subordinate units of sentences, paragraphs, and sections of the report must be made to appear so by the lesser magnitude of development given them by the creative report writer.

Format Presentation

The headings point up the writer's main themes and aid the reader in following the development of the thoughts. Chapter 16 will undertake discussion of problems relating to the written presentation of the report. It may, nonetheless, be stated here that presentation of format figures in report development.

A consistent style for indicating the value of headings is the main device for clearly displaying the relative weights attached to individual parts. No amount of care devoted to headings and format, however, will compensate for a report which does not keep the promises it makes. Where the values indicated by format are not borne out by the material developed, the reader can regard the format only as a misleading contrivance.

Any logically consistent format to indicate the overall and internal design is acceptable. One widely used format consists of:

MAIN HEADING: CAPITALIZED AND CENTERED
Subheading: Separate Line, Flush with Margin, Underlined, Main Words Capitalized
Subsidiary Heading: Paragraphed, Underlined, Main Words Capitalized. The text follows in the same paragraph.

In establishing the format, the report writer can be guided almost completely by the values he has set up in his outline.

✿   ✿   ✿   ✿   ✿

Pattern in final organization and development is as important as the words used in a report, for substance without form is chaos. Visualizations, the subject of the following chapter, carry the idea of organizing and developing material a step beyond the patterns we have been discussing.

14

Graphic Devices

THE WORD OR THE PICTURE?

Expression of ideas by means of visualizations has come fully into its own. Contemporary writers of reports, truly, may ignore use of visual aids only at the hazard of appearing quite out of tune with the harmonics of our times. It may very well be that the importance of graphic presentations in reports has been disproportionately magnified, to the point of placing the written word in peril. Nonetheless, there are abundant valid reasons for the creative report writer to freely use graphic aids to supplement and amplify what he has written.

Graphs, charts, tables, drawings, diagrams, maps, and photographs help to vividly and clearly delineate facts and ideas. Moreover, the impact of movies, television, cartoons, picture magazines, and audio-visual teaching aids has thoroughly attuned the modern mind to all manner and form of pictorialization. Graphic artists have been specially trained in the necessary disciplines, and in a great many corporate, professional, and governmental enterprises, these persons devote all their energies to the making of visualizations. The creative report writer—whether obliged to prepare his own relatively simple graphs and charts or to collaborate with a specialist in making complex visualizations—needs to be adequately equipped with a general knowledge of the different kinds of visual aids.

The more ardent exponents of picture techniques in report writing have taken the position that, since "one picture is worth 1,000 words," the visualizations should be the core of the report, with the text written around them. Let us hope the day when the report writer abdicates in favor of the visualist will never come, for visual aids were not intended to replace the written word and cannot do so. Visualizations are devices of incalculable usefulness to support the report text—but not to supplant it. Excellent visual aids may not be accepted in lieu of the best writing; graphics do not effectively serve to mask poor writing.

GRAPHS

Statistics play a central role in many major reports. So that the abstract ideas embodied in numerals may be given a concrete representation, graphs of various kinds are utilized. (See Figure 14-1, which shows the component parts of the standard graph used in many reports.) In general, graphs serve better than anything else to dramatically compare and contrast sets of numbers and to depict movement or trends in a discernible direction amidst variables.

200

Figure 14-1 Designation of graph components. (*Adapted from R. R. Lutz, Graphic Presentation Simplified, Funk & Wagnalls, New York, 1949. By permission of Dun and Bradstreet, Inc.*)

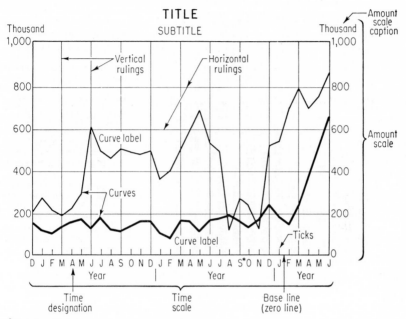

Bar Graphs. Since the bar graph is relatively easy to construct and simple to understand, it is the most popular variety. It consists of bars arranged horizontally or vertically from a "zero" base (see Figures 14-2 to 14-5 and Figure 14-10). Different values are represented by size, length, and sometimes color of the bars. In practice, bar graphs are utilized chiefly for comparing and contrasting—income and wages, quotas and sales, individual output, departmental production, etc. But they may be put to good use in a wide diversity of situations involving different sets of figures.

Figure 14-2   Vertical bar graph. (*Courtesy of Elmer Smith for* Fortune Magazine.)

Executives See Sales Gains Ahead

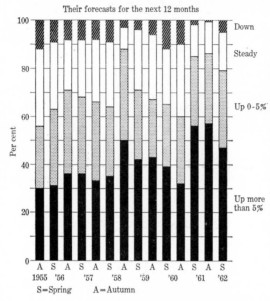

Their forecasts for the next 12 months

Four out of five businessmen responding to FORTUNE's semi-annual survey of the business mood say they expect gains in their own sales over the next year. Executive optimism, therefore, is only slightly less widespread than last autumn or spring (or in the first flush of recovery in the autumn of 1958). Their optimism for the future, though somewhat moderate in tone, is greater today than it was after business gains of a year or more were behind them at comparable points in the upswings of 1955–56 and of 1959–60. The latest reading was taken at the start of spring, prior to the recent spate of encouraging business developments.

Figure 14-3   Vertical bar graph. (*Courtesy of* Monthly Economic Letter, *First National City Bank, New York.*)

DIMENSIONS OF REPORTED UNEMPLOYMENT IN THE UNITED STATES

Figure 14-4 Horizontal bar graph (bottom) used with a curve graph (top). (*Reproduced by permission of National Industrial Conference Board, New York.*)

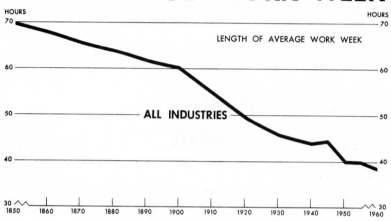

THE AVERAGE WORK WEEK

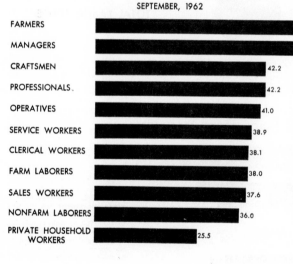

AVERAGE WEEKLY HOURS
SEPTEMBER, 1962

FARMERS	53.3 HOURS
MANAGERS	49.6
CRAFTSMEN	42.2
PROFESSIONALS	42.2
OPERATIVES	41.0
SERVICE WORKERS	38.9
CLERICAL WORKERS	38.1
FARM LABORERS	38.0
SALES WORKERS	37.6
NONFARM LABORERS	36.0
PRIVATE HOUSEHOLD WORKERS	25.5

During the last 110 years, the length of the average work week has declined sharply from about 70 hours per week to about 39 hours per week. The greatest decline occurred between 1900 and 1930, when the work week dropped by about 14 hours. Over the last decade, the work week has leveled off somewhat to just under 40 hours. In September 1962, the longest work week occurred among farmers (53 hours), while private household workers, where part-time work is predominant, had the shortest work week (26 hours).

Sources: Top, Twentieth Century Fund; bottom, Department of Labor

Figure 14-5   Horizontal bar graph (bottom) used with a circle pie graph (top). *(Reproduced by permission of National Industrial Conference Board, New York.)*

WOMEN in the Labor Force

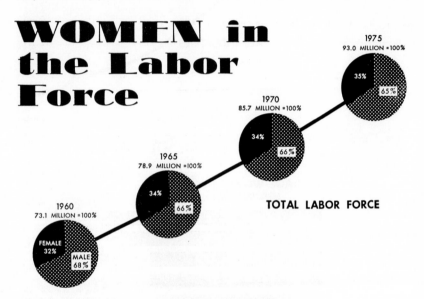

TOTAL LABOR FORCE

CHANGES IN LABOR FORCE, 1960-1975

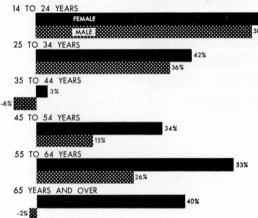

By 1975, it is expected that women will comprise 35% of a total U. S. labor force of 93 million persons. In 1960, by contrast, only 32% of a labor force of 73 million were women. Slightly more than 11 million men and nearly 9 million women will be added to the labor force by 1975, but in relative terms the female work force will increase at a faster rate (37%) than the male work force (23%). The greatest relative growth in the labor force as a whole is expected to take place in the 14 to 24 age group, while the 35 to 44 age group is expected to decrease.

Source: Bureau of Labor Statistics

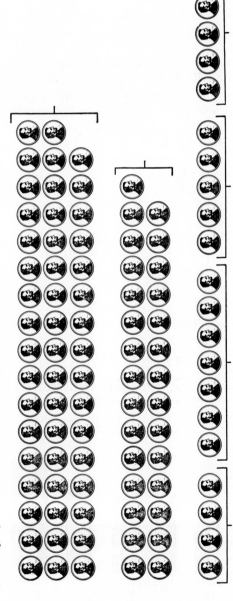

Figure 14-6 Horizontal bar pictorial graph.
(*Courtesy of The Pfizer Scene, Chas. Pfizer & Co., Inc., New York.*)

Bar Pictorial Graphs. As a perhaps more sophisticated refinement of the conventional horizontal or vertical bar graph, the bar pictorial graph is less exact but more interesting (see Figures 14-6 and 14-7). For projecting certain kinds of figures it is most effective. Rather than bars, drawings are chosen to convey the thought. The drawing is usually the object to which the numbers refer—persons, farms, automobiles, money, houses, etc. Numbers or sizes of the illustrations convey proportionate amounts.

Circle Pie Graphs. To depict a breakdown or distribution of particular values, the circle pie chart (shown in Figures 14-5 and 14-8) is exceedingly useful. Circle charts figure largely in corporate and governmental reports charged with explaining how funds have been allocated and spent. Each section or slice of the pie can be colored or shaded to emphasize its percentage of the whole circle.

Line or Curve Graphs. Industrial reports often depend upon the line or curve graph to delineate economic situations and business cycles and trends. However, the line graph has many other applications. As is shown in Figures 14-4 and 14-9, it is put to use to represent various vectors in motion against a particular time and space backdrop.

Figure 14-7 Vertical bar pictorial graph. (*Courtesy of American Pharmaceutical Association, Washington, D.C.*)

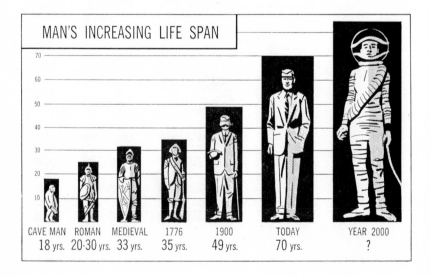

Figure 14-8 Circle pie graph, depicting annual expenditures, shown with the budget of a college (below).

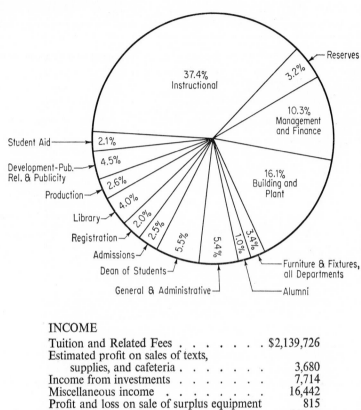

INCOME

Tuition and Related Fees	$2,139,726
Estimated profit on sales of texts, supplies, and cafeteria	3,680
Income from investments	7,714
Miscellaneous income	16,442
Profit and loss on sale of surplus equipment	815
Unrestricted contributions	44,132
Student Aid	3,646
	$2,215,973

DISTRIBUTION OF FUNDS

Alumni	$ 23,161
Building and Plant	357,766
Management and Finance	227,234
General and Administrative	119,359
Instructional	827,395
Library	89,455
Production	57,341
Registration	45,019
Admissions	55,545
Dean of Students	121,458
Development-Public Relations and Publicity	98,795
Furniture and Fixtures—All Departments .	75,732
Reserves	70,244
Student Aid	47,469
	$2,215,973

Figure 14-9 Line or curve graph with explanatory comment. (Courtesy of Fortune Magazine.)

Interest Rates Soften a Bit

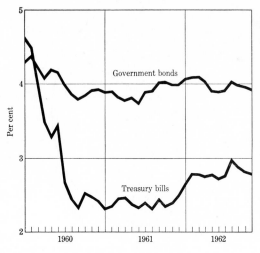

Interest rates were already drifting off last month when the Fed lowered some of the reserve requirements for commercial banks. In the past twenty-four months rates have on net balance varied relatively little altogether, a stability shown in no other postwar business upturn. Long-term government bonds are up less than 0.25 per cent since mid-1960, and rates on corporate and municipal bonds are as low as any time in the past two or even three years. Rates on Treasury bills have been up as much as 0.5 per cent, as they were boosted in order to discourage capital from flowing to foreign countries.

Figure 14-10 Surface-curve graph (left) depicting sales of discount chain operation in relation to total sales, and vertical bar graph (right) showing growth in number of discount stores. (*Courtesy of* Fortune Magazine.)

INTERSTATE DEPARTMENT STORES, INC.

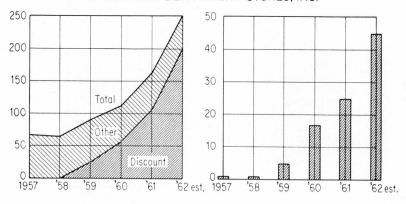

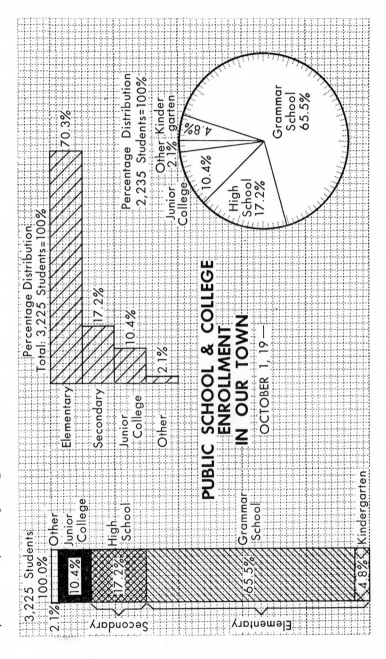

Figure 14-11 Ways in which statistical information may be adapted to three kinds of graphics. (*Courtesy of Polychart Graphic Workshop, Brooklyn Heights, New York.*)

Figure 14-12   Organizational chart of a small college.

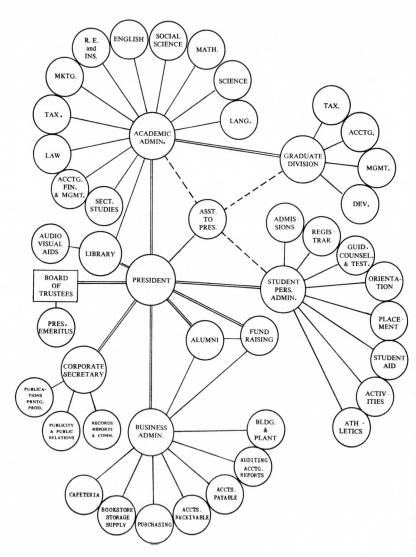

Surface-curve Graphs. By coloring or shading surface areas between selected lines or curves the surface-curve graph (Figure 14-10) is created. As a more elaborate graph, it achieves greater dramatic effects by throwing different values into vivid contrast.

CHARTS

Like the graph, the chart is an instrument commonly used by the report writer to present complex data in compact, interesting visual form. Factual statistical information comprised of masses of data can be more readily comprehended and interpreted when so visualized.

Organizational Charts. Analysis of a complexly structured organization is effectively accomplished with an organizational chart (Figures 14-12 to 14-14). Lines of authority and chains of responsibility can be clearly perceived in their correct sequences and relationships. Each division or component of the structure can be visualized in relation to the complete organizational complex. Words alone could not at once communicate the idea of the whole arrangement of an organization.

Flow Charts. To visualize the idea of movement of objects or the concept of sequential happenings, the flow chart is created. Though the steps in a particular process may be the subject of many written pages, a single flow chart like the one in Figure 14-15 may dynamically summarize the total sequence. Likewise, the history of a particular phenomenon, such as the stages through which a legislative bill must pass from the time of its proposal to the point at which it becomes law, can be visually depicted. Whenever the notion of dynamic flow rather than static fixity appears central to a proposed visualization, a flow chart may be considered.

Statistical Map Charts. The relationship of numbers to geographic locale is often pictorially expressed through the statistical map chart (Figures 14-16 and 14-17). Dispersion and distribution of things or people over a particular region may be effectively depicted for comparative purposes. Arbitrarily chosen symbols (dots, lines, etc.), pictorial symbols (drawings of factories, horses, etc.), numbers, percentage figures, coloring, or shading, may indicate the distribution. The objective is always the same (though the techniques may be interestingly individualized): to display overall proportional numerical relationships in terms of topographic distribution.

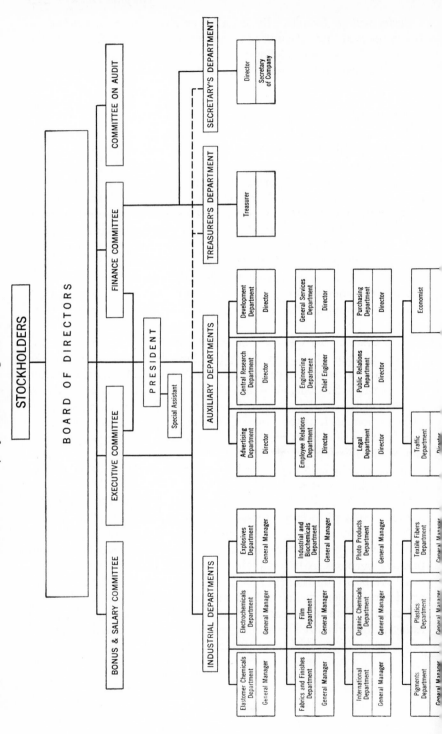

Figure 14-13 Organizational chart of a large corporation. (*Reproduced by permission of National Industrial Conference Board, New York, and E. I. duPont de Nemours and Company, Inc., Wilmington, Delaware.*)

Figure 14-14 Organizational chart of a research laboratory. (*Courtesy of Health News Institute, New York.*)

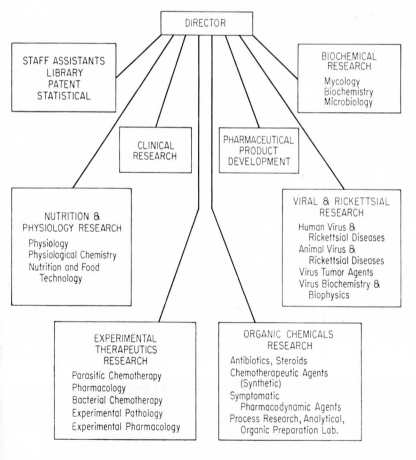

HOW ONE RESEARCH LABORATORY IS ORGANIZED

DIRECTOR

STAFF ASSISTANTS
LIBRARY
PATENT
STATISTICAL

BIOCHEMICAL
RESEARCH

Mycology
Biochemistry
Microbiology

CLINICAL
RESEARCH

PHARMACEUTICAL
PRODUCT
DEVELOPMENT

NUTRITION &
PHYSIOLOGY RESEARCH

Physiology
Physiological Chemistry
Nutrition and Food
Technology

VIRAL & RICKETTSIAL
RESEARCH

Human Virus &
Rickettsial Diseases
Animal Virus &
Rickettsial Diseases
Virus Tumor Agents
Virus Biochemistry &
Biophysics

EXPERIMENTAL
THERAPEUTICS
RESEARCH

Parasitic Chemotherapy
Pharmacology
Bacterial Chemotherapy
Experimental Pathology
Experimental Pharmacology

ORGANIC CHEMICALS
RESEARCH

Antibiotics, Steroids
Chemotherapeutic Agents
(Synthetic)
Symptomatic
Pharmacodynamic Agents
Process Research, Analytical,
Organic Preparation Lab.

TABLES

For the summary presentation of small and great amounts of qualitative and quantitative data, tabular display is recommended. As is shown in Figures 14-18 and 14-19, tables encourage the orderly grouping of statistics into logical patterns. Readers may easily perceive the principle of order—alphabetical, chronologic, numerical, quantitative, qualitative, or combinations of these. Isolated numbers scattered throughout the text quickly take on meaning when gathered together and presented in parallel fashion. Though some tables may be prepared as a preliminary step to the making of a graph or chart, there will be many instances in which the data are likely to be best comprehended through reference to the neat rows and columns of figures themselves rather than to a graph. All cases dealing with statistics cannot be feasibly treated by conventional graphs and charts; tables may usually be utilized without great difficulty.

Figure 14-15   Flow chart of a manufacturing process. Illustrates the number of inspection and quality-control steps that are taken. The white boxes represent manufacturing operations; grey boxes represent quality-control checks; colored boxes represent inspections. (*Courtesy of General Motors Corporation.*)

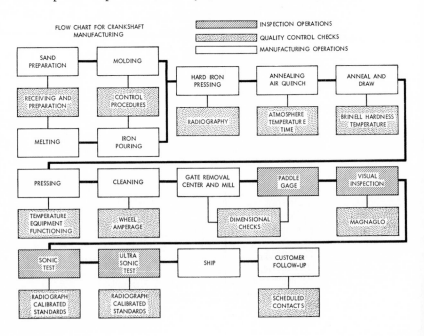

Figure 14-16 A statistical map chart. (*Reproduced by permission of National Industrial Conference Board, New York.*)

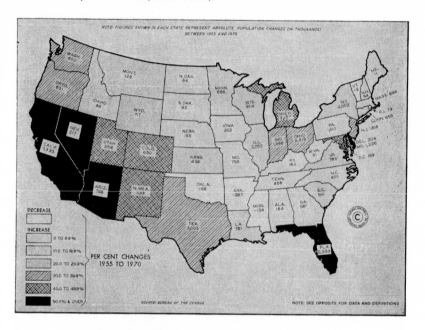

POPULATION PROJECTIONS, BY STATE
1955–1970

Source: Bureau of the Census

	1955	1970		1955	1970
	(*Thousands*)			(*Thousands*)	
Alabama	3,110	3,273	Nebraska	1,394	1,590
Arizona	1,007	1,802	Nevada	235	453
Arkansas	1,802	1,435	New Hampshire	553	648
California	12,961	20,296	New Jersey	5,324	6,942
Colorado	1,547	2,197	New Mexico	793	1,126
Connecticut	2,200	2,859	New York	16,021	20,023
Delaware	390	593	North Carolina	4,344	5,149
District of Columbia	857	1,025	North Dakota	643	710
Florida	3,580	5,912	Ohio	8,945	12,258
Georgia	3,662	4,249	Oklahoma	2,210	2,112
Idaho	612	700	Oregon	1,685	2,317
Illinois	9,301	11,353	Pennsylvania	10,898	12,508
Indiana	4,329	5,715	Rhode Island	817	896
Iowa	2,671	2,874	South Carolina	2,308	2,809
Kansas	2,060	2,498	South Dakota	683	776
Kentucky	3,011	3,172	Tennessee	3,414	3,883
Louisiana	2,934	3,695	Texas	8,748	11,752
Maine	906	916	Utah	797	1,151
Maryland	2,744	3,970	Vermont	370	368
Massachusetts	4,773	5,471	Virginia	3,579	4,362
Michigan	7,326	10,483	Washington	2,607	3,459
Minnesota	3,190	3,856	West Virginia	1,984	2,015
Mississippi	2,133	1,999	Wisconsin	3,702	4,606
Missouri	4,201	4,957	Wyoming	312	379
Montana	629	755	United States	164,303	208,346

The figures shown above represent the civilian population plus the armed forces stationed in each area. Armed forces overseas are excluded. These population figures are not intended to be predictions but projections based upon assumptions of future changes in the components of population change. Data for 1955 are current estimates of the Census Bureau.

The series shown above for 1970 is a new series based upon the following assumptions:

1. *Migration*—1950–55 levels are assumed to prevail until 1960; then, those levels are assumed to change linearly so as to equal the 1940–55 levels by 1970–75.

2. *Fertility*—1954–55 rates prevail until 1960; then, those rates decline linearly to 1950–53 levels by 1970–75. State rates were based on national rates.

3. *Mortality*—Projections are tied in with unpublished United States mortality rates furnished by the Social Security Administration.

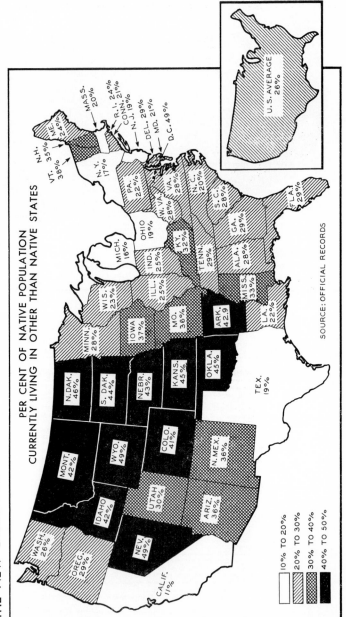

Figure 14-17 A statistical map chart. (*Courtesy of Polychart Graphic Workshop, Brooklyn Heights, New York.*)

Figure 14-18 Table for presenting data, with explanatory headings. (*Courtesy of* Monthly Economic Letter, *First National City Bank, New York.*)

U. S. Balance of Payments, 1958-62
(In Billions of Dollars)

	1958-60 Average	1961 Full year	1961 2nd half*	1962 1st half*
Commercial exports	⎰17.4	17.7	17.8	18.1
Govt. aid-financed exports†	⎱	2.2	2.4	2.6
Imports	—14.3	—14.5	—15.5	—15.9
Surplus on trade	3.1	5.4	4.7	4.8
Services rendered	7.0	7.7	7.8	8.2
Services received‡	— 5.9	— 6.3	— 6.5	— 6.5
Surplus on services	1.1	1.4	1.3	1.7
Surplus on trade & services	4.2	6.8	6.0	6.5
Military outlays§	— 2.9	— 2.5	— 2.4	— 2.0
Economic grants	— 1.6	— 1.9	⎰ — 4.0	⎰ — 3.2
Loans¶	— 0.8	— 0.9	⎱	⎱
Total government outlays	— 5.3	— 5.3	— 6.4	— 5.2
Private long-term capital:				
Inflow	0.3	0.6	0.1	0.3
Outflow	— 2.4	— 2.5	— 2.8	— 2 5
Net	— 2.1	— 1.9	— 2.7	— 2.2
Total government outlays & private long-term capital	— 7.4	— 7.2	— 9.1	— 7.4
Basic deficit	3.2	0.4	3.0	0.9
Private short-term capital:				
Recorded outflow	— 0.6	— 1.5	— 1.2	— 0 8
Errors and omissions	0.1	— 0.6	— 0.4	0.5
Net	— 0.5	— 2.1	-- 1.6	— 0.3
Over-all deficit	3.7	2.5	4.6	1.2

* Seasonally adjusted, raised to annual rate. † Excluding shipments under military aid programs. ‡ Including private remittances and government pensions. § Net of sales of military equipment. ¶ Net of repayments.

Note: Details may not add to totals because of rounding.

Source: U.S. Department of Commerce, *Survey of Current Business.* Figures for the first half of 1962 are educated guesses based on preliminary and incomplete data.

Figure 14-19   Table for presenting data, with explanatory headings. (*Courtesy* of Monthly Economic Letter, *First National City Bank, New York.*)

NET INCOME OF LEADING CORPORATIONS FOR THE YEARS 1960 AND 1961
(Dollar Figures in Thousands)

No. of Cos.	Industrial Groups	Reported Net Income After Taxes 1960	1961	Per Cent Change	Book Net Assets Jan. 1-a 1960	1961	% Return on Net Assets-a 1960	1961	% Margin on Sales-b 1960	1961
15	Baking	$ 68,339	$ 58,536	—14	$ 590,027	$ 607,796	11.6	9.6	3.2	2.7
13	Dairy products	111,692	112,103	+..†	989,319	1,066,722	11.3	10.5	2.5	2.6
18	Meat packing	59,526	44,869	—25	931,969	962,368	6.4	4.7	0.8	0.6
13	Sugar	26,407	27,737	+ 5	418,508	427,066	6.3	6.5	2.8	2.9
79	Other food products	390,807	435,898	+12	3,428,923	3,563,934	11.4	12.2	4.3	4.5
14	Soft drinks	63,344	67,801	+ 7	376,901	428,797	16.8	15.8	6.9	7.0
16	Brewing	37,209	40,228	+ 8	482,938	501,902	7.7	8.0	3.4	3.7
13	Distilling	102,208	109,008	+ 7	1,377,824	1,460,037	7.4	7.5	3.6	3.7
15	Tobacco products	260,881	280,618	+ 8	1,753,713	1,878,980	14.9	14.9	5.8	6.0
59	Textile products	157,002	119,056	—24	1,970,613	2,115,848	7.9	5.6	3.5	2.7
76	Clothing and apparel	63,536	70,957	+12	621,158	642,884	10.2	11.0	3.5	3.6
23	Shoes, leather, etc.	38,118	24,503	—36	431,850	465,970	8.8	5.3	2.9	1.8
45	Rubber and allied products	238,943	248,364	+ 4	2,316,618	2,440,031	10.3	10.2	3.9	4.1
26	Lumber and wood products	75,565	60,928	—19	1,013,577	1,028,591	7.5	5.9	6.7	5.3
34	Furniture and fixtures	27,644	27,063	— 2	348,118	362,849	7.9	7.5	4.1	4.1
78	Paper and allied products	413,408	388,227	— 6	4,539,280	4,836,617	9.1	8.0	5.8	5.2
68	Printing and publishing	112,393	110,990	— 1	806,481	890,872	13.9	12.5	5.3	4.9
85	Chemical products	1,119,821	1,122,720	+..†	9,042,304	9,787,565	12.4	11.5	8.6	8.5
22	Paint and allied products	89,139	86,337	— 3	681,779	719,487	13.0	12.0	6.3	6.1
36	Drugs and medicines	362,582	383,051	+ 6	1,776,353	1,949,195	20.4	19.7	10.7	10.6
34	Soap, cosmetics, etc.	186,181	206,659	+11	1,105,474	1,201,452	16.8	17.2	6.0	6.2
124	Petroleum prod. and refining	3,036,707	3,225,164	+ 6	29,621,282	31,015,039	10.3	10.4	8.1	8.3
21	Cement	95,171	96,181	+ 1	844,330	855,974	11.3	11.2	11.7	11.4
16	Glass products	166,320	146,564	—12	1,238,724	1,322,157	13.4	11.1	7.8	7.0
47	Other stone, clay products	256,335	250,704	— 2	2,120,106	2,287,783	12.1	11.0	8.0	7.7
72	Iron and steel	823,993	700,566	—15	10,017,436	10,880,916	7.8	6.4	5.7	5.1
54	Nonferrous metals	363,447	347,742	— 4	5,031,172	5,181,540	7.2	6.7	6.3	5.9
46	Hardware and tools	74,154	79,653	+ 7	620,194	645,634	12.0	12.3	6.2	6.4
56	Building, heat., plumb. equip.	60,635	52,466	—13	1,138,135	1,164,808	5.3	4.5	2.6	2.3
75	Other metal products	151,302	128,271	— 2	1,937,582	1,987,045	6.8	6.5	2.9	2.8
51	Farm, constr., mat.-hdlg. equip.	171,919	181,162	+ 5	2,951,238	2,996,133	5.8	6.0	3.4	3.6
22	Office, computing equipment	199,607	257,577	+29	1,409,572	1,576,783	14.2	16.3	6.7	7.6
211	Other machinery	418,194	406,713	— 3	4,235,330	4,451,516	9.9	9.1	4.8	4.6
273	Electric equip. & electronics	760,509	735,736	— 3	6,646,838	7,308,312	11.4	10.1	3.9	3.7
14	Household appliances	80,740	84,371	+ 4	807,775	881,404	10.0	9.6	4.4	4.5
12	Autos and trucks	1,453,162	1,339,034	— 8	8,606,175	9,397,620	16.9	14.2	6.7	6.7
42	Automotive parts	136,908	98,511	—28	1,866,959	1,932,368	7.3	5.1	2.4	2.1
14	Railway equipment	58,852	42,635	—28	828,331	847,558	7.1	5.0	4.0	3.3
42	Aircraft and space	155,349	262,996	+69	2,568,512	2,442,637	6.6	10.8	1.4	2.3
79	Instruments, photo goods, etc.	259,551	249,645	— 4	2,019,607	1,913,577	12.9	13.0	7.6	6.9
85	Misc. manufacturing	179,397	180,567	+ 1	1,443,492	1,573,736	12.4	11.5	5.0	4.7
2,138	Total manufacturing	12,886,997	12,891,906	+..†	121,374,557	128,001,703	10.6	10.1	5.5	5.4
18	Metal mining - c	27,629	30,312	+10	307,721	312,010	9.0	9.7	8.3	9.2
20	Coal mining - c	61,066	69,972	+15	921,910	937,350	6.6	7.5	6.1	7.4
13	Other mining, quarrying - c	39,338	39,303	—..†	368,830	365,793	10.7	10.7	18.2	18.4
51	Total mining - c	128,033	139,587	+ 9	1,598,461	1,615,153	8.0	8.6	8.5	9.6
47	Chain stores—food	236,782	238,795	+ 1	1,787,541	1,938,872	13.2	12.3	1.3	1.3
61	Chain stores—variety, etc.	125,884	126,600	+ 1	1,419,383	1,575,190	8.9	8.0	2.7	2.6
63	Department and specialty	220,835	226,539	+ 3	2,269,924	2,385,959	9.7	9.5	2.6	2.6
7	Mail order	225,617	234,313	+ 4	2,126,350	2,229,143	10.6	10.5	3.8	3.9
153	Wholesale and misc.	136,496	137,404	+ 1	1,221,075	1,350,900	11.2	10.2	2.1	1.9
331	Total trade	945,614	963,651	+ 2	8,824,273	9,480,064	10.7	10.2	2.3	2.2
106	Class I railroads - d	444,657	382,444	—14	17,291,787	17,312,733	2.6	2.2	4.7	4.2
18	Common carrier trucking	10,063	18,620	+85	158,975	163,430	6.3	11.4	1.2	2.2
11	Shipping	26,022	26,210	+ 1	578,281	589,687	4.5	4.4	5.5	5.6
17	Air transport	30,625	D-9,356	—..‡	747,569	767,633	4.1	...	1.4	...
53	Misc. transportation	53,876	50,813	— 6	594,077	625,502	9.1	8.1	4.1	3.7
205	Total transportation	565,243	468,731	—17	19,370,689	19,458,985	2.9	2.4	4.0	3.3
223	Electric power, gas, etc. - d	2,178,680	2,299,712	+ 6	21,857,776	23,186,546	10.0	9.9	13.0	12.9
25	Telephone and telegraph - d	1,361,108	1,438,818	+ 6	13,749,546	14,728,939	9.9	9.8	13.9	13.8
248	Total public utilities	3,539,788	3,738,530	+ 6	35,607,322	37,915,485	9.9	9.9	13.3	13.3
47	Amusements	47,651	50,397	+ 6	527,948	552,656	9.0	9.1	4.7	4.3
27	Restaurant and hotel	15,743	15,348	— 3	181,459	192,681	8.7	8.0	2.4	2.2
77	Other business services	106,528	107,508	+ 1	764,219	837,483	13.9	12.8	4.6	4.4
30	Construction	6,767	49,285	+..‡	470,988	468,716	1.4	10.5	0.4	3.3
181	Total services	176,689	222,538	+26	1,944,614	2,051,536	9.1	10.8	3.3	3.8
*	Commercial banks	1,689,000	1,713,000	+ 1	16,264,000	17,398,000	10.4	9.8	...	...
56	Fire and casualty insurance	240,228	255,800	+ 6	4,093,741	4,379,895	5.9	5.8	...	...
214	Investment trusts - e	662,769	704,648	+ 6	21,544,172	22,042,002	3.1	3.2	...	...
82	Sales finance	289,292	302,596	+ 5	2,051,034	2,343,081	13.9	12.9	...	...
51	Real estate	18,587	15,536	—16	197,175	222,380	9.4	7.0	...	...
403	Total finance	2,899,876	2,991,580	+ 3	44,180,122	46,385,358	6.6	6.4	...	...
3,557	Grand total	$21,142,240	$21,416,523	+ 1	$232,900,038	$244,908,284	9.1	8.7	5.6	5.6

a—Book net assets at the beginning of each year are based upon the excess of total balance sheet assets over liabilities; the amounts at which assets are carried on the books are far below present-day values. b—Profit margins computed for all companies publishing sales or gross income figures, which represent about nine tenths of total number of reporting companies, excluding the finance groups; includes income from investments and other sources as well as from sales. c—Net income is reported before depletion charges in some cases. d—Due to the large proportion of capital investment in the form of funded debt, rate of return on total property investment would be lower than that shown on net assets only. e—Figures in most cases exclude capital gains or losses on investments. *—Federal Reserve Board tabulation of all member banks; number of banks (6,113) not included in our totals; assets are annual averages. †—Increases or decreases of under 0.5%. ‡—Increases or decreases over 100% not shown. D—Deficit.

DIAGRAMS

The impulse to mark out by representational lines and forms that thing which one desires to explain is inherent in man. As words are symbols for the object or idea the meaning of which the writer wishes to communicate, so are the hieroglyphics of a diagram symbolic of meaning (see Figure 14-20). The difference is that the lines and shapes of a diagram, being more literal than words, roughly conform to the configuration of the object they are striving to represent; words are by comparison much more figurative and abstract. A concrete representation of a thing by diagram removes some of the problems of semantics and clears the way for a direct meeting of the mind of the diagrammer with the mind of the viewer. While the written word must be seen and understood before the mind can summon up a picture of the thing the word stands for, the diagram once seen makes easier the further processes of recognition and comprehension. Since many of the complex objects which must be explained in contemporary reports do not readily lend themselves to the higher process of word description, diagrams are often not merely desirable but necessary.

PHOTOGRAPHS

The need to show visually the object described in the report may, in selected instances, be satisfied by a photograph (Figure 14-21). Large objects are excluded by the mechanical limitations of the camera itself and by the fact that details of the photographed object will not be adequately revealed for explanatory purposes. In addition, only outer surfaces of an object can be easily photographed while the parts essential to understanding it may be encased within. Nonetheless, even though use of photographs is thus circumscribed, their appearance in many reports, particularly those of a scientific character, adds greatly to the interest and clarity.

IDENTIFICATION

Illustrations insufficiently identified and explained are a nuisance and a bore. If the illustrations are exceedingly deficient in numbering, legends, notes, or other identifying matter, they can effectively ruin the report.

In any individual section or chapter of the report, illustrations should be numbered consecutively throughout. Reference in the text of the report ought to be to the numbers of the illustrations themselves rather than to the pages on which they appear.

The legend which accompanies a graphic device is an integral part of the figure. Wording should be concise and pertinent; the same style and terminology used in the text should be employed in the legend. A meaningful and exact identifying title is an essential part of the legend. The reader must know at once precisely what he is looking at: The illustration title should be boldly and clearly placed.

Many tables and graphs will require explanatory notations. A key may be needed to explicate symbols and abbreviations. Notes may be necessary for explanation of the material visualized and the special techniques or limitations which apply to it. The report writer should assume responsibility for checking carefully to determine whether all labeling and other identifying matter required for full understanding of the graphic properly accompanies it.

Figure 14-20   Diagram and explanation of parts of a unit of a missile. (*Courtesy of General Motors Corporation.*)

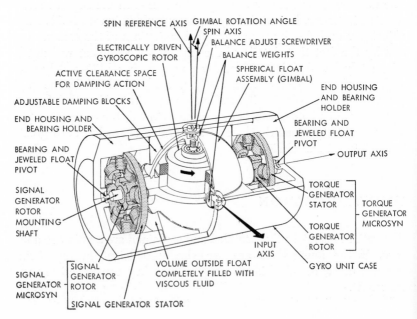

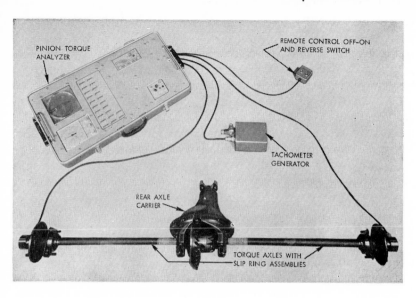

Figure 14-21 Photograph and photographic diagram of an instrumentation system. (*Courtesy of General Motors Corporation.*)

PLACEMENT

Graphics may be interpolated throughout the text or gathered together at the end. Placing them at appropriate points throughout the writing is good in that the visualizations become integrated into the body and at the same time offer the audience a brief rest from reading. A change of pace is always welcome to refresh the attention. Graphics at the end of the report, although they are separate from the text they illustrate, offer an opportunity for final review and summary. Some readers, however, may be annoyed at the necessity for flipping pages back and forth while studying the report.

GRAPHICS—YES OR NO?

There is surely a marked tendency to include a superfluity of pictorial elements in reports. Writers would be wise to rigorously screen their proposed illustrations and to ask whether all of them are truly informative and serve to enhance and clarify the text. One also does well to limit his graphics to those which are pertinent to main themes rather than to side issues. Likewise, the writer should question whether a clear and interesting graphic will result from his planned efforts. If not, then a good description will possibly serve better. All illustrations that may duplicate material that is part of another graphic can probably be eliminated. Balanced treatment is required between the amount of text and the total number of graphics. As with all elements concerned with the report, only the creative writer's best instinct and careful judgment can provide the final answer.

15

The Text of the Report

As distinguished from front matter (letters of authorization and transmittal, etc.) and back matter (appendixes and bibliography, etc.) the text of the report is the *main body of matter*. It is what many persons would call the "report proper." The full panoply of the different elements of front and back matter was analyzed in Chapter 4. How they and the text should be finally presented will be covered in Chapter 16. Methods for organizing and developing the text were, of course, treated chiefly in Chapters 12 and 13 but were also touched upon in Chapters 10 and 11.

In a report, one may think of the main corpus of matter as consisting of three broad areas which we will refer to as the preliminary, core, and terminus sections. In fact, these correspond to the beginning, middle, and end which were discussed in a theoretical sense in Chapter 12. Since a writer is prepared at this point to synthesize his report, final consideration can now be given to these three general parts of the text.

PRELIMINARY PART

Whether the report writer chooses to label his opening section as the introduction or not, the function of this section of the report is clearly fixed. It serves to provide preparatory information leading up to the core. It is designed to orient the reader to his surroundings; it serves to focus on the relation of the report to the world at large as well as to the smaller world of the report's subject matter. In short, the function of the preliminary section is to introduce the reader to the knowledge and experience he will encounter at the core of the report.

Words should not be minced in the preliminary or any other part of the report. From the first word of the opening sentence, the direction should be straight forward. Subject and purpose of the report ought to be unmistakably laid out by the end of the first paragraph. The attention and interest of the reader can be hoped for only if the writer confronts him at once with the business before them.

No pat formulas exist that will show exactly what the preliminary section should contain and how long it should be. These aspects will be determined entirely by the individual writer in view of the specific nature of the report and its main intention. Enough information must be provided to lead the reader into a painless understanding of the body of the report; no more or less material is needed than that which will accomplish this.

Perspicacious writers will take full note of the fact that many contemporary reports present an abbreviated summary of conclusions before anything of a preliminary nature. If so, this summary, labeled simply Summary of Conclusions (or any other appropriate name) may be the very first thing the reader sees of the text. On the other hand, some writers will choose to incorporate their summarized findings into the preliminary section before moving on to the core of the report.

One must choose his own course to follow in these affairs. Surely, much by way of rapport with the reader can be gained by giving him the conclusions right away. This gesture of thoughtfulness for the reader's time may be considered a conventional business courtesy. But if there is a chance that the summarized conclusion may prevent a fair hearing for the rest of the report, one would do well to hold it back until the end. For example, one might hesitate to first present conclusions in a report to the public tracing the relation between lung cancer and smoking. Fear that all the pertinent implications traced in the core of the report would not be followed through might prompt the writer to withhold the conclusion until the full story was told. Reports covering controversial legislation, unpopular rulings, and negative findings in the business setting are, generally, those that might stand to gain full readings only if the conclusion is delayed until the full report has been given. But these considerations hardly apply to the majority of reports, as is seen by the decisive trend toward giving summarized conclusions before, or as a part of, the preliminaries.

What the preliminary section may actually contain will vary widely. In some short, informal reports (Chapter 5) there may be only one sentence, which says, "The purpose of this report is ———." As the report becomes more formal, so will the preliminaries. In a long, fully formal report—one accompanied by some elements of front matter— the preliminary section may commence with reference and a backward look to authorization, acceptance, approval, and transmittal of the document. Depending on how many, if any, of the writer's views have been aired in the front matter, these too may be dealt with in the preliminary section.

As has already been suggested, the preliminary section will almost certainly announce the purposes, objectives, scope, and limitations of the report. Fundamental ground rules, theories, or principles requisite to understanding the report may be stated first. A review of how and where data were gathered may follow. Critically pertinent terms may be defined. An outline of chief methods used for resolving problems may be presented. Citation may be made of particularly valuable sources of material or modes of developing information. A general plan of the report may be sketched in. Any, but probably not all, of these matters might be explored in the preliminary section.

As discussed earlier, material preceding or incorporated into the preliminary text may consist of a summary of findings or results, a statement of main conclusions, or a review of chief recommendations arrived at in the report. At no moment, however, should the writer allow himself to lose sight of the objective and function of the preliminaries, i.e., preparation of the reader for the core of the report. Unless an inviolately logical order of presentation is adhered to, the chaos may put the reader off.

One will see certain headings and subheadings used for the preliminary section. The most common is simply Introduction. Others, which serve to emphasize the nature of the content, are Statement of Purpose, Statement of Objective, Outline of Plans and Procedures, Perspective to the Report, Foreground to the Report, Background to the Report, History of the Problem, Aims and Objectives, Criteria for the Evaluation, and so forth. There is not very much range the writer can exercise in using these headings, and so he might very well expend his ingenuity in saying well and in an orderly fashion whatever goes beneath them.

If the reader does not know for sure what it is all about by the time he completes the preliminary section of the text, the report has already failed. The preliminary part, moreover, should lead by smooth transition right up and into the core of the report.

CORE OF THE REPORT

Figuratively speaking, the core is the essence or most important part of the report. It is the central or inner body of the matter, containing the kernels or seeds. Etymologically, core traces back to the Latin word for heart. And into this vital interior section is distilled the most essential information.

For analytical purposes, the core may be talked about first in terms of materials and methods and then in terms of results.

Materials and Methods

The writer of exposition is obliged to clearly lay out for the reader all the constituent elements that figure in a process. One cannot fully understand what a thing is, or may be, without knowing the substance that comprises it. By unveiling his materials, the report writer is with methodology exposing all the implements, tools, and articles—all the things with which the information in the report is concerned. Without the materials to work with, nothing could be produced, least of all a report.

Thus the materials will be set forth in the report with all their particular characteristics and attributes. Essential differentiae will be presented. Specifications will be articulated. Basic sizes, shapes, designation numbers and formulas, nomenclature, catalog keys, and file references—all the details which make an item one thing in this world and not another—will be provided. Every report wants certain facts, and among these are certainly full facts about the materials.

As the stuff with which the report author has worked, the materials may be just about anything under the sun. In a financial report, the materials will be figures; in a scientific report, they may be masses of data; in a personnel report, they will probably be people; in an architectural report, building supplies and equipment. As will be seen from the example at the last of this section, in a medical report of a clinical nature the materials are patients with certain kinds of diseases and the drugs used to treat them.

The methods section of the report explains what the report writer has done with his materials. The derivation of the word "method" is traced to a classical Greek word which, translated loosely, means 'a going after.' This meaning is especially apt for our purposes. Method is the definite, orderly procedure for going after specific information. Regularity and orderliness in thought and action are needed. Logical procedure in conducting an investigation to gather information for a report is method. Principles of reasoning are applied to inquiry.

Explanation of methods will almost certainly involve an exposition of a number of steps or operations. In dealing with these the writer will remember the patterns of organization (Chapter 12) and the patterns of development (Chapter 13) at his disposal. He will also recall the principles governing logic in the report (Chapter 9), especially those surrounding the inductive method of procedure. Essentially, he will proceed through a series of particular steps, noting results so that a conclusion will be possible. His pattern of research or procedure (Chapter 9) will be explained so that the reader can follow along to the threshold of the conclusion.

We must at this time as emphatically as possible introduce a point of considerable importance. The point has to do with a fundamental aspect of report writing about which there is apparently much confusion and even ignorance. The crux of the difficulty lies in the fact that a great many report writers have a proclivity to introduce into their materials and methods section analysis and interpretation of data. No practice, it seems to the present author, is more counter to logical, "scientific" procedure and is more likely to botch up the report by raising confusion at a critical juncture.

As the core of the report, the materials and methods, as well as results, sections should strive toward as "pure" an expository approach as possible. That is to say, disembodied facts are needed, devoid of any mark of the writer's personal response (interpretation and analysis) to them. (Let us very quickly interpose that interpretation is of overwhelming importance in a report, but *in its place!*) Since an entire structure of information—results, discussion, conclusion, recommendation—will be built upon the facts established in the materials and methods section, the writer owes it to the reader to first get those facts objectively established. Materials and methods, because of their close and almost inextricable relation, may be given in parallel fashion. Though the writer also should, where needed, present in this section his reasons for proceeding in a particular way, he should not offer value judgments regarding the superiority of those reasons.

It is, then, the responsibility of the author to maintain throughout the report a sharp dichotomy between fact and opinion (Chapter 9)— between objective reality and subjective reaction. Both facets of experience will be of towering importance in the report, for indeed, they will *be* the report. But the reader should be given each separately and in the section of the report created for it. Perhaps a most facile writer can successfully, in the same section of the report, present fact and opinion in alternating and opposing pattern. Most writers, however, are not both fully able to maintain segregation between fact and opinion, and adroit in physically handling them under one heading. The superior course is to allow only facts into the core of the report, to keep both analysis and interpretation out of the materials and methods and results sections—to save them for where they properly belong, among the terminal components.

Titles and subtitles together with or in place of the materials and methods heading can be used, though in conventional headings of this kind the range is sharply limited. One will see, and will be free to invent, such titles as these: Procedures Followed, Steps Carried Out, Mode of Attack, Action Taken, Use of Materials, and Operations Performed.

To exemplify some of the points discussed, the following materials and methods section from a report is offered. The report is by a physician for other physicians and is concerned with the clinical value of a pharmaceutical preparation—a tranquilizer—in the treatment of patients with certain kinds of skin diseases. The results, commentary, and conclusion sections from the same report will be presented separately under the appropriate headings in this chapter.

Materials and Methods

Treated in this study program were 233 patients of both sexes. Ages ranged from 15 to 85 years. Various diseases of the skin in which pruritus was a prominent symptom were seen. There were 138 cases of nummular eczema, 33 of atopic dermatitis, and 29 of neurodermatitis. Remaining

patients (33) had seborrheic or eczematous dermatitis, psoriasis, furun-
culosis, lichen planus, dermagraphism, or undiagnosed skin diseases.

In that conventional conservative measures—soothing applications, wet
dressings, barbiturates, and superficial x-ray therapy—had not provided
appreciable relief of itching and burning, these were all judged to be re-
fractory cases. If the patients could gain relief from this destructive cycle
of itching and scratching, attempts at treating the disease might be successful. It was therefore determined to attempt to control the emotional
overlay with the administration of fictioxyzine, the tranquilizer.

An assessment without personal bias was wanted. Accordingly, two
series of patients were established. Series I consisted of 172 patients. To
relieve emotional tension and reduce pruritus, these persons were given
orally the ataractic drug, fictioxyzine, 10 to 25 mg., b.i.d. or t.i.d., depending on the severeness of the condition. Series II was established as
a control group. Either a placebo or fictioxyzine was given on a double
blind basis. Forty-five patients were given fictioxyzine tablets as above;
16 received a placebo tablet.

The report writer has in direct fashion told the reader what materials
he had to work with and what he did with them. Where necessary, he
has stated why he took certain steps. He has provided nothing but the
simple facts of the process, without pausing to interpret or analyze
them. As will be seen shortly, he deals with his results in the same
straight expository fashion, reserving comment for his commentary
section and presenting his conclusion with equal simplicity.

Results

Subjecting the given materials to specific procedures, processes, and
operations according to a purposeful method will produce an effect
(positive or negative) which is the result. This consequent, which is
the end product—that which issues from the calculation or investigation—is of fundamental importance at the core of the report. For the
result, once established and clearly apprehended, will yield up meanings to provide the basis for a conclusion, which in turn will make a
decision possible. A rational course of action (or inaction) in response
to the decision is the last link in this chain of happenings.

Certain real value can, in fact, be gained from thinking of the
results section of the report within the context of the above-described
chain of events. In very precise terms, the results section should truly
be called the effects section (in certain highly scientific reports it is indeed so termed). That which is produced by a cause is, properly
speaking, the *effect*. Carrying this further, the *result* is actually
the last in a series of effects traceable to a given cause. For example,
the effect of swallowing a certain pill may be the return of the body

temperature to normal, which as a consequence provides improved health. The final result will be discharge from hospital. From the report writer's viewpoint, of course, this hairsplitting means that he will commit to the results section no more than the *immediate effects* produced by use of the materials according to the predetermined method. Inferences and implications of these effects will be discussed by him in the commentary section, and deductions from them in the conclusions and recommendations section. The total project is designed to provide information which will permit logical decision and action based on the conclusion.

Presentation of the results—the immediate effects—will be undertaken within the framework of rules of inductive logic as presented in Chapter 9. Attention will be paid to the separateness of fact and opinion, a matter already treated.

Following is the results section of the clinical medical report whose materials and methods section was given above:

Results

Objective and subjective responses were evaluated. Subjectively, one depended upon the patient to report whether the intense itching was greatly, moderately, little, or not relieved. Objectively, improvement in the cutaneous lesions, diminution of eruptive signs, and increase in healing were studied.

By combined objective-subjective criteria, 141 (82%) of the 172 patients in Series I were excellently improved and 13 (8%) were moderately improved. Eighteen patients (10%) gained poor or no relief.

In Series II, 7 of the 16 placebo patients (44%) reported moderate to great relief of pruritus; the other 9 placebo patients (56%) obtained no relief. Of the 45 patients remaining in Series II—those who received the fictioxyzine—29 (64%) experienced moderate to great improvement, and 16 (36%) had poor or no response.

Negligible side effects were encountered in 25 patients (10%). The greatest complaint was of drowsiness, sleepiness, or listlessness. Several persons also said they felt depressed. One person spoke of feeling "drunk" and yet another of feeling "nervous." Mild flatulence, upset stomach, and headache were reported. Adjustment of dosage tended to correct these effects without necessitating cessation of treatment.

In this instance, before the writer is able to present the results he is obliged to explain his criteria for determining them. This will often be the case; frequently a subheading under results will be devoted to criteria for evaluation, and this may constitute a large segment of the report. Elucidation of the criteria is required whenever qualitative grading is made of results. Where possible, accepted standards or scales for grading should be the criteria. However, often these will not exist, and the writer will be obliged to establish his own and to explain them. As above, though, once the evaluative criteria are explained, only straightforward exposition of the immediate effects is wanted.

Visual materials discussed in Chapter 14 will probably be used most extensively in the core of the report, though they may surely also appear elsewhere. In general, tables seem to be most utilitarian in the Materials and Methods section and graphs in the Results section. Schematic drawings and photographs often prove to be of most value in the explanation of methods. But there is no fixed rule for any of this. Since so much of the central meaning of the report is contained in the core, the writer will wish to use freely any of the standard visual tools available to him. Provided that they are accurate as to information and presentation, visualizations have the advantage of lending additional objectivity to that part of the report which most requires it.

With the basic and essential facts laid down objectively on paper—what the materials were, how and what was done with them, and what happened—the core of the report is completed. With the foundations solidly positioned, the superstructure can now be erected.

TERMINAL COMPONENTS

Those sections of the report which it is not possible to prepare until after the core is completed will be referred to arbitrarily as the terminal components. These are the parts of the report that demand, in many ways, the deepest and most original thinking. While mechanical skill, technical proficiency, or established guidelines may serve the reporter in applying proper methods to his materials, only his individual capacity for observation, abstraction, analysis, interpretation, and deduction will enable him to project the report that urgent step beyond. The reader has already been told what the report is trying to do, how it is trying to do it, and what has issued as a result. Now, during the final phases, he must be told not only what the writer thinks all this means, but also what the writer believes should be understood by it and done about it.

Discussion and Commentary

By systematically subjecting the facts at the core of the report to the refining fires of intense analytical scrutiny, the writer creates the discussion phase of the investigation. He launches a comprehensive exploration of all the reasonable meanings the facts may offer up. To discuss in a report is to critically examine, to sift the multiple considerations for and against various possibilities.

The necessity of devoting strict attention to objective realities at the core of the report becomes more vivid in light of the function of the discussion. Facts at the core are susceptible of proof, and probably there can be only small areas for possible disagreement. The reader may, for example, question whether the best method was used or the most revealing materials employed. Such disagreements are often productive of subsequent investigations which represent improvements over the report in question. Nonetheless, the disagreement is confined to factual substance.

As distinct from these relatively concrete matters of material and method, there is the world of personal interpretation and opinion (Chapters 9 and 13). For human experience may be apprehended and understood in many different ways. Where a set of facts may for one individual be invested with one meaning, for another person there may be quite a different interpretation. For example, where there results a certain kind of mold growth from the culturing of a particular organism according to a special method, this fact may to one mind mean something dramatically important and to another something of little or no importance. Only the mind trained to a scientific discipline, in the first place, would see any meaning at all in the fact.

And so it is with the discussion portion of the report. Here the terrain is roped off for intellectual performance by the writer. It is understood that he will flex his cerebral muscles and engage in analytic gymnastics. The reader will expect a brilliant burst of ideational pyrotechnics to light up the cyclorama of the stage. For now it is that the facts will have breathed into them the life of meaning and that their connection with the rest of the world will be effected.

Yet in all this caldron of intellectual ferment, there may be some ideas that do not bubble forth. Moreover, not all the readers will agree with those interpretations that do appear. Perhaps some basic considerations may even have been overlooked. The discussion of the facts and the commentary upon them may, for some reason, fail to come full circle. Or, to take the most hopeful view, perhaps all the readers may assent to all the possible meanings which may be turned up in the discussion. Whatever the outcome, a positive and constructive process has occurred in consequence of this phase of the report: The minds of the writer and reader have been activated to profitable thought about the problem.

In his role as commentator and discussant, then, the report writer has provided critical remarks, explanatory annotations, and exploratory observations upon the text of the report core. All this is by way of the writer's personal views and is designed to project all possible reasonable meanings. Through this ratiocination, the full spectrum of ideas is exposed.

Because of the diversity of implications possible in certain reports, a great variety of headings and subheadings may appear. For example, a report providing information about the shift of urban population to suburban communities might divide its discussion into: Impact on Suburban Real Estate Values, Schools, Economic Growth, City Government, Public Recreation, Taxes, and so on. Each of these could, in turn, present additional ramifications by way of subheadings. The patterns by which they might be proliferated would have to be logically organized, structured, and developed according to principles enunciated in Chapters 9, 12, and 13.

As a brief example of a commentary section from a report, there follows that one from the medical report whose materials and methods and results sections were offered as examples in the foregoing matter.

Commentary

Intensive therapy prior to administration of fictioxyzine had failed to produce remission of cutaneous lesions in persons included in this study. That 154 of 172 such patients (90%) in Series I experienced satisfactory responses with the ataractic offers interesting evidence of the apparent relation between emotional and dermatologic disturbances.

Failure of more than half of the placebo patients in Series II to obtain relief seems to point up the usefulness of fictioxyzine. Conversely, the 7 patients who did improve on placebo could be regarded as testimony to the unpredictably neurotic character of their skin diseases. Even suggestion that a medication would provide emotional calmness helped produce alleviation of pruritus and diminution of eruptive signs in these essentially neurotic individuals.

Favorable results in the patients who received fictioxyzine rather than the placebo in Series II, as can be seen, were generally comparable on a percentage basis with those in Series I. Likewise, clinical failures with fictioxyzine in Series II are of the same general magnitude of those in Series I. These findings tend to corroborate the ratio of success obtained with fictioxyzine in Series I.

It is clear that there are points in the commentary with which readers might disagree. Indeed, quite different analytic interpretations might be placed upon the facts presented at the core. The writer might, for example, have subjected his findings to the chi-square method of statistical analysis, to determine whether any significant differences could be found between results in the two series of patients. Nonetheless, all the personal interpretations presented are preeminently reasonable, and they obviously represent the briefest statements possible of all that the particular reporter believes can be said meaningfully about the facts at the core (materials and methods and results). Since the basic substance is still intact there, it is an easy thing for the reader to return to the core and to test for himself the views in the commentary against it. Had the report author done violence to the facts initially by imposing his views upon them while in the process of presenting them, attempts by the reader to test them would be made unspeakably more complicated.

Though the report above is not such as to require a recommendation section, it does have a conclusion section, which will be presented shortly. Following the discussion, however, many reports will present a Recommendation for Action section. It is that idea, therefore, which we will next explore before taking up the conclusion and other terminal components.

Recommendations

There will be reports which by nature of subject, informality of treatment, or brevity will not require a recommendation section. As a general rule, routine informational reports do not call for recommendations. It might be stated as a loose generalization that as the report tends to be more formal and more special, the likelihood of its requiring a recommendation section seems to increase.

If, as has already been suggested, the conclusions for the report are presented prior to or as an element of the preliminary part, the recommendation may be the terminal component. Even when the conclusion is not given at the outset of the report, some writers will choose to present the recommendation as the very last item of the text, following after the conclusion. In still other reports, both the conclusion and the recommendation will stand as part of the preliminary material.

Since the report requiring recommendations is usually undertaken in the first place to provide recommendations on a specific problem as requested, there is not much doubt for the writer as to whether to include this section. For example, committees called upon to provide recommendations in a given situation will create their reports solely for this purpose. A clinical medical report such as the one used above as an example does not, on the other hand, explicitly call for recommendations. The purpose of that report, in the main, is to present information developed by the writer during his investigation of the clinical efficacy of a certain drug in specific kinds of diseases. It is not his chief intention to recommend whether other physicians should give the same treatment. Therefore, the recommendation section is omitted. Yet recommendations are implicitly offered by virtue of the commentary we saw and the conclusion we shall see.

Persons who are familiar with the complex of paper work in government, industry, and other institutions know to what an acute degree recommendations by persons or groups qualified (presumably) to make them are depended upon. In an ethical sense, those so positioned in any phase of organizational life as to have the power to either accept or reject the offered recommendations are professionally and morally responsible for any decision ultimately taken. But the responsibility for what may occur is truly that of the entire group complex and must be shared equally by the person or persons making the recommendations.

Because of the importance of recommendations in a report as a basis for possible action, the writer offering them will often be (in proportion to the magnitude of the implications of the recommendations) in a responsible position of trust. Clearly, then, recommendations must be presented courageously, confidently, and unequivocally. Few aspects of a report can more discredit the writer than a set of recommendations that are not forthright. Commitments are wanted, and an honest error in judgment, presented unfalteringly, is infinitely better than a set of recommendations offered in a smoke screen of doubt and ambiguity.

Though various satisfactory synonyms for the infinitive "to recommend" might profitably be employed, the connotations attaching to "to advise" and "to counsel" make these the preferred ones. A recommendation in a report as much properly constitutes advice and counsel as commendation. Through exercise of deliberate and prudent judgment of the facts, the writer commits himself to the support of a definite point of view and course of action.

Many report writers will, accordingly, prefer to emphasize their recommendations by ordering them logically by number or letter and by presenting them in the imperative mood of the verb. The modal force of the imperative is, generally, conceived of as command. Other writers commonly employ the subjunctive mood of the verb, conceiving of the recommended action as wish or possibility. While the declarative (indicative) mood will predominate throughout all other portions of the report, it would seem to serve less well for recommendations than the other two moods. The following example demonstrates use of first the imperative and then the subjunctive moods in a set of hypothetical recommendations.

Recommendations

To achieve marketing of this new product by the established market date of July 16, the coordinating committee makes the following recommendations to specific personnel.

1. Advertising manager: Prepare, circulate for approval, and produce all supporting materials by June 20.

2. Sales training director: Orient the field selling force by July 1.

3. Traffic coordinator: Fully stock all warehouses by July 10.

4. Public relations associate: Announce release of the product on July 15 simultaneously in all sectors of the country.

In effecting these actions, it is further recommended that:

a. Each responsible supervisor recognize the coordinating committee as the central control unit.

b. All supervisors submit weekly progress reports on Fridays to the chairman of the coordinating committee.

c. Each supervisor report at once to the coordinating committee any problems threatening to prevent achievement of individual target dates.

So that the individual steps can be efficiently coordinated, this committee, as a final point, recommends that detailed plans of action and timetables be prepared by each group and submitted to the committee chairman by June 1.

Illustrated in the foregoing example are the imperative mood (in the 1, 2, 3, 4 sequence) and the subjunctive mood (in the a, b, c sequence and the statement which follows it). The emphasis on specific details also may be seen in the set of recommendations. Responsibility for advised actions is indicated so that uncertainty will not follow. Vagueness in enunciating the steps could cause delays in action and could hamstring the operation.

Lastly, it should be said of recommendations that they require complete separation from the other elements of the report. Discussion or commentary included with them is singularly distracting. Recommendations such as those offered above as an example could only follow an investigation yielding certain facts which, when duly considered, led to the action commended. But the recommendation section of the report needs to be separate unto itself. By the stage at which recommendations are provided, all necessary explanation and analysis should be well out of the way. Efforts should be bent toward presenting recommendations in a language and a format that provide immediate communication of the important points.

Conclusions

In all reports that contain recommendations as well as conclusions, the substance and spirit of the two sections are closely related. In fact, some reports combine the two sections into one unit and call it Recommendations and Conclusions or Conclusions and Recommendations. Where each is treated separately, one right after the other, which of them comes first is determined by the writer and the nature of the report. In analytical reports, where the conclusion may be treated extensively, it often precedes the recommendations. In informational reports, where the conclusion is chiefly by nature of summary, it often follows the recommendations. By strict definition, the conclusion is the end or close, the terminal component.

Considerations surrounding the logical validity of conclusions reached inductively or deductively were taken up in Chapters 9 and 12. In general, the reporter must be concerned to see that the conclusion does follow from the facts dealt with. By application of reason to the evidence (facts) at the core of the report, the writer must make his final inferences and judgments. What is deduced as the necessary or probable consequence of the relationships among the reported facts is the conclusion.

Mechanics of presenting the conclusion are much the same as those for presenting the recommendations. Use of the straight paragraph form is common, but presentation by enumeration is also a popular technique. If the conclusion is given in the preliminary part of the report, it may be presented in a compact, condensed form. In such a case a more detailed conclusion may be given in the terminal portion of the report. Or the full conclusion may be given at the outset, in which case no further treatment of it will be required. Particularly in reports providing information on an important investigation, the conclusion may be the item of greatest interest to the reader. To satisfy this interest, a general statement might serve at the outset, and an adequately amplified conclusion may be needed at the end.

There is an inevitability about the sequential marching order from materials and methods to results on to recommendations and conclusions. Each grows out of the other. By its very nature, the conclusion embodies a degree of summary in its attempt to bind together all that has gone before. A well-made package should result, with everything neatly wrapped up.

In some preceding sections, examples were given of the materials and methods, results, and discussion sections from a medical report of a drug's efficacy. From the same report there follows now the conclusion section:

Conclusions

An apparent relation exists between the emotional state of some patients and certain pruritic dermatoses. Where conventional dermatologic measures alone fail to produce clinical results, medication with a tranquilizer for the control of emotional tension in these patients is justified for relief of pruritus.

1. The efficacy of fictioxyzine as a tranquilizer, reported by other investigators in the treatment of dermatoses, was confirmed in the present partially double blind study.

2. Control of tension was subjectively and objectively established in the improvement of pruritus of dermatoses in 82% of 172 patients given fictioxyzine in Series I.

3. Sixty-one patients in Series II received either fictioxyzine or a placebo on a double blind basis. Of 45 patients who received the drug

29 (64%) improved; 7 (44%) of 16 who received the placebo also improved.

4. Fifty-six % (9) of the placebo patients experienced no relief of pruritus, while only 36% (16) of the 45 fictioxyzine patients failed to gain relief.

5. Mild side effects, which tended to disappear as dosage was adjusted, were reported in 10% (25) of the 233 patients.

6. Inclusion of fictioxyzine in the program of treatment for pruritic dermatoses is both rationally merited and clinically valuable.

Recapitulation

In a report, a recapitulation is a concise summary of the principal points. Brief restatement of the major phases of the report can serve to provide a final vivid picture. This can be useful in long reports heavy on detail. Blurring of the outline of the principal parts can quite easily occur in the reading, but the final summary can serve to place things in their proper perspective again.

It has already been said that the conclusion necessarily embodies summary; this can be seen in the example above. Recognizing this, some report writers prefer to offer a combined summary and conclusion. Others like the separate treatment, which tends to isolate and emphasize the conclusion. Again, as with conclusions and recommendations, contemporary report-writing practice fully allows placement of the summary as part of the preliminary matter. (Aspects of writing various kinds of summaries are taken up in Chapter 25.)

❖   ❖   ❖   ❖   ❖

At this point we may say that the work of the report is pretty well along. In Phase I the preliminaries and essentials were carried out and the raw materials gathered and shaped. In Phase II, just completed, the materials were organized into final form and were then given logical development and visual treatment within the main components of the text.

The report writer is now prepared to undertake the third and final phase in the creation of the report—that of presenting it in written or spoken form.

V

Creating the Report: Phase III

16

Presenting the Written Report

The Reading Process
General Problems in Presentation
Quotation
Documentation
Shortened Forms and Abbreviations
Latin and English Terms
The Bibliography

THE READING PROCESS

It is most unlikely that an individual can ever become a creative report writer without becoming also a creative reader. Consideration of facets of the reading process is inescapable as the writer prepares the final copy of his report to place before the reader.

Individuals will read the report for different reasons. Some may read it to obtain an overall understanding of the main idea involved in the material. Others may simply search out a specific fact, figure, date, place, or other item. Another reader may wish to obtain such an understanding of the material that it can be recalled in logical sequence for an important meeting. Yet another reader may wish simply to determine the report writer's slant and purpose, to relate these to facts already known, and to establish where points of agreement or difference exist.

The report writer's responsibility is to present his report in both content and format so that all readers may be fully served. Preceding chapters in this book have been devoted to report content—establishing it, amassing it, organizing it, and writing it. The form and arrangement of the presented report must in every way serve to fortify, display, and delineate the content. Whatever the reader's chief purpose, the format should be such that he is able quickly to locate key words, identify main ideas, perceive the broad outline, and isolate the summaries.

Certain report writers forget that all language is symbolic. In fact, a writer never writes a meaning in itself; he writes only symbols in the form of words that stand for the meaning he wishes to convey. The reader does not see on the typed, printed, or written page the meaning the writer wishes to communicate; the reader sees only the symbols the writer has used to represent meaning. Obviously, if the physical format of the report is to any degree deficient in spelling, size of type, arrangement of materials, etc.—in presenting word symbols—the reader's desire to penetrate meanings is to that degree resisted.

The creative reader demands or looks for meaning intended by the writer. Should the reader regard the writer's words only as symbols he has seen before, without understanding what the writer means, reading is not taking place. To the extent that the reader apprehends the writer's intended meaning does the creative writing-reading process occur. All elements of format as well as content should be disposed to underscore the intended meaning.

Yet no writer can easily give the reader precisely his intended meaning. The writer may simply set before the reader well-chosen word symbols, arranged carefully in good order. Though every reader needs to build for himself an understanding of the writer's meaning, the writer must diligently strive through the substance and form of the report to expedite the process. And it would be wise for the accomplished report writer to remember that many persons may not be able to read as well as he writes.

For one does not read reports purely for recreatory purposes. Reports are written and reports are read so that actions which may be of a crucial character can be rationally undertaken. Understanding which the reader achieves must be adequate to serve as a tool for him to use in subsequent straight thinking and rational action. Moreover, the reader, under stimulation of the writer's intended meaning, should be activated to think of legitimate meanings the writer may have overlooked in the report. To read thus critically and analytically, though, the reader needs first to arrive at adequate understanding of what the creative report writer's meaning is. To facilitate this, there are general problems in presentation to be considered apart from content.

GENERAL PROBLEMS IN PRESENTATION

The integral parts which may comprise the various kinds of short and long reports were set forth in Chapters 4 and 5. The order of presentation of the elements was explained. No attempt, however, was made there—and none will be made here—to present comprehensively a manual of style for the format of the report.

For, while overall arrangement is dictated by conventional practices, wide diversity exists in the details of report formats. Differences may be only mechanical and superficial, as related to quality of paper or size of type, or they may be fundamental, relating to length of paragraphs, form of footnotes, or display of subheadings. Attempt to establish a format or manual of style equally applicable to all reports, therefore, is futile. Nonetheless, one may fruitfully explore some general principles of good format and include details of some special problems which surround it. But unless the reader has firmly in mind a picture of the individual parts of which any report may be composed (Chapters 4 and 5) and a picture of the main components of a report as discussed in Chapter 15, a survey of problems in presenting the report is bound to be mostly devoid of meaning.

It is folly for the writer to assume his job is done once the report draft is completed in its last rough form. Shunting off to a secretary the responsibility for the preparation of the final manuscript is just too easy. Only the writer himself can have the necessary knowledge of the text which must dictate the physical appearance of the final typed page. Decisions as to spacing, underscoring, presentation of formulas, or display of selected elements for emphasis or change of pace should be the writer's. Overall appearance of the manuscript must, of course, be such as to invite full reading by someone whose time is precious. But once the reading process is launched, a logical relationship must be discoverable between what is said and the way in which it is disposed on the page. The responsibility is the writer's, despite the well-known fact that a multitude of loyal and competent secretaries truly keep the wheels of industry turning.

There is no substitute for a good-quality and -weight (preferably substance 20) white unlined bond paper of standard 8½ by 11 inches size. Only one side of the page is used; when stencils or plates are prepared for reproducing the report in quantity, both sides of the page may be printed on, provided the text does not show through.

Double spacing is the rule within the body of the text, except for footnotes, extensive quotations, and tabulated matter. This rule is frequently disregarded, particularly in intraorganizational reports, probably in the interest of some false economy. As to the type, one simply uses the typewriter which is available, be it of pica or elite style. The type should be cleaned frequently in any event, to ensure a sharp impression. Generous margins with plenty of white space are wanted at the top, bottom, and sides of typed pages.

Each page of the report is numbered except the title page (see Chapter 4). For the preliminary pages (front matter), use lowercase Roman numerals (ii, iii, etc.). These numbers are centered about ½ inch from the bottom of the page. One should begin numbering with ii, since the title page is i but no number appears on it. Pagination for the balance of the report is in Arabic numerals, unpunctuated. The numbering of these pages should begin with 1 and run consecutively throughout the report. Numbers of first pages of all sections are centered ½ inch from the bottom of the page. Numbers of subsequent pages, however, are placed ½ inch from the top of the page and aligned with the right margin. It is common practice to insert a blank unnumbered page between the cover and the title page and also between the last page of the report and the back cover.

In the text of the report, main divisions are called chapters, sections, topics, or parts, according to the choice of the writer. Whichever he selects, the author should be consistent throughout when making reference to such divisions. Titles as they appear at the beginning of each division should correspond to titles as given in the table of contents. Each main division should start on a new page.

Subtitles are of great utility in reports. Despite the view to the contrary of some authorities, subtitles may be used frequently and freely in reports, even in those only one or two pages in length. Since the busy man may suffer frequent distractions from his reading, subtitles may serve as guides to get him back on course. Few devices serve to improve the report's readability as well as wisely used subtitles. Subheads help much to point up the content which follows. In addition, they are good indicators of the divisions in the writer's plan and good reminders to the reader of the relationship of one piece of information to the full outline. Subheads, moreover, take cognizance of the short attention span of contemporary readers. Large numbers of pages of unbroken text do not endear the report to a hard-pressed reader. Subtitles do help dispose the report reader favorably, in a psychological sense, to the business of reading at hand.

QUOTATION

Though frequent use of long quotations is inadvisable (the reader is tempted to pass them by), a report can gain strength through the words of an authority. Also, quotations are useful in transmitting important ideas through somebody else's apt phrasing. Perhaps most important, quotations are used to cite sources for facts that may be in doubt or dispute. As will be seen shortly, however, credit must always be given for borrowed ideas, whether they are quoted directly or paraphrased.

It is mandatory that quoted material correspond exactly to the source in spelling, phrasing, punctuation, etc. No report writer wishes to be guilty of inaccurate, sloppy use of somebody else's material. However, if the first word in a quotation is the first word in its original source but is linked grammatically with the report text that precedes it, it need not be capitalized. For example: The assertion was made that "the package with the brightest colors is usually selected." If, on the other hand, the quotation is introduced by a complete sentence, the capitalization is retained: "The package with the brightest colors is usually selected."

Where quotation marks are used, a comma or period at the end is always enclosed within them, regardless of whether or not a comma or period was part of the original source. Semicolons and colons are always placed outside the quote marks at the end. Exclamation points and question marks, if they are part of the quoted matter, are enclosed within, but they are otherwise placed outside.

Practice varies according to the individual writer and organization as to whether short and long quotations are integrated into the text or relegated to the footnotes. The preferred practice is to place quoted matter in the text, provided that the quotation is not so long as to seriously prolong the reading process. In either case, quotations of three to four typed lines are incorporated into the body of the regular paragraph of which they may be a part, and quotation marks are used. But when there are more than five lines of quoted material, the quoted matter is set off from the body of the text with extra spacing, indented so that the margins are wider than those of the text, and single-spaced. There is no need to use quotation marks at the beginning and end of a long, indented, single-spaced quote; the format just described identifies it as a quotation.

Omission of irrelevant words, phrases, or sentences from a quotation is permissible on the grounds of brevity so long as the original meaning is not distorted. Ellipsis marks consisting of three periods with a space before and after each period are used to show such an omission. Where omitted matter itself contains a period, it should be added to the ellipsis marks, making four periods.

DOCUMENTATION

Though there is occasionally a tendency in business reports to be casual about documentation or to develop strange new forms for presenting it, standard practice should prevail. A creative report writer should be at pains to acknowledge quotations, ideas, opinions, and statements of fact not original to him. Not to so do involves both moral and legal difficulties.

Documentation may be presented as citation within the text or as reference to a bibliography. The classic and most widely used method of documentation calls for footnotes. Notes at the foot of the page on which reference is made to them provide the writer with a flexible method for acknowledging the source of information, supporting arguments, providing additional material for the reader, identifying quoted material, or elaborating on the meaning within the text. Footnotes are single-spaced, but double spaces are used between them. Each note is indented to conform to paragraph indentation on the page.

Numbers, typewriter symbols, or printing symbols are used as an index of reference from the text to a footnote. The numeral or symbol is placed at the appropriate point above the line of writing and corresponds, of course, to the number of the footnote to which it refers at the bottom of the page. Classically, the number is raised one-half space above the line; in actual practice, to save time this number may be and often is raised a full space or is not raised at all in the footnote.

Footnote numbers in the text and at the foot of the page are not punctuated or placed within parentheses.

Various kinds of sources for notes require different treatments. Also, while very complete detail is needed in the initial reference to a source, an abbreviated form is used in subsequent reference to the same source. Footnote sources may be books, reports, newspapers, manuscripts, public documents, journal articles, legal references, unpublished material, letters, and interviews. The essential elements in the first reference to a particular source consist of identification of the author, the work referred to, facts of publication, and specific reference to the page within the source.

The final authority for the form of an author's name is always the title page of his book, or the way in which it appears in whatever printed source is used. This indicates not only the proper spelling but whether full name, names, or initials are to be used. The given first name or initials precede the surname.

Following are examples of various ways in which authors' names may appear for their initial entry in footnotes:

One author

[1] T. S. Eliot, *Title* (Facts of Publication), page reference.

Two authors

[2] Cleanth Brooks and Robert Penn Warren, *Title* (Facts of Publication), page reference.

Three authors

[3] Gerald Dewitt Sanders, John Herbert Nelson, and M. L. Rosenthal, *Title* (Facts of Publication), page reference.

More than three authors

[4] Felix Upalavich et al., *Title* (Facts of Publication), page reference.

[4] Felix Upalavich and others, *Title* (Facts of Publication), page reference.

Author is an association

[5] Modern Language Association of America, *Title* (Facts of Publication), page reference.

Author is a committee

[6] Committee on Legislative Procedure, American Management Association, *Title* (Facts of Publication), page reference.

Author is a public body

[7] U.S. Congress, House of Representatives, *Title* (Facts of Publication), page reference.

[7] New York State Department, Division, *Title* (Facts of Publication), page reference.

[7] East Hampton Township, Division, *Title* (Facts of Publication), page reference.

No author, but an editor

[8] Rutherford Q. Schmit (ed.), *Title* (Facts of Publication), page reference

No author

[9] *Title* (Facts of Publication), page reference.

[9] Anonymous, *Title* (Facts of Publication), page reference.

Titles should be given exactly in the form in which they appear in the source. While articles from periodicals or chapters from books are placed within quotation marks, titles of books, bulletins, periodicals, newspapers, published reports, lectures and proceedings, encyclopedic works, legislative acts and bills, and unpublished theses and dissertations are underlined.

Following are examples of various titles properly presented for the initial entry in a footnote:

Subdivisions of whole publications, such as articles in periodicals

[10] Author, "The Use of Tranquilizers in Neurotic Report Writers," *Journal of the American Medical Association*, XIV (date), page reference.

Chapters or sections in books

[11] "George Bernard Shaw," *Encyclopædia Britannica*, IX, edition, page reference.

[12] Author, *Stories from Six Authors* (Facts of Publication), page reference.

Bulletins

[13] World Health Organization, *Bulletin No. 112* (Facts of Publication), page reference.

Periodicals

[14] Author, "Sex Life on the Moon," *Journal of Business*, XIX (date), page reference.

N.B. In order to save space and reduce printing costs, names of journals are often not presented in entirety. There are standard abbreviations for the scholarly, professional, and scientific journals in every field of endeavor. Report writers will come to know those accepted abbreviations for the periodicals and journals related to their own field. Full listing and information regarding standard abbreviations for journals are obtainable in the library.

Newspapers

[15] Author (if any), "Huge Stock Market Advance Delights Wall Street," *New York Times* (date), page reference.

Legislative acts and bills

[16] New York Rev. Stat. (date), c.23, Paragraphs 397, 398.

Unpublished theses and dissertations

[17] Author, *Arthur Symons: Critique et Poete*, (unpublished Doctorate of University of Paris thesis, Sorbonne, Paris, 1949), page reference.

Separately published reports, lectures, proceedings, etc.

[18] Women's Christian Temperance Union, *Annual Report* (Facts of Publication), page reference.

Encyclopedic works

[19] Author (if any), "French Drama," *Encyclopedia Americana*, XIX, edition, page reference.

As with authors' names and the titles of various published works, information regarding the imprint or facts of publication should also be accurately given in the documentation. Publication facts included in a reference to books are enclosed in parentheses and followed by a comma. Some of the facts of imprint which may be included in a reference to a book, depending on the individual circumstances and the available information, are the total number of volumes, number or name of edition (if other than the first), name of series of which reference is a part, place of publication, name of publisher, and date of publication.

Different combinations of the foregoing facts of publication come into play at different times. Various hypothetical examples of how the imprint may be shown in footnotes are:

[20] Author, *Title* (16 vols., 2d rev. ed., Princeton Classics; Cambridge, Mass.: The Puffy Co., 1939), page reference.

[21] Author, *Title* (2d ed.; New York: Goom-Ball, Inc., 1953), page reference.

[22] Author, *Title* (3d rev. ed.; Chicago, 1959), page reference.

[23] Author, *Title* (3 vols.; Eastern Municipal Association, 1948), page reference.

[24] Author, *Title* (2d ed., 1907), page reference.

Documentary references to articles in periodicals or to other subdivisions of whole publications require the volume number in Roman numerals or Arabic numbers (depending on how it is shown on the publication itself) and the month and year of publication, or the year of publication alone, followed by a comma. Examples are:

[25] Author, "Title of Article," *Name of Periodical*, XIV (April, 1953), page reference.

[25] Author, "Title of Article," *Name of Periodical,* 14 (April, 1953), page reference.
[25] Author, "Title of Article," *Name of Periodical* (April, 1953), page reference.

Regarding documentary citation of the specific reference within a particular source, examples which follow cover the most common cases in both periodicals and books:

[26] Author, "Title of Article," *Name of Journal,* XVII (March, 1956), p. 39.
[26] Author, "Title of Article," *Name of Journal,* XVII (1956), p. 39.
[27] Author, *Title* (Chicago: The Acme Press Co., 1949), II, p. 179.
[28] Author, *Title* (New York: Dapper and Co., 1931–1953), IV, p. 241.
[29] Author, *Title,* III (Boston: Booze and Co., 1941), p. 14.
[30] Author, *Title* (Edinburgh, 1881–1897), III, Part II, p. 7.
[31] Author, *Title,* Vol. II, Book III, chap. 19.

The following examples indicate how pages may be cited in footnotes:

Reference to a single page: p. 9.
Reference continues from a given page to the following page: pp. 9 f.
Reference continues from a given page to pages that follow: pp. 9 ff.
Reference to successive pages: pp. 9–28.

Shortened Forms and Abbreviations

Once a work has been cited in full detail, shortened footnote forms may be used in referring to it in subsequent notes. Formerly, Latin terms and their abbreviations were used in scholarly documentation for reports. Though the use of Latin forms still persists among many writers who were brought up on them, and among others who seem simply to prefer them, the decided trend in recent years has been to Anglicize all terms and abbreviations used in footnotes and bibliography.

When a note refers to the title cited in the footnote immediately preceding it, the Latin term *Ibid.* (always capitalized, underscored, and followed by a period) may be used. The capitalization is needed because the term stands at the beginning as the first word in a sentence, the underscoring indicates that it is a foreign word, and the period marks the fact that the term is an abbreviation of a longer word, *ibidem,* meaning 'in the same place' or 'from the same work.' Examples:

[1] H. W. Fowler, *A Dictionary of Modern English Usage* (Oxford, 1958), p. 39.

[2] *Ibid.* (identical with previous reference)
[3] *Ibid.*, pp. 49–50 (identical source, but different pages)

Modern practice, infinitely to be preferred, eliminates *Ibid.* by handling the same situation as follows:

[1] H. H. Fowler, *A Dictionary of Modern English Usage* (Oxford, 1958), p. 39.
[2] Fowler, p. 39.
or
[2] *Dictionary*, p. 39.
[3] Fowler, pp. 49–50.
or
[3] *Dictionary*, pp. 49–50.

The short form of the author's name or title is fully acceptable in contemporary practice.

Much the same applies to use of *op. cit.*, 'in the work cited,' and *loc. cit.*, 'in the place cited.' These terms were conventionally used in nonconsecutive footnotes citing a previously documented work and referring either to pages different from those in the initial citation (*op. cit.*) or to the same pages as before (*loc. cit.*). Examples:

[1] H. W. Fowler, *A Dictionary of Modern English Usage* (Oxford, 1958), p. 39.
[2] *Ibid.*
[3] Cleanth Brooks and Robert Penn Warren, *Modern Rhetoric* (New York, 1949), pp. 114–121.
[4] Fowler, *op. cit.*, p. 190 (same work as in notes 1 and 2, but different page)
[5] Brooks and Warren, *loc. cit.* (same work and same pages as in note 3)

Contemporary practice would treat notes 4 and 5 above as follows:

[4] Fowler, p. 190.
or
[4] *Dictionary*, p. 190.
[5] Brooks and Warren, pp. 114–121.
or
[5] *Modern Rhetoric*, pp. 114–121.

If these Anglicized forms were used, it would also be necessary to eliminate *Ibid.* from note 2 and to use

[2] Fowler, p. 39.

in its place. Whichever forms a report writer prefers to adopt, it is necessary for him to be consistent throughout his report: He must not mix his terms.

Latin and English Terms

Without doubt, every book that discusses documentation gives treatment to Latin forms and abbreviations far beyond their importance. The report writer will discover that in practice he is obliged to utilize shortened Latin or English forms and abbreviations most infrequently. But use them he must on certain occasions. Moreover, even though a writer may himself adopt Anglicized forms and abbreviations, he will often encounter the Latin forms, particularly in older works. For that reason, the list below gives some of the Latin terms frequently encountered in documentation. It is followed by a similar list of English terms.

Abbreviation	*Word*	*Definition and commentary*
. . . . . .	*ante*	before
ca.	*circa*	about (used with dates, e.g., *ca.* 1906)
et al.	*et alibi*	and elsewhere
et seq.	*et sequens*	and the following
ibid.	*ibidem*	in the same place; from the same work
. . . . . .	*idem*	the same; the same as that mentioned above
. . . . . .	*infra*	below (should not be substituted for *ibid.* or *op. cit.*)
loc. cit.	*loco citato*	in the place cited; in the passage last referred to
op. cit.	*opere citato*	in the work cited
. . . . . .	*passim*	everywhere; all through, here and there
. . . . . .	*post*	after
. . . . . .	*sic*	thus (inserted in brackets within a quotation and after a quoted work or words to indicate that the preceding expression, strange or incorrect as it may be or seem, is exactly quoted)
s.v.	*sub verbo*	under the word or heading above
. . . . . .	*supra*	above (should not be used in place of *ibid.* or *op. cit.*)
. . . . . .	*vide*	see
viz.	*videlicet*	namely, to wit

The following abbreviations consist of Anglicized terms (although some are based on Latin words) which are used freely in writing and documenting reports:

Abbreviation			
Singular	*Plural*	*Word*	*Definition and commentary*
art.	arts.	article(s)	
bk.	bks.	book(s)	If Roman numerals follow this abbreviation, it should be capitalized, e.g., Bk. II; if Arabic numerals follow, the abbreviation is not capitalized, e.g., bk. 2
bull.	. . . . . .	bulletin	
cop.	. . . . .	copyrighted	e.g., cop. 1920
cf.	. . . . .	compare	
chap.	chaps.	chapter(s)	
col.	cols.	column(s)	
diss.	. . . . . .	dissertation	
ed.	eds.	edition(s)	e.g., 2d ed.
ed.	eds.	editor(s)	or, edited by
e.g.	. . . . . .	*exempli gratia*	for example
et al.	. . . . . .	*et alii*	and others
f.	ff.	following	and following page(s), e.g., pp. 5f. means page 5 and the following page; pp. 5ff. means page 5 and following pages
fig.	figs.	figure(s)	e.g., fig. 2 or Fig. II
i.e.	. . . . . .	*id est*	that is
illus.	. . . . . .	illustrated	or, illustration
l.	. . . . . .	line(s)	
MS	MSS	manuscript(s)	may be written ms. or mss.
n.	. . . . . .	footnote(s)	e.g., "see n. 5" means to refer to footnote number 5
n.b.	. . . . . .	*nota bene*	note well; take notice
n.d.	. . . . . .	no date	
no.	nos.	number(s)	
n.p.	. . . . . .	no place	used in bibliography
N.S.	. . . . . .	new series	
p.	pp.	page(s)	
par.	pars.	paragraph(s)	
proc.	. . . . . .	proceedings	
pt.	pts.	part(s)	e.g., pt. 5 or Pts. V, VI
q.v.	. . . . . .	*quod vide*	which see; reference is made to it
rev.	. . . . . .	revise	or, revised, or revision
sec.	secs.	section(s)	
trans.	. . . . . .	translated	or translation, translator
vol.	vols.	volume(s)	e.g., vol. 4, or Vol. IV, or 6 vols.

THE BIBLIOGRAPHY

For some readers and for many other persons who may consult the long formal report containing documentation, the final bibliography can be the component of greatest interest and importance. The bibliography is particularly valuable for transmitting cumulative knowledge to future researchers and writers. It often saves other searchers hours and even weeks of duplicated effort.

It is well known that practice varies widely among individuals as to the scope of material included in the final bibliography. The preliminary bibliography (see Chapter 26) prepared on file cards contains all references likely to provide helpful material. It is a working bibliography. The final bibliography, as included in the report, lists only those sources which actually yielded relevant material for the report.

But the report writer ought to exercise good judgment in deciding which items to finally include. He should avoid a bibliography so broad that it contains items of peripheral or questionable relevance. Yet he should not prune his listing so extensively that only sources cited in notes are included, for there are likely to be certain valuable sources which were consulted but which did not yield information worked directly into the report.

Fullness of bibliographic listing, in the final analysis, is determined by the nature and breadth of the report. In short reports destined for publication, just those references actually cited in the text are usually shown at the end of the report. Printing costs make longer bibliographies prohibitive and also necessitate elimination of footnotes as such. Since such a relatively incomplete numbered listing is not a true bibliography, it is usually headed Cited References. Other bibliographies, particularly those in large reports and those which review all pertinent literature on a subject, may very well be of considerable length.

In preparing the final bibliography the writer must decide on a classification system with appropriate subheadings, the order or sequence of the items included under the headings or subgroupings, and the manner of presentation of the references themselves.

The number and variety of entries determine whether a single consecutive bibliographic listing or a classified listing is needed. Classification may simply provide a breakdown between book references and periodical (journal) references. The book listings may include such items as monographs, pamphlets, material from composite works, encyclopedia articles, etc. It is not uncommon in far-ranging reports to list a third bibliographic category for primary source materials such as public documents, manuscripts, documents and working papers in private unpublished collections, personal diaries and accounts, newspapers, manuscripts, etc. Only when the final bibliography begins to exceed twenty or so entries is it necessary to consider any system of classified listings with or without subheadings.

By far the most common order or sequence of bibliographic listing is alphabetical by authors' surnames. In short reports this alphabetical order is both desirable and convenient. Alphabetical order also frequently prevails in bibliographies of some length and breadth. But the listings are presented by subdivisions of the subject, with each separate list in alphabetical order. Another possible arrangement is a chronological listing, sequenced by date of publication. Where the system of referring to Cited References is used in place of the usual footnote arrangement, the references will be listed numerically, and the numbers used in the text will refer to the listing. This last is the least desirable arrangement, but, as pointed out in Chapter 4, it is acceptable and is growing in popularity.

The manner of presenting the references themselves differs in several respects from the manner of presenting footnotes. In the bibliography the author's surname always precedes his forename or initials. Also, punctuation and capitalization in the bibliography are somewhat different from that in footnotes. Proper listing for a final bibliography as it might appear in a creative report may be seen in the following example.

Sample Bibliography on Report Writing

Part A. *The Communication Process in Creative Report Writing*
  Books
    Ball, John, and Cecil B. Williams, *Report Writing*, Ronald, New York, 1955.
    Hayakawa, S. I., *Language in Thought and Action*, Harcourt, Brace & World, New York, 1951.
    Lee, Irving J., *How to Talk with People*, Harper & Row, New York, 1952.
    Marsten, Evertt C., Lorring M. Thompson, and Frank Zacker, *Business Communication*, Macmillan, New York, 1949.
    Osborn, Alex F., *Applied Imagination, Principles and Procedures of Creative Thinking*, Scribner, New York, 1953.
    Redfield, Charles E., *Communication in Management*, The University of Chicago Press, Chicago, 1953.
  Articles
    "Economic Facts for Executives," *Modern Industry*, December, 1952, vol. 24, pp. 48–51.
    Johnson, Wendell, "Fateful Process of Mr. A. Talking to Mr. B.," *Harvard Business Review*, January, 1953, vol. 31, pp. 49–56.

Part B. *Phases in the Preparation of a Creative Report*
Books

Blankenship, Albert B., editor, *How to Conduct Consumer and Opinion Research,* Harper & Row, New York, 1946.

Bradford, Ernest S., *Marketing Research,* McGraw-Hill, New York, 1951.

Hertz, David B., *The Theory and Practice of Industrial Research,* McGraw-Hill, New York, 1950.

Parten, Mildred, *Surveys, Polls and Samples: Practical Procedures,* Harper & Row, New York, 1950.

Payne, Stanley L., *The Art of Asking Questions,* Princeton, Princeton, N.J., 1951.

Articles

Blankenship, Albert B., Archibald Crossley, and others, "Questionnaire Preparation and Interviewer Technique," *The Journal of Marketing,* October, 1949, vol. 14, pp. 399–433.

Robinson, R. A., "How to Boost Returns from Mail Surveys," *Printers' Ink,* June 6, 1952, vol. 239, pp. 35–37.

Worthy, James C., "Attitude Surveys as a Tool of Management," *General Management Series* no. 145, American Management Association, New York, 1950.

Part C. *Presentation Problems in Creative Report Writing*
Books

Chase, Stuart, *Power of Words,* Harcourt, Brace & World, New York, 1954.

———, *The Tyranny of Words,* Harcourt, Brace & World, New York, 1938.

Graves, Robert, and Alan Hodge, *The Reader over Your Shoulder,* Macmillan, New York, 1944.

Guthrie, L. C., *Factual Communication,* Macmillan, New York, 1948.

Articles

Davis, K., and J. O. Hopkins, "Readability of Employee Handbooks," *Personnel Psychology,* Autumn, 1950, vol. 3, pp. 317–326.

Public Documents

Style Manual, Government Printing Office (rev. ed.), GPO, Washington, D.C., 1953.

Part D. *Special Kinds of Reports*
Books

Bell, William H., *Accountants' Reports* (4th ed.), Ronald, New York, 1949.

Doris, Lillian, *Modern Corporate Reports to Stockholders, Employees and Public,* Prentice-Hall, Englewood Cliffs, N.J., 1948.

Nelson, J. Raleigh, *Writing the Technical Report* (3d ed.), McGraw-Hill, New York, 1952.

Turbian, Kate L., *A Manual for Writers of Dissertations,* The University of Chicago Press, Chicago, 1947.

Whyte, William H., Jr., *Is Anybody Listening?* Simon and Schuster, New York, 1952.

Articles

Allison, T., "Employee Publications: There's Room for Improvement," *Personnel Journal*, July, 1954, vol. 31, pp. 56–59.

Inglis, John B., "Recent Statements Show New Techniques in Annual Reporting Are Being Widely Used," *Journal of Accounting*, December, 1950, vol. 90, pp. 474–478.

Paterson, Donald G., and James J. Jenkins, "Communication between Management and Employees," *Journal of Applied Psychology*, February, 1948, vol. 32, pp. 71–80.

✿   ✿   ✿   ✿   ✿

Bibliography, documentation, quotation, and the general problems in presentation of the report have been reviewed with attention to the process of reading. Although most reports are prepared primarily to be read, there are diverse occasions when the creative report writer will need to present his product orally. How to do this is the subject of Chapter 17.

17

Presenting the Oral Report

THE LISTENING PROCESS

Many creators of written reports will be called upon to present their work orally—to the boss, to a committee, to the entire sales force, to a professional-society meeting. Those reporters skilled in speaking will probably welcome the opportunity to communicate their findings directly to the group. Quite properly, they will believe that where the written report might not be given a complete and fair reading, the oral report is at least assured of a full hearing. Lamentably, "hearing" is often not "listening."

If there are inherent in our culture and daily lives, as suggested at the beginning of the preceding chapter, a staggering number of distractions from careful reading of a report, there are an equal or greater number of forces conspiring against careful listening. The unsophisticated maker of an oral report may easily defeat his purpose by the naïve belief that because his words are being poured into the hearers' ears, they are being listened to.

Effective listening requires the putting aside of all prejudices, preconceived judgments, taboos, and any other activities; only a small number of disciplined hearers are true listeners. There is a great difference between active and passive listening. An active listener to reports (like an active reader) listens wholly—with his senses, attitudes, beliefs, thoughts, and intuitions—as a requisite for understanding. The passive listener is merely a receptor for sound—an organ without self-perception, personal involvement, discrimination, or live curiosity.

Since, in the nature of business, professional, and academic situations, the oral reporter is destined to be confronted by passive rather than active listeners on most occasions, he is wise to make peace with the problem beforehand. Where the reporter may have expended prolonged time and effort in preparing the report, he will have only the briefest interval (ten minutes? twenty minutes?) in which to verbalize it. What will he select to present? How can he extract and communicate only the most germane ideas? How much can he realistically hope to make his preponderantly passive audience understand? What are the ways in which he can hope to attract and hold audience attention long enough to get across even a few main ideas?

VISUAL AIDS

One might expect discussion of visual aids to constitute the terminal portion of a chapter on oral report making. Actually, visual aids are so central to the challenge of engaging the attention of passive audiences that they should be the first order of business in planning an oral report. Though the written report may creak through on its own (be it dull, pedestrian, and a chore to read) without the graphic devices discussed in Chapter 14, the contemporary business or professional oral report can hope for only the smallest success without visual devices. And the failure of the speaker is a painful public spectacle.

From his written report the speech planner should initially extract the most pertinent data with a view to presenting these visually in his talk. Most probably, the material will already be visualized in an appropriate chart, graph, drawing, or table in the written report. The job will then simply become one of adapting the visualization to a form suitable for use during a speech. Will slides and a projector do the job? Can a slide be made of the photograph or map? Is a filmstrip or a movie available to support the presentation? Can a large easel or magnetic board be utilized to display a large graph? Is a blackboard at the disposal of the speaker? Should sufficient copies of the visualization be duplicated beforehand for distribution to the audience? These considerations must be part of planning the oral report.

It may be that the speaker will be able to build his presentation around an actual object—a miniature version of the new pump, a scale model of the proposed building, a cutaway plaster mold of the human heart. Whatever ingenious uses of form, color, and motion the speaker can make to engage and maintain the jaded attention of his audience are satisfactory, provided the visual device does not draw attention only to itself rather than to the speech it is a part of. The speaker is not operating a sideshow; he is simply taking intelligent cognizance of the fact that visual devices increase understanding and facilitate recall of information. Time, effort, and money expended in their preparation are usually well spent.

Flash cards have been used advantageously by many oral reporters. These are no more than cardboard cards containing a key idea—a word, phrase, or sentence. The card is flashed before the audience to bring home a point. Perhaps the key ideas of the report can be reduced to three or four symbolic words and each of these placed on a flash card. As aids in establishing an outline and directing attention to major points in the explanation, flash cards should be seriously considered by the talker.

The striptease poster is similar in principle to the flash card. Each major point on the poster is covered with a protective piece of paper or cardboard. As the speaker makes a point, the covering is quickly stripped away to expose the key word or phrase. The advantage, of course, is that this technique permits the audience to gain cumulative knowledge while the words and ideas are constantly before them.

When the covers have been stripped, the oral reporter has all his key words on the poster exposed and available for use in summary.

If one excludes loudspeaker equipment, there are few audile aids available to the maker of oral reports. The wire recorder, the phonograph, the tape recorder, though readily accessible in most instances, have few applications in the majority of expository speeches. Remarks, interviews, sessions, etc., can be recorded, and sounds—for example, the working of a pump—can be transcribed; but the number of oral reports in which these audile techniques may be exploited are few in number.

Turning his attention to the visual aspects of the oral report has for the speaker the additional advantage of directing his thought to the main purpose of his speech. When this has been clearly established in his mind, he may then proceed to organize his information in terms of presenting it with the visual aid as the heart of his presentation.

OVERALL ORGANIZATION OF THE ORAL REPORT

Only some of the problems of organizing the oral report are the same as those for the written report. (Aspects of organization of the written report are covered in Chapters 9, 10, 12, and 15.) The very permanence of the written document imposes structural and developmental requirements of its own. The oral reporter must consider the evanescent, abstract quality of the spoken word which, like music, plays quickly upon the outer and inner ear and then is gone. Selectivity in material, with stress upon interrelationships, therefore becomes a prime concern if the speaker hopes to succeed in explaining and informing.

General patterns of arrangement of the oral report can be approached in terms of the written report (see Chapters 12 and 15). However, with the core of the information visualized for the speech, the speaker must consider whether a new order is needed to best give the visualization prominence. The emphasis must be upon greater simplification and upon elimination of developmental material—material necessary to the amplification of the written report but an encumbrance to rapid covering of main points in an oral report.

The Introduction

Introductory remarks in an expository report should strive to characterize the nature of the topic the speaker intends to explain, to stimulate interest in the subject, and to give the listeners a brief preview of the reporter's purpose and direction. Opening comments may be judged successful if they direct the attention of the listeners to the speaker and lead that attention naturally and easily into the topic to be explained.

Ideally, the introduction should help the speaker establish good rapport with his listeners. In a business or professional setting, common ground can usually be established quite quickly through direct expression of the mutual interests and purposes uniting talker and listener. Unlike introductory remarks in other speaking situations, those in a report ought to be just as brief and direct as feasible—if possible, perhaps, one short, simple sentence. The oral reporter who respects his listeners' time and is, though pleasant and courteous, businesslike in directly attacking his subject, will win their approval quickly.

There are standard devices for effecting a direct introduction to the oral report. These are a reference to the subject or the occasion, the use of the rhetorical question, the inclusion of an interesting or startling statement, a reference to recent or current events, or introduction of a quotation from the literature on the subject.

In referring to the subject the speaker might, for example, state, "A major problem we in engineering have sought to solve is that of reduction of friction between rotating wheels." In referring to the occasion the speaker might say, "I feel certain this annual sales meeting will lead to fuller cooperation between the advertising and marketing departments." The rhetorical question, of course, is a question the speaker introduces to arouse interest but which he proposes to answer himself, if an answer is in fact possible. The speaker might ask: "Can you tell me exactly how much work time could be saved by eliminating the coffee break throughout this company?"

An interesting or startling statement may be particularly useful in arousing an apathetic group of listeners. Usually it will be a statement of fact, an unusual conjecture, or an unusual opinion; but it should be closely related to the speaker's topic lest it divert attention from the business at hand. Some examples might be: "If we teachers of English want to save the language, we are going to have to get sledgehammers and destroy every television set in the land." "I believe a Soviet Russian will be seated in the White House by 1985 unless . . . ." "It is my guess that this machine, properly used, will put more than 100,000 people out of jobs in the next ten years."

A recent current event likely to be familiar to a reasonably well-informed audience may provide a brief introductory formulation. The speaker is merely obliged to attach to such an event a general principle which may be covered by the report in a particular way. For example, "Gentlemen, Governor Slimy's recent reelection proves that a mediocre product can make its way in the marketplace if it carries an appealing slogan." Or "Last week's Wall Street advance should indicate to us, as accountants, that our present techniques for establishing working budgets are inadequate."

Authorities acknowledged as leaders in a particular business, professional, or academic field may be quoted to provide a succinct introduction to an oral report. Preferably, a noncontroversial figure should be cited. Examples are: "Professor Adelbert Mummer maintains, in his most recent scholarly article, that 'Automation in the mortician's field is certain to revolutionize present processes.'" "'Contemporary methods of refining wheat are inefficient in the amount of 3 billion dollars annually,' says the editor of *Wheat Age*, the leading publication in our field." The old war-horse of using literary quotations or popular proverbs is, happily, losing popularity in introductions to oral business reports. Generally, it is a corny method; for example, "A review of last year's sales figures on product X reminds me of the line, 'Is this the face that launched a thousand ships?'" This technique can become as tiresome as that of starting out with a humorous story or anecdote, usually slightly off-color, in the immature, misguided attempt to win audience attention. These appeals are unworthy of serious adults.

Having made a bid for the attention of his audience by one of the foregoing techniques, the oral reporter should move swiftly to keep it. The wisest way to do this is to state forthrightly in summary fashion the three or four main points the report will cover. Such a summary serves as a preview and as a plan the listeners may follow. Moreover, if their attention should meander, they have at least heard the main points one time at the beginning.

Once the plan of the main body has been clearly stated in introductory fashion, the reporter may move logically along to an articulation of each of his ideas. The visual aid may be used as the focal point of interest. Brief but lucid remarks must be made to show relationships between each of the main ideas. Strict effort must be exerted neither to digress nor to dwell too long upon a single item. Respect must constantly be paid to the clock. The reporter should endeavor to talk to his listeners and not to his visual aid. He should have absolute knowledge of his subject and full control of his materials. When the exposition of his main points has been achieved, the oral reporter should not be reluctant to proceed directly to his conclusion.

The Conclusion

It is not a counsel of despair to say that the conclusion of an oral report offers the last chance to make sure that the listeners understand the facts. In the light of the explanation given in the main body of the report, moreover, the conclusion of an oral report should be the ultimate synthesis of the report's materials.

Crisp recapitulation of the main ideas in sequential order is probably the ideal way to tell the listeners, "This is the end." Repetition, therefore, figures largely in the conclusion as a means of unifying the speech and gaining final emphasis for the explanation. Very often there will be an implicit or explicit call to action in the report. If so, the nature of the expected action must be clearly and unequivocally stated in the conclusion. The means of carrying out the action should be articulated in concrete terms, and the steps in carrying out the action should be presented as a simple rather than a complex process.

Summary reiteration as a concluding device may consist either of an exact restatement of the purpose and main divisions of the oral report, or of a restatement in different terms. There may be more imaginative but certainly not more effective means than to numerically restate points as "First . . . second . . . third." Reiterative summary is simple, it makes ideas clear, and it states the ideas with new meaning and interest in view of their relation to the explanation of which they are a part.

Use of a pertinent quotation from an authority is also appropriate in the conclusion to an expository speech. A good quote can add credence to the substance of the talk, fortify the need for action, or suggest the proper frame of mind in which to evaluate the remarks. As an example, "Dean Strudelmeyer has said, 'We cannot accept the traditional view of automation if we are to be free to develop productive means of meeting the present challenge. New ideas and new approaches must be explored if we are not to outlive our usefulness.'"

An illustration by example may, on some occasions, serve to aid in calling for action or emphasizing a main point. For example, "During the war, American Marines in the South Pacific learned how to make their own liquor from alcohol intended for other uses. Many a boy enjoyed a cheap drunk, but just as many experienced convulsions and died. Using archaic equipment and poor materials may seem an economically feasible way to create this new product, but it may also be the best way to kill off our industry."

Impressive or challenging final statements may likewise find a place in the conclusion. The remark is helpful if it serves to underscore the importance, seriousness, or other significance of the presentation. One might say, "Precautions taken against explosion hazards in the operating rooms of this hospital are probably as complete as those in any hospital in this country. Nonetheless, the personal professional damage to the physician who may be guilty of relaxing these precautions would be nothing like the despair of his conscience if an accident were to result."

Humor, also, may certainly find its place in the conclusion of a serious oral report. In our way of life, few occasions are deemed so sacrosanct as not to admit of a lighter touch; humor may relieve the strain of close attention which was demanded and leave the listeners in a good frame of mind. However, the humor should be neither low, irrelevant, nor strained. It should certainly not belittle any racial or religious group.

ORAL REPORTS: FORMAL OR INFORMAL?

According to the type of preparation and mode of delivery, there are four kinds of oral reports: (1) those fully written out and memorized, (2) those fully written out and read from manuscript, (3) impromptu reports, and (4) extemporaneous reports.

The memorized speech is generally reserved for formal occasions of oratory—a lecture, a sermon, etc.—but it may be used on any occasion, provided the reporter has the time and inclination to memorize. Manuscript reports which are read, within the purview of the business, professional, or academic setting, are presented at meetings of the various professional and learned societies. An impromptu report is one which is given on a moment's notice and which allows for no specific preparation. An impromptu report may be called for during a committee meeting, during a group discussion, or in the course of a dialogue with another person.

It is the extemporaneous kind of talk which best suits most oral reporting situations encountered in business. This is the carefully organized speech which is neither written out nor memorized. The reporter has his objectives firmly in mind; he knows his materials and the relationships among the parts. The pattern of the report is logically outlined in detail, but only a card containing heads and subheads of the outline is referred to during the speech. The talk may be practiced and timed beforehand. Perhaps a specific opening and a specific closing line, but not more, may be committed to memory.

Though extemporaneous reporting has some disadvantages, it is, on the whole, the most advantageous method. Generally, it allows the reporter to choose his specific words at the moment of delivery and thereby to achieve a desirable measure of spontaneity. The speaker is able to create a more natural, informal, and relaxed environment and to talk without artifice or oratorical airs which may prejudice the audience against him. In reporting extemporaneously, the speaker is free to maintain a conversational attitude and direct eye-contact with his audience. In terms of self-discipline, the extemporaneous report challenges the speaker to organize his ideas for oral utterance, to think on his feet, to concentrate on communication, and to adapt his speaking to the demands of the audience situation.

There is always the danger that the extemporaneous speaker will prepare insufficiently; then the result is pitiable chaos. The talk will meander, the order of presentation will be illogical, the points will not be covered, and the time will run out. Such travesties happen sometimes because the oral reporter has not understood the nature of extemporaneous speaking. Actually, only the choice of words should be left until talk time; everything else should be meticulously predetermined.

IV

Special Kinds of Reports

18

How to Evaluate a Report

A Critical Methodology for Evaluating Reports
The Nature of Science
Steps in the Scientific Method

A CRITICAL METHODOLOGY
FOR EVALUATING REPORTS

The well-educated man, one definition holds, is he who can appreciate excellence and recognize mediocrity in all things. A well-rounded chemist can appreciate an excellent poem, an educated insurance actuary can recognize a poorly designed chemical experiment, a cultivated marketing executive can perceive the flaws in the philosophy of Nietzsche, and so on. In this age of intense specialization, such a criterion for marking the civilized man is severe but appropriate.

For it is indeed the urgent specialized demands of our technocracy which have impelled us toward progress while erecting communication barriers between us. Perpetuation of our institutions necessitates educating a vast body of persons intensively trained to master the intricacies of one specific area of learning. Taken cumulatively and used cooperatively in an organized pattern, these units of information developed in isolation are able to advance us. If one specialist cannot talk to another, however, breakdown occurs, and if all specialists cannot report to the people, we are rehearsing for Babel.

A corps of practitioners qualified in their specialties but capable of effective reporting is much wanted. In the training of such a corps for report writing, instruction in a critical method necessarily comes first. A man is unable to evaluate and improve his own reports unless he has a grasp of some first principles which may be critically applied to all kinds of writing.

Emphatically, there is no such thing as "good report writing," "good technical report writing," or "good business writing"—there is only good writing. Everybody who maintains otherwise is wrong. All good writing is a creative art which cannot be served up in a formularized package. And the very same principles of literary criticism which apply to a novel by William Faulkner, a poem by Robert Frost—or to an advertisement, a syndicated newspaper column, a piece of propaganda, or a story in the *Saturday Evening Post*—apply equally to reports. Distinctions among these widely different kinds of writing were emphasized in Chapter 2, but all purposeful writing may be productively analyzed by the same critical apparatus.

Application of critical method to any piece of serious writing involves many steps, but these may, in very broad outline, be grouped into four phases. Since literary criticism employs analytical questioning, the phases can be posed as questions applied to any specific report.

Phase 1. What, exactly, is the report trying to do?
Not to pose and answer this question at the very start, before any-

hing else, is to violate a fundamental tenet of rational criticism and, most probably, to render the analysis ultimately invalid. It is critically amateurish to fail to begin with this first question. And the answer, to be truly sound, should be fully articulated, completely expressed, and reduced to a single, carefully phrased sentence. Sidestepping this phase leads to denying the report a fair hearing and to censuring the writer for not doing what he never tried to do; it is quite stupid to condemn an apple for not being an orange, but it makes sense to reject a bad apple for a good one. A creative thinker cannot critically analyze a report without fully knowing what it is, what it is trying to be, and what its writer intended it to do and say.

Is the specific objective of the report to present a workable program for long-term training of promising young executives for top-management posts? To offer a $3,000 budgetary plan for a year-around direct-mail advertising campaign for a small insurance agency? To outline and analyze the financial advantages of an automated inventory control system? To recount an experiment designed to test the clinical efficacy of a new tranquilizer in the treatment of psychotic children? If it is the last, for instance, the report cannot be condemned for not reporting on the effectiveness of the drug with mentally retarded children; this the report did not try to do. Just as the excellence of any one apple can be fully appreciated only when it is compared with other apples, so a report on a tranquilizer used with psychotic children can be adequately judged only when compared with other reports of exactly the same kind.

Many writers, in tackling the question of what someone else's report is trying to do, will prefer first to skim through it once lightly to get the general feel before pursuing a detailed scrutiny. The front matter, including the table of contents, is reviewed, and introductory and concluding portions are spot-checked. The writer of the report under analysis, if competent, will have clearly stated his objective in the opening paragraphs. Many times, though, the critical reader will uncover unfortunate discrepancies between what the writer says his objective is and what he has actually done. It is the very purpose of the critical method to penetrate to the substance of any such deviations.

Any negative feelings or biases against the report subject or author must be carefully put down by the critic. The answer to the question of what the report is trying to do has absolutely no concern with whether the critic approves or disapproves, agrees or disagrees. The critical method, in a later phase, permits ample opportunity for value judgments about the report. But to meet the problem squarely, these judgments must be directed at the core of the writer's own objective. Only the foolish critic will attack or defend a report the objective of

273

which he has not troubled to establish. Don Quixote attacking the windmill while thinking he was charging a dragon perpetuated himself in our hearts forever, but Quixote would probably not be elected to a corporation's board of directors.

Since no one can reasonably proceed by the critical method without a clear answer to what, exactly, the report at hand is trying to do, the reader ought to give this problem the effort it deserves. As he learns good practice and acquires critical experience, this initial step will require less time but not less care.

Phase 2. How does the report try to achieve what it sets out to do?

In this second phase, the critical methodology for evaluating reports now involves dissecting the report at hand. Though all reports—like all poems and novels—have many things in common, each also has its individuality. Of the many standard components and elements which go into all reports, each subject will call for its own particular recipe, to be formulated by the creative writer. Just as one painter on canvas will employ bright colors, hazy facial contours, and many straight lines to express a certain subject, so will a competent report writer mold and shape his materials to serve the particular need of the subject, audience, and materials at hand.

Familiarity with the standard components of reports is, of course, necessary to carrying out this phase of the critical process. Such knowledge is gained only through reading and writing many reports. It is not a magical intuition bestowed upon a chosen few, but information assimilated through continuous effort over a period of time. Presumably, those reading this book are sufficiently motivated to undertake to gain this experience. Many readers have already had varying degrees of experience with the critical approach. Still others have already raised the question as it applies to other forms of writing, to paintings, and to music. It is only that small multitude of marvelously proficient, technically superior but absolutely uncritical persons who permeate our culture who must start from scratch to learn this process.

A checklist of some of the chief methods by which a creative report writer may go about trying to achieve his particular ends can be prepared. Again, as a guide this is inadequate, for all the items will come into play at different times. But the perceptive critic will undertake to isolate the emphases, the balances, the tones, the proportions adopted by the creative report writer to serve his individual needs.

A Checklist for Critically Analyzing How an Individual Report Undertakes to Achieve Its Particular Purpose

Circumstances and Purpose of the Report
   1. Who asked for it? When? Why? Was it done on the writer's initiative?

2. Why did this particular person undertake it? Who is he? What are his qualifications? What is his relationship to the person requesting the report: employee? client? paid writer? Is the report for external or internal circulation, or both? Is it intended for a horizontal or a vertical up-or-down readership?
3. Who is the intended audience: one reader? many? Are the readers specialists—scientists, management consultants? Is readership general?
4. Is the report seeking only to inform or explain? Does it seek to argue? To plead? Does the situation allow for truthful, unbiased presentation?

Form of the Report
1. Why is the report informal—a letter report, a memorandum, a short report? Is the form appropriate to the function, occasion, and readership? Is the form adopted for some special reason: to underplay the seriousness of the subject? to dramatize it? to evade responsibility? to seek undeserved credit?
2. Is a long, formal report really required? Are all the necessary formal-report components included? Is the long report justified by the total picture—importance of subject, scope of treatment, length of study, intended readership? Is the format in keeping with the substance?

Substance of the Report
1. Are there a sufficient number of facts? Has there been an adequate search for materials? Are all pertinent sources included? Is the research up to date? Have the best sources been explored? The most authoritative and objective? Is the experiment logical, complete, and well designed?
2. Is there a valid inductive or deductive pattern of organization? Is the sequence clear? Are the conclusions justified by the facts? Are the recommendations reasonable and just? Are there fallacies in the sequence of reasoning?
3. Is there a clear style of writing? Is it grammatical? Is the style too breezy or pompous? Is it appropriate to the subject, occasion, and purpose? Does the style interfere with the ideas, or reinforce them? Are language, sentences, and tone proper? Are they too technical? Too colloquial?
4. Are graphic illustrations well used to clarify meanings? Are charts, tables, and graphs well integrated with the text?

Through exploration of matters like these, a critic of a report can begin to see into the principles and techniques which have guided the writer. The report under scrutiny will cease to be a formidable sheaf of papers and will become a written communication capable of being mastered.

As the critical method is applied to several different reports, it will become more clear that each piece of writing must be analyzed on its own terms. Some subjects will depend mainly, for example, upon intricate graphs and charts for a complete exposition. The critic, therefore, may focus his chief analytical efforts upon these. The nature of another report may be such that a lucid unraveling of the steps in a particular process is the major concern of the writer; hence, the critic can bear down analytically the most heavily on these. Intellectual probing by the critic can, in due course, turn up the major clue to how an individual report necessarily undertakes to express its particular purpose.

When the "what" and "how" phases of the critical process are out of the way, the critic may move on to Phase 3, which allows for value judgments.

Phase 3. Does the report succeed or fail to do what it set out to do?
The critic enters most deeply into the analytical process in Phase 3, and he comes eventually to some fine considerations. Phases 1 and 2 of the critical method were taken up with the total architecture of the report under study—its whole purpose, design, and personality, its general relationship to the world at large, and the relationships of its parts to one another. Now he is obliged to attentively examine appropriate individual components of the report to determine whether each was successfully executed and how this success or failure influenced the attainment of the report's goal.

As with many intellectual processes, Phases 2 and 3 of the critical method merge into one another. It is truly only for academic reasons that they need to be artificially dichotomized. For example, in noting that a certain report must rely on the clarity of its explanation of steps in a particular process as the main device for realizing its purpose, the critic at the same time forms a judgment as to whether these steps are indeed clearly explained or not. But in Phase 3, the critic must put his finger precisely upon the cause of the lack of clarity, if such there is.

Is it that certain of the steps are out of order? Is it that transitions between the steps are not provided? Is it that insufficient divisions exist among the material and that each step is inadequately delineated? Is it that there is a flaw in the procedure being explained? Is it that basic terms are insufficiently or inaccurately defined? Is it that not enough background information has been supplied to place the explanation in proper perspective? Or is it that the writer's style is awkward and obscures the expression of his ideas, which are in themselves excellent?

In the business world or out of it, a person may not say simply, "I liked it," or "This is a poor excuse for a report," and be unprepared to logically indicate precisely why. Others must be made to see the basis for a critic's judgment and even the reasons for it, and there can be no rational base for discussion unless the critic is able to offer tangible evidence that his is not simply an emotional response. Vague, generalized feelings, positive or negative, have no place in the critical method. If the report critic cannot articulate adequately what seem to him to be precise defects and virtues in the work, he has not really determined whether or not the report has succeeded or failed within the framework it set for itself. The critic's reaction may be correct, and people may agree with him, but a critical process has not been executed.

Execution of Phase 3 provides the intellectual means that will allow the critic to say not only if the report is a success but exactly to what degree. Herein are the bases for appreciating excellence and recognizing mediocrity, because the sum total of the report's strengths and weaknesses—seen objectively and understood in relation to one another—yield the answer.

If the report, however painfully, somehow gets its message across despite a series of deficiencies noted by the critic, then to that degree the report is a success. And this will, pathetically enough, be the case with most reports analyzed by the critical method. They will be recognized as the quintessence of mediocrity, being unimaginatively conceived and executed, stultifying to read, depressing to think about. By the same token the critic will come to appreciate the excellence of those few reports done creatively in the desire to set up a dynamic equilibrium between writer and reader. These will, by the satisfaction they give in the reading, be the touchstone for the critic's own report writing. He will have become educated to appreciate excellence and recognize mediocrity—at least, in reports.

Phase 4. Was the report worth doing in the first place?

It might appear that this ought to be the first question in the critical process rather than the last. Or, perhaps, it may not be readily apparent why this question need be raised at all. Yet the process of criticism, being discussed here as the basis for establishing criteria for evaluating reports, is not fully rounded out until Phase 4 is accomplished.

Moreover, a meaningful answer to this question is not possible until the other three phases have been dealt with. A critic is unable to determine the ultimate worth of a report until he knows what it tries to do, how it tries to do this, and whether it succeeds or fails. Clearly, there will be many reports that fail which were nonetheless well worth doing; and there will be many reports that succeed but which never should have been done in the first place.

Readers of this book already know that a report is a purely utilitarian, pragmatic—albeit creative—piece of writing in response to a concrete need. It does not exist for its own sake. It exists to serve a useful purpose in the everyday world of men; it is something which is beneficial, serviceable, helpful, advantageous—something which has practical utility in advancing the work of this world. In other words, a magnificently prepared, well-mounted report that undertakes to say beautifully something that already has been said, or something which, in the opinion of the critic, should not be said because it serves no useful purpose, is worthless.

The sophisticated critic must look around him and recognize the mountains of utterly useless reports which surround us. He must ask whether a ten-page report on his desk, no matter how well done, distributed to twenty-five people, could not have been avoided by a five-minute conversation between, perhaps, two people. He must ask whether a report calculated to cover up a costly error, to promote a lost cause, or to puff up somebody's ego (even though the report in question is successful within its own framework) was a report worth doing. In view of the urgent, original, and necessary work waiting to be done in all fields, and in view of the important work which is being done and reported in all fields, the answer is too apparent.

A report critic, then, must know what has been done already and what remains to be done in his own field. He cannot otherwise definitely know whether a report was worth doing or not. He must also be prepared to recognize that a poor report on an important, original, and difficult project is a report worth doing. This kind of report can be a spur to somebody else to carry the work forward, to complete—"to strive, to find, not to yield."

      ✿   ✿   ✿   ✿   ✿

For our purposes, the critical method applied to reports is, of course, not an end in itself. It is a logical and necessary foundation to appreciating all good writing—and to attempting to do creative report writing.

The quality of a man's work and of his thought are inseparably bound up with the quality of his reports. There is no avoiding the recognition that a report *is* the man—an expression of his personality, an extension of his very self. Moreover, in the vast and shifting complexity of modern institutional life, a report may very well be the only way that a man becomes known to others within and without his organization. It pays to undertake report writing creatively.

THE NATURE OF SCIENCE

Examination of contemporary reports in business, in government, in the professions, and in the colleges reveals a gaping deficiency with disastrous potentialities: The majority of report writers have limited comprehension of the nature of science and of steps in the scientific method of investigation. Causes of this frightening circumstance are traceable to a variety of forces. Chief among them, naturally, is the education given in this country, including education in the sciences themselves. Though a patient report reader in quest of a grain of verifiable truth and himself possessing a modicum of scientific critical apparatus might, for example, find it possible to drag through the unscientific morass of many business reports, he can only yield up the problem in despair when a report prepared by a scientist is lacking fundamentally in scientific method.

An investigator may be said to have a scientific attitude when he is truly prepared to reject conventional systems of ideas as an ultimate basis for truth. Essential to a report embodying scientific approaches is an investigator with a thorough knowledge of some small group of facts, of their relationship to each other, and of the laws which express their sequences. The aim of science is to ascertain truth in every possible branch of human knowledge. Characteristics of the scientific method may be said to be (1) critical discrimination, (2) generalization and system, and (3) empirical verification.

In the attempt to obtain and present a comprehensive account of a subject, critical discrimination is needed so that one can get at bare facts. The investigator must not be influenced by surface appearances or popular notions. To say that a scientific frame of mind is needed for a proper investigation and valid report is not merely to repeat a meaningless shibboleth.

An open, critical mind is needed because the nature of science is to seek to ascertain the common characteristics of types of objects, as well as of the general laws or conditions of events. Elucidation of many such general laws leads us on to a conception of the total pattern. As to generalization and system, science is not concerned with individual objects or phenomena but with types, kinds, or classes of objects and events. The scientist seeks to provide descriptions of classes of objects and phenomena and to explain these phenomena by designating relationships which exist among them.

Empirical verification is likewise characteristic of the scientific method. If a suggested explanation cannot be confirmed through observation, it is not a scientific explanation; it may be an explanation which seems to be correct, which satisfies needs and even solves problems, but it is not a scientific explanation until empirically verified. It is in the nature of the scientific method to begin with facts of observation and then to verify explanations by returning to observations. That which cannot be substantiated by experience and experimentation is not a scientific fact. There are, indeed, many branches of learning which are of inestimable value and which are not scientific. But they do not have to do with report writing, the subject of this book.

Steps in the Scientific Method

Reports are written to explain or to inform (Chapter 4). Though they embody both facts and opinions, these are separate, since opinions are not possible until the facts are established (Chapter 6). Logic is used in expressing the facts (Chapters 6 to 8) and in ordering them for presentation (Chapter 9). Since facts are the raw materials from which reports are created, the writer must be at pains regarding the quality and quantity of them. The very process of gathering facts and reporting them is, of course, essentially a scientific activity. No matter what the source of his facts—bibliographic research, experimentation, questionnaires, or interviews—the report writer should be aware of steps in the scientific method while gathering them.

The scientific method being talked about here is not the technical or technological method involving ingenious instruments in a laboratory. It is rather the method of reasoning logically according to the data obtained. Technical methods and apparatus differ from one science to another, but logical methods are common to all sciences.

Science, as we have said, begins with the observation of selected parts of nature. Observation then leads to description. As phenomena are described, an explanation of cause and effect between them is sought. This involves analysis (breaking down separate parts) and synthesis (putting them together). The next step is to form a hypothesis—a trial explanation concerning the nature and connection of the observations.

The hypothesis is, in other words, a possible explanation of or solution to the problem. It is the hypothesis that guides the gathering of data. The data then serve to prove or disprove the hypothesis, to solve or not solve the problem.

In all, scientific method as a foundation for report writing may be viewed in six general stages: (1) Formulating a specific hypothesis or questions for investigation, (2) designing an investigation to prove the hypothesis or answer the question, (3) accumulating data according to the design, (4) classifying the data, (5) developing generalizations from them, and (6) verifying the results. Harking back momentarily to Chapter 10 on the preliminaries and essentials for a report, the reader will discover familiar terms in a new dressing. The "objective" in Chapter 10 is now seen as the hypothesis, and the "protocol" as the design of the investigation.

✿   ✿   ✿   ✿   ✿

The chapters which follow will be almost completely uninstructive to the casual reader. This book has provided cumulative treatment of the various phases of report writing. Unless the reader can come to the following chapters with a full knowledge of the principles of organizing, developing, writing, and presenting a report as unfolded in Chapters 1 through 17, he is advised to start at the beginning.

Except for introductory headnotes, Chapters 19 through 25 consist chiefly of illustrative samples of special kinds of reports. The exhibits are offered as admirable specimens of their respective genres, worthy of the scrutiny of serious readers. But no one of them is without some minor defect of organization, style, or language. Chapter 26, in presenting the library research paper, offers information on the preliminary bibliography, the library, and note taking. As a further guide to research techniques for the inexperienced report writer—and as a review for others—the Appendix presents ideas on designing an experiment, making a questionnaire, and using an interview.

19

The Business Letter

If the reporter can obtain briefness and clearness in his everyday business correspondence, he is likely to achieve these—together with goodwill—in his reports. Though many otherwise well-informed businessmen are unaware of it, a total revolution in the writing of business letters has occurred in recent decades. The contemporary business letter is anything but the sterile, formalized digit interchanged between two automatons.

A business letter is a bridge between two people with a common interest or problem. Attempts should be made at every turn to make the letter human—natural, personal, warm, and friendly. The barrage of vapid clichés and ready-made phrases of yore is today quite unacceptable (see Chapter 7 for a review of some of the problems of language). Various studies have shown that the simple average daily business letter now costs a company about $5 in terms of personnel, time, office space, equipment, and mailing. Costs of doing business may spiral when letters written by the firm are ineffective.

Each letter must be planned before it is written or dictated. Major points should be covered immediately. Possible objections of the reader should be anticipated and dealt with, as should reasonable questions which may arise. Total information must be provided so that the correspondent is free to act without further ado. Information given must be not only complete but accurate in detail. Whatever action is wanted of the addressee should be shown to be logical and advantageous to his particular situation.

But it is in the conception of the overall approach that the letter may fail or succeed. The writer must grasp the idea that though he is writing in an institutionalized capacity—as a company representative—to a client or customer, he is not blindly acting out a predetermined role established by Fate. To the extent that the letter writer exercises his own creativeness, individuality, and judgment within the established business framework, to that degree will his letter be a human document satisfying a unique business purpose.

SPECIMENS*

CHASE MANHATTAN BANK

hattan Plaza, New York 15, New York

December 27, 19__

. J. J. Black, Treasurer
own Corporation
ndusky, Ohio

ar Joe:

lliam Smith mentioned a few days ago that you were interested in acquiring
ompany that would allow you to utilize your excess space.

th this in mind, we contacted the Smith Corporation without giving Brown's
me. We know the Smith people well. They told us that they are definitely
erested in hearing from potential buyers. However, time may be a factor.
ey are presently in the preliminary stages of bargaining with another pro-
ective buyer.

m enclosing a summary of the company's operations, its history, and their
ndensed figures. I will have to admit that it is a heavy situation to say the
st but they take in a lot of dollars and I thought you might be interested.

you would like any further information or want us to arrange for the two
mpanies to get together, please let me know.

ppy New Year!

Sincerely yours,

John

John J. White
Assistant Vice President

closures 2

* Reproduced with permission.

New York Life Insurance Company . . . 51 MADISON AVENUE, NEW YORK 10, ℕ

November 17, 19__

Mrs. Robert Vansworth
75-24 Springfield Boulevard
Bayside 64, New York

Dear Mrs. Vansworth:

Thank you for counting to ten as you wrote your letter. I have a feeling, though, that you'd stopped counting by the time you came to the postscript.

Please let me try to explain the situation to you. To the lay person, power of attorney is an all-embracing instrument authorizing the agent to exercise and enjoy all the rights and privileges of the grantor. Unfortunately, this is not so. The rights of the attorney are specific and limited to the terms of the authorization. As a matter of fact, in your letter, you point out that the power of attorney filed with the . . . . Insurance Company is an insurance power of attorney, and through it, you have encountered not the least difficulty. The power of attorney we have filed with us is a general power of attorney. Does this not suggest to you that the fault might lie in the inadequacy of the document itself rather than any lack of consideration or disservice on your part?

We're just people here, Mrs. Vansworth. Nothing could be more apparent to us than Captain Vansworth's intention that you act for him in his absence. But our contract is with Captain Vansworth, and until he tells us otherwise, we're bound to protect his interest -- right down to the small print! If you look on page 2 of the policy, you'll find that only the insured may change the beneficiary. That's a standard policy provision, one that you'll find in pretty nearly every life insurance policy issued in the United States. It's a very special right reserved to the insured alone because it is so vital to the control of the ownership of the policy, which is, in effect, personal property. Even as assignee, to whom all right, title and interest has been transferred by an absolute assignment, may not effect a change in beneficiary. When our Office of the General Counsel examined your power of attorney and found that this specific act was not enumerated, they had to suggest the alternative procedure.

Mrs. Robert Vansworth -- page 2   November 17, 19__

But I have another suggestion that might work. Write to the
. . . . .Insurance Company and ask them to send you a photostat of
the power of attorney in their file. When you receive it, read it carefully.
If it isn't limited by its terms to the specific policy with their company,
then by all means, send it directly to this office, and we will be glad to
look it over. Just for luck, I'll send along the change of beneficiary form
you wish, and keep my fingers crossed.

I do hope I've been able to make our position clear and that you no
longer feel we acted arbitrarily or without consideration. And may I
send with this letter the sincere wish that your husband be returned very
soon, safe and sound, to these shores.

Yours very truly,

Vincent Verro

Vincent Verro
Policy Contract Changes Division

VV:MEE1

Electronics World *formerly* RADIO & TV

One Park Avenue   New York 16, New York   ORegon 9-7

December 19, 19___

Mr. Samuel Bogart
Components Company
142 Main Street
Brewster, Maine

Dear Mr. Bogart:

You were certainly correct in feeling disappointed about the position of your advertisement in our December issue. I was quite irritated myself when I saw it but, at that point, it was too late to do anything for you. On rare occasions this kind of positioning does occur. You can be sure I'll do what I can to prevent any recurrence.

Your January ad, however, is another matter. It was in a good spot and experience has shown that either right or left hand positioning is equally effective.

You can be sure of our special attention so far as positioning is concerned for any future ads of Components Company. With this assurance, you should have no hesitation in returning to our magazine at the earliest possible time.

Cordially,

ELECTRONICS WORLD

Richard J. Halpern
Advertising Department

RJH:AM
cc: Mr. Tom Smithers
      Oriole Advertising Co.

VOLKSWAGEN OF AMERICA, INC.

ENGLEWOOD CLIFFS, N. J.

January 7, 19__

Mr. George Parker
1522 North Shore Drive
Milwaukee, Wisconsin

Dear Mr. Parker:

Our general manager is currently in Germany, and I do not like to keep you waiting too long for a final decision on the proposal by Trinity University for a research project on the influence of the automobile on the community.

We have had several discussions here about it and feel that there is need for such a research, but we do not feel that Volkswagen of America should be the sole contributor to such a program. I would suggest that the University try to interest the Automobile Manufacturers Association in Detroit in it, since obviously the American automobile manufacturers have had the most influence on the community. Another possible area for support would be the National Automobile Dealers Association.

Volkswagen of America will be happy to participate in sponsoring such a plan if the majority of the American manufacturers would go along with it also. We feel it is presumptuous for us (that is, Volkswagen) to underwrite a study in the United States of the effects of the automobile on American society. This is something which we have played such a very small part in that I believe it would not be in our interest to sponsor such a study alone.

Sincerely,

Arthur R. Railton
Public Relations Manager

ARR:ksw

20

The Business Report

The business report may be all things to all people; the term, though perhaps originally meaningful, is now somewhat ambiguous. "Business report" is presently used generically to characterize any written communication directed to a particular reader or readers for a specific business purpose. No distinction is usually made regarding the category of the report by function or composition (see Chapters 4 and 5) or by the nature of the business—law, advertising, or plumbing.

Business is that which occupies the time, attention, or labor of men for the purpose of profit or improvement. The professions, labor, and all commerce, trade, and industry may be included in this definition of business. It becomes evident why nobody can say precisely what a business report is.

In order to help establish a more exact definition of a report dealing with business, the present text proposes that the term be limited to explanatory or informational communications encompassing the subject matter of economics, industrial management, corporation finance, investment, money and banking, marketing, and retailing.

Anatomy of Corporate Planning

A new framework for researching and understanding top-management planning problems.

By Frank F. Gilmore and Richard G. Brandenburg

One of the last strongholds of the art of management is the crucial task of top-management planning. The difficulties of determining overall objectives, formulating product-market strategies, and evaluating the joint effects of combined programs have not yet given way to those advances in analytical techniques which are becoming so effective in operating decision areas such as production planning and inventory control. Naturally, this has not been of management's choosing, and many managers have expressed a need for new analytical tools and for an improved understanding of the many business variables which are involved in the top-management planning process. But before new approaches can be developed to assist executives, the major problems must be defined more systematically and with greater precision than they have been in the past.

One of the first steps toward an effective solution of top-management planning problems is to discover a better way of

Anatomy of Corporate Planning

By FRANK F. GILMORE AND RICHARD G. BRANDENBURG

FRANK F. GILMORE is Professor of Business Administration and Director of the Executive Development Program, Cornell University. RICHARD G. BRANDENBURG is a member of the faculty, Graduate School of Industrial Administration, Carnegie Institute of Technology.

REPRINTED FROM

HARVARD BUSINESS REVIEW

NOVEMBER–DECEMBER 1962

* Reproduced with permission of *Harvard Business Review*, 40:61 (November–December), 1962.

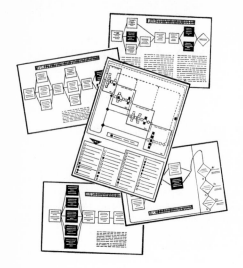

exploring the anatomy of the planning process and determining just what goes on. Such an approach will require a consistent vocabulary of definitions and concepts, expressed in terms which are meaningful to business executives. In addition, it is important to have a detailed description of the major planning decisions that are made in most businesses, the interactions among them, and the important considerations involved in each one. Finally, these factors must be integrated within an adequate, logical scheme which enables a clearer understanding of the major characteristics of top-management planning.

AUTHORS' NOTE: This article is based on a research project carried out by the authors during the period from September 1960 through June 1962. It was sponsored by Cornell University's Graduate School of Business and Public Administration under a grant of funds from the Ford Foundation. We are indebted to Dr. H. Igor Ansoff for introducing the concept of synergy to us and for his assistance in clarifying a number of steps in our planning framework.

Setup for Planning

Our purpose in this article is to present a top-management planning framework which can serve as a start toward meeting these needs. This framework, as we call it, was developed over a two-year period. Our project began with an intensive study of the military decision-making process at the U.S. Army Command and General Staff College at Fort Leavenworth, Kansas. Based on this study, a crude business analog of the military model was then created and discussed with a number of businessmen and experts in management science.

The final step was to compare and modify our model in light of the top-management planning process employed over the past five years by the Lockheed Aircraft Corporation, which has been carrying out a major diversification program. During this step, we worked closely with one of the participants in the company's top-management planning group. This exploration of actual experience in terms of our model enabled us to sharpen our concepts and definitions and to bring our ideas more nearly in line with actual planning practices.

The Benefits

It is our feeling that this framework, even though it is just the beginning of a larger project involving many case studies over the years to come, will yield several practical benefits to top-management planners. Specifically:

• It should be useful in organizing and classifying the wealth of existing business planning experience.
• It can aid in evaluating the extent to which the available results of management research are useful for top-management planning.
• It may serve as a guide for new research by helping to isolate important problem areas and to suggest hypotheses for empirical investigations.
• It can provide a unified conceptual outline for improving the planning capabilities of managers being trained in executive development programs and for teaching potential new managers in graduate schools of business administration.
• It will provide an improved system for integrating current knowledge about business planning, the lack of which has severely handicapped the teaching of business policy formulation.
• Finally, as the framework gradually is refined and tested, it should enable executives to organize their thinking and actions more effectively as they carry out the difficult job of planning in the complex modern business environment.

While none of the individual elements of the framework are new in themselves, the *degree* of subdivision and the *definition* of relationships do bring forth a new opportunity: not only is the way paved for greater application of analytical techniques, but also there is the possibility of making a conscious search for *synergy*.

In top-management planning, synergy refers to the phenomenon wherein joint performance of several programs is superior to the sum of the performances of the individual programs before combination. For example, $10,000 worth of advertising plus $10,000 worth of salesmen's efforts may produce more than $20,000 worth of either one separately. In business, synergistic (or greater-than-the-sum-of-the-parts) effects are more likely to result if tests for synergy are applied at appropriate points in the planning process. These test points will be developed in the following exhibits (shown as black boxes in contrast to the white boxes), and then discussed further in the text.

Master Plan

In this article, the relationship between the company and its competitive environment is expressed by the master plan of the enterprise. Three basic components comprise the master plan: *economic mission, competitive strategy,* and *program of action.* These, plus the *reappraisal* component, are defined as follows:

1. Formulating the *economic mission* is concerned with the kind of business the firm should be in, and what its performance objectives should be.
2. The problem of determining *competitive strategy* is that of finding the right product-market-sales approach combination for effective accomplishment of the

economic mission, and deriving associated goals in the various functional areas of the business.

3. Specification of *program of action* involves a search for efficient means of implementing the competitive strategy.

4. The *reappraisal* phase reflects the need to answer the question of when and to what extent the master plan should be modified.

Each of these components of the master plan represents a major decision phase in the proposed planning framework. In the rest of the article, these phases will be examined in greater detail. A flow diagram, depicting the network of interrelated planning problems as questions for management, is presented for each (Exhibits i through iv). Where necessary, additional definitions are supplied by notes appended to the individual steps. Then, after the four major phases have been defined, the top-management framework will be presented as a whole (Exhibit v), and the significance of some of its features for top managment will be summarized in the balance of the text.

Significance of Framework

Our effort in these charts has been to develop a step-by-step framework for depicting the anatomy of top-management planning. Since we feel strongly that a definition of the problems involved is prerequisite to a more systematic approach to planning, we have attempted to recognize and define key elements in the four stages of the planning process (Exhibits i–iv) and then to integrate them into a total, logical sequence by means of the final, master chart (Exhibit v).

You will notice on this master chart that Exhibit iv actually becomes the first phase of the total process (as a result of the fact that most large corporations already will have some sort of master plan in operation). The purpose of this *reappraisal phase* is to monitor the internal and external environment of the firm in search of problems and opportunities which are triggering circumstances that might demand some change in the current master plan. Fundamental to the effectiveness of this phase is maintenance of the master plan of the enterprise in currently valid condition; remember that what is involved is reappraisal of the plans by which the company is really operating, not of some hypothetical or idealistic set of objectives.

Evaluating the Phases

The significance of the reappraisal phase in the top-management planning process was emphasized by Robert B. Young in a recent article on the causes of industrial growth.[1] Young stressed the importance of utilizing a program of environmental surveillance to identify and size up future changes in the corporate environment and to sense the specific product opportunities and threats implicit in these changes.

[1] "Keys to Corporate Growth," HBR November–December 1961, p. 51.

EXHIBIT 1. FORMULATION OF ECONOMIC MISSION

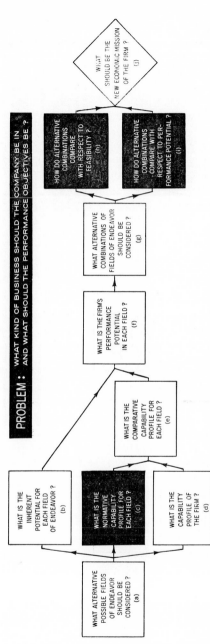

PROBLEM: WHAT KIND OF BUSINESS SHOULD THE COMPANY BE IN AND WHAT SHOULD THE PERFORMANCE OBJECTIVES BE?

WHAT SHOULD BE THE NEW ECONOMIC MISSION OF THE FIRM? (j)

HOW DO ALTERNATIVE COMBINATIONS COMPARE WITH RESPECT TO FEASIBILITY? (h)

HOW DO ALTERNATIVE COMBINATIONS COMPARE WITH RESPECT TO PERFORMANCE POTENTIAL? (i)

WHAT ALTERNATIVE COMBINATIONS OF FIELDS OF ENDEAVOR SHOULD BE CONSIDERED? (g)

WHAT IS THE FIRM'S PERFORMANCE POTENTIAL IN EACH FIELD? (f)

WHAT IS THE COMPARATIVE CAPABILITY PROFILE FOR EACH FIELD? (e)

WHAT IS THE INHERENT POTENTIAL FOR EACH FIELD OF ENDEAVOR? (b)

WHAT IS THE NORMATIVE CAPABILITY PROFILE FOR EACH FIELD? (c)

WHAT IS THE CAPABILITY PROFILE OF THE FIRM? (d)

WHAT ALTERNATIVE POSSIBLE FIELDS OF ENDEAVOR SHOULD BE CONSIDERED? (a)

NOTES

(a) A field of endeavor is a sphere of business activity within which a firm operates. It may be characterized by a common thread such as technology or product-market orientation. For a small company, a segment of an industry may constitute its field of endeavor, and it may be thought of as specialized. A larger firm may be active in several related fields of endeavor within an industry and be considered integrated. Or a company may be acting in several unrelated fields of endeavor and be thought of as diversified.

(b) Inherent potential defines the extent to which a field of endeavor offers the possibility of achieving objectives in four critical areas of performance: (i) growth —both rate of growth and outlook for continuance of growth; (ii) flexibility in relation to the uncertainties of technological change; (iii) stability in resisting major declines in the business cycle; and (iv) return on investment. The performance of leading firms in the field offers some indication of the potential inherent in the field.

(c) A normative capability profile is a composite statement in quantitative and/or qualitative terms of what it takes to be successful in a field of endeavor. Measures are needed in such functional areas as research and development, marketing, production, finance, and management. A study of the capabilities and sources of synergistic strength of the leading firms in each field can provide a point of departure in estimating requirements for success.

(d) The firm's capability profile is a statement in quantitative and/or qualitative terms of the firm's capabilities in the functional areas defined in the normative capability profile.

(e) Relating the firm's capability profile to the normative capability profile for each field of endeavor will serve to develop comparative profiles which indicate how well the firm's capabilities match the requirements for success in each field.

(f) The firm's performance potential in each field may be derived by matching the comparative capability profiles with inherent potential in each field with respect to growth, flexibility, stability, and return on investment.

(g) It may be desirable for the firm to be active in more than one field of endeavor. If integration or diversification appears attractive, possible combinations of the more promising fields should be formulated at this point.

(h) Alternative combinations of several fields of endeavor may be evaluated with respect to feasibility by comparing resource requirements. Resource requirements will reflect the degree to which synergy is realized under each alternative.

(i) Also, alternative combinations of fields of endeavor may be evaluated with respect to growth, flexibility, stability, and return on investment. Particular note should be paid to the degree to which synergy is realized under each alternative.

(j) The final decision with respect to the combinations of fields of endeavor (together with associated performance goals) defines the economic mission of the enterprise. The foregoing analyses are concerned with the problem of choosing a combination of fields of endeavor and objectives from an economic point of view. To this information base top management must add noneconomic considerations and business judgment in order to arrive at a final decision.

EXHIBIT II. FORMULATION OF COMPETITIVE STRATEGY

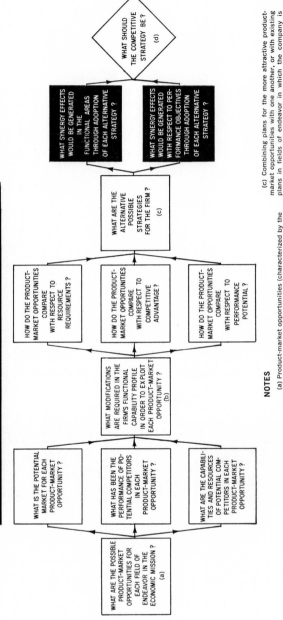

PROBLEM : HOW SHOULD THE FIRM PURSUE ITS OBJECTIVES IN EACH FIELD OF ENDEAVOR SPECIFIED IN THE ECONOMIC MISSION ?

NOTES

(a) Product-market opportunities (characterized by the significant features that are expected to influence their outcome) are specific combinations of product-market-sales approaches which define possible ways of exploiting a field of endeavor.

(b) Based on the information developed in the preceding three steps, an analysis may be made of the firm's functional capabilities with respect to research and development, marketing, production, finance, and management. Changes required for successful implementation of each alternative product-market opportunity may be defined as product-market plans.

(c) Combining plans for the more attractive product-market opportunities with one another, or with existing plans in fields of endeavor in which the company is already operating, will serve to develop alternative strategies for the firm as a whole.

(d) The decision as to the competitive strategy of the firm defines the directions in which the company will move toward its objectives in each environment included in the economic mission. The particular ways in which performance objectives will be pursued in each field of endeavor, together with the functional goals necessary for their accomplishment, are specified, thus providing the framework for development of a program of action.

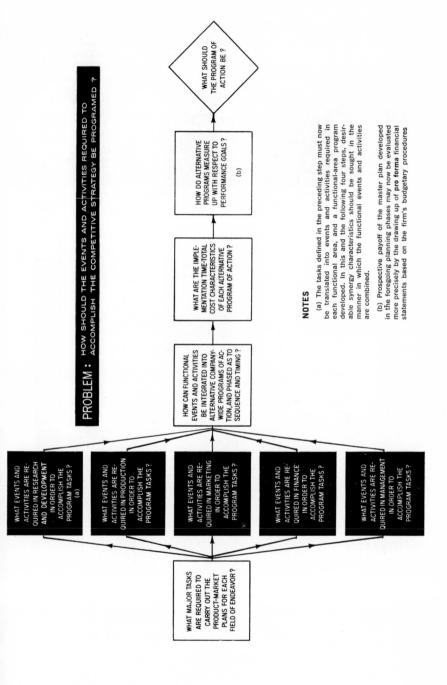

PROBLEM : HOW SHOULD THE EVENTS AND ACTIVITIES REQUIRED TO ACCOMPLISH THE COMPETITIVE STRATEGY BE PROGRAMED ?

WHAT MAJOR TASKS ARE REQUIRED TO CARRY OUT THE PRODUCT-MARKET PLANS FOR EACH FIELD OF ENDEAVOR ?

WHAT EVENTS AND ACTIVITIES ARE REQUIRED IN RESEARCH AND DEVELOPMENT IN ORDER TO ACCOMPLISH THE PROGRAM TASKS ? (a)

WHAT EVENTS AND ACTIVITIES ARE REQUIRED IN PRODUCTION IN ORDER TO ACCOMPLISH THE PROGRAM TASKS ?

WHAT EVENTS AND ACTIVITIES ARE REQUIRED IN MARKETING IN ORDER TO ACCOMPLISH THE PROGRAM TASKS ?

WHAT EVENTS AND ACTIVITIES ARE REQUIRED IN FINANCE IN ORDER TO ACCOMPLISH THE PROGRAM TASKS ?

WHAT EVENTS AND ACTIVITIES ARE REQUIRED IN MANAGEMENT IN ORDER TO ACCOMPLISH THE PROGRAM TASKS ?

HOW CAN FUNCTIONAL EVENTS AND ACTIVITIES BE INTEGRATED INTO ALTERNATIVE COMPANY-WIDE PROGRAMS OF ACTION, AND PHASED AS TO SEQUENCE AND TIMING ?

WHAT ARE THE IMPLEMENTATION TIME-TOTAL COST CHARACTERISTICS OF EACH ALTERNATIVE PROGRAM OF ACTION ?

HOW DO ALTERNATIVE PROGRAMS MEASURE UP WITH RESPECT TO PERFORMANCE GOALS ? (b)

WHAT SHOULD THE PROGRAM OF ACTION BE ?

NOTES

(a) The tasks defined in the preceding step must now be translated into events and activities required in each functional area, and a functional-area program developed. In this and the following four steps, desirable synergy characteristics should be sought in the manner in which the functional events and activities are combined.

(b) Prospective payoff of the master plan developed in the foregoing planning phases may now be evaluated more precisely by the drawing up of **pro forma** financial statements based on the firm's budgetary procedures

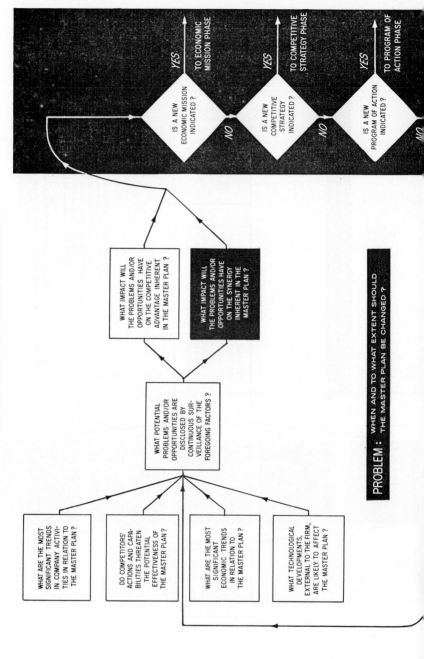

EXHIBIT IV. REAPPRAISAL OF MASTER PLAN

WHAT ARE THE MOST SIGNIFICANT TRENDS IN COMPANY ACTIVITIES IN RELATION TO THE MASTER PLAN ?

DO COMPETITORS' ACTIONS AND CAPABILITIES THREATEN THE POTENTIAL EFFECTIVENESS OF THE MASTER PLAN ?

WHAT ARE THE MOST SIGNIFICANT ECONOMIC TRENDS IN RELATION TO THE MASTER PLAN ?

WHAT TECHNOLOGICAL DEVELOPMENTS, EXTERNAL TO THE FIRM, ARE LIKELY TO AFFECT THE MASTER PLAN ?

WHAT POTENTIAL PROBLEMS AND/OR OPPORTUNITIES ARE DISCLOSED BY CONTINUOUS SURVEILLANCE OF THE FOREGOING FACTORS ?

WHAT IMPACT WILL THE PROBLEMS AND/OR OPPORTUNITIES HAVE ON THE COMPETITIVE ADVANTAGE INHERENT IN THE MASTER PLAN ?

WHAT IMPACT WILL THE PROBLEMS AND/OR OPPORTUNITIES HAVE ON THE SYNERGY INHERENT IN THE MASTER PLAN ?

IS A NEW ECONOMIC MISSION INDICATED ?

YES → TO ECONOMIC MISSION PHASE

NO

IS A NEW COMPETITIVE STRATEGY INDICATED ?

YES → TO COMPETITIVE STRATEGY PHASE

NO

IS A NEW PROGRAM OF ACTION INDICATED ?

YES → TO PROGRAM OF ACTION PHASE

NO

PROBLEM : WHEN AND TO WHAT EXTENT SHOULD THE MASTER PLAN BE CHANGED ?

EXHIBIT V. TOP-MANAGEMENT PLANNING FRAMEWORK

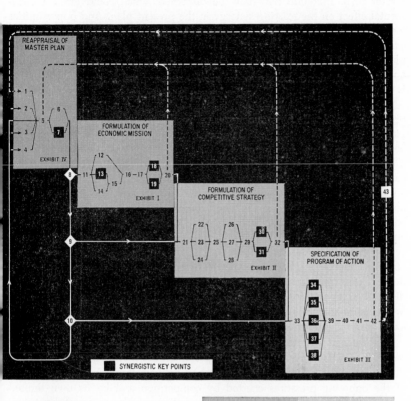

KEY			21 Product-market opportunities	33 Program tasks
			22 Potential market	**34** R & D events and activities
1 Company activities	11 Fields of endeavor		23 Competitors' performance	**35** Production events and activities
2 Competitors' actions	12 Inherent potential		24 Competitors' capabilities	**36** Marketing events and activities
3 Economic trends	**13** Normative capability profile		25 Functional changes	37 Finance events and activities
4 Technological developments	14 Firm's capability profile		26 Feasibility comparisons	38 Management events and activities
5 Potential problems and opportunities	15 Comparative capability profile		27 Competitive advantage comparisons	39 Program integration
6 Impact on competitive advantage	16 Performance potential		28 Performance potential comparisons	40 Time-cost characteristics
7 Impact on synergy	17 Combinations of fields		29 Alternative strategies	41 Performance goal evaluation
8 New economic mission?	**18** Feasibility comparisons		**30** Functional synergy	42 Program of action
9 New competitive strategy?	**19** Performance potential comparisons		**31** Performance synergy	43 Operations
10 New program of action?	20 Economic mission		32 Competitive strategy	

In this phase, synergy needs to be considered for the first time in the planning process. The answers to the first five questions in Exhibit iv would provide the necessary data to re-evaluate synergy in the existing master plan. Problems may now be discerned which could exert a detrimental effect on the existing synergy in the present plan. And opportunities may have developed which might conceivably yield an improvement over existing synergy. Thus, a synergistic test made at this early phase of the planning process can serve to sharpen management's judgment as to whether a new economic mission, new competitive strategy, or new program of action is called for.

The purpose of the second phase, that of formulating the company's proper *economic mission,* is to select the new external competitive environment for the firm, and to establish valid over-all goals as targets for company performance in that environment. Synergy considerations are significant, also, in two parts of this phase: (1) The estimate of the normative capability profile for each field of endeavor should be complemented by an examination of the sources of synergistic strength manifested in the activities of leading firms. (2) The synergy that may result from each of various alternative combinations of fields of endeavor needs to be weighed and the results used as a basis for deciding on the economic mission.

The purpose of the *competitive strategy* phase is to specify just how the company should go about pursuing its objectives in its competitive environment. The correct strategy will establish the proper relationship between the distinctive capabilities of the firm and problems and opportunities in the firm's environment. The search for the correct interrelationship is at the heart of strategy formulation.

The concept of strategy in business planning is being given increasing recognition these days. James Brian Quinn defines a strategy as a plan that determines how the organization can best achieve its desired ends in light of the opposing pressures exerted by competition and by its own limited resources.[2] He suggests that the essence of strategic planning is the marshaling of an organization's resources so that its strengths are emphasized and the competitors' strengths minimized. Watson carries this point further by observing that the choice of a proper niche in the market is the key to planning a strategy that will give the firm some kind of competitive advantage.[3] As he puts it, management needs a plan based on the characteristics of the market, the resources of the firm, and the conditions of the economic environment.

Synergy considerations enter the strategy formulation phase at two points: (1) in each functional area when synergy is sought in the weighing of alternative combinations of product-market plans; and (2) when these synergistic effects are evaluated with respect to how well they contribute to

[2] "Top Management Guides for Research Planning," in *Technological Planning at the Corporate Level,* edited by James R. Bright (Boston, Division of Research, Harvard Business School, 1962).

[3] Edward T. P. Watson, "Diagnosis of Management Problems," HRB January–February 1958, p. 69.

the performance objectives of the company as a whole. For example, some combinations may produce beneficial synergistic reactions in the short run but may actually prove detrimental to other long-range objectives.

The purpose of the *program of action* phase is to specify, sequence, and schedule the major activities and events necessary to accomplish efficiently the strategy agreed on in the previous step. In this phase, operations research is beginning to offer increasingly useful techniques for top management. Critical path planning and scheduling, mathematical programing for resource allocation and capacity planning, capital budgeting models, and simulation, all can be of value in comparing alternatives.[4] In this phase, synergistic effects are sought when the combinations of events and activities required in each functional area to implement the product-market are evaluated.

Difficulties Encountered

Thus, by dividing the top-management planning process into specific stages, we have focused attention on the problem of achieving the most beneficial combinations of actions which will produce synergistic effects. However, it should not be inferred from this discussion of synergy that the segments of a master plan can be characterized completely in quantitative terms and that the optimum combination of segments can be selected according to some precise analytical method. The questions posed throughout this framework show the formidable problems involved in estimating the feasibility and performance potential of a single segment of a plan. Immensely greater difficulties are encountered when the joint or synergistic effects associated with combinations are considered.

Even though the evaluation of these effects is today not amenable to precise analytical attack, it is still useful to highlight, as we have done in EXHIBIT V, the key points where synergy plays a role, rather than to allow synergy considerations to remain buried in the top-management planning process.

Conclusion

This exploration of the anatomy of top-management planning has subdivided the process (1) into subsections of the complete plan according to different product-market arrangements, and (2) into subsections according to key decision areas.

The product-market breakdown is important because each of its elements forms an essential part of the over-all pattern which characterizes the relationship of the firm to its competitive environment. Each element is an area of company activity for which there must be an organized program that covers planning, operations, and control.

[4] See Robert W. Miller, "How to Plan and Control with PERT," HRB March–April 1962, p. 93; Edward G. Bennion, "Econometrics for Management," HRB March–April 1961, p. 100; James C. Hetrick, "Mathematical Models in Capital Budgeting," HRB January–February 1961, p. 49.

The key-decision-area breakdown is important because each of the four major phases is a significant part of the process by which the master plan of the firm is determined. Each phase is logically related to the other phases, involves recognition of particular key planning variables, and is an integral part of an over-all process which is cyclical and recurring in nature.

We hope that this effort to develop a useful framework for exploring the anatomy of top-management planning will make a contribution to meeting the need for better descriptions of major planning problems as a prelude to the development of improved techniques. While such techniques will be of great value in making improved planning decisions, the role of vision, imagination, and keen executive judgment will remain essential. The ability of experienced managers to perceive new alternatives and to make risk-taking decisions in "ill-structured" situations will continue to be a vital ingredient in effective top-management planning.

By proposing a planning framework, this article is an attempt to organize concepts which can contribute to the body of useful definitions and assumptions about business cited by Peter F. Drucker as prerequisites for a more effective discipline of management.[5] This attempt is offered as a step toward meeting a growing challenge to business management—that of evaluating and planning the company's future operations in light of a real appreciation of the changing environment in which it will have to survive.

[5] "Potentials of Management Science" (Thinking Ahead), HRB January–February 1959, p. 25.

21

The Technical Report

Applied science in industry, business, government, and education is the substance of the bulk of modern technical reports. There is also the technical report based on pure or basic science—the technical report which develops laws and theorems. Writers of reports dealing with applied science will have technical proficiency in their particular discipline. However, attempts to explain the methods and mechanics by which principles of science may be industrially applied are foredoomed unless the technologist also possesses broad scientific knowledge.

Though dispassionate objectivity has been repeatedly stressed as a requisite for all report writing (see Chapters 2 and 4 to 10), nowhere is the need for it more emphatic than in the technical report. Yet the technologist must not accept this fundamental dictum naïvely and assume that facts speak for themselves. They don't. Without the creative writer to interpret and expound their meaning, the facts are of value only to people who like to read catalogs. Detached assurance by the writer of a technical report is a positive signal to the reader that there has probably been a legitimate explanation-interpretation made of the data.

W. S. DORN

Generalizations of Horner's Rule for Polynomial Evaluation*

Abstract: Polynomials are generally evaluated by use of Horner's rule, sometimes referred to as the nesting rule. This rule is sequential and affords no opportunity for parallel computation, i.e., completion of several of the arithmetic operations simultaneously. Two generalizations of Horner's rule which allow for parallel computation are presented here.

Schedules and, in some cases, machine codes for evaluating a polynomial on a computer with several parallel arithmetic units are developed. Some advantages of the generalized rules in sequential computations on a computer with a single arithmetic unit are presented.

1. Introduction

The prospect of high-speed digital computers possessing several arithmetic units which may operate simultaneously requires a reappraisal of many of the standard methods and techniques of numerical analysis. Indeed, these

* Presented at the 16th National Conference of the Association for Computing Machinery, Los Angeles, California, September 5–8, 1961.

306

Reprinted from

IBM **Journal of research and development**

Vol. 6 | No. 2 | April 1962

W. S. Dorn

Generalizations of Horner's Rule for Polynomial Evaluation*

* Reproduced with permission of the *IBM Journal of Research and Development*, 6:239 (April) 1962.

methods were all developed with a sequential mode of operation in mind. Classical numerical methods were designed for an individual using either paper and pencil or a desk calculator. Even modern refinements were tailored for digital computers in which only one arithmetic operation could be performed at any given time.

Many of these classical methods should not be expected to be well adapted to computers having several parallel arithmetic units. The purpose of this article is to investigate one classical problem—that of the evaluation of a simple polynomial from this point of view. A complete analysis is given for this problem which is so prevalent in modern computing.

Polynomials are usually evaluated by Horner's rule, sometimes referred to as the *nesting rule*. This rule, however, is entirely sequential in the sense that none of its arithmetic operations may be performed simultaneously. After a brief review of Horner's rule (Section 2), two generalizations which allow for simultaneous arithmetic are derived in Section 3. Schedules which evaluate a polynomial in minimum time on computers with two, three or four arithmetic units are given in Section 4. Actual machine codes are written for a certain class of parallel computers, and estimates are given regarding the maximum number of arithmetic units which may be used efficiently.

Finally, Section 5 describes some advantages that the generalized Horner's rules provide even for sequential computers with a single arithmetic unit. In particular, the problem of integrating a rational function by use of Gauss quadrature is shown to require fewer arithmetic operations if the generalized rule is utilized in the computation.

2. Horner's rule

Consider a polynomial $p(x)$ of degree n

$$p(x) = a_0 + a_1 x + \cdots + a_n x^n \tag{2.1}$$

and divide $p(x)$ by a linear factor $x - x_0$

$$p(x) = (x - x_0)(b_1 + b_2 x + \cdots + b_n x^{n-1}) + b_0. \tag{2.2}$$

The remainder, b_0, and the coefficients, $b_1, b_2, \cdots, b_n$, in the quotient are readily obtained by equating the coefficients of like powers of x in (2.1) and (2.2) as follows:

$$b_n = a_n \tag{2.3}$$
$$b_j = a_j + x_0 b_{j+1} \qquad j = n - 1, \cdots, 0. \tag{2.4}$$

The b_j may be computed recursively from (2.3) and (2.4). Moreover, it follows from (2.2) that

$$p(x_0) = b_0. \tag{2.5}$$

This method for evaluating the polynomial $p(x)$ at $x = x_0$ is *Horner's rule* and may be expressed alternatively by

$$p(x_0) = a_0 + x_0\{a_1 + x_0[a_2 + \cdots + x_0(a_n) \cdots]\}. \tag{2.6}$$

Horner's rule requires n multiplications and n additions for the evaluation of $p(x_0)$.

It can be shown that at least n additions are required to compute $p(x_0)$. It is also generally accepted that a total of $2n$ operations (additions and/or multiplications) are necessary to compute $p(x_0)$. No proof of this latter fact exists, however, except for $n \leq 4$ (Ref. 1).

The minimum number of multiplications necessary to evaluate $p(x_0)$ is likewise an open question. Again for $n \leq 4$ at least n multiplications are necessary.[1] Motzkin[2] has shown that for $n = 6$ only $n/2 = 3$ multiplications are required. Motzkin does not state the number of additions required by his algorithm.

It is clear from (2.4) that Horner's rule is sequential in the sense that for any j, b_j cannot be computed until all the b_i for $i = n, n - 1, \cdots, j + 1$ have been computed. It follows that none of the arithmetic operations may be performed in parallel. Thus the availability of a computer with several arithmetic units which can operate simultaneously would not decrease the time in which $p(x_0)$ could be calculated.

In the following section two generalizations of Horner's rule which allow for simultaneous operation of arithmetic units will be developed.

3. Generalizations of Horner's rule

To obtain Horner's rule the polynomial $p(x)$ was divided by a linear factor $x - x_0$, and the remainder was, therefore, $p(x_0)$. An obvious generalization is to divide $p(x)$ by a polynomial $q(x)$ which has x_0 as a root, i.e., $q(x_0) = 0$. Then the remainder, evaluated at $x = x_0$, is $p(x_0)$.

In particular, choose $q(x) = x^k - x_0^k$ where $k \geq 1$.

$$\begin{aligned} p(x) &= (x^k - x_0^k)(b_k + b_{k+1}x + \cdots + b_n x^{n-k}) \\ &+ b_{k-1}x^{k-1} + \cdots + b_1 x + b_0 . \end{aligned} \tag{3.1}$$

By equating the coefficients of like powers of x in (2.1) and (3.1) it follows that

$$b_j = a_j \qquad j = n, \cdots, n - k + 1 \tag{3.2}$$
$$b_j = a_j + x_0^k b_{j+k} \qquad j = n - k, \cdots, 0 . \tag{3.3}$$

Moreover,

$$p(x_0) = b_{k-1}x_0^{k-1} + \cdots + b_1 x_0 + b_0 . \tag{3.4}$$

The computation of the b_j in (3.3) and the subsequent evaluation of $p(x_0)$ in (3.4) requires n additions and $n + k - 1$ multiplications. For $k = 1$ this reduces to Horner's Rule. The generalized rule given by (3.2) and (3.3) will be referred to as the kth *order Horner's rule*.

Notice now that once the b_i have been computed for $i = n, n - 1, \cdots, j$ (where $j \leq n - k + 1$) then $b_{j-1}, b_{j-2}, \cdots, b_{j-k}$ can all be computed simultaneously. That is to say, k arithmetic units operating in parallel could compute k of the b_j in one addition time plus one multiplication time.

For large n, the time to compute $p(x_0)$ on a computer with k arithmetic units which operate in parallel is of the order of n/k multiplication times plus n/k addition times using the kth order Horner's rule. A detailed analysis of the exact time requirements for several values of k is given in Section 4.

Another generalization of Horner's rule which allows for parallel computation has been given by Estrin.[3]

First compute

$$c_i^{(0)} = a_i + x_0 a_{i+1} \qquad i = 0, 2, \cdots, 2\lfloor n/2 \rfloor \tag{3.5}$$

where $\lfloor y \rfloor$ denotes the largest integer less than or equal to y. Then successively compute

$$
\begin{aligned}
c_i^{(1)} &= c_i^{(0)} + x_0^2 c_{i+2}^{(0)} & i &= 0, 4, \cdots, 4\lfloor n/4 \rfloor \\
c_i^{(2)} &= c_i^{(1)} + x_0^4 c_{i+4}^{(1)} & i &= 0, 8, \cdots, 8\lfloor n/8 \rfloor \\
&\;\;\vdots \\
c_i^{(m)} &= c_i^{(m-1)} + x_0^{2^m} c_{i+2^m}^{(m-1)} & i &= 0, 2^{m+1}, \cdots, 2^{m+1}\lfloor n/2^{m+1} \rfloor .
\end{aligned}
\tag{3.6}
$$

The process will terminate when $m = \lfloor \log_2 n \rfloor$ and, moreover,

$$p(x_0) = c_0^{(m)} . \tag{3.7}$$

This procedure also may be expressed by

$$
\begin{aligned}
p(x_0) = {} & a_0 + a_1 x_0 + x_0^2(a_2 + a_3 x_0) + x_0^4[a_4 + a_5 x_0 \\
& + x_0^2(a_6 + a_7 x_0)] + x_0^8\{a_8 + a_9 x_0 \\
& + x_0^2(a_{10} + a_{11}x_0) + x_0^4[a_{12} + a_{13}x_0 \\
& + x_0^2(a_{14} + a_{15}x_0)]\} \\
& + x_0^{16}{<}a_{16} + \{[\cdots + (a_{30} + a_{31}x_0)]\}{>} \\
& + \cdots
\end{aligned}
\tag{3.8}
$$

Now notice that for each j all $c_i^{(j)}$ may be computed simultaneously in one addition time plus one multiplication time. Since there are $\lfloor \log_2 n \rfloor + 1$ values of j, the minimum time to compute $p(x_0)$ using this algorithm is

$$T = (\lfloor \log_2 n \rfloor + 1)(t_a + t_m),$$

where t_a is the time required for one addition, and t_m is the time for one multiplication.

In order to achieve this minimum time, however, it is necessary that the computer possess sufficient arithmetic units to compute all $c_i^{(j)}$ simultaneously for any j.

The maximum number of $c_i^{(j)}$ for any j occurs for $j = 0$, and there are $\lfloor n/2 \rfloor + 1$ of the $c_i^{(0)}$. If n is even the final $c_i^{(0)}$ is

$$c_n^{(0)} = a_n$$

and does not require any computation. The number of $c_i^{(0)}$ which must be calculated, therefore, is given by $\lfloor (n+1)/2 \rfloor$. In order to calculate the $c_i^{(1)}$, however, x_0^2 must also be calculated. This can be done at the same time as the $c_i^{(0)}$ are computed. Thus $\lfloor (n+1)/2 \rfloor + 1 = N$ arithmetic units must be used initially. With N arithmetic units, all of $c_i^{(0)}$ and x_0^2 can be computed in one addition and one multiplication time.

For $j \geq 1$ the $c_i^{(j)}$ are fewer than $N-1$ in number, so all of the $c_i^{(j)}$ and x_0^{2j+1} can be calculated in one addition time and one multiplication time on N parallel arithmetic units.

If fewer than N arithmetic units are available a nontrivial scheduling problem arises if the computing time is to be minimized. This scheduling problem is discussed elsewhere[4] and will not be considered here.

4. Schedules for parallel computers

From the discussion of the previous section it appears that for a computer with k parallel arithmetic units the kth order Horner's rule provides the fastest way to evaluate a polynomial. In general, it is to be expected that there will be relatively few arithmetic units available. Therefore, a detailed analysis for the case of two, three or four parallel arithmetic units will be given here. It will be assumed that all arithmetic units are identical.

• A. *Second-order Horner's rule*

The second-order Horner's rule is

$$b_n = a_n$$
$$b_{n-1} = a_{n-1}$$
$$b_j = a_j + x_0^2 b_{j+2} \qquad j = n-2, \cdots, 0 \tag{4.1}$$

and

$$p(x_0) = b_0 + b_1 x_0 . \tag{4.2}$$

This is equivalent to evaluating two polynomials in x^2 of degree $n/2$ by a first-order Horner's rule as follows

$$\begin{aligned} p(x_0) = &<a_0 + x_0^2\{a_2 + x_0^2[\cdots + x_0^2 \; (a_{2\lfloor n/2 \rfloor})]\}> \\ &+ x_0 <a_1 + x_0^2\{a_3 + x_0^2[+ x_0^2 \\ &\times (a_{2\lfloor n-1/2 \rfloor} + 1)]\}> . \end{aligned} \tag{4.3}$$

The formulation (4.3) was previously given by K. Ralston (see, e.g., Ref. 3).

If two parallel arithmetic units are available, the process is started by computing x_0^2 on one unit while the second sits idle. Then $x_0^2 a_n$ and $x_0^2 a_{n-1}$ are computed simultaneously followed by $b_{n-2} = a_{n-2} + (x_0^2 a_n)$ and $b_{n-3} = a_{n-3} + (x_0^2 a_{n-1})$. The complete schedule is given in Appendix I. Notice that the terminal steps vary depending on whether n is even or odd, but in either case a total of $n+2$ steps is necessary. The total time, T_2, is given by

$$T^2 = (\lfloor n/2 \rfloor + 1)t_a + (\lfloor (n+1)/2 \rfloor + 1)t_m, \tag{4.4}$$

where again t_a and t_m are the addition and multiplication times respectively. If the multiply and add times are equal $(t_m = t_a = t)$ this reduces to

$$T_2 = (n + 2)t .$$
(4.5)

The utilization U is defined to be

$$U = \frac{\text{total time all the arithmetic units are in use either individually or collectively}}{\text{total time all the arithmetic units are available}} .$$

The utilization then is a measure of how efficiently the arithmetic units are used. A utilization of 1 indicates no idle time on any unit. The utilization, U_2, of the schedule given in Appendix I is

$$U_2 = \frac{2n + 1}{2(n + 2)}$$
(4.6)

for the case $t_m = t_a$.

For large n, T_2 approaches nt, and U_2 approaches 1.

Notice that the foregoing discussion has neglected all hardware considerations. For example, no mention has been made of the number of memories the computer possesses or the access to these memories. Such considerations may significantly affect the validity of the computing time stated in (4.5). In order to determine the effect of these factors consider a mythical parallel computer of the type described in Appendix II with two arithmetic units. Suppose for the moment that $r = 1$, i.e., the arithmetic operations of addition and multiplication require 1 time cycle, as do the FETCH and STORE operations.

A program may be written for this computer (see Appendix III) which evaluates the nth degree polynomial $p(x)$ in $2n + 9$ time cycles. The utilization is

$$U = \frac{4n + 7}{4n + 18} .$$

This program uses the second-order Horner's rule. For comparison, a similar computer with one arithmetic unit requires $4n + 2$ time cycles for a program based on the first-order Horner's rule. The utilization for the latter program is 1.

Thus for large n, the time required by two arithmetic units is one-half that required by one arithmetic unit, and the utilization in both cases is 1.

Additional arithmetic units, however, will not serve to further decrease the computing time. A justification and discussion of this fact will be deferred until the third- and fourth-order rules have been considered in detail.

• B. *Third-order Horner's rule*

The third-order Horner's rule is

$$
\begin{aligned}
b_j &= a_j & j &= n, n-1, n-2 \\
b_j &= a_j + x_0{}^3 b_{j+3} & j &= n-3, \cdots, 0
\end{aligned}
$$
(4.7)

which can be expressed as

$$p(x_0) = a_0 + x_0{}^3[a_3 + x_0{}^3(a_6 + \cdots)]$$
$$+ x_0\{a_1 + x_0{}^3[a_4 + x_0{}^3(a_7 + \cdots)]\}$$
$$+ x_0{}^2\{a_2 + x_0{}^3[a_5 + x_0{}^3(a_8 + \cdots)]\}. \tag{4.8}$$

For a computer with three parallel arithmetic units a schedule can be constructed which evaluates $p(x_0)$ in a total time of

$$T_3 = (n - \lfloor n/3 \rfloor - \lceil n/3 \rceil + 1)t_a + (\lceil n/3 \rceil + 2)t_m , \tag{4.9}$$

where $\lceil y \rceil$ is the smallest integer greater than or equal to y and it is assumed that $t_m \geqq t_a$. If $t_m = t_a = t$ then

$$T^3 = (n - \lfloor n/3 \rfloor + 3)t \quad \text{(See Appendix IV)}. \tag{4.10}$$

The utilization in the latter case is

$$U_3 = \frac{2n + 2}{3(n - \lfloor n/3 \rfloor + 3)} \tag{4.11}$$

which approaches 1 for large n.

Consider now the parallel computer described in Section 4A but with three parallel arithmetic units ($r = 1$). The number of time cycles required to evaluate $p(x_0)$ is still of the order $2n$, and the maximum utilization for large n is $2/3$. That is to say, the addition of the third arithmetic unit does not decrease the computing time. This is due to the fact that when one of the three arithmetic units has completed an addition or multiplication it must stand idle for one time cycle awaiting a memory access. This delay is necessary because there are now three units accessing the memory and only one may have access at any given time.

On the other hand, if $r = 2$ (addition and multiplication require two time cycles each) then the time requirement is approximately one-third that of a computer with a single arithmetic unit, and the limiting utilization is 1.

• C. *Fourth-order Horner's rule*

A similar analysis may be given for the fourth-order Horner's rule. The schedule using this rule on a computer with four parallel arithmetic units requires a computing time of

$$T_4 = (\lfloor n/4 \rfloor + 2)t_a + (\lceil n/4 \rceil + 2)t_m , \tag{4.12}$$

where again $t_m \geqq t_a$.

For $t_a = t_m = t$ this becomes

$$T_4 = (\lfloor n/4 \rfloor + \lceil n/4 \rceil + 4)t \tag{4.13}$$

and the utilization then is

$$U_4 = \frac{2n + 3}{4(\lceil n/4 \rceil + \lfloor n/4 \rfloor + 4)} .$$

Again for the parallel computer described in Section 4A ($r = 1$) but with *four* parallel arithmetic units, the number of time cycles required to evaluate $p(x_0)$ is of the order of $2n$. In this case each unit is idle two time cycles after each arithmetic operation awaiting a memory access, and the maximum utilization is 0.5. Not until $r \geq 3$ will it be profitable time-wise to add the fourth unit and use the fourth-order rule.

5. Use of sequential computers

The discussion thus far has been directed toward polynomial evaluation on parallel computers with multiple arithmetic units. The generalized Horner's rule also offers certain advantages for computation on sequential computers with a single arithmetic unit.

Notice from (3.1) that

$$p(\theta_j x_0) = r(\theta_j x_0) ,\tag{5.1}$$

where

$$r(x) = b_{k-1} x^{k-1} + \cdots + b_1 x + b_0\tag{5.2}$$

and θ_j are the kth roots of unity. Since θ_j is, in general, a complex number, additional $k - 1$ multiplications and $k - 1$ additions are all that are required to evaluate $p(\theta_j x_0)$ for any j once the coefficients $b_{k-1}, \cdots, b_0$ have been computed. All of the k values of $p(\theta_j x_0)$ can be obtained in $n + k(k - 1)$ multiplications and $n + (k - 1)^2$ additions. In contrast, k applications of the first-order rule for complex $\theta_j x_0$ would require $n + 2n(k - 1)$ multiplications and a like number of additions.

Of particular interest is the case where $k = 2$. Then

$$p(-x_0) = b_0 - b_1 x_0 .\tag{5.3}$$

Thus if $p(x_0)$ has been computed using the second-order Horner's rule, equations (4.1) and (4.2), then $p(-x_0)$ is obtained by one addition and no multiplications.

The evaluation of $p(x_0)$ *and* $p(-x_0)$ using the second-order Horner's rule requires a total of $n + 1$ multiplications and $n + 1$ additions. By way of comparison, the first-order Horner's rule requires $2n$ multiplications and $2n$ additions.

In this same connection consider the problem of evaluating the definite integral of a rational function by Gauss quadrature.

$$\int_{-1}^{1} \frac{p(x)}{q(x)}\, dx = \sum_{i \neq 1}^{N} W_i \frac{p(x_i)}{q(x_i)} ,\tag{5.4}$$

where x_i are the roots of the Legendre polynomial of degree N

$$P_N(x) = \frac{1}{2^N N!} \frac{d^N}{dx^N} (x^2 - 1)^N$$

and the weights w_i are defined as

$$w_i = \frac{1}{\prod\limits_{\substack{j=1 \\ j \neq i}}^{N} (x_i - x_i)} \int_{-1}^{1} \prod\limits_{\substack{j=1 \\ j \neq i}}^{N} (t - x_i)\, dt .$$

Here $p(x)$ and $q(x)$ will be assumed to be polynomials of degree n and m, respectively.

The roots x_i of the Legendre polynomial $P_N(x)$ are symmetrically placed about the origin. To evaluate the right-hand member of (5.4) then $p(x_i)$, $q(x_i)$ and $p(-x_i)$, $q(-x_i)$ are required. Using the first-order Horner's rule requires

$N(m + n + 1)$	multiplications
$N(m + n + 1) - 1$	additions
N	divisions.

On the other hand, using the second-order Horner's rule requires

$(N - \lfloor N/2 \rfloor)(m + n + 1) + 3 \cdot \lfloor N/2 \rfloor$	multiplications
$(N - \lfloor N/2 \rfloor)(m + n) + N - 1$	additions
N	divisions.

For example, for $m = n = 4$ and $N = 10$ the number of arithmetic operations are

	First-order rule	Second-order rule
Multiplications	90	60
Additions	89	49
Divisions	10	10

6. Conclusions and remarks

The schedules for the evaluation of a polynomial in minimum time may be classified as follows:

If the number of parallel arithmetic units, $k \geq 1$, is relatively small compared with the degree of the polynomial, n, then the kth-order Horner's rule should be used.

If the number of arithmetic units, k, is of the same order as the degree of the polynomial, n, then the generalization due to Estrin, equations (3.5) to (3.7), should be used.

These are, however, only general guides, and a detailed analysis of the schedule on the particular computer is necessary to assure efficient use. In particular, the timing of the memory accesses will dictate the number of parallel units which can be used advantageously, and hence the computational rule to be used. In the example considered in Section 4, only $r + 1$ arithmetic units could be used if the arithmetic operations required r times the time required by the memory accesses.

Regard'ess of the number of parallel arithmetic units, the kth-order Horner's rule will complete some computations in minimum time. Evaluation of the definite integral of a rational function by Gauss quadrature, for example, can be most quickly computed by using an even-order Horner's rule as demonstrated in Section 5. Other problems requiring the evaluation of the same polynomial at values proportional to the kth roots of unity can be similarly speeded up by use of the kth-order rule.

Appendix I: Schedule for second-order Horner's rule

The schedule of operations on two identical arithmetic units which operate in parallel using the second-order Horner's rule is:

Step number	Unit 1	Unit 2
1	$x_0 \cdot x0$	Idle
2	$x_0^2 \cdot a_n$	$x_0^2 \cdot a_{n-1}$
3	$a_{n-2} + (a_n x_0^2) = b_{n-2}$	$a_{n-3} + (a_{n-1}x_0^2) = b_{n+3}$
.	.	.
.	.	.
.	.	.
.	.	.

For n even

Step number	Unit 1	Unit 2
$n-1$	$a_2 + (b_4 x_0^2) = b_2$	$a_1 + (b_3 x_0^2) = b_1$
n	$x_0^2 \cdot b_2$	$x_0 \cdot b_1$
$n+1$	$a_0 + (b_2 x_0^2) = b_0$	Idle
$n+2$	$b_0 + (b_1 x_0) = p(x_0)$	Idle

For n odd

Step number	Unit 1	Unit 2
$n-1$	$x_0^2 \cdot b_3$	$x_0^2 \cdot b_2$
n	$a_1 + (b_3 x_0^2) = b_1$	$a_0 + (b_2 x_0^2) = b_0$
$n+1$	$x_0 \cdot b_1$	Idle
$n+2$	$b_0 + (b_1 x_0) = p(x_0)$	Idle

Appendix II: Description of a parallel computer

Consider a computer with k identical arithmetic units which operate in parallel and with one memory which is available to all arithmetic units. Only one of the arithmetic units may have access to the memory at any given time. For example, if one unit is in the process of storing a word and a second unit then requests a word from memory, the second unit must wait until the store operation is completed.

The individual arithmetic units operate in the following way: Each unit possesses two registers, called A and B, which may be loaded from memory by the instruction FETCH (F) or stored into memory by the instruction STORE (S). The fetch instruction does not destroy the memory contents, nor oes the store instruction destroy the register contents. The instruction ᴜʟᴛɪᴘʟʏ (M) forms the product of the contents of registers A and B and laces the result in register A. Similarly, the instruction ᴀᴅᴅ (A) places the ım of the contents of the two registers in register A.

The sᴛᴏʀᴇ and ғᴇᴛᴄʜ instructions require one cycle of time, and the ᴜʟᴛɪᴘʟʏ and ᴀᴅᴅ instructions each require r cycles of time.

The following table of instructions will be used:

— A, m	Fetch the contents of memory location m in memory to register A. Leave location m unaltered.
— B, m	Fetch the contents of memory location m in memory register B. Leave location m unaltered.
— A, m	Store the contents of register A in location m of memory. Leave register A unaltered.
I, —	Multiply the contents of registers A and B and place the product in register A.
, —	Add the contents of registers A and B and place the sum in register A.

ppendix III: A program for a parallel computer with two arithmetic units

Consider a computer of the type described in Appendix II with two arithmetic units and with $r = 1$. The following program evaluates an nth degree polynomial $p(x) = a_0 + a_1 x + \cdots + a_n x^n$ using the second-order Horner's ule.

Let $a_0, a_1, \cdots, a_n$ be stored in memory locations $A, A + 1, \cdots, A + N$ respectively, and let x_0 be stored in memory location X.

Time cycle	Unit 1	Unit 2
1	$F - A, X$	Idle
2	$F - B, X$	Idle
3	$M, -$	Idle
4	$S - A, X2$	Idle
5	Idle	$F - A, X2$
6	Idle	$F - B, A + N - 1$
7	$F - B, A + N$	$M, -$
8	$M, -$	$F - B, A + N - 3$
9	$F - B, A + N - 2$	$A, -$
10	$A, -$	$F - B, X2$
11	$F - B, X2$	$M, -$
.	.	.
.	.	.

	Time cycle	Unit 1	Unit 2
For n even	$2n$	$M, -$	$F - B, A + 1$
	$2n + 1$	$F - B, A + 2$	$A, -$
	$2n + 2$	$A, -$	$F - B, X$
	$2n + 3$	$F - B, X2$	$M, -$
	$2n + 4$	$M, -$	$S - A, R$
	$2n + 5$	$F - B, A$	Idle
	$2n + 6$	$A, -$	Idle
	$2n + 7$	$F - B, R$	Idle
	$2n + 8$	$A, -$	Idle
	$2n + 9$	$S - A, R$	Idle
For n odd	$2n$	$A, -$	$F - B, X2$
	$2n + 1$	$F - B, X2$	$M, -$
	$2n + 2$	$M, -$	$F - B, A$
	$2n + 3$	$F - B, A + 1$	$A, -$
	$2n + 4$	$A, -$	$S - A, R$
	$2n + 5$	$F - B, X$	Idle
	$2n + 6$	$M, -$	Idle
	$2n + 7$	$F - B, R$	Idle
	$2n + 8$	$A, -$	Idle
	$2n + 9$	$S - A, R$	Idle

The value of $p(x_0)$ is stored in memory location R.

Appendix IV: Schedule for third-order Horner's rule

The schedule of operations on three identical arithmetic units which operate in parallel using the third-order Horner's rule is:

Step Number	Unit 1	Unit 2	Unit 3
1	$x_0 \cdot x_0^2$	Idle	Idle
2	$x_0 \cdot x_0$	Idle	Idle
3	$a_n \cdot x_0^3$	$a_{n-1} \cdot x_0^3$	$a_{n-2} \cdot x_0^3$
4	$a_{n-3} + (a_n x_0^3) = b_{n-3}$	$a_{n-4} + (a_{n-1} x_0^3)$ $= b_{n-4}$	$a_{n-5} + (a_{n-2} x_0^3)$ $= b_{n-5}$
.	.	.	.
.	.	.	.
.	.	.	.

Case 1, $n = 3m$

	Unit 1	Unit 2	Unit 3
$2m$	$a_3 + (b_6 x_0^3) = b_3$	$a_2 + (b_5 x_0^3) = b_2$	$a_1 + (b_4 x_0^3) = b_1$
$2m + 1$	$b_3 \cdot x_0^3$	$b_2 \cdot x_0^2$	$b_1 \cdot x_0$
$2m + 2$	$a_0 + (b_3 x_0^3) = b_0$	$(b_1 x_0) + (b_2 x_0^2)$	Idle
$2m + 3$	$b_0 + (b_1 x_0 + b_2 x_0^2)$ $= p(x_0)$	Idle	Idle

Case 2, $n = 3m + 1$

$2m$	$a_4 + (b_7x_0{}^3) = b_4$	$a_3 + (b_6x_0{}^3) = b_3$	$a_2 + (b_4x_0{}^3) = b_2$
$2m + 1$	$b_4 \cdot x_0{}^3$	$b_3 \cdot x_0{}^3$	$b_2 \cdot x_0{}^2$
$2m + 2$	$a_1 + (b_4x_0{}^3) = b_1$	$a_0 + (b_3x_0{}^3) = b_0$	Idle
$2m + 3$	$b_1 \cdot x_0$	$b_0 + b_2x_0{}^2$	Idle
$2m + 4$	$b_1x_0 + (b_0 + b_2x_0{}^2)$	Idle	Idle
	$= p(x_0)$		

Case 3, $n = 3m + 2$

$2m$	$a_5 + (b_8x_0{}^3) = b_5$	$a_4 + (b_7x_0{}^3) = b_4$	$a_3 + (b_6x_0{}^3) = b_3$
$2m + 1$	$b_5 \cdot x_0{}^3$	$b_4 \cdot x_0{}^3$	$b_3 \cdot x_0{}^3$
$2m + 2$	$a_2 + (b_5x_0{}^3) = b_2$	$a_1 + (b_4x_0{}^3) = b_1$	$a_0 + (b_3x_0{}^3) = b_0$
$2m + 3$	$b_2 \cdot x_0{}^2$	$b_1 \cdot x_0$	Idle
$2m + 4$	$(b_1x_0) + (b_2x_0{}^2)$	Idle	Idle
$2m + 5$	$b_0 + (b_1x_0 + b_2x_0{}^2)$	Idle	Idle
	$= p(x_0)$		

In all three cases the total number of time steps is:

$$n - \lfloor n/3 \rfloor + 3.$$

References

1. A. M. Ostrowski, "On Two Problems in Abstract Algebra Connected With Horner's Rule," in *Studies in Mathematics and Mechanics Presented to Richard von Mises*, Academic Press, 1954, pp. 40–48.
2. T. S. Motzkin, "Evaluation of Polynomials," *Bull. Amer. Math. Soc.*, **61**, 163 (1955).
3. G. Estrin, "Organization of Computer Systems—The Fixed Plus Variable Structure Computer," *Proceedings Western Joint Computer Conference*, May, 1960, pp. 33–40.
4. W. S. Dorn, N. C. Hsu and T. J. Rivlin, *Some Mathematical Problems in Parallel Computation*, IBM Research Report (forthcoming).

22

The Legal Report

Though it would be foolish to conjecture which of the professions words are most important to, law must certainly be high on any such list. A whole conception of law involves the written record, set down in permanent form for all to read and interpret. It is ironical that contemporary law school graduates have received only cursory, if any, formal training in report writing.

In the conduct of their everyday affairs, advocates write formal reports mainly of two sorts, briefs and memoranda of law. Then there is the special legal report which offers an opinion on matters of broad principle and doctrine—tracing the precedents, examining the immediate foreground, and projecting the effects.

The brief, of course, consists of written legal argument upon the questions before the court for decision. The trial brief for counsel is prepared by the advocate for his own edification and guidance; it is chiefly a mapping of strategy. Of necessity and by tradition, the trial brief consists of the table of contents and authorities cited, a statement of facts, a digest of the pleadings, the grounds for challenging the jury and jurors, the evidence required to establish the case, a list of witnesses and exhibits, a digest or statement of witnesses, the proof required by opposing counsel and the key questions in aid of cross-examination, a brief on the legal questions presented, and requested charges to the jury.

The appellate brief must contain the essential facts of the client's case; the issues raised on the appeal; the questions of law involved; the principles of law, discussed under appropriate points, that the advocate maintains governs the determination of issues; and the desired particular application by the court of governing legal principles in the manner urged by the advocate. As essential components, the foregoing parts are set forth as the title, the preliminary statement, the questions presented, the statement of facts, the argument, the conclusion, and the signature of the lawyer.

Memoranda of law are generally of two sorts: those prepared by the lawyer for the purpose of advising a client on a legal question concerning which the client has made inquiry, and those prepared for submission to a court on a legal question that may have arisen during a trial. The office memorandum, the first kind, contains a title, the question presented, a brief answer, the statement of facts, a discussion, and a conclusion. The court memorandum of law consists of the title, the question presented, the argument, and the conclusion.

The special legal report, which might be termed a review or a survey of the law, though it is not of the routine nature of a brief or a memorandum, figures heavily in the thinking of an advocate who may be involved in a particular application of the broad principle. The same

322

THE PROBLEM OF MALAPPORTIONMENT:
A SYMPOSIUM ON BAKER v. CARR

Reprinted from the Yale Law Journal
Volume 72, Number 1, November 1962
Copyright 1962

* Reproduced with permission of *Yale Law Journal,* 72:64 (November) 1962. This report was one of several contributed by various authorities to a general symposium on malapportionment.

sense of logical organization and the same unbending, stern zeal for accuracy and precision must illuminate this important legal report.

Malapportionment and Judicial Power

THOMAS I. EMERSON†

THE Supreme Court's decision in *Baker v. Carr*[1] promises to be one of the most important of the century. Like the segregation decisions,[2] it brings constitutional principles and judicial institutions to the solution of one of the fundamental problems of American society. Unlike the decisions in the Smith and McCarran Act cases,[3] which have no future in the democratic process, it moves broadly in the direction of developing and supporting procedures necessary for the effective operation of a modern democratic system. The decision is of interest and significance on various levels. The major ones are (1) its importance in terms of legal doctrine; (2) its bearing on the actual solution of the malapportionment problem; and (3) its broader implications concerning the role of law and legal institutions in the democratic process.

I. IMPLICATIONS FOR LEGAL DOCTRINE

The failure of five Justices to agree upon an opinion necessarily limits the significance of *Baker v. Carr* in doctrinal terms. Moreover, the strong dissent of Justices Frankfurter and Harlan, and the grudging acquiescence of Justices Clark and Stewart, confirmed the close division of the Court over issues of the sort presented. The retirement of Justices Whittaker and Frankfurter, and their replacement by Justices White and Goldberg, whose constitutional views have not yet become apparent, makes speculation on the Court's future direction additionally hazardous. Nevertheless, the decision in *Baker v. Carr* does throw some light upon possible developments in the three main legal doctrines raised in the case: equal protection, justiciability, and the guaranty clause.

In applying the broad constitutional requirement of equal protection of the laws, the Supreme Court has, with a few sharp exceptions, moved with the utmost caution. The chief exception is, of course, in the area of racial discrimination. Here the Court, at least since *Brown v. Board of Education*,

---

† Lines Professor of Law, Yale Law School.

This article, with certain additions, is being published simultaneously in *Law in Transition.*

[1] 369 U.S. 186 (1962).

[2] Brown v. Board of Education, 347 U.S. 483 (1954), 349 U.S. 294 (1955).

[3] Dennis v. United States, 341 U.S. 494 (1951). See also, Scales v. United States, 367 U.S. 203 (1961); Communist Party v. Subversive Activities Control Board, 367 U.S. 1 (1961).

has enforced the provision vigorously, even when necessary to extend the doctrine of "state action" to unprecedented and still unforeseen lengths.[4] It has also invoked the principle in the field of criminal procedure, as evidenced by its line of decisions requiring the states to afford equal opportunity for indigent defendants to invoke facilities for appeal.[5] Beyond these limited sectors, however, the Court has traditionally been extremely reluctant to set foot in what has seemed to it the bottomless quagmire of equal protection.[6] All government action involves discrimination between persons affected and those not affected, or between those affected in certain ways and those affected in others. To separate the appropriate from the inappropriate differences in treatment has undoubtedly appeared a dubious exercise in judicial supervision from which the Court has naturally shrunk. Yet the requirement of equal protection of the laws constitutes a fundamental principle of a democratic society, and one more subject to disregard or violation as government controls over society expand. It remains one of the few areas where the courts can legitimately exercise some degree of control over the substantive results of the working of the democratic process. Narrower than substantive due process, which the courts have, quite properly, largely abandoned, an increased supervision over equality of treatment by the state in exercising its manifold powers could become a vital function of our judicial system.

In *Baker v. Carr* a majority of the Court did not, of course, officially reach the merits and hence did not treat the application of the equal protection clause to apportionment cases. But it held that the clause was applicable, in that a "substantial question" was raised under it.[7] And the plain implication of the decision was that an apportionment as seriously distorted as that of Tennessee was most likely a violation of equal protection. Despite the enormously difficult problem of working out standards for utilizing the equal protection provision in apportionment cases—a difficulty the dissenters played to the hilt—the majority felt impelled to enter the field. And, just as in the race discrimination cases the Court found it necessary to give a wholly new meaning to "state action," so here it was not deterred by the novel and dangerous problem of fashioning adequate relief. The fact that the Court was dealing with the right to vote, a fundamental and special area, indicates that one should perhaps not make too much of this new use of the equal protection clause. Yet the decision does suggest that the concept of equal protection may well in the future receive increased attention in its application to other aspects of our national life.

[4] Brown v. Board of Education, 347 U.S. 483 (1954); Burton v. Wilmington Parking Authority, 365 U.S. 715 (1961).

[5] Griffin v. Illinois, 351 U.S. 12 (1956). See also Smith v. Bennett, 365 U.S 708 (1961); Burns v. Ohio, 360 U.S. 252 (1959); Eskridge v. Washington Bd. of Prison Terms & Paroles, 357 U.S. 214 (1958).

[6] See, *e.g.*, McGowan v. Maryland, 366 U.S. 420 (1961); Salsburg v. Maryland, 346 U.S. 545 (1954); Goesaert v. Cleary, 335 U.S. 464 (1948); Kotch v. Board of River Port Pilot Comm'rs, 330 U.S. 552 (1947). *But cf.* Morey v. Doud, 354 U.S. 457 (1957).

[7] 369 U.S. at 198–204.

With respect to the justiciability doctrine, the fact that the Court agreed to decide the apportionment issue is in itself momentous. For it did so in the face of the violently partisan nature of the problem, the elusiveness of standards, the possible repudiation of judicial efforts to frame a remedy, the long line of contrary decisions behind which it could have hidden[8] and much scholarly advice to stick to the "passive virtues."[9] Plainly, the realm of nonjusticiability has been narrowed. It will not be quite the same again.

More specifically, the Court's treatment of the "political question" is likely to result in some crystalization and confirming of that amorphous concept. Mr. Justice Brennan's opinion first eliminates from coverage of the doctrine all matters concerning "the federal judiciary's relationship to the States," limiting it to "the relationship between the judiciary and the coordinate branches of the Federal Government. . . ."[10] It then rejects blanket application of the doctrine to any broad areas of categories of cases, such as "[f]oreign relations," "[d]ates of duration of hostilities," validity of procedures in enacting constitutional amendments or statutes, and "[t]he status of Indian tribes."[11] To the contrary, it stresses "the need for case-by-case inquiry," "the necessity for discriminating inquiry into the precise facts and posture of the particular case, and the impossibility of resolution by any semantic cataloguing."[12] Further, the opinion goes on to enumerate the specific elements which make an issue into a "political question."[13] There is a strong implication that the list given is exclusive. But even if not, the listing compresses the doctrine into a far more rigid form. Hereafter litigants will not be faced with a completely open-ended concept, but will have the opportunity to argue their way out of each individual element. It is to be noted that Justices Clark and Stewart did not question these features of the Brennan opinion, and that Mr. Justice Douglas went beyond.

The Court's handling of the "political question" issue thus has significant implications in other areas. For example, it may well prove important in such matters as the Court's function in dealing with state attempts to invoke martial law, provided no head-on clash between the Court and Congress or the President is involved. Similarly, it may even open up such questions as federal court enforcement of section 2 of the fourteenth amendment, providing for reduction in the congressional representation of states which deny their citizens the right to vote.[14]

Less surely, but potentially of more importance, the decision in *Baker v. Carr* may have significance in the Court's future treatment of the guaranty

[8] Colegrove v. Green, 328 U.S. 549 (1946), and following cases, discussed 369 U.S. at 234–37.

[9] See Bickel, *The Supreme Court, 1960 Term—Foreword: The Passive Virtues,* 75 Harv. L. Rev. 40 (1961).

[10] 369 U.S. at 210.

[11] 369 U.S. at 211–17.

[12] 369 U.S. at 210–11, 217.

[13] Summarized in 369 U.S. at 217.

[14] See Bonfield, *The Right to Vote and Judicial Enforcement of Section Two of the Fourteenth Amendment,* 46 Cornell L.Q. 108 (1960).

clause. The provision in article IV, section 4, guaranteeing each state a republican form of government, was originally designed as a basic feature of our constitutional structure. It was intended to mean more than that the federal government had the power and duty to protect the states against insurrection or invasion, for these protections were included in the same section as separate guaranties. At the time of Dorr's Rebellion in 1841–42 the guaranty clause was invoked as the basis for a claim which would have required the Supreme Court to decide which one of two competing Rhode Island governments was the legitimate one. In *Luther v. Borden*,[15] however, the Court held, in a sweeping opinion, that this issue was non-justiciable. The guaranty clause was utilized after the Civil War as the major constitutional basis for the program of Reconstruction enacted by Congress. But in the following decades the guaranty clause became in practice largely superseded by the fourteenth amendment. In 1912, in *Pacific States Tel. & Tel. Co. v. Oregon*,[16] the guaranty clause was relied upon as a ground for arguing that the Oregon initiative and referendum law was invalid as inconsistent with a republican form of government. The Court, again in a broad opinion, held this issue non-justiciable. Since then the traditional rule has been that all claims presented to the Court under the guaranty clause are non-justiciable.[17]

Mr. Justice Brennan purported to leave guaranty clause doctrine unchanged. But his treatment of the issue may in fact have reopened the question. The Brennan opinion does not take the position that the guaranty clause is to be interpreted as vesting enforcement only in Congress or the Executive. On the contrary, it expressly states that the sole reason the guaranty clause is not enforceable by the courts is that the issues raised under it are "political questions."[18] Mr. Justice Frankfurter agreed.[19] But since Mr. Brennan repudiates the notion that "political questions" are to be determined by blanket categories and makes clear that each case must be determined on its own facts, it would seem that the issue of justiciability

---

[15] 48 U.S. (7 How.) 1 (1849).

[16] 223 U.S. (1912).

[17] The rule presumably does not mean that action taken by Congress or the President upon the basis of the guaranty clause is not subject to any review whatever by the courts; this would allow the legislative and executive branches, through the mere formality of invoking the clause, to evade judicial review and, in fact, would come close to destroying the whole institution of judicial review. Indeed, in Coyle v. Smith, 221 U.S. 559 (1911), the Supreme Court held unconstitutional an attempt by Congress, relying on the guaranty clause, to specify the location of Oklahoma's capital as a condition of admission to the Union. See also 369 U.S. at 226 n.53. But the extent of review by the Supreme Court over the exercise of power by the other branches in reliance on the guaranty clause has never been clarified.

For an historical account of the guaranty clause, see Bonfield *The Guarantee Clause of Article IV, Section 4: A Study in Constitutional Desuetude*, 46 MINN. L. REV. 513 (1962).

[18] 369 U.S. at 218, 228–29.

[19] 369 U.S. at 297.

under the guaranty clause would likewise tu:.: on whether the essential elements of a "political question" are present in any particular case. Furthermore, Mr. Justice Brennan concedes that a question of republican form of government does not always become a political one by reason of "the lack of criteria" for judgment.[20] Once these two objections are eliminated, it is hard to see why the Court should not treat questions under the guaranty clause the same as other alleged "political questions." On this view, the Court would hold guaranty clause cases non-justiciable only where a decision would involve a direct clash with Congress or the President, or involve one of the other elements of a "political question" listed by Mr. Justice Brennan. Clearly Mr. Justice Brennan did not draw this conclusion. But it seems implicit in his analysis. The other Justices forming the majority did not challenge this approach. And Mr. Justice Douglas was obviously thinking in these terms.[21]

For these reasons it appears possible that the Court might in the future consider apportionment issues under the guaranty clause. As we argue later, there would be many advantages in doing so. Beyond this, were the Court to entertain claims under the guaranty clause, in cases where none of the Brennan elements of a "political question" were present, it would open up an important new line of constitutional growth. While the original purpose of the guaranty clause was primarily to assure that the states did not take on an aristocratic, monarchistic, or despotic form of government, the interpretation of republican form of government in the light of modern developments would extend the application of the provision to numerous significant areas. Thus, issues such as the closing of public schools might be dealt with in terms of maintaining a republican form of government. Such a development of constitutional doctrine would be entirely consistent with the Court's current role as an institution for supporting and vitalizing the mechanisms of the democratic process without undertaking to supervise the results reached by that process.[22]

II. Extent of Solution of the Apportionment Problem

What does *Baver v. Carr* portend as to the Supreme Court's handling of the apportionment problem when it reaches the merits? Will the Court confine itself to certain kinds of cases? What standards will it apply in determining the validity of an apportionment system? What will be the nature of the remedy decreed? And to what extent is judicial action likely to solve or alleviate the basic problem?

It would be foolhardy to attempt detailed answers to these questions. No one is now in possession of all the facts. The issues are varied and complex;

[20] 369 U.S. at 222–23 n.48.

[21] 369 U.S. at 242–43 n.2. For an elaboration of this argument, see Bonfield, *Baker v. Carr: New Light on the Guarantee of Republican Government*, 50 Calif. L. Rev. 245, 246–52 (1962).

[22] On the current potential of the guaranty clause, see Bonfield, *supra* note 17, at 560–69.

many cannot now be clearly defined or anticipated. The degree to which state political machinery is capable of reforming itself cannot be known. Public response, and hence the effective power of the Supreme Court, is not fully foreseeable. The ultimate solution, if one is ever completely achieved, must be hammered out by a long process of discussion and compromise in accordance with the democratic tradition. At most, therefore, it is possible to note some of the major issues, consider some tentative solutions, and perhaps indicate the general direction of events.

A. Types of Situations Open to Judicial Consideration

Baker v. Carr involved (1) state legislative districts; (2) state constitutional provisions basing apportionment in both houses roughly on equal population, the apportionment to be made by the legislature on a decennial basis; (3) failure by the legislature to reapportion over a long period of years; and (4) no available method, other than action by the legislature, by which the constitutional mandate could be carried out. There is nothing in the decision to indicate, however, that a justiciable constitutional cause of action will be found only where all these elements are present.

The two other situations in which a claimed malapportionment of state legislative districts might occur would clearly seem to fall within the principles enunciated by the decision. Where the asserted inequality arises from affirmative action of the legislature, rather than failure to act, the case for judicial review would appear even more plain. Indeed, here the problem of devising a remedy may be less difficult. Where the state constitution itself creates the alleged malapportionment—the so-called *de jure* case—no additional theoretical problems are presented. It is immaterial whether state action denying equal protection derives from statutory or constitutional sources. And, while the framing of a remedy might be more troublesome, it is unlikely that such difficulties would be sufficiently greater to alter the Court's position. The remand of the Michigan and New York cases indicates that the *de jure* situation will also reach decision on the merits.[23]

With regard to inequality in congressional districts, there is language in the Brennan opinion which might suggest that *Baker v. Carr* is not decisive on the issue of justiciability. As already mentioned, the opinion takes pains to point out that the doctrine of "political questions" does not apply to relations of the federal courts to the states, but rather is a matter of the relationships between the coordinate branches of the federal government.[24] And in the case of congressional districts, Congress enters the picture under its power to determine the qualifications and supervise the election of its own members. Yet it seems most unlikely that the Supreme Court will refuse to entertain cases of this nature. The possibility of open conflict with Congress is remote. Practical remedies, as will be seen shortly, are more readily avail-

[23] WMCA, Inc. v. Simon, 370 U.S. 190 (1962); Scholle v. Hare, 369 U.S. 429 (1962).

[24] See text at note 10 *supra*.

able. *Colegrove v. Green*,[25] the main obstacle to the Court's new position, was not distinguished on this ground. Moreover, the momentum engendered by *Baker v. Carr* would seem to assure that the Court will not go out of its way to create distinctions that would in practice appear entirely artificial, imposing greater restrictions on districting state legislative seats than congressional seats. Finally, Mr. Justice Brennan expressly declared, speaking for three members of the Court, that prior cases "settled the issue in favor of justiciability of questions of congressional redistricting."[26]

Nor does there seem to be any doubt that the principles of *Baker v. Carr* are applicable to primary elections. Under the *Classic* case and the white primary cases primaries are treated as integral parts of the election process and equally subject to the requirements of the fourteenth amendment.[27]

There remain for consideration those situations in which a remedy other than through action of the state legislature itself might be available. In the few states where statutes provide for apportionment by administrative commission or similar device, the Supreme Court will undoubtedly insist upon exhaustion of state administrative remedies before federal relief can be sought. And in certain cases where doubtful questions of interpretation of state constitutional provisions are involved, the Court might require state judicial remedies to be pursued. Otherwise, there would appear to be little justification for the Court to refuse consideration of the merits on the ground that other remedies are available. Individual rights accruing under the equal protection clause are not normally dependent upon exhaustion of state judicial remedies. Relief by way of initiative and referendum laws, available in some states, is too cumbersome and uncertain to serve as the basis of any doctrine of exhaustion. The difficulty under such procedures of framing a detailed constitutional amendment or statute acceptable to a majority of voters, the lack of opportunity for amending or compromising the initial proposal, the effort and expense of collecting a large number of valid signatures, and similar inflexibilities and technicalities render such devices of dubious practicality.[28] Similar considerations apply to state constitutional provisions for popular initiative in calling a constitutional convention. It is to be noted that only Mr. Justice Clark put any stress on the absence of other forms of relief. At most the existence of such devices might be one factor to be considered in determining whether to afford discretionary equitable relief; it should scarcely be decisive of the issue.

In sum, it would seem that *Baker v. Carr* has opened to judicial consideration all aspects of the malapportionment problem, regardless of the source of the claimed inequality.

[25] 328 U.S. 549 (1946).

[26] 369 U.S. at 232. *But cf.* Wesberry v. Vandiver, 206 F. Supp. 276 (N.D.Ga. 1962) (dismissing a congressional district case).

[27] United States v. Classic, 313 U.S. 299 (1941); Terry v. Adams, 345 U.S. 461 (1953).

[28] See, for example, the problems of securing relief through the initiative in Oklahoma, recited in the amicus brief filed by the Governor of Oklahoma in *Baker v. Carr*, at pp. 14–17.

B. *Standards*

The formulation of "judicially manageable" standards for decision of future cases on the merits poses a difficult and intriguing problem. The majority in *Baker v. Carr* did not undertake to solve it, and those Justices who discussed the question were in agreement only on the proposition that the equal protection clause prohibits "invidious discrimination." Efforts by lower courts and commentators to work out an acceptable formula have not progressed very far. The issue will yield to solution only on a case-by-case basis.

Certain aspects of the problem, however, would not appear too difficult. In a case, such as *Baker v. Carr* itself, where the state constitution provides for legislative districts of roughly equal population, either in both houses or only one, the failure by the legislature to maintain such districts would constitute a classic form of denial of equal protection. The case would be no different from any other in which state officials administered state law on a discriminatory basis.[29] The standard for complying with the equal protection clause would therefore be the creation of legislative districts consisting of substantially equal number of voters. Variations by reason of observing county lines, handling fractions, and the like would exist, but only to the extent necessary to meet practical problems. According to expert estimates such variations should not exceed ten to fifteen per cent. In a case of this nature, in short, there is no reason why the Supreme Court should not require the state to adhere to the basic requirements of the state constitution.[30]

The standard applicable to congressional districting would likewise not appear to involve any great difficulty. The federal constitution, particularly in providing that members of the House of Representatives are to be elected by "the People of the several States," would not seem to contemplate that in choosing such representatives the vote of one qualified citizen should carry substantially less weight than that of another.[31] Certainly it is the general expectation that congressional districts be formed of roughly equal population. The Supreme Court may therefore properly hold that the creation of congressional districts of unequal voting strength constitutes a denial of equal protection. And the standard for measuring adherence to this constitutional requirement is simply that the districts be, within practical limits, equal in population.

[29] See, *e.g.*, Snowden v. Hughes, 321 U.S. 1 (1944).

[30] Justices Frankfurter and Harlan argued in *Baker v. Carr* that the fact that the Tennessee apportionment was in violation of the Tennessee Constitution did not in itself constitute a violation of the equal protection clause. 369 U.S. at 325–27, 332. It is difficult to follow this reasoning. It is true that a state constitutional provision creating unequal districts might violate equal protection, just as a statute would, and in this sense the distinction between constitution and statute is immaterial. But it does not follow that a statute denying rights established by the state constitution might not constitute a separate and different violation of the equal protection clause.

[31] Art. I, § 2.

Once the Court gets involved beyond this point, however, the difficulties increase. When the state constitution, or the state legislature acting within the state constitution, takes into account factors other than population, the problem of deciding when the inequality in terms of numbers becomes so egregious as to outweigh the value of the other factors, thereby becoming "invidious discrimination," is not easily answered.

At the outset, one must ask the question whether this problem is not better conceived as an issue of republican form of government than of equal protection. There is much force in Mr. Justice Frankfurter's argument that equal protection implies some basic standard from which to measure deviation, and that the determination of this standard is essentially a question of republican form of government.[32] In any event there can be little doubt that the Court, in seeking a solution of the apportionment problem, will actually be thinking in terms of republican form of government. That concept is indeed well designed for coping with the question. Historically the idea of a *republican* form of government was closely tied in with the system of legislative representation; it has become even more so today as the right to the franchise has widened. On the other hand, the equal protection requirement is limited by the doctrine that the state is entitled to make a "reasonable classification." But, as Mr. Justice Harlan comes close to showing, the application of "reasonable classification" is hardly adequate to solve the apportionment problem and, in this area, will have to be badly strained or abandoned. Thus the republican form of government concept is both more relevant and more precise. It would certainly serve as a better vehicle through which the Court could articulate and justify its conclusions.[33]

The Court may well, however, hesitate to add to its burdens by making such a seemingly radical departure as to revive the guaranty clause. And it must be admitted that all that it needs, or possibly wants, to do can be crammed within the formula of "invidious discrimination." We must therefore examine the problem on the assumption that the Court adheres to the equal protection formulation.

It has been urged that the Court, in applying the equal protection clause, should rule out all factors which have the effect of creating any substantial deviation from a system of legislative districts consisting of equal population. This position has been taken by the American Civil Liberties Union.[34] There is much to be said in its favor. When one comes to examine the factors other than population—and there are actually far fewer than the "host" of which Mr. Justice Frankfurter speaks—the argument for giving them weight in a modern system of state apportionment is far from persuasive. The major ones are recognition of political subdivisions, weight according to density of population, representation of various communities of interest, and historical factors. Others, such as stability of the apportion-

---

[32] 369 U.S. at 299–301.

[33] For further elaboration of the argument, see the two Bonfield articles, *supra* notes 17 and 21.

[34] American Civil Liberties Union Weekly Bulletin, Mar. 20, 1961, pp. 1–2.

ent system, retaining honored incumbents, and the like are purely sec-
ndary. It is not possible here to analyze these various factors in detail but
rious questions can be raised as to their value in outweighing the right
f each citizen to an equal vote in electing his state legislature.

Thus, recognition of political subdivisions is not a matter of first im-
ortance today in the internal affairs of a state. There is no real analogy
ere to the position of the states at the time of framing the federal con-
itution, when claims of sovereignty forced acceptance of a system of two
enators from each state. Moreover, subdivisional lines can be respected
ithout unduly distorting the voting population of the districts, provided
ere is no requirement that each subdivision have a whole vote. The argu-
ent for giving greater weight to areas of thin population is that density
f population gives an advantage in political organization. But the revolu-
on in transportation and communication, and the phenomenal growth of
rganization generally, have radically altered this situation. Indeed, it can
e argued that social pressures leading to political cohesion are more likely
o be found in rural than urban areas, and that legislators representing the
eady clientele of rural areas have advantages over their colleagues represent-
g more volatile urban constituencies. The theory that any particular "com-
unity of interest" should be given greater representation in the state legis-
ture than its numbers entitle it to is essentially inconsistent with our
otions of democratic process. The theory is little more than a throwback
o the days of property-holding qualifications on the right to vote. The
dvantages of veto power potential and protection of minority rights are
fforded through other features of our political system. The historical argu-
ent, developed at great length by Mr. Justice Frankfurter, is at first sight
mpressive. But actually it proves too much, for it assumes the validity of
olitical ideas and practices long since repudiated. The historical trend
as been entirely in favor of equality of the franchise.

It will be urged that considerations of this nature are matters of policy
or legislatures and the framers of constitutional amendments, not for
ourts. This is in part true. And it is perhaps doubtful that such arguments,
ven if fully supported by empirical evidence, will persuade the Supreme
ourt in the near future to establish a standard of equal protection based
pon voting population alone. Nevertheless, it is relevant to the Court's func-
on that the argument for representation founded upon such other factors is
 dubious one. For, as we point out later, unless the Court adopts some
echanical formula of allowable deviation in apportionment cases, it will
e forced into some consideration of the validity and weight of the reasons
ffered for qualifying the underlying right to equality in voting. If the
ropositions here advanced are sound, the Court should at least scrutinize
on-population factors with care and require proponents of such a system
o establish their case with precision. To this extent the doctrine that the
urden of establishing unconstitutionality rests upon those challenging the
egislative classification should be modified.

If we turn to less speculative matters, the problem still remains of giving
ome content to the test of "invidious discrimination." It seems clear that

the Court will not adopt Mr. Justice Harlan's rule of a scintilla of r
tionality.[35] As Mr. Justice Harlan himself demonstrates, such a doctri
would never, or hardly ever, result in a decision that the equal protecti
clause had been violated. It is likewise very doubtful that a majority of t
Court will accept Mr. Justice Clark's "crazy quilt"[36] principle, or even t
"without-any-possible-justification-in-rationality" formula[37] of Mr. Justi
Stewart. Such approaches do not go very far toward solving the proble
and the Court seems committed at least to making a serious attempt. Rathe
it is more likely that the Court will look at the situation in terms of wheth
or not factors other than population operate so as unduly to subordina
the basic right to equality in exercising the franchise.

What, in practice, would the adoption of some such intermediate formu
mean? In the first place, the Court should refuse to legitimize all facto
that are non-democratic in character. Thus an apportionment system bas
on racial factors would clearly constitute a denial of equal protection. On t
same theory the New Hampshire system, under which senatorial distric
are formed in accordance with the proportion of district taxes paid, *i.e.*, c
the basis of wealth, would appear vulnerable.[38] Very likely an attempte
justification for giving special weight to particular economic or other interes
would fall within the same ban.

Secondly, the Court might accept the proposition that at least one hou
of the legislature must be apportioned on an equal population basis. Th
is the federal system. All but eleven states, at least in theory, now su
stantially meet this requirement.[39] And the average citizen would certain
feel that a system in which neither house was elected on a one-man, one-vo
basis could not be reconciled with equal protection of the laws.

Yet, if the Court stopped here, the apportionment problem would st
be far from settled. It would give a majority of voters a veto power, but
would not assure them legislative strength to take affirmative action. Th
crucial issue, therefore, becomes how far would deviations from a populatio
basis be allowed in the second house. There is probably substantial agre
ment on the chief elements to be considered in measuring the extent
deviation. They are (1) the proportion of the total voters who are ab
to elect a majority of the representatives to that house; and (2) the relativ
value of a vote in the larger districts as compared with the smaller one
measured either by direct comparison or by comparison with an averag
But there is no agreement on the formula for determining at what poi
these discrepancies are sufficiently great to violate the equal protectic
clause.

Various standards have been proposed. In the Georgia county unit ca
the three-judge court formulated the rule that the discrepancy existing wi
respect to any county would be valid if no greater than "the disparity th

[35] 369 U.S. at 336–37, 345–49.
[36] *Id.* at 254.
[37] *Id.* at 265.
[38] N.H. CONST. pt. 2, art. 26.
[39] See BAKER, STATE CONSTITUTIONS: REAPPORTIONMENT 5–8, 63–70 (1960

exists against any state in the most recent electoral college allocation, or under the equal proportions formula for representation of the several states in the Congress. . . ."[40] This formula would apparently make the Georgia county unit system untenable.[41] Mr. Bonfield has suggested that deviation in the first element mentioned above should not exceed that existing at the time of entry of the state into the Union, or that suffered by any state through its representation in the United States Senate, whichever standard is higher.[42] The test of Senate representation would invalidate all state systems in which less than 16.5 per cent of the voters elected a majority of representatives; the historical test would vary with each state but generally would call for more equality than presently exists. A further possibility is that the Court simply accept some fixed percentage of deviation as permissible or impermissible.[43]

It is doubtful that the Supreme Court will accept rigid standards of this nature. If it does not, then it must undertake a more thorough exploration of the merits of each case. It would have to take into account all relevant factors, including the claimed justification for deviations from equal population, and render a general verdict as to whether the system does or does not unduly subordinate equality of voting power. Eventually such a method may come to form a pattern which can be generalized into a more specific standard. Under such an approach, much will depend upon the extent to which the Court is willing to scrutinize the justifications advanced in support of deviations. If the conclusion stated above is correct, that such justifications are not persuasive, the trend of decision would be strongly in the direction of an equal population standard.[44]

It should be noted that the Court's difficulties in devising a standard could be lightened by congressional assistance. The power of Congress to provide specific standards for the creation of congressional districts would not seem open to question. And under the guaranty clause,[45] Congress could also frame standards for state legislative districting. There would be some advantages in action by Congress to this end, for it would permit fuller consideration of policy issues in devising standards and place the prestige of the federal legislature behind the Court's effort to solve the apportionment

[40] Sanders v. Gray, 203 F. Supp. 158, 170 (N.D. Ga. 1962).

[41] N.Y. Times, June 19, 1962, p. 1, col. 2.

[42] Bonfield, *supra* note 21, at 257–62.

[43] See, *e.g.*, *Scholle v. Hare* on remand, in which two of the four majority justices said: "When a legislative apportionment provides districts having more than double the population of others, the constitutional range of discretion is violated." 367 Mich. 176, —, 116 N.W.2d 350, 355 (1962).

[44] We do not here undertake to consider the standard that would be applicable in cases where the populations of voting districts are roughly equal but with district lines gerrymandered to the advantage of one political party. The problems overlap because the professed desire to achieve equal population could be used as a device to achieve an invidious gerrymander. The factors to be taken into account in formulating a standard for dealing with this type of manipulation, however, are somewhat different from those relevant to the equal population issue.

[45] U.S. CONST. art. IV § 4.

problem. Yet the difficulties of formulating adequate standards to cover the varied systems of state legislative apportionment would still remain. And divergence between congressional and judicial views would give rise to still further problems.

C. Remedies

The greatest danger facing the courts in dealing with the question of remedies has been that legislative or executive officials would refuse to comply with remedial decrees. The spectre of open conflict between the courts, "possessed neither of the purse nor the sword," and officials of other branches, fired with partisan zeal and threatened in their very political existence, has continually haunted the judiciary. Actually, these fears have proved groundless. Such conflict did not occur in situations where state courts, before *Baker v. Carr*, undertook to formulate a remedy.[46] And there has been no sign of this sort of opposition in the many cases that have already followed *Baker v. Carr*.[47] In contrast to the hostile response which greeted the segregation decisions in the South, the apportionment decision has met with general support throughout the country and, indeed, has proved to be a highly popular one. The pattern of acceptance thus far demonstrated is likely to become more deeply rooted as time passes and the role of the courts becomes more permanently fixed. In this context the problem of remedies, if not simple, by no means appears insoluble.

Mr. Justice Clark, in his opinion in *Baker v. Carr*, objected to federal courts' assuming jurisdiction of reapportionment cases "in the hope that such a declaration, as is made today, [would] have the direct effect of bringing on legislative action and relieving the courts of the problem of fashioning relief"; in his view "this would be nothing less than blackjacking the Assembly into reapportioning the State."[48] Yet something of this sort must necessarily be a court's initial step. A declaratory judgment or an opinion holding the existing system invalid, with postponement of further decree until the legislature can act, would normally be the court's opening move. Such a procedure has the advantage of placing the burden of affirmative action where it belongs, on the legislative or constitutional amending process, and reserving to the court the veto, modifying and approving function. The possibility of delay is not the all-important factor here that it may be in other types of litigation. And the court, by retaining jurisdiction, can act quickly to render a decision on the validity of the modified system. Many of the district courts confronted with the problem of remedies in the flood of litigation after *Baker v. Carr* have adopted this approach, including those

---

[46] See, *e.g.*, Lewis, *Legislative Apportionment and the Federal Courts*, 71 Harv. L. Rev. 1057, 1066–70, 1087–90 (1958); 369 U.S. at 250 n.5.

[47] For discussion of the cases up to the first week of September, see Goldberg, *The Statistics of Malapportionment*, 72 Yale L.J. 90 (1962). The best source of information concerning current cases is the National Municipal League, 47 East 68 St., New York 21, N.Y.

[48] 369 U.S. at 260.

in Florida, Colorado, Georgia, Pennsylvania, and in the Tennessee case itself on remand.[49]

In this connection, an important issue may be whether modification of a system based on the state constitution can be undertaken by the legislature. The amending process is, in some states, an elaborate one which may take several years to complete. In such circumstances, however, there would seem to be no constitutional reason why the legislature could not, at least temporarily, change the system to meet federal constitutional requirements, pending action by the more time-consuming procedures of amendment.

In order for the initial judicial step to be successful, forcing the job of framing a valid system on the legislature, it is necessary that the court have in reserve some positive form of action which renders its "threat" plausible and exerts the requisite pressure on the legislature to act. Perhaps the most effective instrument for this purpose is the power of the court to order an election-at-large. In the case of congressional districts this weapon is a readily administerable one. The same is true in the county-unit cases, and in fact the district court has already compelled an election-at-large for governor in Georgia.[50] Where the issue concerns state legislative districts, the use of the election-at-large raises more troublesome problems. But as a temporary measure it is entirely feasible, particularly if only one house is involved. The prospect of an election-at-large, in any of these situations, is bound to exert enormous pressure to effectuate a valid apportionment. The forces at work in local machine politics, the expense to local candidates of state-wide elections, the possibility of defeat for the political interests opposing reapportionment (by definition likely to be a minority), and other factors all tend in this direction. The technique of ordering an election-at-large is readily enforceable by decrees directed against state election officials in charge.

The major alternative open to the court, either as a means of forcing action by other institutions of government or as directly resolving the problem, is for the court itself to frame the changes necessary in the apportionment system. In earlier discussion of the problem the notion that a court would affirmatively undertake the task of reapportionment was virtually inconceivable. Mr. Justice Frankfurter reflected this climate of opinion when he observed, "Surely a Federal District Court could not itself remap the State. . . ."[51] But thinking on the subject has moved with unexpected rapidity. Mr.

---

[49] Sobel v. Adams, Civ. No. 182–62–M, S.D. Fla., decided July 23, 1962; Stein v. General Assembly of Colorado, No. 20240, Sup. Ct. of Colo., decided July 9, 1962; Toombs v. Fortson, 205 F. Supp. 248 (N.D. Ga. 1962); Butcher v. Trimarchi, No. 2431, Equity, No. 151, Commonwealth Docket, Court of Common Pleas, Dauphin County, Pa., decided June 13, 1962; Baker v. Carr, 206 F. Supp. 341 (M.D. Tenn. 1962). For more details on these cases see Goldberg, *supra* note 47.

[50] Sanders v. Gray, 203 F. Supp. 158 (N.D. Ga. 1962). *Cf.* N.Y. Times, Sept. 13, 1962, p. 21, col. 4.

A lower court in Kansas has likewise ordered state-wide elections. See Goldberg, *supra* note 47, at 98 n.42.

[51] 369 U.S. at 328.

Justice Clark's concurrence, otherwise not of a radical bent, suggested such a solution. And it has already been utilized by courts in Alabama and Mississippi.[52] To the degree that the standard of equal protection approaches one of equal population the feasibility of this form of remedy increases.

Beyond these methods there are other possibilities available. One is for the court to enjoin election officials in particular counties from conducting an election in which more than a specific number of representatives are to be elected. Another is for the court to act only with respect to one house, retaining jurisdiction as to the other. More radical is the proposal that the court permit elections as before but order a system of weighted voting in the legislature, a favorite device of some political scientists. Other improvisations are possible to fit the particular case. The courts will certainly retain flexibility in devising an appropriate remedy.[53]

All in all, then, the problem of remedies does not seem as difficult of solution as originally appeared. Indeed, the normally rigid judicial process seems about to yield to innovation and ingenuity. Such a development would be in line with the recent expansion of judicial techniques in some other areas, such as the administration of anti-trust decrees and of pupil assignment laws.

D. *The General Prospects for Judicial Solution*

When the decision in *Baker v. Carr* came down, perceptive analysts were careful to point out that the case decided only that the federal courts had jurisdiction in apportionment matters and that the extent to which the courts would actually do something about the apportionment problem was a question for the uncertain future.[54] This warning must still be heeded. Yet an appraisal of the situation in light of the above analysis, and particularly in light of developments since the original decision, indicates that the prospects for substantial reform are bright. The decision certainly opens up all forms of malapportionment to judicial scrutiny. Much will depend upon whether the standards of equal protection adopted move in the direction of assuring one house fully, and the other substantially, apportioned on an equal population basis. For the reasons already given, this should be the trend

---

[52] Sims v. Frink, 205 F. Supp. 245 (M.D. Ala. 1962); Fortner v. Barnett, No. 59,965, Chancery Court, First Judicial District, Hinds County, Miss., decided June 7, 1962. *Cf.* Wisconsin v. Zimmerman, Civ. No. 3540, W.D. Wis., July 3 & Aug. 14, 1962. In the latter case the court appointed a master to draw the reapportionment plan. After hearings, the master recommended dismissal without prejudice to further action after the 1962 elections, a recommendation accepted by the court. See N.Y. Times, July 4, 1962, p. 1, col. 2; July 26, 1962, p. 24, col. 8; Aug. 6, 1962, p. 22, col. 3. See Goldberg, *supra* note 47, at 95.

[53] It has been assumed, probably with justification, that state election laws may be modified by judicial decree in order to conform to constitutional requirements.

[54] See, *e.g.*, Lewis, "Decision on Reapportionment Points Up Urban-Rural Struggle," N.Y. Times, April 1, 1962, § IV, p. 3; Bickel, "The Great Apportionment Case," New Republic, April 9, 1962, p. 13.

of decision. The problem of devising effective remedies can be solved. Popular response has been most favorable. And, in the cases already brought in more than thirty states, judicial response has on the whole been aggressive. But the ultimate outcome, of course, remains uncertain.

III. The Role of Law and Legal Institutions

It will have become clear by now that the main significance of the decision in *Baker v. Carr* lies not in what was actually decided, or in what was expressly said, or even in the promise held forth of assisting in the solution of the malapportionment problem. Rather it lies in the far-reaching implications of the Supreme Court's action with respect to the function of law and legal institutions in modern American life. Essentially the decision marks a momentous step forward in utilizing law and legal principle for the maintenance and invigoration of the democratic structure of our society and in the assumption of a positive role by the Supreme Court in that task. In this respect the decision was indeed a "massive repudiation" of the school of thought of which Mr. Justice Frankfurter has been the intellectual and spiritual leader.

This is not to say that the Supreme Court has abandoned the time-honored forms of the judicial process. On the contrary, Mr. Justice Brennan's opinion is written entirely in terms of technical legal doctrine. To the man from Mars it would surely appear startling that a decision abruptly reversing the whole position of the Court on a vital and fundamental issue of substance should be couched exclusively as a discourse on abstract legalisms of jurisdiction, standing, justiciability and "political questions." Nowhere does Mr. Justice Brennan find it necessary to mention the actual facts or issues at the heart of the problem. Moreover, in the best tradition of the judicial process Mr. Justice Brennan carefully demonstrates that no change has occurred at all, that the outcome is wholly in line with, not to say compelled by, past precedents of the Court. And, again, the Court respects the judicial tradition by deciding only the narrowest possible issue, leaving development of the new area opened up by the decision to future elaboration on a case-by-case basis.

Nevertheless, the meaning of the Court's action is plain. As the nation has been transformed from a relatively individualistic to a highly organized society, and as industrialization, urbanization and bureaucratization have come to be the chief characteristics of the modern way of life, the part played by law and legal institutions in protecting the rights of the individual and maintaining the basic procedures of the democratic process has sharply altered. No longer are such rights and procedures the automatic by-product of economic and political laissez-faire. Their main support must rather rest upon a conscious growth of legal principles and institutions, designed to give strength and vitality to the ideals and mechanisms of democratic living.

The problem of malapportionment is one which peculiarly fits such a judicial role. For the usual methods by which a majority can constitutionally gain its ends are blocked. The issue thus goes deeper than the ordinary questions facing a democratically organized community. It raises a problem which is, in effect, anterior to the operation of the democratic process, namely the form and content of the basic political units which make up the system. The functioning of a democratic state assumes agreement upon this fundamental issue. When disagreement develops, apart from resolution by the judiciary, the only recourse is voluntary relinquishment of political power or recourse to extra-constitutional means. If the disagreement is irreconcilable the result is a break up of the structure in revolution, as happened in the Civil War or on a lesser scale in Dorr's Rebellion. Within the democratic structure it is primarily the courts which are in a sufficiently independent position to effect a rational, peaceful and constitutional solution. In terms of democratic theory, therefore, there are weighty reasons for the courts, despite the manifest difficulties, to utilize their prestige, powers and procedures in attempting to resolve questions of malapportionment.

Thus the decision in *Baker v. Carr* is wholly in line with the direction that the Supreme Court must take and, with some lapses to be sure, has been taking for the past quarter of a century. In the impetus given this crucial development lies the real significance of the decision.

23

The Medical Report

A large proportion of medical reporting is clinical, e.g., it has to do with the experience of doctors in treating patients with particular drugs or by specific methods. Medical reports of laboratory experimentation, that is, of basic research with test animals or primary substances, tend to be technical reports in whatever the appropriate discipline—chemistry, biology, physics, zoology, etc. Reports of both in vivo (human) and in vitro (laboratory) experience are scientific in nature (see particularly Chapter 9, The Logic of Reports, and Chapter 18, which contains a discussion of the nature of science and steps in the scientific method).

Medical doctors scrutinizing a clinical report by one of their colleagues wish to know the set of treatments selected for comparison, the specifications of the experimental units to which treatment are applied, the rules by which treatments are allocated to the experimental units, and the specifications of the measurements or other records made on each unit.

Therefore, in designing his experiment and in writing his report, the reporter-physician must confront himself with certain questions: What query is the experiment planned to answer? To what population shall the results be applicable? What subjects will be chosen for the experiment? The report must yield up clear-cut answers essentially to two questions: Did the patient benefit from the treatment, and did the patient show any toxic side effect?

Preanesthetic Medication
with Intravenous Hydroxyzine *

*A double-blind study to verify a
pilot program and uncontrolled trial*

DANTE BIZZARRI, M.D.   FRANK E. FIERRO, M.D.
FRANCIS S. LATTERI, M.D.   JOSEPH GIUFFRIDA, M.D.
ALBERT SCHMOOKLER, M.D.   HOWARD C. BERGER, M.D.
New York, New York†

THIS REPORT, one portion of a comprehensive program of investigation of hydroxyzine hydrochloride (Atarax®), deals only with its intravenous administration. A subsequent report will deal with intramuscular administration of this compound.

* Atarax®, product of J. B. Roerig & Company, Division Chas. Pfizer & Co. Inc.
† New York Medical College—Metropolitan Medical Center, New York, New York.

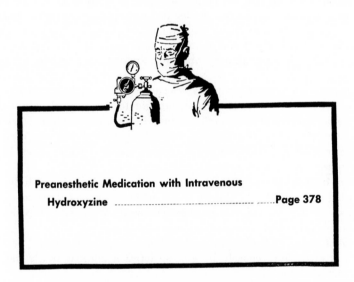

Anesthesia AND Analgesia

.....CURRENT RESEARCHES

Preanesthetic Medication with Intravenous
Hydroxyzine .... Page 378

Journal of the International Anesthesia Research Society

Volume 40, Number 4   JULY-AUGUST, 1961

* Reproduced with permission of *Anesthesia and Analgesia*, 40:378 (July–
August) 1961.

GENERAL DESIGN: OBJECTIVES, COMPONENTS, PROCEDURES

Broad Objectives—This study was carried out to determine the clinical effects of hydroxyzine when given prior to the induction of anesthesia. Effectiveness was measured by results with hydroxyzine in providing a state of preanesthetic ataraxia in patients without adversely affecting the status of the physiologic mechanisms at the time of surgery. Ataraxia here is meant to designate calmness of mind and emotions, a somewhat-detached serenity without depression of mental faculties or clouding of consciousness. Our premise is that the tranquil patient in a state approximating complete homeostasis is better able to bear the burden of anesthesia and surgery.

Evaluative Criteria—Throughout the over-all study, specific physiologic effects upon patients' vital signs were studied. These included blood pressure, pulse, and respiration before premedication; 15, 30, and 45 minutes after premedication; and while on the operating table. Also evaluated were effects of hydroxyzine upon the action of anesthetic agents and the anesthetic management;* upon rate and nature of recovery;† upon pain when present; and, as to presence or absence of allergic manifestations, vessel thrombosis, mania, convulsions, pain upon administration, or other untoward reactions or side effects. Total effects of hydroxyzine were evaluated through the foregoing physiologic signs; through objective observations;‡ and by subjective criteria.§

Patients—Adult female patients selected for this study required emergency surgery and were, in general, brought to the hospital only a short time prior to surgical intervention. Thus, being under neither other preanesthetic medication nor the stress of prolonged hospitalization, they lent themselves well to a study of hydroxyzine under acute circumstances. Invariably, apprehension was manifest.

Series of Patients—In all, 621 patients were included in this study. The following series were established: I. 300 patients—a pilot dose range-finding study; II. 221 patients—an uncontrolled-efficacy study; III. 100 patients—a double-blind study.

Administration of Hydroxyzine—About an hour prior to surgery, hydroxyzine was given intravenously by glucose infusion injected slowly into the intravenous tubing.

---

* Was cough, vomiting, struggling, laryngospasm, excessive secretions, or unintentional apnea present?

† What was the time of arousability? Was there mild, moderate, or no restlessness, excitement, or pain? Did premedication produce amnesia?

‡ Comfortable or uncomfortable, worried and appehensive or toubled, excited or relaxed, happy and euphoric or serene, drowsy and sleepy or awake, talkative or quiet, nauseated or not, able to open eyes, able to grasp hand firmly, able to touch nose with index finger with eyes closed?

§ Was patient comfortable, worried, tense, unusually happy, or sleepy? Did he vomit? Is his stomach upset? Does he feel tired? Does he see double? Does he have pain?

MATERIALS, METHODS AND RESULTS

I. Pilot Dose Range-Finding Study—Though considerable information on oral forms of hydroxyzine was available at the time this study was first undertaken, and though papers on the drug in premedication[1-6] have in the interval appeared, not a great deal about effective dosages of the intravenous medication was then known. All the many publications on hydroxyzine in varied fields of medicine, however, emphasize the safety and lack of side effects from the drug. A pilot study was nonetheless undertaken to determine the optimal dose and rate of infusion of hydroxyzine so that these could be used in subsequent phases of the experiment.

Hydroxyzine was used with 300 patients in doses ranging from 20 mg. to 350 mg., allowing from 1 to 20 minutes for intravenous infusions.

The optimal dose for preanesthetic ataraxia was found to be 100 mg. of hydroxyzine in 20 cc. of saline infused during a 1 to 2-minute interval. All patients were observed for cardiovascular effects throughout this phase, but no data were recorded.

When higher concentrations of hydroxyzine were used, or when more rapid delivery was allowed, patients complained of a burning sensation at the entry site. Higher dosages delivered more rapidly, moreover, provided no appreciable improvement in the desired preanesthetic status of the patient, and lower dosages, in the judgment of the investigators, did not prove adequate.

II. Uncontrolled-Efficacy Study—In 221 women treated as above, surgery required was dilatation and curettage, except in 7 cases as noted in table 1. General anesthesia was produced as shown in table 2. Age groups are shown in table 3.

The anesthesiologist who evaluated the effects of hydroxyzine in all patients in this series, using the criteria described earlier, judged that this drug produced excellent to good results in 204 patients (92.0 per cent); fair results in 15 patients (7.0 per cent); and poor results in 2 patients (1.0 per cent) (Graph 1).

Table 1
SURGERY IN 221 WOMEN GIVEN HYDROXYZINE AS PREMEDICATION IN EFFICACY STUDY

Type of surgical procedure	Patients
Dilatation and curettage	214
Incision and drainage	2
Excision of Bartholin cyst	1
Hysterectomy	1
Appendectomy	1
Repair of ruptured uterus	1
Conization	1

Table 2
ANESTHESIA EMPLOYED IN 221 WOMEN
GIVEN HYDROXYZINE AS PREMEDICATION
IN EFFICACY STUDY

Anesthesia	Patients
Cyclopropane-oxygen	196
Pentothal® sodium-cyclopropane-oxygen	6
Pentothal sodium-nitrous oxide-oxygen	11
Nitrous oxide-oxygen	3
Pentothal sodium-Fluothane®	2
Spinal	1
Caudal	1
Epidural	1

Table 3
AGE DISTRIBUTION OF 221 WOMEN
GIVEN HYDROXYZINE AS PREMEDICATION
IN EFFICACY STUDY

Age ranges	Patients
10 to 19	27
20 to 29	134
30 to 39	44
40 to 49	13
50 to 59	1
60 to 69	1
70 to 79	1

Effects upon vital signs were observed during this series, those occurring in blood pressure and pulse being recorded for analysis. A change in blood pressure and/or pulse by 20 per cent greater or less than the initial readings was considered significant.

According to the foregoing, no significant changes in blood pressure or pulse occurred in 204 patients (92.5 per cent). By these same criteria, only 17 patients (6.5 per cent) experienced significant changes.* However, these important objective signs produced no alteration in the total clinical picture presented, produced no other observably adverse effect upon the patient, and did not unfavorably alter the course of recovery. No significant respiratory embarrassment occurred.

* Ten of these alterations were in pulse only; six in blood pressure only; and one in both pulse and blood pressure.

The anticipated minor difficulties in anesthetic management seen in any patient population, regardless of drugs used, were encountered in 8 patients in this series. Likewise, typical effects invariably seen among some of any large number of patients during recovery were recorded here for 9 patients. These were occasional vomiting, stormy emergence, coughing, and laryngospasm. None of these commonly-encountered, non-life-threatening phenomena proved prolonged or uncontrollable, and none altered the otherwise favorable prognosis for any patient.

III. Double-Blind Series—Hydroxyzine or Saline Solution Alone as Placebo—Another series of tests, using a double-blind technique, was run. In this test the anesthesiologist making the evaluations did not administer the premedication (neither hydroxyzine nor the placebo), but simply evaluated the patients' status immediately prior to the induction of anesthesia. The anesthesiologist administering the premedication also did not know what he was giving, since all material was coded. This added series of patients, moreover, was used to determine whether the occasional non-threatening cardiovascular manifestations seen transitorily in the preceding group could be statistically related to hydroxyzine administration.

Of 100 patients included, 64 received hydroxyzine and 36 were given a placebo. Evaluated effects by the same anesthesiologist are shown in table **4.**

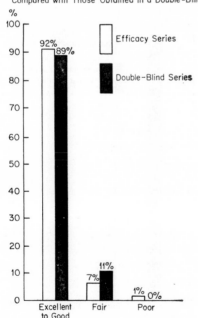

Graph 1
EFFECTIVENESS OF HYDROXYZINE
IN PROVIDING DESIRED PRE-ANESTHETIC ATARAXIA
Percentages of Results Obtained in an Uncontrolled Efficacy Study
Compared with Those Obtained in a Double-Blind Study

The evaluator was correct in 86 of 100 instances as to whether the patient received hydroxyzine or the placebo. Of the patients who received hydroxyzine intravenously, 89.1 per cent were rated by the investigator as being either good or excellent prior to surgery, compared to 47 per cent of those who received the placebo. The difference between these two groups was found to be significant (Pth < .01) (Graph 2).

In judging that 27 of 36 patients who had received the placebo were nonetheless good or fair preoperatively, the evaluator was 75 per cent correct. Where he guessed incorrectly, these guesses appeared consistent with good or bad results obtained with the placebo.

It is interesting to note that of the 5 incorrect guesses made when patients had actually received hydroxyzine, only 1 patient had been rated as good, while the other 4 had been rated as fair. Conversely, of the 9 patients who had been given the placebo and were incorrectly guessed by the evaluator, 3 had been rated excellent and 6 good, prior to surgery. One may not, of course, from this conclude that the anesthesiologist made his judgment as to the drug used from his rating of the patient or that he judged the drug first and then rated.

The foregoing results were compared with those obtained in the uncon-

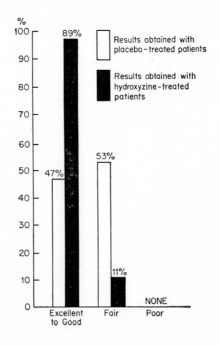

Graph 2
RESULTS OBTAINED WITH HYDROXYZINE
COMPARED WITH THOSE IN PLACEBO–TREATMENTS

Table 4
RESULTS OF DOUBLE-BLIND TEST

| | Hydroxyzine intravenous | | | | Placebo | | | |
| | Total | | Guesses | | Total | | Guesses | |
			Correct	Incorrect			Correct	Incorrect
Excellent	20	31.3%	20	—	3	8.3%	—	3
Good	37	57.8	36	1	14	38.9	8	6
Fair	7	10.9	3	4	19	52.8	19	—
Poor	—	—	—	—	—	—	—	—
	64	100.0%	59	5	36	100.0%	27	9

rolled-efficacy series. Comparing the 89.1 per cent who were rated good or excellent in the double-blind series with the 92.0 per cent so rated in the efficacy series, no significant difference in results of treatment was observed (P > .05). The efficacy of hydroxyzine was thus clearly confirmed as it became apparent that the results obtained and the evaluations made during the uncontrolled efficacy series were thoroughly justified and logically attributable to the drug (Graph 1).

Next, statistical evaluation was undertaken to determine whether or not the isolated cardiovascular manifestations observed in both series II and III could be related to hydroxyzine or were merely "normal" for any preoperative population. Since all the data in series III were procured in a side-by-side fashion in a controlled manner, and the lowest expected value obtained was 6.8, the procedure meets the criterion for a valid chi-square test. It was possible to conclude that the cardiovascular effects observed under the conditions of the experiment are no greater than would be expected if hydroxyzine had not been administered.

SUMMARY

Through a pilot program with 300 patients, it was established that 100 mg. hydroxyzine in 20 cc. saline solution infused during a 1 to 2-minute interval about an hour prior to surgery is the optimal dose for preanesthetic ataraxia. The optimal dose provided a calm mind and emotions without significant depression of mental faculties or vital signs, thereby rendering the patient both cooperative and easily arousable.

With this technique, dose, and rate of infusion in a subsequent series, satisfactory preanesthetic ataraxia with hydroxyzine was produced in 204 of 221 patients (92.0 per cent), without untoward reactions. Significant changes in blood pressure or pulse were recorded for 17 patients but did not influence adversely the clinical course.

In a double-blind study with an additional 100 patients, 89.1 per cent who received the drug and not the placebo were adjudged by the same evaluator to be in excellent to good preanesthetic status, compared with the 92.0 per cent so rated in the uncontrolled series.

Chi-square condensation of data regarding all cardiovascular manifesta- tions seen with hydroxyzine compared with data obtained from placebo- treated patients indicate that the cardiovascular effects observed under the conditions of the experiment were no greater than would be expected if hydroxyzine had not been administered.

Hydroxyzine, by providing an eminently desirable status of preanesthetic ataraxia in more than 90 per cent of tested patients without affecting vital signs, appreciably advances the search for an ideal preanesthetic agent.

REFERENCES

1. Steiner, L., et al.: The Preoperative Sedation of Children; presented at Southern Society of Anesthesiologists, Birmingham, Alabama, April 1959.

2. Grady, Robert W. and Rich, Alvin R.: A Preliminary Report on the Use of Hydroxyzine (Vistaril) as a Premedicant for Surgical Patients. *J. M. A. Alabama* 29:377 (April) 1960.

3. Carbone, M. and Mazzarella, B.: The Use of Hydroxyzine in Anaesthesia for Neurosurgery. *Panminerva Medica* 2:234 (May) 1960.

4. Grady, R. W., et al.: Clinical Evaluation of Parenteral Hydroxyzine (Vistaril) for Preoperative Medication; presented at the Southern Society of Anesthesiology, Washington, D.C., April 1960.

5. Steinberg, Nathan and Holz, Wilbur, G.: Preoperative Preparation for Tonsillectomy with Hydroxyzine Hydrochloride in Pediatric Patients. *New York J. Med.* 60:691 (March 1) 1960.

6. Mulla, N.: An Evaluation of Hydroxyzine Hydrochloride (Atarax) in Ob- stetrical Practice. *J. Internat. Coll. Surgeons.* In press.

24

The Accountancy Report

Formal reports of accountants are, very generally, of two sorts: financial statements and audit reports. The financial statement consists of a balance sheet, an income statement, a statement of application of funds, and any supporting statement or other presentation of financial data derived from accounting records. The audit report is an auditor's statement of the work he has done in an audit and his expression of belief or opinion as to the propriety of the financial statement.

Accountancy reports depend upon accountancy systems. General requirements of an accountancy system are that it give the figure results clearly, quickly, and with continuous, accurate, and full explanations of what has occurred both daily and annually. The system must allow ready comparison with the prior year's figures and must signal all variations from ratios and standards. Within the system there should be a design to deter employee frauds, wastes, errors, and spoilage. It is essential that any system permit prompt filing of accurate reports and tax returns required by the government. Beyond these necessities, the accountant's system should help develop an efficient sales policy by, for example, showing up the more profitable sales for concentrated effort, finding the best markets for profits, and determining what promotion and selling effort to use. Accountancy systems also help in purchasing and controlling stock and in establishing the cost of distribution.

As a direct reflection of the system, the accountancy report form must be governed by the person served. To present and interpret the information, every method—charts, graphic devices, and symbolization—is used (see Chapter 14). The report must utilize the simplest language permitted by the complexity of the subject matter and must be intelligible to the widest possible audience. An accountant's report will include all items deemed essential by the creative writer of the report, but there must also be consistency and continuity with the preceding report of the same type.

By Arthur M. Cannon

Financial Statements for a Church

A REPRINT FROM

THE

JOURNAL

OF

ACCOUNTANCY

* Reproduced with permission of *The Journal of Accountancy*, 114:43 (September) 1962.

Financial Statements for a Church

A CPA treasurer of a church in a small community outlines the procedures used, with samples of financial reports

SOME years ago in THE JOURNAL OF ACCOUNTANCY for May 1957, Lowell Larsen published an article on church accounting. I am told that it became one of the most reprinted articles THE JOURNAL ever ran, possibly indicating how many of our readers become church treasurers. When I became treasurer of Christ Church parish (Episcopal) in Oswego, Oregon. I quickly found my problems just where Professor Larsen indicated they would be—internal control and preparation of statements. This article sets forth the results I have come up with.

This church is in a suburban town of about 10,000 population, located ten miles from the center of the Portland metropolitan area. There are about five hundred family memberships in the church, of whom about three hundred, fifty make regular annual pledges. Total pledges are about $60,000 per annum, and that is the approximate annual budget. Plate collections and miscellaneous receipts are about enough to offset a 10 per cent shrinkage in pledge collections. The church and adjoining parish house, rectory and office buildings, together with equipment, cost about $250,000 about ten years ago. Mortgage debt against the properties has been reduced to under $20,000.

The church has four full-time employees—rector, assistant, secretary and sexton, and three part-time employees—another assistant, the bookkeeper and the organist. Total payroll is $21,600 a year and other wage costs include social security, clergy utilities and rent, and pension assessment (15 per cent of total wage cost of clergy). The church pays the diocese an annual assessment and quota of $11,000. Mortgage payments and capital improvements for the current year were budgeted at $10,000.

The church carries around $10,000 in cash funds, mostly in savings accounts. The principal asset other than land and buildings and cash consists of pledges receivable, which as described later are fully reserved until collected.

Internal control—receipts

The principal problem here is, of course, with loose plate collections. We follow the practice of having an ushers' committee for each service, headed by a vestryman. In addition to the usual nonburdensome tasks of ushering, the committee counts the collection immediately after the principal Sunday service, fills out and signs a report (Exhibit I), and makes out a deposit slip in triplicate. The ushers open the pledge envelopes and check or enter the amount enclosed on the outside of each envelope and, at least in theory, balance the pledge collections with a tape of the envelopes. The deposit is locked in a canvas bag and placed in a local bank night depository together with the deposit slip in duplicate. Triplicate of the deposit slip and the ushers' report together with pledge envelopes are left for the bookkeeper's attention. It is important to list checks by name as well as by bank number on the deposit slip and to segregate the loose plate checks from those included in envelopes. (The loose plate checks are usually intended to be credited to pledges.) This is the principal means by which the bookkeeper can check back on errors or such disputes as may arise, and we find it is a very helpful practice.

Exhibit I

Ushers' Report
Christ Church Parish, Oswego, Oregon

Date_____19____

Remember

1. Count loose plate collection separately from pledge envelopes. List loose checks *first* on deposit slip.
2. Make deposit slip in triplicate: two to bank; one with report and pledge envelopes. Leave in box in counting room.
3. Stamp and list checks on deposit slip by *name, bank number and amount*. List the checks which are *not* in pledge envelopes *first*, and draw a line under this group before proceeding to list the checks from pledge envelopes.
4. Run tape of pledge envelopes, compare with total as counted, wrap tape around envelopes and fasten with rubber band.
5. Take deposit (with two copies deposit slip) to night depository at bank in locked bag. Return keys to box in counting room.

Attendance

9:15 A.M. Service_____ 11:00 A.M. Service_____

Collection	Loose Plate	Pledge Envelopes	Totals
Currency	_____	_____	_____(A)
Silver	_____	_____	_____(A)
Checks	_____(C)	_____	_____
TOTALS	_____	_____(B)	_____(A)

(A) Should agree with deposit slip.
(B) Should agree with tape of pledge envelopes.
(C) Must be listed first on deposit slip. See 3 above.

Ushers' Signatures:

_____   _____

For Office Use only:
Loose checks: Pledge_____ Open_____

A weekly report (Exhibit II, below) is sent to the ushers' committee chairman and others showing how the ushers' count agreed with the bank's count.

Receipts that come in the mail are deposited directly by the secretary with duplicate deposit slip to the bookkeeper, listing names (for credit to pledges) as well as bank numbers.

Pledge control

When the finance committee completes its annual autumn "Every Member Canvass," a list of the pledges is turned over to the bookkeeper and set up as a memorandum control. A standard printed pledge record available from church supply houses provides a carbon-copy monthly statement which

---

Exhibit II

Report to Usher's Committee Chairman

Dear Sir:

Most of the income of the church comes in the Sunday offerings and thus most of the church income accounting derives from the ushers' reports and accompanying material—pledge envelopes and deposit slips. Because of the great importance of accuracy in this work, I have asked the bookkeeper to inform each Sunday's usher captain of the results of the bank's recount of the deposit, and the bookkeeper's recheck of pledge envelopes.

ARTHUR M. CANNON,
Parish Treasurer

The results for Sunday, ... were as follows:

Collection	Per Ushers' Report	Per Bank
Silver	$_____	$_____
Currency	$_____	$_____
Checks	$_____	$_____
Total	$_____	$_____
	Per Ushers' Report	*As rechecked*
Pledges	$_____	$_____

Yours very truly,
Bookkeeper

cc: Chairman, Usher Committee
    Usher Captain
    Treasurer
    Rector
    File

P.S. The attendance count at *each* service is equally important for our church records. For this particular Sunday, the ushers did not report the attendance for each service.

is mailed to members. The cards are kept in a compression type binder just as with any simple accounts-receivable system. The memorandum pledge control is carried forward from month to month, entering new pledges or cancellations as well as collections as recorded in the cash book, and the pledge control is balanced with pledge card balances each month. The total of the control appears on the balance sheet. There are usually two years' controls outstanding at any one time. Early in the year we will have prior year and current year and then later in the year, current year and next year. Before we start the next year's pledge control, we will customarily have written off all prior year balances. Write-offs are by the vestry on recommendation of the finance committee, which supervises collections and reviews the monthly trial balance of outstanding pledges, on which delinquencies are noted.

Internal control—disbursements

We make all disbursements by check on invoice approved by an appropriate person, usually the rector, with checks prepared by the bookkeeper and signed by the treasurer. Bank statements come direct to the treasurer's downtown office from the bank, and the treasurer reconciles the bank account and examines cancelled checks and returned duplicate deposit slips. This is a real weakness—someone else should reconcile the bank account. Our only protection is through the bookkeeper, and annual audit. A small petty cash fund is kept by the secretary, reimbursed from time to time by the bookkeeper under usual procedures and controls for such funds.

Both cash receipts and cash disbursements are recorded by the bookkeeper in a standard printed bound book providing columns matching up with the requirements of the annual report to the diocese which are also reflected in the receipts and disbursements statements to follow.

Financial statements

I get out a treasurer's report each month to the rector, wardens, vestry, and a number of parishioners—anyone who asks and all above a certain pledge amount. That for October 1961, is reproduced in Exhibit III. It consists of three pages—a covering letter of comments, comparative balance sheets, and comparative statements of cash receipts and disbursements.

The statements are on a cash receipts and disbursements basis in that no consideration is given to depreciation, accounts payable, or expense accruals. However, the balance sheet does include pledges receivable, fixed assets at cost, payroll taxes withheld, and the various designated gifts and special funds, etc., as well as long-term debt.

The covering letter of comments summarizes for the nonaccountants on the vestry (all but myself) the financial situation and results of operations for the month and year-to-date, all in a standard form, changing only the figures from month to month with perhaps a sentence or two of special comment as called for. An important part of this letter is the reconciliation of capital investment for the year-to-date. This reconciliation starts with the January First balance, adds income receipts and deducts budgeted disbursements, with adjustments for the two items in budgeted disbursements that nevertheless do not reduce net worth: capital improvements and mortgage principal payments, and any other special adjustment that may be necessary.

Balance sheets

The monthly report includes balance sheets as at the end of each of the two prior years and the current month-end. The month-end balances are not prepared from any general ledger (we do not have one), but from the bank reconciliations, pledge controls, memorandum controls over designated gifts, special funds, etc.,* and the mortgage balances as appearing on the mortgagees' statements, which, of course, we check and reconcile with the net worth statement. Payroll taxes withheld are carried forward from the previous month, adjusting plus or minus for the net amount of such items in the cash disbursements book. Fixed assets are carried forward from the previous month, adjusted when necessary for the appropriate amount appearing in the net-worth reconciliation.

As previously mentioned, pledges receivable are under control. The balance sheet item is reduced by a reserve for estimated uncollectibles, which starts at 10 per cent of each year's initial total of pledges (based on prior experience), and is reduced in round amounts for pledges written off by vestry action. The net balance of pledges receivable after deducting the reserve for uncollectibles is exactly offset on the liability side of the balance sheet as deferred income, the result being to fully reserve the pledges until collection and take into income only the cash receipts thereon.

Receipts and disbursements statement

As set out herewith this statement shows comparative information for the current month, this year and last, and for the year-to-date, this year and last, in simple tabular form starting with the beginning balance, adding the receipts and deducting the disbursements. The amounts come directly from column totals in the cash receipts and cash disbursements books respectively and from the bank reconciliation. Cents are dropped, rounding off to dollars (in the statement, but not in the books). It is important to separate the receipts as between "income receipts"—plate, pledge, Sunday School and miscellaneous income items, and nonincome receipts which include those for designated gifts, special collections, exchanges, and transfers from savings accounts. (This is a statement of receipts and disbursements of the general bank account only, which seems to suit our purposes, but it would work just as well if the savings account balances were included also.)

---

* I am told that it is common to keep these restricted funds in a special bank account but we find it more convenient to use just one, keeping track of the funds by memorandum accounts controlled in the balance sheet.

"Exchanges" comprise such in-and-out items as personal long distance telephone tolls on the rector's utility bill paid by the church, collections for the diocesan fund which sometimes stray into the church plate, etc. These are accounted for along with the designated gifts and special collections in a

---

Exhibit III

Christ Church Parish (Episcopal)
Lake Oswego, Oregon

Treasurer's Report as of October 31, 1961

November 13, 1961

Comments

To the Rector, Wardens and Vestry,
Christ Church Parish:

On October 31, 1961, the Parish had $912 in its general bank account, plus $50 in petty cash fund and $6,500 in insured savings account and savings and loan association. Total pledges receivable amounted to $15,594, including $14,329 of current year's pledges, and before deducting an estimated provision for uncollectibles of $5,000. Total assets amounted to $268,665. After deducting liabilities and uncollected pledges, the net capital investment was $239,136 as shown on the balance sheet.

The statement on page 48 shows that there was collected in October, $5,798, including $500 from savings account, and in the ten months through October 31, $54,153 (including $2,500 from savings account). Disbursements for the same periods were $6,060 and $64,277 respectively (including rectory mortgage paid off, $3,116, and $9,000 transferred to savings accounts during the year). Income receipts for the ten months were $49,236, and budgeted disbursements $52,832, being $1,094 over the budget for the year to date (due to early payoff of rectory mortgage as mentioned).

Total 1961 pledges were $61,931 (including pledges added since January 1) as compared to $60,277 for 1960.

Reconciliation of capital investment account for the year-to-date follows:

Balance January 1, 1961	$230,174
Add: Income receipts	49,236
(Less) Budgeted disbursements	(52,832)
Other items:	
Capital improvements purchased	2,045
Parish house furnishings donated	1,310
Mortgage payments	9,253
Write-off of account receivable	(50)
Balance October 31, 1961	$239,136

Yours very truly,
ARTHUR M. CANNON
Parish Treasurer

memorandum control posted from the appropriate columns in the cash receipts and cash disbursements books each month.

Similarly, it is important to segregate the disbursements between those which are budgeted and those which are not. The latter comprise withheld payroll taxes and the offsets to the nonincome receipts mentioned previously—designated gifts, special collections, exchanges, and transfers to savings accounts.

It will be noted that the current year's budget together with a year-to-date allocation thereof (an even one-twelfth per month in all but one case) is tabulated immediately adjoining the disbursements section. Thus the vestry can run down the parallel columns of disbursements for the year-to-date and the budget for the year-to-date as a ready check on disbursements. Any major deviations would be commented on in the covering letter.

The accumulated totals for the year-to-date are carried forward right in the cash receipts and disbursements books by adding to each month's totals the accumulated totals from the previous month.

As previously noted, all receipts are handled by either the ushers or the church secretary. The bookkeeper keeps the pledge records and control and the cash receipts and disbursements books and writes the checks. She also drafts the monthly statement directly on an extra copy of the statement for the previous month or the corresponding month of the previous year, as may be convenient. The treasurer checks the statement draft and then the bookkeeper or secretary mimeographs it. The treasurer, as noted, also signs the checks and reconciles the bank account. He checks the pledge balance against the control occasionally. The rector reviews and approves bills from creditors except where vestry action may be thought desirable because of the size or character of some item. The vestry on recommendation of the finance committee exclusively handles any pledge write-offs, and these are entered only from the vestry minutes.

Certainly there are thousands of readers of THE JOURNAL who have faced the same problems I have encountered as a parish treasurer. I should be glad to have their comments and suggestions.

Christ Church Parish (Episcopal)
Lake Oswego, Oregon

Balance Sheets, December 31, 1959 and 1960, October 31, 1961

Assets	*12-31-59*	*12-31-60*	*10-1-61*
Cash and Investments	$ 7,906	$ 11,136	$ 7,462
Cash in Bank (Citizens)	7,666	11,036	912
Petty Cash	50	50	50
Savings Account (Citizens—3%)			1,500
Savings & Loan Account (Benj-Franklin—4%)			5,000
Note Receivable	190	50°	—

Pledges Receivable	$ 53,613	$ 48,505	$ 10,594
Prior Year			1,265
Current Year	6,109	7,426	14,329
Next Year	56,504	51,079	—
Reserve for estimated uncollectible #	(9,000)	(10,000)	(5,000)
Fixed Assets (@ cost)	$244,666	$247,254	$250,609
Equipment	391	1,179	1,669
Automobile	800	2,600	2,600
Church furnishings	17,116	17,116	17,116
Parish House furnishings	5,215	5,215	6,525
Church	102,085	102,085	102,777
Parish House	55,257	55,257	56,081
Rectory	25,220	25,220	25,220
Annex	28,065	28,065	28,104
Land	10,517	10,517	10,517
Total Assets	$306,185	$306,895	$268,665

Liabilities and Capital

Payroll Taxes Withheld	$ 403	$ 578*	$ 185
Designated Gifts, Special Funds and Exchanges	$ 630	$ 1,670	$ 2,034
Church School	$ 500	$ 500*	$ 500
Church Women	—	1,000	21
McVey Memorial	—	—	200
Steeble Memorial	—	—	50
Lenten-Self-Denial	—	—	237
Choir Fund			30
Church Development Program	—	—	1,000
Miscellaneous	130	170	(4)
Mortgage Loans Payable	$ 33,669	$ 25,968*	$ 16,715
Church (U.S.N. Bank—4%)	12,828	7,121*	2,185
Rectory (U.S.N. Bank—4½%)	4,484	3,466	—
Annex (Prudential—5%)	16,357	15,381	14,530
Deferred Income—Pledges	$ 53,613	$ 48,505	$ 10,594
Capital Investment (@ cost)	$217,870	$230,174*	$239,136
Total Liabilities and Capital	$306,185	$306,895	$266,665

* Corrected.

\# Recent experience indicates about 10 per cent of each year's total pledges will not be collected. Reserve is uncollectible balance of two years as shown—at 12-31-59; $6,000 for 1960 plus $3,000 for 1959; at 12-31-60 $5,500 for 1961 plus $4,500 for 1960. Total pledges were $60,277 for 1960 and $61,931 for 1961 (revised to date). As pledges are written off by Vestry action, both the amount receivable and the reserve (rounded) are reduced. As we approach the end of the year, the reserve tends to bear a larger relationship to the remaining uncollected balances.

Christ Church Parish (Episcopal)
Lake Oswego, Oregon

Cash Receipts and Disbursements
Periods Ended October 31, 1960 and 1961

	Month of October		Ten Months to 10-30		Budget-1961	
	1960	*1961*	*1960*	*1961*	*10 mos.*	*Year*
BEGINNING BALANCE	$ 7,279	$ 1,174	$ 7,666	$11,036		
Receipts						
Plate	259	554	2,354	2,962		
Pledges	4,948	4,605	42,140	45,029		
Prior Year	—	6	2,856	2,458		
Current Year	4,948	4,599	39,284	42,571		
Next Year	—	—	—	—		
School (est.)	125	125	797	784		
Miscellaneous	5	8	917	461		
Income Receipts	$ 5,337	$ 5,292	$46,208	$49,236		
Designated Gifts	—	—	1,169	499		
Special Collections	—	5	415	763		
Exchanges	26	1	297	1,155		
Transfer from Savings	—	500	—	2,500		
Total Receipts	$ 5,363	$ 5,798	$48,089	$54,153		
Disbursements						
Salaries	$ 1,856	$ 1,784	$16,838	$17,846	$18,000	$21,600
Clergy		1,092		10,917	10,918	13,100
Sexton		150		1,546	1,500	1,800
Organist		208		2,123	2,082	2,500
Office		334		3,260	3,500	4,200

Pensions-Clergy						250
Social Security	58	63	222	257	213	1,625
Insurance	17	17	1,424	1,129	1,354	3,000
Utilities	61	65	2,629	2,556	2,500	1,800
Church and Office Sup.	53	37	1,062	1,297	1,500	250
Altar Supplies	9	84	121	301	208	100
Choir & Music	107	—	158	211	83	1,000
Church School	122	164	400	710	833	1,300
Auto & Travel	161	95	1,068	807	1,083	900
Telephone	70	74	753	772	750	700
Miscellaneous	10	14	482	420	583	500
Discretionary	—	—	500	500	500	300
Gifts	—	—	250	228	250	2,250
Repairs	91	247	2,356	1,155	1,875	1,080
Interest	108	70	1,178	847	900	750
Taxes	—	—	35	—	625	1,200
Rent	100	110	900	1,090	1,000	3,919
Assessment (Diocese)	294	326	2,940	3,266	3,265	7,100
Quota (Missionary)	446	600	4,459	5,900	5,917	2,000
Capital Improvements	2,234	863	2,916	2,045	1,666	8,010
Mortgage Payments	649	588	6,399	9,253	6,675	$61,984
Budgeted Disb.	$6,873	$5,683	$49,242	$52,832	$51,738	
Withheld (Taxes, etc.)	250	372	126	393		
Designated Gifts	98	—	98	1,428		
Special Collections	—	—	366	505		
Exchanges	26	5	529	119		
Transfer to Savings	—	—	—	9,000		
Total Disb.	$7,247	$6,060	$50,361	$64,277		
ENDING BALANCE	$5,395	$912	$5,395	$912		

25

Abstracts and Résumés

ABSTRACTS

That discourse which presents the substance or general idea in brief of a longer discourse is variously called an abstract, a summary, a digest, a précis, a brief, a condensation, or a résumé. There are certain implications and denotations attaching to each of the particular nouns which provide a modicum of differentiation among them. Common to all, however, is their objective of presenting in compact, reduced size the fundamental points of a longer treatise.

The abstract itself is a summary or an epitome containing the substance, general view, and principal heads of a longer writing. Developmental and illustrative matter in the original is shorn away to leave just the essence of the writer's thought. No fundamental points of the original are omitted, nor are new points introduced by the abstracter. Yet the abstract is a complete discourse in itself, containing full sentences and necessary transitions.

How the abstract should be organized and how long it should be are for the writer to decide, with reference to the purpose for which the abstract is intended. Either the order of organization of the original text may be followed, or a new method may be introduced. A new order may be preferred in that the writer of the original text probably organized his material with a view to its place in a fuller frame of reference.

Nor is there an ironclad formula for the length of an abstract. Some authorities timorously venture to suggest the abstract may be about one-third as long as the original, but this may be too large or too small for a particular purpose. An abstract accompanying a published report (see specimen report in Chapter 21) may be just two or three sentences long, in line with its purpose of indicating to a prospective reader whether or not the scope of the article is within his sphere of interest. An abstract (or précis) for use by the abstracter in a report (see Chapters 9, 10, and 11) or a research paper (see Chapter 26) he is preparing may contain a certain proportion of the illustrative matter of the original.

Always the abstract will be in the abstracter's own words, and it should not contain "guide words" such as "according to the author," or "Jones states," or "it is the contention of the author that." The assumption is that all the ideas in the abstract are those of the original writer, and all the words are those of the abstracter, unless set off with quotation marks.

Ability to abstract is a prerequisite to gathering material for a report or a research paper. Once the report itself is completed, the writer will probably wish to abstract at least his major findings so that these may be presented at the outset (see Chapters 4, 13, and 15). Moreover, with the explosive proliferation of published information in all fields, but especially in the arena of science, readers themselves must depend on abstracts in order to keep abreast of current developments.

SPECIMENS*

1JL26M. McLeish, John. (U. Leed) Exhibitionism. *Med. World, Lond.,* 1960, 93(8), 126–128. Sex perversion occurs when some childish activities, which lead up to procreative acts, separate and substitute for normal intercourse, bringing entire sexual release. Constitutional weakness or poor training in childhood prevents normal sex development. The exhibitionist cannot explain why exposing his body brings sexual pleasure. He is no sex-crazed rapist; he is an infantile impotent person. Imprisonment neither deters nor reforms him. Failure to integrate may be due to a punishing mother, or to early lack of sympathy and understanding working on an enfeebled psychosexual constitution. Psychiatric therapy and use of drugs to reduce potency are valueless. This problem is a challenge to cooperative research by psychiatrists, psychologists, and family doctors.—F. A. Cooksley.

(Reproduced with permission of Psychological Abstracts.)

THE SEARCH FOR COHERENCE: T. S. ELIOT AND THE CHRISTIAN TRADITION IN ENGLISH POETRY

(Order No. 62-1897)

George Mathewson, Ph.D.
Princeton University, 1961

The following study seeks to trace the development of T. S. Eliot as a poet and critic, and to assess his position as a man of letters. Beginning with a discussion on an early poem, *The Death of Narcissus,* which it relates to *Prufrock* and *The Waste Land,* it treats Eliot's youthful skepticism; his conversion to Anglo-Catholicism; and the effect of his conversion on his later poetry and thought. It deals with the problems of a Christian artist writing religious poetry for a public which may not share his religious convictions; and shows how such an artist may, through his general awareness, meet the demands of his public. It then seeks to indicate the philosophic basis of Eliot's critical position, and to clarify his attitude towards romanticism and classicism—or liberalism and orthodoxy—by surveying his comments on a single romantic poet, Shelley. It attempts to give a record of Shelley's reputation in the 'twenties and 'thirties, and to relate Eliot's pronouncements to the judgments of other critics of Shelley. It discusses the relationship of

* Reproduced with permission.

368 *Special Kinds of Reports*

Eliot's critical theory to his practice of poetry, and tries to show how his theory and practice coalesce. An effort is made to show Eliot in his role of arbiter of taste, and to give an idea of his conception of the classic in art.

Continuing with a discussion of the function of the Christian artist in the present century, it deals with Eliot's role as a Christian propagandist by means of an analysis of *Murder in the Cathedral*. It compares this festival drama with his other plays; and his plays with his non-dramatic verse. Having observed Eliot as poet and critic and dramatist, it tries to show how he has been able to fill the traditional position of the English man of letters for our time. After discussing briefly Eliot's work as an editor, and dealing with some of his polemical writings, such as *The Idea of a Christian Society* and *Notes towards the Definition of Culture*, it attempts to contrast him with previous men of letters; and to describe his theory of the function of the poet.

Microfilm $2.95; Xerox $10.35.   227 pages.

(Reproduced with permission of Dissertation Abstracts.)

The relation between thermal expansion coefficients and apparent densities of carbons. Tetsuo Yamaguchi (Tokai Electrode Mfg. Co., Ltd., Nagoya). *Kogyo Kagaku Zasshi* 62, 1719–21(1959). Tests were made on specimens cut from the centers and in the direction of the axes of cylindrical graphite electrodes 16 in. in diam. Specimens taken from the same electrodes were compared; in most cases, higher thermal expansion coeffs. went with higher apparent ds. and therefore with higher elec. conds. This relation was not found, however, between specimens tested in pairs from different electrodes of the same manuf. A section was cut from each of 2 electrodes, perpendicular to their axes. One of these electrodes was identical to the 16-in. electrodes used in the previous tests, and the other was a semimanufd., baked product. A no. of specimens were taken from each of these 2 sections, parallel to their axes, and from all parts of the sections. Higher thermal expansion coeffs. were observed in most specimens with higher apparent ds. The relation resulted from some causes which varied simultaneously both with the thermal expansion and the apparent d. of the C or the graphite. It was confirmed during the production of C in the lab. that one of these causes was the use of pitch binder in making the C.   CA

Industrial separation of metals in columns by the exchange extraction method. P. I. Bobikov and L. M. Gindin (Mining-Met. Combine, Noril'sk). *Izv. Sibirsk. Otd. Akud. Nauk SSSR* 1962, No. 6, 46–53. The metathetic equil. between the chloride of one metal and the monocarboxylate of another in a system contg. immiscible aq. and org. solvents permits the operation of a countercurrent extn. system in a packed column. The order of decreasing tendency of metals to enter the org. phase is $Sn^{4+} > Bi^{+++} > Fe^{+++} > Pb^{++} > Al^{+++} > Cu^{++} > Cd^{++} > Zn^{++} > Ni^{++} > Co^{++} > Mn^{++} > Ca^{++} > Mg^{++} > Na^{+}$. Distribution coeffs. were developed where the org. radical was a C_7–C_9 com. aliphatic monocarboxylic acid. The aq. phase consisted of aq. HCl + dissolved metal chlorides, and the org. phase consisted of the free org. acid and its metal salts. The distribution coeffs. were: $Na^{++}-Co^{++}$ 1.8, $Zn^{++}-Co^{++}$ 5.0, $Cd^{++}-Co^{++}$ 35.0, $Co^{++}-Mn^{++}$ 1.4, $Cu^{++}-Co^{++}$ 100–500, $Fe^{+++}-Co^{++}$ 10,000, $Co^{++}-Na^{+}$ 100–200. Values $\geqq 100$ vary with concn. The extn. column is illustrated for Co–Ni sepn. The $CoCl_2-NiCl_2$ mixt. is fed into the center of the column. NaOH is fed in at some point below it, the C_7-C_9 acid is introduced at the bottom of the column, and HCl at the top. The product streams consist of $NiCl_2$ soln. withdrawn above the point of $CoCl_2-NiCl_2$ entry, and $CoCl_2$ soln. withdrawn below it. Free C_7-C_9 acid is removed from the top of the column and recycled to the bottom. The NaCl removed at the bottom is electrolyzed to yield the recycle NaOH stream, and the H and Cl are recombined for the recycle HCl stream. Operating parameters are developed for pulsed flow in Raschig ring-packed columns.

C. H. Fuchsman

(Reproduced with permission of Chemical Abstracts.)

RÉSUMÉS

In response to the rather special needs of a complex system for getting people jobs, the term "résumé" has come to have a particular meaning. It is unlikely that a person today seeking white-collar employment in a large American city can be maximally successful without a résumé.

A résumé is a carefully constructed report which provides a profile and summing up of the personal data, work experience, and educational background of an individual. It is prepared by a job seeker for perusal by a prospective employer. As an abstract of the fundamental facts about a person which are pertinent to his suitability for employment in a particular job, the résumé has become a helpful instrument to both employee and employer.

There are no fixed rules for presenting a résumé. Major practice suggests that only one or two sheets of standard 8½- by 11-inch paper should be used. Also, it is common to present information about experience and education chronologically in reverse, starting with the most recent facts and working back. Reference to race or religion is not only regarded as unessential but is forbidden by law in some states.

If the résumé is transmitted to a prospective employer directly by the job seeker rather than by a personnel employment agency, it should be accompanied by a short transmittal letter. The letter ought to indicate the point of contact (newspaper ad, personal friends, etc.), the precise nature of the job being sought, and a commentary on the special qualifications of the writer. The letter should, of course, end by saying when the writer is available for a personal interview.

Reference to salary requirements, either in the résumé or accompanying letter, is open to individual choice. Good arguments exist for and against inclusion of this information. The present author favors the mentioning of salary, but preferably within ranges ($10,000 to $11,500, for example), so long as the figures are realistic at both extremes.

SPECIMENS*

BREWSTER L. KNAPP
PHYSICIST

EDUCATIONAL QUALIFICATIONS

Presently attending St. John's University, Jamaica, Long Island. Candidate for Degree of Master of Science in Physics in June, 1964.

Curriculum –   Theoretical Physics

Wave Mechanics

Graduated from Queens College in June 1961 with Degree of Bachelor of Science in Physics.

Major:	Mechanics
	Electricity & Magnetism
	Optics
	Modern Physics
	Thermodynamics
	Electronics
Minor:	Chemistry
	Differential Equations
	Advanced Calculus
	General Relativity

Concentrated on Machine drawing and drafting at home. Pursued the designing and construction of electronic circuits as a hobby. Capable of operating small machine shop.

EXPERIENCE QUALIFICATIONS

June 1961/Feb. 1963 – Employed by Explosions Engineering, Inc.,
Windsor, Conn.

(Critical Facilities Nuclear Division)

Assisted in designing, constructing and performing experiments on Nuclear Reactors.

Familiar with IBM FORTRAN Data Reduction and experienced in

---

* Reproduced with permission of Allwin Resume Service, New York. Names of individuals and other personal data are fictitious.

criticality calculations and analysis of experimental results.
Also have knowledge of electronic instrumentation.
MILITARY: Presently under student deferment.

24 years of age   Single
          3465 Nasturtium Blvd., Amagansett, N. Y.
              Telephone: Amagansett 6-3412

Melvin R. Morse   34 Lovatt Drive
                                               Stamford, Connecticut
                                               DAvis 3-4115
     CHIEF ACCOUNTANT — ASSISTANT CONTROLLER — CONTROLLER
     *   *   *   *   *   *   *   *   *   *   *   *   *   *   *

Nearly twenty years of progressive experience, through a number
of responsible positions, in all elements of accounting; a
well rounded knowledge of other phases of business operations.

          *   *   *   *   *   *   *   *   *   *   *   *   *   *
                    RECORD OF EXPERIENCE
          1942 to Present ROUND LINE, INC., New York City

1961 – Present: ASSISTANT TO THE COMPTROLLER (100 Employees)
     Assist the Comptroller in the administration of the Accounting
     Department and responsible for the department in his absence.
     Liaison between Accounting Department and the Treasurer,
     between the Accounting Department and the Executive Vice
     President. In charge of special projects — cash flow studies,
     review of investments vs. bonds for best utilization of cash,
     study of cash reports for control of accounts payable, analysis
     of cargo handling costs for establishment of most advantageous
     rates, policy on charges acceptable by agents, drawing up of
     agency contracts, special systems studies, analysis of financial
     statements, review of operating and capital budgetary controls,
     etc.

1959-1961 MANAGER, ACCOUNTING LEDGERS DEPARTMENT
          (60-36 Employees)
     Responsible for the administration, personnel and production
     of ledgers sections covering stevedore and vessel payrolls,
     accounts payable, agency and vessel disbursements, claim
     payments, government contract invoices, freight and mail
     revenue accounts, passenger revenue accounts, property,
     securities, cash, insurance, etc., and all other accounts
     through and including a corrected trial balance. Responsible

for Terminal, Advertising and General and Administrative
Profit and Loss Statements and their comparison to budget.
Familiar with I.B.M. accounting. A complete systems and
procedures study under my supervision resulted in a reduction
in staff from 57 to 33 in two years and a savings of almost
$100,000. per year in departmental overhead costs.

1958-1959 NINE MONTHS EXECUTIVE TRAINING PROGRAM
Actual working experience, observation and instruction in
every phase of the company including operations, traffic,
claims, and insurance, treasurers and sales.

1955-1958 ASSISTANT SECTION HEAD, FINANCIAL REPORTS SECTION
(7 Employees)
In addition to complete responsibility for intricate accountings
on government contracts on a current basis, prepared monthly,
quarterly and annual financial statements, on both individual
and consolidated basis, prepared Capital Employed statements,
handled reserve fund accounts, property and security accounts
and numerous special reports and analyses such as cash flow,
analyses of surplus and net worth, industry reports, proposed
mergers, 10 and 20 year projections, budget material, etc.
Due to illness of superior assumed full responsibility for
section, closing of books and preparation of financial
statements for year 1958. Accounting changed in this period
from Remington Rand bookkeeping machines to full IBM
accounting.

1953-1955 SECTION HEAD, SUBSIDY ACCOUNTS SECTION (3 Employees)
Complete responsibility for review and audit of the books of the
company and its subsidiaries and submission of revised
financial statements under provisions of U. S. Government
contract for Operating Differential Subsidy. The section
worked itself out of a full time job and function was absorbed
by Financial Reports Section.

1948-1953 ASSISTANT SECTION HEAD, PASSENGER ACCOUNTS SECTION
(13 Employees)
General accounting, "trouble shooting," and administrative
work in section of 13 employees handling passenger sales, bar,
slop chest baggage and baggage insurance accounting as well as
master and pursers accounts. Immediate superior had heart
attack; assumed many of the administrative burdens he
ordinarily carried.

1945-1948 MILITARY SERVICE – U.S. NAVAL RESERVE
Port operations officer at advanced bases in Pacific area.
(Present status: Lieutenant, USNR (Retired))

1944-1945 ASSISTANT CASHIER AND SUPERVISOR
Assistant cashier and supervisor of Accounts Receivable
Section amounting to $50,000,000. a year. Experience in
extension of credit and credit ratings.

1942-1944
Experience in Bill of Lading Department and Freight Cashiers.

EDUCATION
1937/1941	Carver College – Bachelor of Arts Degree
1942/1943	Columbia University Graduate School – Course in Export-Import Traffic Management.
1943/1944	Coast Guard School, New York – Mathematics, Seamanship, Meteorology, Navigation – Jr. Navigators certificate
1957/1958	Alexander Hamilton Institute – Business Administration
1958/1959	School of World Trade – Course in steamship operation
1958/1959	N. Y. University Graduate School – Course in Marketing
1959/1960	Various A.M.A. seminars.

CIVIC ACTIVITIES:
1949/1961	Community Chest Drive
1954/1955	Stamford Health Association Drive
1961	District Captain – American Red Cross

PERSONAL DATA:
43 years old, married – 4 children, U.S. citizen, in excellent
health.

CLARENCE J. WETHERILL   ATTORNEY-AT-LAW

125 Buckingham Road   Admitted to the Bar of the State of
Bronx 19, New York   New York
Telephone: BL-4-6593   December 5, 1961

EDUCATION:

1957/1961:   Received LL.B. degree in June, 1961 from St. John's
University School of Law, Brooklyn, N. Y. Standing in class:
Top quarter. Activities: Phi Delta Phi Legal Fraternity.
Awards: American Jurisprudence Prize in Evidence.

1951/1955:   Columbia College, Columbia University in New York
City. Received A.B. degree with Major in Ecomomics and minor in
Government. Standing in class: Top third. Activities: Played
Freshman and Varsity Football, member of Tau Epsilon Phi
Fraternity.

LEGAL EMPLOYMENT:

1961/Present: IRVING SMATHER, ESQ.
                  319 7th Avenue, New York, New York
Legal Assistant.
Position involves researching legal problems; preparation of
pleadings, primarily for the Federal Courts; calendar calls
and other appearances at Court and the general duties of a law
clerk.

EMPLOYMENT WHILE ATTENDING LAW SCHOOL:

1959/1961:   MEXICAN FARM LOYALTY INSURANCE GROUP
             141 Livingston Street, Brooklyn, N. Y.
Casualty Claims Adjuster
Position entailed the investigation and adjustment of personal
injury and property damage liability claims.

1958/1959:   ALL GRADES INSURANCE COMPANY
             71 West 23 Street, New York, N. Y.
Automobile Property Damage Claims Examiner
Position included the handling of subrogation claims against
third parties.

1957/1958:   MINNEAPOLIS-SWEETROLL MODIFIERS COMPANY
             Long Island City, N. Y.
Administrative Assistant to the Branch Office Manager.

1950/1955:   Held various part-time and summer positions in order
             to augment the financing of A.B. degree.

MILITARY SERVICE:

1955/1957:   U.S. NAVY – Lieutenant (Junior grade.) Served as
Communications Watch Officer for COMFLEACTS YOKOSUKA, JAPAN.
Hold final top-secret/cryptographic clearance. Responsible
for plain language and crypto centers, supervising 3 officers
24 enlisted men.

PERSONAL: Born: April 6, 1934 in Mamaroneck, N. Y. Married, one child. Health: Excellent. Height: 5'10. Weight: 170 lbs.

HARLAN ROBBINS
COMMUNICATIONS ENGINEER

Business	Home
LST Surface Communications	36 Forest Avenue
75 Varick Street	Elizabeth
New York 13, N. Y.	New Jersey
Walker 5-3716, Ext. 563	Becker 9-4747

TYPE OF WORK DESIRED:
1. Communication Systems Planning
2. Communication Equipment Development
3. Electronic Equipment Research and Design
4. Communication System Operations

QUALIFIED BY

35 years experience in communication engineering and operations. Service in Philippines (6 years), Tangier, Africa (7 months)
Last five years close contact with USAF, and U.S. Army Communication System Design.

EXPERIENCE HISTORY
Private

SENIOR DESIGN ENGINEER – LST COMMUNICATIONS, INC., (1928 - 1948)
Started as a student engineer and became thoroughly familiar with all phases of the radio communications from an engineering and commercial aspect. Designed and constructed high powered HF, MF, and VLF transmitters, HF directive antennas, high speed keying systems, data transmission. Designed and installed complete radio stations at Manilla, P. I. and Tangier, Africa.

SENIOR PROJECT ENGINEER – REDFER RADIO CO., (1948-1950)
Developed diversity receiving and frequency shift transmitting equipment and system.

SENIOR PROJECT ENGINEER – GAS AFFILIATES, INC. (1950-1951)
Developed AN/GRC 26 Radio Equipment for Signal Corps.

SENIOR PROJECT ENGINEER – US Department of State (1951-1954)
Developed anti-jam equipment and techniques. Chief – Propagation and Frequency Section.

RESEARCH ASSOCIATE – BUSTER LABORATORIES, INC. (1954-1956)
Developed classified military equipment (ECM and SSB).
Developed commercial carrier telephone equipment.

HARLAN ROBBINS

EXPERIENCE
HISTORY
(Cont'd)

PRIVATE CONSULTING ENGINEER (1956 to 1959)
Specialized in transistor applications to carrier equipment, telephone instruments, paging receivers, data transmission over long wire lines, DC to DC power supplies for mobile and airborne equipment, SSB transmitters and receivers.

SENIOR PROJECT ENGINEER, ROBERT AIRCRAFT CO., Communication Division (1959-1962)
Specialized in System Design and Equipment Development. Primarily concerned with HF and UHF facilities for SAC and NORAD for planes and missile complexes. Considerable work in ECM and reliability fields.

SENIOR PROJECT ENGINEER, LST Surface Communications (1962 to present)
Specialized in System Design for U.S. Army (UNICOM). Work primarily in long haul radio circuits for high speed data transmission. Familiar with current and proposed modulation techniques to combat jamming and multipath.

<u>Military</u>	Present Rank – CAPTAIN, United States Naval Reserve Active duty 1941-1946 Executive Officer, Design Division, Bureau of Ships, 1941/44 Staff Radio Officer, COMSOPAC 1944/45 Commanding Officer, Shore Radio Section, BuShips 1945/46 Commanding Officer – Naval Reserve Electronics Company 3-36 1957 to 1960.
PROFESSIONAL AFFILIATIONS	SENIOR MEMBER – Institute of Radio Engineers PGCS Member Chairman Membership Committee 1958-1959 PGAP Member, AFCEA Member, American Legion Member.
PATENTS	#2,084,740 Filter Circuits #2,171,243 Frequency Control System #2,236,195 Automatic Control Device #2,248,770 FM/PM Modulation System #2,283,617 Antenna System (Folded Radiators) #2,968,718 Diversity Signal Selector Pending Communication System (Anti-Multipath) Pending Vehicle Identification System Pending Transistor crystal oscillator
PAPERS	"Geo-Magnetic Absorption" IRE/URSI Washington, D. C., 1954. Many classified reports and surveys
SECURITY CLEARANCE	Top Secret – 1960
AVAILABILITY	30 days or less.
REFERENCES	Any or all past employers may be contacted for information. Names on request.

<u>CHARLES S. VALENTINE</u>

43-56 Garden Street
Garden City, L.I., N. Y.

```
EXECUTIVE ASSISTANT  -  TREASURER
CONTROLLER  -  CHIEF ACCOUNTANT  -  AUDITOR
```

- . . . 31 years old, married, B. S. in Business administration, veteran.
- . . . Over 6 years diversified experience culminating in the position of Senior Accountant with internationally known firm of certified public accountants.
- . . . Fully experienced in all phases of preparation of financial statements, audit reports, state and federal taxes.
- . . . Adept at working well with management and subordinates.
- . . . Broad knowledge of varied types of businesses, particularly in the public utility, service organization, and investment fields.

RECORD OF EXPERIENCE

September, 1953 – Present	STEWART, ALLISON & GOLDBRIAR
(Includes military service leave)	34 Broadway, New York, N. Y.

Started with this international firm of Certified Public Accountants as a Junior Accountant and moved progressively to Semi-Senior and Senior Accountant at an above-average rate of advancement.

As a Senior Accountant, my responsibilities include being in full charge of audits of financial statements, the preparation of audit reports, and the supervision of staff assistants assigned to me. In addition to these responsibilities, I have prepared state and federal tax returns for gas and electric utility companies, investment funds, service organizations, manufacturing companies, etc., and also worked closely with the controllers and treasurers of the respective companies on these various assignments.

Through my work, I have gained a broad knowledge of business and financial procedures, and have become familiar with the operating of general accounting, budget, and cost systems.

It is now my desire to obtain a position in a business organization. My employer is aware of my plans to seek such employment.

EDUCATION and EXTRA-CURRICULAR ACTIVITIES
1950 – 1953 MIAMI UNIVERSITY, Oxford, Ohio

Graduated 1953.   Bachelor of Science in Business Administration.
Major in accounting.   Courses in Accounting, Business, Finance,
Business Law, Economics, Mathematics, etc.

Attended 1951 summer sessions at Mount Union College, Alliance,
Ohio, with courses in Economics.

Member of Theta Chi Fraternity.   Held office as Chapter Marshall.

Photographer for College Newspaper and Yearbook.

MILITARY SERVICE
December, 1953 – December, 1955 U.S. Army

Graduated from Army Finance School as Disbursing Specialist.
Assigned as Supply Clerk and subsequently placed in charge of
company supply office at Ft. Benjamin Harrison, Indiana.

While in service, worked nights in the Transit Department,
Alabama National Bank, Indianapolis, Indiana.   Employed as
an IBM Proof Machine Operator.

Honorable discharge.

26

The Library Research Paper

By utilizing the full resources of the library, the research paper draws its materials from diverse printed origins. Facts and ideas on a particular subject are assembled and studied with a view to interpreting them and drawing a conclusion. From scattered sources the researcher brings together all known materials into a fresh pattern of interpretation.

Since the phrase "library research paper" is chiefly used to describe that famous term paper which hundreds of thousands of college undergraduates and graduate students undertake each semester, a certain caution must be directed to them. The admonition is a reminder that library research is far from the rotelike, mechanical exercise which students often take it to be. One does not rather dumbly gather all the books about him and automatically commence copying out information into a kind of crazy quilt.

The library research paper is discriminatingly controlled and directed at all times toward a specific predetermined objective. Information is gathered, noted, sifted, weighed, and collated in terms of its applicability and suitability to the precise research aim. Only those library materials likely to fix an illuminating glow upon the exact topic at hand should be allowed into the final manuscript. Research is a highly creative, individualized process throughout which the perceptive imagination must be fully exercised. Balanced judgment must be used in selecting and placing the materials in a fine state of equipoise. The finished library research paper ought to be a reasonable arrangement of the materials, a self-sufficient document that fully satisfies the research objective and reflects the originality of the researcher.

THE PRELIMINARY BIBLIOGRAPHY

Making a preliminary bibliography is the most important step in Phase I of creating a library research paper.

Before any report of consequence can be written, preliminary bibliographic research is essential.

As the repository for the accumulated wisdom of the race, the library must necessarily become familiar terrain to the reporter. In a business setting, the executive faced with a decision must keep abreast of current policies and procedures developed by other organizations in the field. He will probably wish to trace the historical development of the problem with which he is faced. Or he may need to acquire extensive background on a new subject. Need for bibliographic research in reports for business and for all fields is abundantly manifest.

The preliminary bibliography should provide for the report writer a full picture of all the work hitherto published in the field. To undertake a report without knowing this could be disastrously wasteful. It would be dismal to devote hours of arduous effort in preparing a report on something that another writer has already fully treated in a publication.

Though each writer will develop his own method of procedure, it is probably best to assemble and record the preliminary bibliography before attempting to actually examine any of the material. First, the mechanics of using the library and of compiling and recording the preliminary bibliography will be taken up. Then, how to take notes from the materials will be discussed. (How to shape the data was discussed in Chapter 11.)

THE LIBRARY

A library has three principal kinds of holdings: (1) a general collection of books, (2) a collection of reference works, and (3) a collection of periodicals, newspapers, magazines, journals, bulletins, and pamphlets. The report writer, to gain a comprehensive view of the available knowledge on his subject, must adequately explore all three areas.

The General Collection

In this classification will be found most of the books in the library—those available for general circulation. Small libraries may place most of their general collection on open shelves where the books are accessible to all. Large libraries usually keep their collection in stacks, access to which is not possible for the public. The person wanting to obtain a book from such a library must first fill out a call slip bearing the call number of the book he desires, the name of its author, and the title. To obtain this information, he must first go to the card catalog.

The card catalog provides an index to the entire library. It lists every book and every bound magazine, whether it is in the stacks or on the open shelves of the reference room.

The report writer will, of course, find that the card catalog consists of 3- by 5-inch cards arranged alphabetically in drawers. For most books, there will be at least three separate cards in the catalog: (1) an author card, (2) a title card, and (3) a subject card. Therefore, if one knows the surname of the author, he may obtain full information necessary to withdraw the book with a call slip by consulting the author card. If one knows only the title of a book, full information may be had from the alphabetically filed title card. Or, as will frequently be the case at the outset of the research, if one knows only the general subject about which he is seeking information, he will find all the available books listed under that subject.

Following is a specimen author card from the card catalog, filed alphabetically according to the surname of the author:

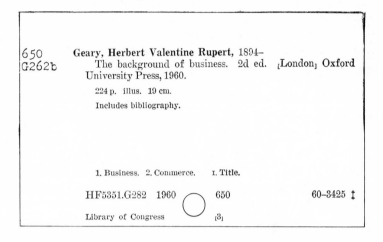

The key to the information on the author card above is as follows:

a.   650—Call number of the book
G262b

b.   Geary, Herbert Valentine Rupert, 1894   —Name of the author, date of his birth; he is still living.

c.   The background of business. 2d ed. [London] Oxford University Press, 1960.—Full title of the book, edition, place of publication, publisher, and date of publication.

d.   224p. illus. 19 cm.—Book contains 224 pages and is illustrated; it is 19 centimeters high (an inch is 2.54 centimeters).

e.   Includes bibliography.

f.   1. Business. 2. Commerce. I. Title.—The book is also listed in the card catalog under these subject headings, and there is also a separate title card for it. (Arabic numerals are used to indicate subject headings and Roman numerals title headings.)

g.   HF5351. G282 1960 —Library of Congress call number with the date of publication.

h.   650—Dewey decimal system call number of the card.

i.   60–3425—Order number used by librarians to order the book.

j.   Library of Congress—book has been housed in and cataloged by the Library of Congress.

k.   3—A printer's key to the card.

The title card is a copy of the author card, with the title typed in just above the author's name. The title card is filed in the catalog according to the first important word in the title.

Each of the subject cards is also a copy of the author card shown above, with the subject typed in (usually in red) above the author's name. It is filed alphabetically by subject. Since the subject listing provides all the books available, it is, as we have said, the most likely classification the report writer undertaking a preliminary bibliography will first explore.

The key to the call number shown on the specimen author card above is the Dewey decimal system, the system used in classifying books. The ten classes of the Dewey system were given in Chapter 13 in the course of the discussion on the concept of classification. The other system of classification used in America, especially by large libraries, is the Library of Congress system, which divides books by letters into the following classes:

A General works	M Music
B Philosophy—Religion	N Fine arts
C History—Auxiliary sciences	P Language and literature
D Foreign history and topography	Q Science
E–F American history	R Medicine
G Geography—Anthropology	S Agriculture
H Social sciences	T Technology
J Political science	U Military science
K Law	V Naval science
L Education	Z Bibliography—Library science

Each of these sections is further divided by letters and numbers which show the specific call number of a particular book.

Obviously, the more familiar and experienced the report writer becomes in locating source materials quickly through use of the card catalog, the less painful becomes his task. Adequate knowledge of the working order of the card catalog is necessarily prerequisite to any degree of competence in library research.

Reference Works

The report writer who can find his way among the invaluable reference works available, usually, on the open shelves of the library's main reading room is well launched on his project. There is certainly no better way to effectively gain a broad overall view of a new subject one is just starting to explore than through use of reference works.

One engaged in report writing gradually adds to his knowledge of reference books through experience. Though it merely serves to skim the surface in selected areas, the following list presents some reference works useful in report writing.

Guides to Reference Books

Cook, M. G. *The New Library Key*. New York: H. W. Wilson, 1956.

Murphey, Robert W. *How and Where to Look It Up; A Guide to Standard Sources of Information*. Consultant: Mabel S. Johnson. Foreword by Louis Shores. New York: McGraw-Hill Book Co., 1958.

Russell, H. G., R. H. Shove, and B. E. Moen. *The Use of Books and Libraries*. Minneapolis: University of Minnesota Press, 1958.

Shores, Louis. *Basic Reference Books*. Chicago: American Library Association, 1954.

Winchell, C. M. *Guide to Reference Books*. Chicago: American Library Association, 1951. Supplements, 1951–52, 1953–55, 1956–58.

General Encyclopedias

Columbia Encyclopedia. 2nd ed. Ed. by William Bridgwater and Elizabeth J. Sherwood. New York: Columbia University Press, 1950.

Encyclopedia Americana. New York: American Corporation, 1956. 30 vols.

Encyclopaedia Britannica, 14th ed. New York: Encyclopaedia Britannica, Inc., 1956. 24 vols.

New International Encyclopedia. 2nd ed. New York: Dodd, Mead and Company, 1914–16. 24 vols. Plate revision, 1922. Supplements, 1925, 1930.

Dictionaries, Word Books

Dictionary of American English on Historical Principles. Ed. by Sir W. A. Craigie and J. R. Hulbert. Chicago: The University of Chicago Press, 1936–44. 4 vols.

Fowler, Henry W. *Dictionary of Modern English Usage*. New York: Oxford University Press, 1934.

New Standard Dictionary. New York: Funk and Wagnalls Company, 1952.

Oxford English Dictionary. Ed. by A. H. Murray *et al.* Oxford: The Clarendon Press, 1888–1933. 10 vols. and supplement. Reissue, corrected, 1933. 12 vols. and supplement. The original issue is known as *New English Dictionary*.

Perrin, Porter G. *Writer's Guide and Index to English*. 3rd ed. Chicago: Scott, Foresman and Company, 1959.

Roget's International Thesaurus. New ed. New York: Thomas Y. Crowell, 1946.

Webster's Dictionary of Synonyms. Springfield, Massachusetts: G. & C. Merriam Company, 1942.

Webster's New International Dictionary. Unabridged. Springfield, Massachusetts: G. & C. Merriam Company, 1954.

Year Books

Americana Book of the Year, 1924 to date. New York: Americana Corporation, 1924—.

Britannica Book of the Year, 1938 to date. Chicago: Encyclopaedia Britannica, Inc., 1938—.

Facts on File. A weekly digest of world events. New York: Person's Index, Inc., 1940—.

New International Year Book, 1907 to date. New York: Dodd, Mead and Company, 1908–31; Funk and Wagnalls Company, 1932—.

Stateman's Year Book, 1864 to date. London: The Macmillan Company, 1864—.

World Almanac and Book of Facts, 1886 to date. New York: The New York World-Telegram, 1886—.

Atlases

Columbia-Lippincott Gazetteer of the World. New York: Columbia University Press, 1952.

Commercial Atlas. Chicago: Rand, McNally and Company. Issued annually.

Cosmopolitan World Atlas. 2nd ed. Chicago: Rand, McNally and Company, 1951.

Encyclopaedia Britannica World Atlas. New York: Encyclopaedia Britannica, Inc. Frequently revised.

Webster's Geographical Dictionary. Rev. ed. Springfield, Mass.: G. & C. Merriam Company, 1955.

General Biography

Biography Index. New York: H. W. Wilson Company, 1946—.

Cattell, Jacques. *American Men of Science*. 9th ed. Lancaster, Pennsylvania: The Science Press, 1955. 3 vols.

————. *Directory of American Scholars*. 3rd ed. Lancaster, Pennsylvania: The Science Press, 1957.

Current Biography: Who's News and Why. New York: H. W. Wilson Company, 1940—. Published monthly with half-year and annual cumulations.

Dictionary of American Biography. Ed. by Allen Johnson and Dumas Malone. New York: Charles Scribner's Sons, 1928–37. 20 vols. and index. Supplements, 1944, 1958.

Dictionary of National Biography. Ed. by Leslie Stephen and Sidney Lee. London: Smith, Elder and Company; Oxford University Press, 1885–1937. 63 vols, supplements.

International Who's Who, 1936 to date. London: Europa Publications, 1936—.

Webster's Biographical Dictionary. Springfield, Massachusetts: G. & C. Merriam Company, 1956.

Who's Who, 1848 to date. London: A. & C. Black, 1849—.

Who's Who in America, 1899–1900 to date. Chicago: A. N. Marquis Company, 1899—.

Books of Quotations

Bartlett, John. *Familiar Quotations.* 13th ed. Ed. by Christopher Morley and Louella Everett. Boston: Little, Brown and Company, 1955.

Mencken, H. L. *A New Dictionary of Quotations on Historical Principles from Ancient and Modern Sources.* New York: Alfred A. Knopf, 1942.

Stevenson, Burton. *The Home Book of Quotations.* 5th ed. New York: Dodd, Mead and Company, 1947.

Business and Trade Directories

For almost every special field of business and industry there exist directories. Only large libraries and those specializing in business information attempt to secure many of the special trade directories. An annotated listing of a sharply limited number of the most useful is given here:

Thomas' Register of American Manufacturers and First Hands in All Lines: Annual. Classified list by product, arranged geographically under each classification. Alphabetic list with home and branch officers. Trade names with the manufacturers of each.

N. W. Ayer & Son's Directory of Newspapers and Periodicals: Annual. Useful to the advertiser for geographical arrangement of periodicals, with frequency, day of publication, size of page, name of publisher, and circulation. Classified lists in supplement. Alphabetic index by title. Also gives industrial information under each place.

Moody's Manual of Investments, American and Foreign; Banks, Insurance Companies, Investment Trusts, Real Estate, Finance and Credit Companies: Useful as a directory for addresses of general offices and names of officers.

Poor's Financial Records: Fiscal manual. Useful as a directory for addresses of general offices and names of officers.

Periodical Literature

While older issues of periodicals—that is, magazines, journals, and newspapers—are usually bound in volumes and shelved in the stacks, recent issues are often kept in the open shelves of the reading rooms.

It is appalling to discover how regularly report writers fail to utilize periodical literature. This is particularly lamentable in that the most recent word on a subject will oftentimes be found in the periodical literature. Many reports are noticeably lacking in contemporaneity because the writer has not explored the various general and special guides to current periodical literature. Any preliminary bibliographical research which excludes periodic literature is woefully deficient.

A representative list of general and special periodical indexes follows:

General Indexes

Poole's Index to Periodical Literature, 1802–81, supplements through January 1, 1907. This is a subject index only; no author entries are given.

Reader's Guide to Periodical Literature, 1900 to date. This is published monthly; each year the accumulated issues are bound in volumes. The *Reader's Guide* gives entries under author, title, and subject.

International Index to Periodicals, 1907 to date. This index deals with more scholarly publications than the *Reader's Guide.* Although most of the periodicals it indexes are American, it also covers many foreign publications.

Special Indexes

These indexes list articles published in periodicals devoted to special fields. A few also list books.

Agricultural Index, 1916 to date. A subject index, appearing nine times a year and cumulated annually.

Applied Science and Technology Index, 1958 to date. (Formerly *Industrial Arts Index.*)

The Art Index, 1929 to date. An author and subject index.

Articles on American Literature, 1900–1950. (Ed. by Lewis Leary.)

Business Periodicals Index, 1958 to date. Monthly. (Formerly *Industrial Arts Index.*)

Dramatic Index, 1909–1949. Continued in *Bulletin of Bibliography,* 1950 to date. Annual index to drama and theater.

The Education Index, 1929 to date. An author and subject index.

Engineering Index, 1884 to date. An author and subject index.

Essay and General Literature Index, 1900 to date. Semiannual, with annual cumulations.

Industrial Arts Index, 1913–1957. An author and subject index, monthly, with annual cumulations. (In 1958 this index was split into *Applied Science and Technology Index* and *Business Periodicals Index.*)

Index to Legal Periodicals, 1908 to date. A quarterly author and subject index.

The New York Times Index, 1913 to date. A monthly index to news stories in *The New York Times.*

Public Affairs Information Service Bulletin, 1915 to date. Weekly, with bimonthly and annual cumulations. An index to materials on economics, politics, and sociology.

Quarterly Cumulative Index Medicus, 1927 to date. A continuation of the *Index Medicus,* 1899–1926. Indexes books as well as periodicals.

Indexes to Bulletins and Pamphlets

Boyd, Anne M. *United States Government Publications.* 3rd ed. New York: H. W. Wilson Company, 1949.

United States Government Publications: Monthly Catalog, 1895 to date.
Washington, D.C.: Government Printing Office, 1895 to date.

Vertical File Service Catalog: An Annotated Subject Catalog of Pamphlets,
1932–34. New York: H. W. Wilson Company, 1935. Supplements, 1935
to date.

BIBLIOGRAPHY CARDS

As the report writer makes his way through the card catalog, the reference shelves, and the guides to periodical literature, it is important that he make adequate records. Use of 3- by 5-inch file cards is recommended. So that full information will be available, obviating the need to return again to the bibliographic source, basic data—including the call number—should be copied out. A separate card should be made for each item; it may be that the preliminary bibliography cards will become several hundred in number, all arranged alphabetically by the author's surname. A sample bibliography card prepared by the report writer would probably look something like the following:

With the preliminary bibliography in hand, and with the objective, the preliminary plan, and the work schedule laid out, the writer is ready to begin amassing his data, the raw material for the report.

SEARCHING THE LITERATURE

Regardless of the nature of the report, a thorough search of the literature must be the first step carried out. It is not in keeping with scientific method to plunge right into the midst of an investigation without knowing all that has been published before on the subject. The human race advances through accumulated wisdom. Moreover, in view of the urgency today for American researchers to expend their efforts rapidly, efficiently, and wisely, repeating somebody else's work is positively immoral. If the report has already been written by somebody else, another report on the same work can only clutter up the literature.

Since the mechanical process of preparing the preliminary bibliography has just been explained, it remains to discuss the techniques of library-research note taking. If, as is the most common practice, the writer has put his preliminary bibliography on 3- by 5-inch file cards, there will be little need for further use of the card catalog, except occasionally to check items of information. Many researchers will have all their library call slips filled out in advance, so that note taking can proceed uninterruptedly from the flow of requested books.

As the researcher now actually undertakes to obtain and examine each item in his preliminary bibliography, there are certain steps he can follow to save time. Once any book is in his hands, he can quickly check both the table of contents and the index to determine the scope of treatment given to his subject. Also, by skimming through the prefatory material, he can determine whether the aims of the book fall within his own circle of interest. It will develop that many sources thus will be discarded as not useful to the project at hand. Perhaps the writer will actually cull only ten to fifteen usable sources from a preliminary bibliography which had consisted of one hundred or more items. Some books will contain only a chapter or chapters for scrutiny, while other whole works will have to be read. Except in totally uncharted areas of research, there will be several basic works already published with which the writer will be obliged to gain intimate familiarity.

It is at this point that careful reading and note taking must start. Skill in reading accurately for full comprehension is an invaluable asset. One should grow to be able to quickly recognize the main points in a discourse and to separate them from developmental matter. As the reading proceeds, one takes notes. Again, common practice is to use file cards; where 3- by 5-inch cards are used for the preliminary bibliography, the 5- by 8-inch cards are preferred for research note taking.

The accuracy and objectivity that the total report may ultimately have can only reflect the accuracy and objectivity with which notes are taken from individual sources. No violence may be done to source material. In note taking, it is the writer's responsibility to "scientifically" record and not to distort or interpret his sources. Whether he agrees or disagrees with the information he records is of small import; the account he renders must be true to the original. It is totally outside the spirit of research and report writing to attack or defend the position of another writer on some issue without first showing objectively what that position is. Every source must be given as disinterested and dispassionate a treatment as the report writer is capable of.

In note taking, the report writer essentially must intellectually grasp the main gist of his source, assimilate it, and then write it down—concisely and none the worse for wear—in his own words on the note card. Occasionally, an idea will be stated with such cogency and clarity in the source that to paraphrase it would be to do it injustice. However, where the report writer elects to use the words of the original, he must not overlook quotation marks and a footnote reference. The writer who fails to include these may be called intellectually dishonest by some and a plagiarist by others. Avoidance of either of these disagreeable situations may best be achieved at the note-card level. Quotation marks should be placed on the card around those portions of the writing to which they apply. At the bottom of the card, keyed to the quotes, should be all the requisite information for eventual incorporation into the footnotes. (The preparation of footnotes is taken up in Chapter 16.) Rather than take time to copy out all the footnote information onto the research note card, the report writer may adopt a system of cross-referencing with his bibliography cards. If each bibliography card is assigned a code number, this number may be recorded in a corner of the appropriate research note card. Thus, the writer will have the full bibliographic information at his disposal when it is needed. It is likewise a good plan to show someplace on the note card a code indicating where the recorded information is likely to fit into the working outline. Regarding the controlling and shaping of data as it is accumulated, more was said in Chapter 11.

Following is a sample research note card. The number in the upper left-hand corner is the report writer's key to his own final bibliography. The numeral in the upper right-hand corner refers the writer to that section of his plan or outline into which the recorded information will eventually be incorporated.

37   IV. 2. (2)

Common Market, Food Plan

[Summary
and
Paraphrasing]
    Food-exporting nations
may be excluded from world's
largest single market.

        Common market "... has
[Direct Quotation]
removed the last major obstacle
in the economic integration & possibly
the political unification of the Western
Continent."

[Writer's
Commentary]
            Fails to fully account for
N. Y. Times   most recent views of French gov't.

SPECIMEN *

A SHORT INTRODUCTION TO SEMANTICS

A Report Offered in Partial Fulfillment
of the Requirements of the Graduate Course
Advanced Composition
English 181

By
Frances Marder

C. W. Post College
Greenvale, Long Island, New York
Department of English

March, 19—

TABLE OF CONTENTS

INTRODUCTION

In a recent essay, Charlton Laird made a number of interesting statements about the words we use.

We use words as though we all agree as to what they mean and what they are good for. On that ill-founded but useful assumption, mankind make laws and enforces them, builds houses and sells them, proposes marriage, and discusses God. . .[1]

Another of his comments was:

We use words as though they were dippers, the same dipper for everybody, but the stuff that is dipped up with the dipper depends upon the body of stuff from which it is dipped. And when we use words, we are always dipping into ourselves.[2]

These remarks, by making us aware of simple truths we may never have thought about, compel us to stop, think, and come to a logical conclusion. This is precisely the attitude that semanticists would have us adopt toward all communication; and it is the main technique in the practical application of semantics.

In other words, the principal purpose of semantics, the promotion of more effective communication between individuals and between groups, has been fulfilled if it leads people, when exposed to words of any kind (written, oral, or mental) used by themselves or others, to pause briefly, to consider the words being employed, to analyze them as to intent and context, and then to act on the basis of their own reactions to what the words stand for — not to the words themselves.

This is the primary lesson of semantics, a science in which a word has no meaning in any strict sense, but only in the sense in which it is used. Semantics emphasizes that a word has many different meanings, depending upon its context, the accumulated experiences of the user, the varied experiences of the hearers, the time and place, and a host of other variable factors, A word can have only one meaning at a time, however, and, when we use it, we must be certain, if we are to avoid misunderstanding and ambiguity, that it means the same thing to our particular audience (at a particular time) that it does to us. We cannot afford to take the high-handed attitude of Humpty-Dumpty, who told Alice, "When I use a word, it means just what I choose it to mean — neither more nor less."[3]

---

[1]Charlton Laird, "Thinking About Words," in Introductory Readings on the English Language, ed. by Richard Braddock, (Prentice-Hall, Inc., Englewood Cliffs, N. J., 1962), p. 235
[2]Laird, p. 234
[3]Alan Shapiro, "As Humpty-Dumpty Told Alice," Scholastic Teacher, (Feb. 22, 1957), p. 8-T

HISTORY

Semantics was originally "significs," the science of meanings or the study of significance. The word comes from the Greek semantikos: significant meaning; but long before it was coined, scholars as far back as Aristotle had been concerned about language problems such as generalization, abstraction, inconsistencies in logic, and loose meanings generally.[4]

The name was used for the first time in 1900 by Michel Breal, a French philologist,[5] and in 1903, Lady Viola Welby officially launched modern semantics with a scholarly work entitled, What is Meaning?[6] Later, philosophers such as A. N. Whitehead and Bertrand Russell dealt with language and verbal logic, the latter demonstrating how most propositions are both true and false, depending on time and place, and calling them "propositional functions."[7]

When the Freudian viewpoint was introduced into the historical study of meaning, it created a new surge of interest in semantic research[8] culminating in the publication of I. A. Richards and C. K. Ogden's classic, The Meaning of Meaning, famous for its phrase, "find the referent" and for its "triangle of reference." Meanwhile, Count Alfred Korzybski published Science and Sanity and established a new science of general semantics, which deals not only with words and their referents (the objects pointed to) but also with their effects on human behavior. The differences between general semantics and semantics in general will be more fully dealt with in the next section, but it should be noted that in the last twenty years, all the best-known semanticists have been disciples of Korzybski. Men like S. T. Hayakawa, Stuart Chase, Wendell Johnson, Irving J. Lee, and Anatol Rapoport have been concerned with the relationship of language, thought, and action and have followed the principles of general semantics as originally set forth by Korzybski.

Today, semantics is taught in innumerable schools and colleges and, surprisingly, in many elementary schools. It boasts two active professional groups: the Institute for General Semantics and the International Society for General Semantics. The latter publishes (under the editorship of S. I. Hayakawa) a quarterly

---

[4]Stuart Chase, The Power of Words, (Harcourt, Brace & Co., N. Y., 1953), p. 181
[5]Hugh R. Walpole, Semantics, (W. W. Norton & Co., Inc., N. Y., 1941), p. 24
[6]Chase, p. 181
[7]Chase,
[8]Stephen Ullman, The Principles of Semantics, (Basil Blackwell, Oxford, England, 1957), p. 2

review called ETC., which, by its name (a semantic device)
warns its readers that it is not the sum total of all wisdom.

DEFINITIONS

Semanticists hold that dictionary definitions are merely words
about other words: dictionaries give the erroneous impression
that words have fixed meanings and that the dictionary usage is
the only accepted one.[9] Webster's definition, lengthy and
scholarly but not very edifying, bears out their contention:

> The science of meanings of words as contrasted with phonetics,
> the science of sounds; the historical and psychological study
> and the classification of changes in the signification of
> words or forms, viewed as normal and vital factors in
> linguistic development.[10]

Semanticists themselves should be the ideal source for
enlightenment on this subject, but they, unfortunately, rarely
agree about the "meaning" of anything, not even semantics. A
montage of their views, however, does provide an explanation
of what semantics is: it "explores theoretically all the
problems which come up when we compare two ways of saying the
same thing";[11] being interested in the senses of words, it may
be looked upon as "a body of questions touching upon the
connections between language and thought";[12] it is "the study of
techniques by which to accomplish purposes through the uses of
words. . . and strives for a more mature and more human use of
language in order to communicate effectively";[13] from the
semantic point of view, "to inquire into the real meaning of a
word is useless because words have a variety of unrelated
meanings, not inherent in the words themselves but in their usage
(or experience) in the world";[14] "it makes the question 'What do
you mean?' a request to share the experiences associated with
the words you are using";[15] it emphasizes the "language situation,"
a set of relationships involving facts, someone evaluating the
facts in a certain way, and a language which represents the

[9]Irving J. Lee, Language Habits in Human Affairs, (Harper & Bros.,
N. Y., 1941), p. 39
[10]Webster's New International Dictionary of the English Language,
Second Edition, (G. & C. Merriam Co., Springfield, Mass., 1959),
p. 2273
[11]Walpole, p. 14, (Introduction by I. A. Richards).
[12]Walpole, p. 34
[13]Bess Sondel, The Humanity of Words, (World Publ. Co., N. Y.,
1958), pp. 19-20
[14]Anatol Rapoport, "Science and the Goals of Man," in
Introductory Readings, ed. by Braddock, pp. 264-65
[15]Rapoport

evaluation.[16]   In other words, semantics is the science which deals with the different uses and meanings of words and language and with the relationships among words, language, thought, and behavior.

Semantics differs from general semantics in that the former is the study of meaning in all its branches, whereas the latter "connotes the study of the psychological, sociological, and political implications of meaning."[17]   General semantics is "the relationship between how we talk, therefore how we think, and therefore how we act."[18]   Hayakawa explains this by saying that it is interested in the human responses to words or "semantic reactions,"[19] which are the "internal residue" of all our habits, traits, contacts, education, and experiences. He therefore redefines general semantics as "a comparative study of the kinds of responses people make to the symbols and signs around them — or the study of how not to be a damn fool."[20]

SPECIFIC TECHNIQUES

There can be many causes of communication failure, as Stuart Chase points out. Some of these are: confusing words with things, failing to check abstract terms with concrete events (find the referent), guilt-by-verbal association, over-generalization, gobbledygook, and confusing facts with inferences and judgments.[21] Korzybski proposed his semantic devices of "stop, look, and listen" to avoid these and other misuses of language and to help in evaluation. The devices are:

1. Dating — placing an object at some point in time so that one does not assume it is for "all time." This avoids great, sweeping statements about men and events.[22] For example, the president 1938 is not the same as the president 1964.

2. Index numbers — to show uniqueness and that there is no complete sameness between two of anything. But our language should show similarities as well as differences in things. The use of this device breaks up false identification. For instance,

---

[16]Irving J. Lee, The Language of Wisdom and Folly, (Harper & Bros., N. Y., 1949), p. xvi
[17]Laird, p. 236
[18]S. I. Hayakawa, The Use and Misuse of Language, (Fawcett Publ., Greenwich, Conn., 1962), p. vii
[19]S. I. Hayakawa, "How Words Change our Minds," Saturday Evening Post, (Dec. 27, 1958), pp. 22, 72-4
[20]Hayakawa, "How Words Change Our Minds."
[21]Chase, p. 11
[22]Lee, Language Habits, p. 76

Man$_1$ (man and wife) is not the same as

Man$_2$ (he's a real man) is not the same as

Man$_3$ (ancient man), etc.

3. Use of the hyphen — to show relatedness of words.

4. Quotes — as a signal for attention, especially to abstract terms. They say slow down and look at the context carefully.

5. Use of "etc." — to remind us of the characteristics left out. It indicates that there is more to a statement than can be said.

The core of Korzybski's work was his attempt "to give ordinary talk some of the benefit of the new talk in science"[23] and his effort to bring "the structure of language closer to the structure of the space-time world."[24] He often used the simile of the map, explaining that a map of the territory is not the territory itself. So, too, language is not the world around us, but a guide to that world. However detailed a map may be, it can never tell all about the territory. Similarly, language cannot tell "all" about an event; some characteristics will always be omitted.[25] While Korzybski did not achieve a great deal through physical research, his work was an important contribution to the field of communication because he was the first to devise and explain the principles and because he started many controversies, stimulating much interest in the behavior of words and causing people to look to their terms.

The "triangle of reference," devised by Ogden and Richards, is another technique for clarifying "what we mean." The triangle involves three aspects of meaning — words, thoughts, and things, and it shows the relationship of these three, the components of every communication process.[26]

There is no base in this triangle because there is no direct relation between words and things, but the circuit is not completed until words are referred through thoughts to things. The main point is that the symbol is not the referent; the word is not the thing. Semantically, the important thing is that a human being is at the center of the process, showing that a word is slightly different for each human being. The obligation of the user, therefore, is to know just what his words refer to out in the world, and each participant must find out what the key words of the user refer to. Communication takes place only when the words of a user refer the thoughts of all participants to the same object.[27]

[23]Chase, p. 124
[24]Chase, p. 127
[25]Chase, p. 137
[26]Sondel, p. 48
[27]Sondel

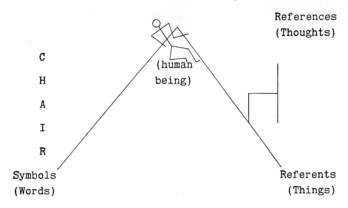

References
(Thoughts)

C

H

A

I

R

Symbols
(Words)

Referents
(Things)

The triangle is restricted to referential language because
emotive words (referring to attitudes or feelings) are not symbols,
but fictions. When listening to words, therefore, if we think
of the triangle, it is possible for us to pick out and check the
"references" and to ignore the emotions. Awareness of these
different characteristics of words (map) and what they stand for
(territory) should lead to the understanding that all utterance
is to be neither blindly accepted nor blindly rejected.[28]

Just as it is easy to make a map without surveying the territory,
it is easy for people to verbalize at random, but:

a map is not the territory,
a word is not the thing in all its senses,
A P P L E   is not

Each word must be considered only in its context, and this context
may be verbal, physical, or psychological.

CONCLUSIONS

This is an age of words. We are constantly being bombarded
by them via every conceivable medium. Conversely, we need
constantly to use them for purposes of our own. This being the
case, it is evident that semantics can help us to understand
better what we hear, read, and say, to talk and write more
effectively, and to think more accurately.[29] By applying
semantic techniques, we can recognize ambiguous and distorted
uses of words and judge whether this use is deliberate. Through
a knowledge of semantics, we get new insights into the causes of
prejudice and mental blocks, and we can see the dangers inherent in

---

[28]Lee, Language Habits, p. 22
[29]Walpole, p. 28

generalizing and in identifying and classifying things arbitrarily without valid reasons. Above all, semantics teaches us to avoid misuses of language and to encourage the best use of words for the accomplishment of human goals.

These benefits are important on an individual basis; when applied to groups and nations, however, their value is immeasurably greater. Clement Attlee has said, "The people of the world are islands shouting at each other over seas of misunderstanding."[30] An understanding of semantics could do much to alleviate miscomprehension among nations by emphasizing clear thinking and by establishing common grounds for discussion.

Semantics has run ahead of the grammarians whose science is still rooted in archaic Greek and Latin,[31] and it continues to develop because there is no end to the study of the "intricate relationships between language, thought, and action and because the insights and training it provides are useful in almost every field."[32]

Semantics does not offer the answer to all problems of language and behavior. It is not a cure-all. And certainly the general public cannot be expected to employ specific semantic techniques every time they speak, write, or listen. In this field, however, it is awareness that counts most. Semantics should be part of every high school curriculum so that our young people can learn to be aware of the functions of language. Only in this way, "by becoming sensitive to the relationships between language and behavior"[33] and by acquiring skill in recognizing and thinking about these relationships, can we "gear ourselves to reality and free ourselves from what Stuart Chase called the 'tyranny of words'."[34]

SELECTED GLOSSARY OF TERMS USED BY SEMANTICISTS

Because semantics is of interest to mathemeticians, logicians, physicists, anthropologists, lawyers, physicians, psychiatrists, philosophers, sociologists, educators, artists, literary critics, and grammarians and because it encompasses all areas of language, meaning, and behavior, it would obviously be impossible to go into detail about the diverse aspects of semantics in actual operation in a report as limited as this one. I have,

---

[30]Chase, p. 185
[31]Chase, p. 76
[32]Hayakawa, Use and Misuse, p. ix

[33]Wendell Johnson, Your Most Enchanted Listener, (Harper & Bros., N. Y., 1956), p. 174
[34]Johnson

therefore, appended this glossary of the vocabulary peculiar to semantics in order to help clarify some of the concepts which have been discussed. These terms have been drawn chiefly from the works by Briggs, Sondel, Hayakawa, and Rapoport (please see bibliography).

Abstracting — the process of selecting certain characteristics of "reality" and leaving others out. When we call a Boston terrier, a bulldog, a chihuahua, and a wolf-hound, dogs, we have abstracted what is common to them all, ignoring for the time being the differences among them.

Abstraction Ladder — a device for illustrating the process of abstraction, with the most specific reality at one end and the most abstract at the other. Semanticists see danger in our tendency to use words so far abstracted from reality that their reference is not clear. Hayakawa lists the following words as more and more abstract: Bessie the Cow, cow, bovine, quadruped, animal, organism.

Classification — naming something and putting it in a group. An individual object or event has no name and belongs to no class until we put it in one. Semantically, classification tells us not only what individuals in a class have in common, but that certain characteristics are left out.

Connotation — implied meaning.

Definition — a particular road which takes the hearer from a common referent to one that is new to him. There are many ways of defining, such as: "this is it . . ., this is similar to . . ., this is the opposite of . . .," etc.

Delayed Reaction — stopping to think things over; a sign of emotional maturity.

Denotation — the same as "extensional meaning" and "referent."

Emotive Language — affective language; language of feeling, as used in poetry.

Extensional Meaning — the object in the "real" world. The meaning is the object which we can point to.

Extensional Orientation — the tendency to check statements by facts, by personal observation, and inspection prior to making statements.

Fiction — a word which refers to an invention of the mind; not the name of an object or specific sense-experience (i.e., democracy, friendship, justice).

Identification — treating as identical all occurrences of a given word or symbol without discriminating among them; assuming that the "thing" is just what the word says it is and acting as if words and what they represent have some inherent natural connection. If we treat all cases alike, when their differences are important, there is something wrong with our semantic habits. (i.e., all Jews or Negroes or Russians are the same because of the label attached to them).

Inference – a guess.

Intensional Meaning – connotation; the words that are associated in our minds with any particular word; definition by synonym or classification.

Intensional Orientation – the tendency to rely too much upon words, not enough upon observation and careful, unbiased examination of facts and reality.

Judgment – an evaluation; an expression of approval or disapproval. This is what we do most of the time, instead of describing what we see.

Loaded Words – words that appeal to emotional bias or prejudice.

Metaphor – the comparison, in one word, of two things from different fields. When we speak metaphorically, we carry over memories of one thing to the contemplation of another (i.e., "that girl is a cat.")

Multi-valued Orientation – the tendency to recognize numerous degrees or gradations; discernment; the opposite of two-valued orientation.

Operational Definition – tells what to do in order to experience or recognize the thing to which the word refers. It is the best type of definition and should be used whenever meaning is not completely clear.

Referent – the object pointed to or symbolized by a term.

Referential Language – the language of fact, used in business, science, and discussion.

Report – a kind of writing that attempts to exclude judgments, inferences, and loaded words; it may be verified, that is, proved to be either false or true.

Sign – a word, object, gesture, or happening that (if true) indicates the presence of something else; it is the part of an experience which, coming back to one's attention, has the same effect that the complete experience had in the past.

Signal – a word, object, number, or action that is used to produce action.

Signal Reaction – an automatic, unthinking reaction to a signal. Contrast with "symbol reaction."

Slanting – the biased use of words. Often the bias is unconscious.

Symbol – a word used referentially; used to represent something else that may or may not be present. By using words as symbols, we may think and speak of things not present, of ideas, qualities, etc., but a symbol has meaning only in its context.

Symbol Reaction – a thoughtful reaction; sometimes a skeptical reaction due to a realization that the symbol may be misleading (the symbol "ghost," most people would agree, is a fiction).

Two-valued Orientation – the tendency to recognize only the two extremes, such as good and bad, with no intermediate degrees; the "either-or" type of thinking. Often, however, it is necessary in making practical decisions.

BIBLIOGRAPHY

Braddock, Richard, editor, Introductory Readings on the English Language, Prentice-Hall, Inc., Englewood Cliffs, New Jersey, 1962.

Briggs, Harold E., Language, Man, & Society (Readings in Communication), Rinehart & Co., New York, 1949.

Chase, Stuart, The Power of Words, Harcourt, Brace & Co., New York, 1953.

Hayakawa, S. I., "How Words Change our Minds," Saturday Evening Post, December 27, 1958.

Hayakawa, S. I., editor, The Use and Misuse of Language (Selected Essays from ETC., a Review of General Semantics), Fawcett Publications, Greenwich, Conn., 1962.

Johnson, Wendell, Your Most Enchanted Listener, Harper & Bros., New York, 1956.

Lee, Irving J., Language Habits in Human Affairs, Harper & Bros., New York, 1941.

Lee, Irving J., editor, The Language of Wisdom and Folly, Harper & Bros., New York, 1949.

Shapiro, Alan, "As Humpty-Dumpty Told Alice," Scholastic Teacher, Volume 70, No. 4 (February 22, 1957).

Sondel, Bess, The Humanity of Words, World Publishing Co., New York, 1958.

Ullman, Stephen, The Principles of Semantics, Basil Blackwell, Oxford, England, 1957.

Walpole, Hugh R., Semantics (The Nature of Words and Their Meaning), W. W. Norton & Co., New York, 1941.

Webster's New International Dictionary of the English Language, Second Edition, G. & C. Merriam Co., Springfield, Mass., 1959.

VII

Bibliography

A Selected Bibliography of Report Writing

I. A General Reference Shelf for Report Writers

Bartlett, John, *Familiar Quotations*, 13th ed., Little, Brown, Boston, 1955.

Barzun, Jacques & Henry F. Graff, *The Modern Researcher,* Harcourt, Brace & World, New York, 1957.

Clark, Donald T. & Bert A. Gottfried, *Dictionary of Business and Finance,* Crowell, New York, 1957.

Dictionary of Foreign Words and Phrases, Maxim Newmark, ed., Philosophical Library, New York, 1950.

Encyclopaedic Dictionary of Business and Finance, Prepared by the Editorial Staff, Prentice-Hall, Englewood Cliffs, N.J., 1961.

Fowler, H. W., *Modern English Usage,* Rev. ed., Oxford, Fair Lawn, N.J., 1954.

Gates, Jean, *A Guide to the Use of Books and Libraries,* McGraw-Hill, New York, 1962.

Long, Ralph B., *The Sentence and Its Parts,* University of Chicago Press, Chicago, 1961.

Manley, Marion Catherine, *Business Information: How to Find It and Use It,* Harper & Row, New York, 1955.

Manual of Style, 11th ed., University of Chicago Press, Chicago, 1949.

Murphey, Robert W., *How and Where to Look It Up: A Guide to Standard Sources of Information,* McGraw-Hill, New York, 1958.

The New Roget's Thesaurus, Norman Lewis, ed., Garden City, New York, 1961.

Nicholson, Margaret, *Dictionary of American-English Usage,* Oxford, Fair Lawn, N.J., 1957.

Russell, Harold, *Use of Books and Libraries,* University of Minnesota Press, Minneapolis, 1958.

Strunk, William, Jr. & E. B. White, The *Elements of Style,* Macmillan, New York, 1959.

Tauber, M. F., *Technical Service in Libraries,* Columbia, New York, 1954.

Turabian, Kate L., *A Manual for Writers of Term Papers, Theses & Dissertations,* University of Chicago Press, Chicago, 1955.

Tver, David F., *Dictionary of Business and Scientific Terms,* Gulf, Houston, 1961.

Vishanathan, C. G., *Public Library Operations and Services,* Taplinger Publishing Company, Inc., New York, 1961.

Wentworth, Harold & S. B. Flexner, *Dictionary of American Slang,* Crowell, New York, 1959.

World Almanac: 1963, Harry Hansen, ed., World-Telegram & Sun, New York.

II. Business and Business Report Writing

Anderson, C. R., Alta G. Saunders & Francis W. Weeks, *Business Reports,* 3d ed., McGraw-Hill, New York, 1957.

Aurner, Robert R., *Effective Communication in Business,* South-Western Publishing Company, Cincinnati, 1958.

Babenroth, Adolph C., *Modern Business Communication,* Prentice-Hall, Englewood Cliffs, N.J., 1957.

Ball, John & Cecil B. Williams, *Report Writing,* Ronald, New York, 1955.

Bell, Reginald William, *Write What You Mean,* G. Allen, London, 1954.

Boyd, William P., *Productive Business Writing,* Prentice-Hall, Englewood Cliffs, N.J., 1959.

Brown, Leland, *Effective Business Report Writing,* Prentice-Hall, Englewood Cliffs, N.J., 1955.

Business Executive's Handbook, 4th ed., Stanley M. Brown, ed., Prentice-Hall, Englewood Cliffs, N.J., 1953.

Douglass, Paul Franklin, *Communication through Reports,* Prentice-Hall, Englewood Cliffs, N.J., 1957.

Drach, Harvey E., *American Business Writing,* American Book, New York, 1959.

Santmyers, Selby S., *Practical Report Writing,* International Textbook, Scranton, Pa., 1950.

Schutte, William M., *Communication in Business and Industry,* Holt, New York, 1960.

Shurter, R. L., *Written Communication in Business,* McGraw-Hill, New York, 1957.

Sigband, Norman B., *Effective Report Writing for Business, Industry and Government,* Harper & Row, New York, 1960.

Writing for Business: Selected Articles, Irwin, Homewood, Ill., 1955.

Writing in Industry, Siegfried Mandel, ed., Putnam, New York, 1960.

Zetler, Robert L. & W. George Crouch, *Successful Communication in Science and Industry: Writing, Reading and Speaking,* McGraw-Hill, New York, 1961.

III. Technical Report Writing

Baker, C., *Technical Publications,* Wiley, New York, 1955.

Baker, J. C. Y., *Guide to Technical Writing,* Pitman, New York, 1961.

Bleckle, Margaret B. & Kenneth W. Houp, *Reports for Science and Industry,* Holt, New York, 1958.

Brown, James, *Casebook for Technical Writers,* Prentice-Hall, Englewood Cliffs, N.J., 1961.

Clarke, Emerson, *How to Prepare Effective Engineering Proposals,* T. W. Publishers, 1962.

Comer, David B. & Ralph R. Spillman, *Modern Technical and Industrial Reports,* Putnam, New York, 1962.

Fountain, A. M. & others, *Manual of Technical Writing,* Scott, Foresman, Chicago, 1957.

Godfrey, James W. & Geoffry Parr, *Technical Writer,* Wiley, New York, 1959.

Hicks, Tyler G., *Successful Technical Writing,* McGraw-Hill, New York, 1959.

———, *Writing for Engineering and Science,* McGraw-Hill, New York, 1961.

Kelly, R. A., *The Use of English for Technical Students,* Harrap, London, 1962.

Mandel, Siegfried & David L. Caldwell, *Proposal and Inquiry Writing: Analysis, Techniques and Practice,* Macmillan, New York, 1962.

Marder, Daniel, *Craft of Technical Writing,* Macmillan, New York, 1960.

Menzel, Donald H., Howard Mumford Jones & Lyle G. Boyd, *Writing a Technical Paper,* McGraw-Hill, New York, 1961.

Miller, Walter J. & Leo C. A. Saidla, *Engineers as Writers,* Van Nostrand, Princeton, N.J., 1953.

Mills, Gordon H. & John A. Walter, *Technical Writing,* Holt, New York, 1954.

Mitchell, John, *Handbook of Technical Communication,* Prentice-Hall, Englewood Cliffs, N.J., 1962.

Nelson, J. Raleigh, *Writing the Technical Report,* 3rd ed., McGraw-Hill, New York, 1952.

Piper, H. Dan & Frank E. Davie, *Guide to Technical Reports,* Holt, New York, 1958.

Production and Use of Technical Reports, Fry, B. M. & J. J. Kortindick, eds., Catholic, Washington, D.C., 1955.

Racker, Joseph, *Technical Writing Techniques for Engineers,* Prentice-Hall, Englewood Cliffs, N.J., 1960.

Rathbone, Robert R. & James B. Stone, *Writer's Guide for Engineers and Scientists,* Prentice-Hall, Englewood Cliffs, N.J., 1961.

Schultz, Howard & Robert Webster, *Technical Report Writing: Sourcebook and Manual,* Longmans, New York, 1961.

Sherman, T. A., *Modern Technical Writing,* Prentice-Hall, Englewood Cliffs, N.J., 1961.

Souther, J. N., *Technical Report Writing,* Wiley, New York, 1957.

Style Manual for Technical Writers and Editors, S. J. Reisman, ed., Macmillan, New York, 1962.

Technical Editing, Ben H. Weil, ed., Reinhold, New York, 1958.

Ulman, Joseph N., Jr. & Jay R. Gould, *Technical Reporting,* Holt, New York, 1957.

Weisman, H. M., *Basic Technical Writing,* Merrill, Englewood Cliffs, N.J., 1962.

Welloon, G. P. & others, *Technical Writing,* Houghton Mifflin, Boston, 1961.

Winfrey, Robley, *Technician and His Report Preparation,* Iowa State University Press, Ames, Iowa, 1961.

Zall, Paul M., *Elements of Technical Report Writing,* Harper & Row, New York, 1962.

IV. Scientific and Professional Writing

Accountants' Handbook, 4th ed., Rufus Wixon, ed., Ronald, New York, 1956.

Davidson, Henry Alexander, *Guide to Medical Writing,* Ronald, New York, 1957.

Enberger, Meta R. & Marian R. Hall, *Scientific Writing*, Harcourt, Brace & World, New York, 1955.

Feiser, Louis Frederick & Mary Feiser, *Style Guide for Chemists*, Reinhold, New York, 1960.

Foster, John, Jr., *Science Writer's Guide*, Columbia, New York, 1962.

Gilman, William, *Language of Science*, Harcourt, Brace & World, New York, 1961.

Gensler, Walter J., & Kinereth D. Gensler, *Writing Guide for Chemists*, McGraw-Hill, New York, 1961.

Government Printing Office Style Manual, Rev. ed., GPO, Washington, D.C., 1953.

Hammond, Kenneth R., *Writing Chemical Reports*, Prentice-Hall, Englewood Cliffs, N.J., 1953.

Henn, Thomas R., *Science in Writing*, Macmillan, New York, 1961.

Huber, Jack T., *Report Writing in Psychology and Psychiatry*, Harper & Row, New York, 1961.

Hunter, Laura Grace, *The Language of Audit Reports*, U.S. General Accounting Office, Washington, D.C., 1957.

Industrial Accountants' Handbook, Wyman P. Fiske & John A. Beckett, ed., Prentice-Hall, Englewood Cliffs, N.J., 1954.

Kiely, James J., *Suggestions for Writing Accountant's Reports*, Bentley School of Accounting and Finance, 1954.

Klopfer, W. G., *Psychological Report*, Grune & Stratton, New York, 1960.

Palen, Jennie M., *Report Writing for Accountants*, Prentice-Hall, Englewood Cliffs, N.J., 1955.

Peterson, Martin S., *Scientific Thinking and Scientific Writing*, Reinhold, New York, 1961.

Trelease, S. F., *How to Write Scientific and Technical Papers*, Williams & Wilkins, Baltimore, 1958.

V. Business Letter Writing

Bender, James F., *Make Your Business Letters Make Friends*, McGraw-Hill, New York, 1952.

Buckley, Earle A., *How to Write Better Business Letters*, McGraw-Hill, New York, 1957.

Business Letter Writing Made Simple, Irving Rosenthal, ed., Garden City, New York, 1955.

Eckersley, Charles E., *English and American Business Letters*, Longmans, London, 1954.

Frailey, Lester E., *Practical Business Writing*, Prentice-Hall, 1955.

Hagar, Hubert Adonley, *Business Letter Writing*, McGraw-Hill, 1953.

Menning, J. H., *Writing Business Letters*, Rev. ed., R. D. Irwin, 1959.

Murphy, Karl M., *Modern Business Letters*, Houghton, Mifflin, 1956.

Naether, Carl Albert, *The Business Letter; Principles and Problems*, W. C. Brown Company, 1952.

Riebel, John P., *How to Write Successful Business Letters in 15 Days*, Prentice-Hall, 1953.

Sheppard, Mona, *Plain Letters: The Secret of Successful Business Writing*, Simon and Schuster, New York, 1960.

Smart, Walter Roy, *Business Letters*, Harper & Row, New York, 1950.

VI. Précis (Abstract) Writing

Aughterson, W. V., *Precis Writing*, Whitcomb & Tombs, Ltd., Christchurch, New Zealand, 1944.

Bennetton, J. H. & D. H. Smith, *Precis and General Knowledge*, 2d ed., Gregg, New York, 1951.

Charlton, J. M., *Preparation and Practice of Precis Writing*, Macmillan, New York, 1951.

Fielden, F. J., *Guide to Precis Writing*, 4th ed., University Tutorial Press, 1961.

Glassey, S. C., *Groundwork of Precis*, Oxford, Fair Lawn, N.J., 1938.

Gourley, J. J., *Precis*, Blackie, Glasgow, 1948.

Mathews, A. M. & others, *Handbook of Precis Writing*, 4th ed., Careers, 1939.

McDonald, Evans, *Preparation and Practice of Precis Writing*, Macmillan, New York, 1951.

Partridge, E., *Precis Writing*, Routledge, London, 1940.

VII. Graphic Devices

Adams, Douglas Payne, *An Index of Nomograms*, M.I.T., Cambridge, Mass., and Wiley, New York, 1950.

Hall, Arthur Stanley, *The Construction of Graphs and Charts*, Pitman, New York, 1958.

Heacock, Frank A., *Graphic Method for Solving Problems*, Edwards, Ann Arbor, Mich., 1952.

Kepler, Harold B., *Basic Graphical Kinematics*, McGraw-Hill, New York, 1960.

Kerley, James J., *Design Nomographs*, Golibart Press, 1953.

Kulmann, C. Albert, *Nomographic Charts*, McGraw-Hill, New York, 1951.

Masuyama, Motosaburo, *Graphical Method of Statistical Inference*, Maruzen Company, Ltd., New York, 1954.

Appendix: Further Notes on Research Techniques

DESIGNING THE EXPERIMENT

The design of the experiment will be determined by the objective of the research. The experiment consists of an arranged, systematic series of objective observations which are accomplished under controlled conditions, which are designed to answer particular questions, and which are repeatable and verifiable. The first step in planning an experiment is to determine the kind of event to be studied and the nature of the variables which prior information suggests may be the controlling ones. Variables will be of two kinds—those which can be controlled and those which cannot be.

Controls are needed in experimentation to help correct for the effect of variables which may be changing in an unknown or uncontrollable way during the experiment. Controls may be thought of as similar test specimens which are subjected to as nearly as possible the same treatment as the objects of the experiment, except for the change in the variable under study. Randomization is required in choosing which member of a pair is to be the subject and which the control; to eliminate possible bias, a coin should be tossed in determining this.

To ensure against bias in human test subjects, it is best that they not know whether they are being used as controls or subjects. Bias in the experimenter himself can be eliminated in this same way. If he is "blind" as to the subjects or controls—human beings, animals, bacteria, or chemical compounds—and as to the identity of the coded materials used, objectivity in observing and recording data is more likely.

Once an experiment has been designed to elicit certain information, it is wise to prepare a checklist prior to actually executing the plan. Errors costly in time and spirit can probably best be averted that way.

When the search for data is under way, the experimenter must know as much as possible about the object of the search and use the most efficient method of detection. He must be certain that he would see his object if and when he encountered it. This necessitates systematic instead of haphazard searching. Not only should the experimenter be constantly watching for observational features which can be used in solving the problem in hand, but he should also be on the alert for new phenomena of all kinds.

MAKING THE QUESTIONNAIRE

Extremely diverse kinds of information for reports may be obtained through surveys. Questionnaires can procure data on simple, objective facts or on complex attitudes with regard to persons, things, situations, or events.

The three major types of questions used in questionnaires are (1) free-answer, (2) two-way, and (3) multiple-choice. Various other types of questions and combinations of questions are also used. Although most of these utilize the concepts of the three major types, consideration of them would require specialized treatment outside the scope of the discussion here.

Free-answer Questions

In this type of question the respondent is left free to offer any idea or ideas he may think of. "When you think of the three or four most famous universities in America, which ones come to mind?" "If you were going to buy a small car, which one would you choose?" "What do you think of the new city sales tax?"

In the overall preparation of a questionnaire, free-answer questions serve well at the beginning to introduce the subject. Even though they are relatively nondirective, they are useful in leading into the subject by indicating the general nature of the topic. Follow-up questions can then provide elaboration. "Which of these famous universities is best known for doing atomic research?" "Why is car A your choice?" "Would you like to see this tax extended to cover taxicab fares?"

Unless he is engaged in the preparation of specialized and far-ranging social surveys and polls, the report writer reading this book is most likely to wish to obtain facts rather than opinions for his document. Here the free-answer question can serve him very well. "Where did you spend your vacation last summer?" "What newspapers do you read most regularly?" "What kind of work do you do?" "What kind of public transportation did you use in getting to work this morning?" "What do you think a bottle this size should sell for?"

Free-answer questions can provide uninfluenced replies which are likely to be the sort of hard-core raw data that reports require for substance. Also, the free-answer question allows a broad range of responses helpful in delineating the scope of the problem and the many possibilities for its solution. Within the framework of a specific questionnaire, the free-answer question serves not only to open the survey but also to elicit answers which can be used as background for interpreting answers to other questions. In the creative process of amassing data, the report writer may employ the free-answer question to develop suggestions, obtain elaboration, probe reasons, evaluate arguments, sift knowledge, and classify respondents. Beyond this, free-answer questions provide quotable individual responses which, mixed

417

into the final report, add richness and substance. Unfortunately, with all these merits, the free-answer question is extremely difficult to code and classify because of the great variety of answers.

Two-way Questions

When the information desired is of the either-or, right-wrong, fair-unfair, good-bad, true-false, yes-no, and agree-disagree sort, the two-way or dichotomous question is used. This kind of question is the most common form used in questionnaires. In that it is intended to suggest only two possible alternatives, it is at the other extreme from the free-answer question.

Frequently, provisions are made for more than merely two responses. Where the respondent may check "no opinion," "don't know," or "neither," he may prefer not to take a definite stand on a difficult issue. Other variations allow for qualified answers such as "too far," "about right," "not far enough," and "in between," and "no difference," "both," and "neither." Information so broken down can render more categorical indications at the extremes, with rating or intensity scales in between.

Only when the respondent may readily and realistically choose one or the other of the alternatives offered is the two-way pattern suitable. Otherwise, replies may seem definite when they are not. Forcing opinion into the questioner's own preconceived notion of possible categories will not provide accurate information. Yes or No to, for example, "Would you favor a six-hour work day?" without qualifications regarding wages and national needs would make it impossible for many to reply. Where categoric replies were obtained, the interviewer might well doubt that the respondent knew much about the subject.

The following questions demonstrate sounder versions of the two-way pattern:

1. Do you think the United States should support or oppose the admission of Red China to the United Nations?
2. Are you for or against resumption of nuclear testing by the United States?
3. In the event of war, would you build your own family fallout shelter?
4. Do you own your own home?
5. Did you buy any stocks or bonds during 1963?

The first three questions call for opinions and the last two for facts. In questions 1 and 2, the alternatives are stated (support-oppose, for-against); in questions 3, 4, and 5, the alternative is implied (would you–would you not, own–or not, buy–or not). Whether stated or implied, alternatives should be as mutually exclusive as possible. They may be made mild (approve-disapprove) or strong (demand-reject). Often the degree of strength of the alternatives will influence the number of qualified or undecided responses obtained.

Multiple-choice Questions

Generally, the multiple-choice question is used (1) when the issue clearly splits more than two ways, or (2) when gradations—ratings of intensity—are wanted regarding the opinions, attitudes, and facts. Multiple-choice questions are sometimes called "cafeteria" questions.

All degrees of opinion may be expressed if the multiple-choice question is well set up. The choices offered must be complete enough to cover the whole range of possible responses. Yet the specified alternatives must be sufficiently mutually exclusive so that the respondent can make a choice between several that may appear desirable.

Where the choices are a list of numbers, it has been shown that respondents are prone to choose those near the middle of the list. Interestingly enough, when the choice is among multiple ideas of statements, respondents are disposed to select statements at the extremes and to favor the top more than the bottom of the list. For this reason, questionnaires containing the same choices in different order are generally used for equal numbers of respondents in a large survey.

As a most formal query, the multiple-choice question requires diligence in preparation. Listing of alternatives serves to call them all to each respondent's attention, a feature of great usefulness in seeking facts and in testing. All the informants are known to have the same information as presented in the questions and therefore to be on a par except for judgment.

In indicating a degree or gradation of feeling, the gradated multiple-choice question can provide helpful information as to the respondent's probable course of action. Example:

1. It is absolutely essential to have a man like Johnson for President.
2. There may be some reasons against having Johnson as President for another four years, but on the whole it is the best thing to do.
3. While Johnson has done some good things, the country would be better off under X for the next four years.
4. The reelection of Johnson for another four years would be a very bad thing for the country.

Framing the Questions

Every report writer should give full consideration to the usefulness of questionnaires in gathering data. But, as a vast literature on this subject by social scientists, psychologists, and statisticians suggests, framing the questions is no job for lightweights.

Questions must be couched in the simplest, most familiar words possible, and they should be as concisely phrased as is consistent with clarity. So that they will yield exactly the information desired for tabulation and statistical analysis, queries must be carefully formulated: The more specific the wording the better. Each question ought to cover only one point, and each question should be thoroughly unambiguous. Moreover, the wording should not suggest answers in line with the questioner's own biases.

The language of questionnaires must avoid words with emotional connotations that tend to arouse the respondent's prejudices (see Chapters 2 and 6 on this point.) Name-calling and extremist words are most malappropriate. One must also exercise care to avoid phrases which may reflect unfavorably upon the prestige of the informant—his educational or social status.

In arranging the order of the questions, patterns which are logically or psychologically valid should be employed. Confusion and misunderstanding may be generated if the sequence seems out of order. It is good practice to have an opening question of wide human-interest appeal to engage the respondent's attention. Opening questions should be easily answerable; they should also not give the impression that the questioner has a vested interest or is selling something. Questions which might embarrass the informant, or raise a point to which he may be sensitive, should be placed toward the middle or end of the questionnaire. Where both general and specific questions are used, general ones should precede. Since continuity in the stream of queries is desired, thought should be given to transition questions.

Elements of the Questionnaire

Regardless of the mode of distribution, the questionnaire should contain certain basic information which identifies and explains it for the respondent. A necessary first element should be an indication at the top of the form of the source or sponsorer of the survey: Squeedunk College Alumni Association, 14 Rabies Square, Eyewash 79, South Dakota. Next should come the title, indicating the general nature of the subject matter: Job and Family Survey. Simple and clear instructions should follow: According to the facts, please place check marks (√) in the appropriate spaces.

The numbered questions should follow, with the required check-off boxes or write-in spaces. At the end of the questionnaire an open question may be provided for further remarks: What additional advice would you give to today's freshman entering college? Corollary or supporting facts may be sought at the beginning or end. Personal data regarding the respondent's age, sex, marital status, military status, income group, etc., provide a basis for cross-tabulating answers to analyze the influence of these factors upon results. The corollary data also provide a check upon the quality of representativeness of the sample.

Depending on the nature of the sample and of the questionnaire, the respondent may or may not be asked to give his name and address on the form. For a survey, let us say, like that for the Kinsey Report, anonymity would be mandatory. When people are asked any kind of personal question, they are unlikely to cooperate if requested to identify themselves.

Questionnaires distributed via mail may have a short covering letter explaining the nature of the survey. The more fully the respondent comprehends the purposes and values of the program, the more likely he is to participate freely and honestly. If any direct or indirect benefits may accrue to him as a result of the knowledge gained through the report, these should be pointed out in the covering letter. Results of the survey can be offered to him if he wishes to receive them when the report becomes available. Instructions for completing the questionnaire may be placed in the letter. Also, assurances may be made regarding the confidential treatment to be given the replies.

Choosing a Sample

After the questionnaire is constructed, it is subjected to tests. Small test-sample groups can provide an index to the overall value of the questionnaire in eliciting the desired information. Weak points of the questionnaire in organization, instructions, or wording can be uncovered. Once revisions are completed, the investigator must make his final decisions regarding the kind and size of the sample which will be used in the final test.

In surveying a large group of persons, of course, only a part of the total group is chosen to receive the questionnaire. Results in this sample, the assumption goes, will be representative of the whole group. Market surveys and opinion polls will seek to sample the entire population. Surveys for informational, factual reports, however, will probably cover special groups whose common connection with a particular question is assumed because of their job (union officers or schoolteachers, for example), their age group (teen-agers or retired persons over sixty), or some other common denominator.

Sources for lists commonly used to form a sample are:

Censuses
Telephone directories
Subscribers to other public
utilities (gas, etc.)
Automobile registrations
Lists of voters
Tax assessors' lists
City directories
Magazine subscriber lists
Stockholders' lists

Clients of social or other
public agencies
Members of organizations and
societies
Graduates of schools and
colleges
Credit lists
Payroll lists
Professional directories

Special lists may be prepared from such general sources as these by the investigator himself, or they may be purchased from firms whose business it is to compile them.

Once the general list is determined upon, there are, according to the method of selection, various kinds of sampling—random, stratified, and proportionate.

Random sampling means that each individual in the entire list has an equal chance of being chosen. One way to select randomly, for example, is to draw lots from a container. Other methods are used which assure selection by chance.

Stratified sampling involves first dividing the list into two or more classes or strata. For example, one might break his lists into three classes of individuals: Protestants, Catholics, and Jews. To secure, let us say, a 10 per cent stratified sample, the investigator draws a sample of one in ten from each list.

In proportionate sampling the selection is controlled so that the characteristics of the entire group are proportionately represented by the sample. If 75 per cent of the list are college graduates and 25 per cent are high school graduates, then three-fourths of the sample is drawn from the one group and one-fourth from the other. This is done only if the difference between the classes would influence the conclusions or responses. If not, then random or stratified sampling will serve.

USING THE INTERVIEW

When basic information required for a report may best be obtained through direct exchange with one or several persons to whom the facts—history, practices, problems, policies—are known, personal interviews may be arranged. As with all methods of data gathering, a personal interview may yield imperfect data. But its usefulness in overcoming misunderstandings, interpreting questions, obtaining rounded, complete replies, and gaining impressions can be quantitatively and qualitatively great. Reports for management (on personnel, time study, industrial relations) and for the professions (law, medicine, social work, guidance counseling) often employ the interview technique in gathering data. In particular personal interviews are utilized in market research, industrial relations, and personnel projects.

Personal interviewing, again, is a complex process surrounded by a massive literature by sociologists, psychologists, and other specialists. Since the desideratum is to create a report presenting the optimum in objective truth, the investigator must strive to procure data susceptible to scientific analysis. Attempts need to be made to control as much as possible the variable factors which might statistically invalidate the results. Standardization must be sought relative to the interviewer, the setting of the interview, the interviewee, the method of questioning, and the system for recording data.

Personal interviews are of two kinds—surface and depth. In the surface or fact-finding interview, a wide range of objective and sub-jective data may be sought through yes-no questions. The depth in-terview is intensive and seeks to explore why the answers are yes or no—it probes the underlying reasons, causes, motives, sources. Surface personal interviews may be conducted by telephone to gain wide cov-erage of representative random samples; they are useful in obtaining data from many respondents at a given time, say between 7 and 9 P.M. on the Thursday before election. Telephone interviews have come into wide use in rating audience response to television and radio shows.

Prior to the interview, considerable preparation is undertaken. Great care is expended in preparing a questionnaire so that the precious op-portunity of a personal interview is exploited to maximal advantage. One may not return for a second personal encounter; all pertinent data must be garnered in one sitting, ranging from ten minutes to, perhaps, ninety minutes. Since missing data may weaken a whole section of the report, the interviewer requires a deep, lucid understanding of exactly what information he needs and for what specific purpose. In addition, he must have a rich knowledge of the full subject. All the details and ramifications of each question he frames should be within the reporter's grasp. Whatever background information—biographical or professional facts—about the interviewee the interviewer can obtain beforehand will be helpful in establishing rapport and providing a yardstick for interpreting responses.

The interviewer, during the interview, must keep control of the exchange while guiding the informant to discuss facts freely and thoroughly. Qualifying probes may be made so that full meanings with all their pertinent implications are apparent in each response. Keeping in mind that very specific information of a certain kind for a special purpose is wanted, the report writer should be prepared to occasionally depart from his schedule to pursue an unanticipated lead developing from a casual remark of the informant. Ability to discriminate between pertinent and irrelevant points is needed by the interviewer.

Whether on separate cards for each question or on a prepared check list, the interviewer will record the information as it is obtained. His form should be designed so that as little note taking as possible is needed during the interview. Usually, however, the interviewee will understand the nature of the situation and sit quietly during the moments required by the report writer for note taking.

Immediately following the interview, it is wise for the report writer to review his data and make note cards, much like those used in recording information obtained through bibliographic research. While all the forms filled out during interviews may be placed in a report appendix, usually just an exhibit of the questionnaire will suffice. If four, eight, or a dozen interviews are held, the report writer will gain cumulative experience; doubtless the final interviews, free of the errors made in the earlier ones, will be the most successful in providing full and accurate information.

Index